Kidnapped Souls

KIDNAPPED SOULS

National Indifference
and the Battle for Children
in the Bohemian Lands, 1900–1948

Tara Zahra

Cornell University Press

ITHACA AND LONDON

First published 2008 by Cornell University Press
First printing, Cornell Paperbacks, 2011

Printed in the United States of America

Library of Congress Cataloging-in-Publication Data

Zahra, Tara.
   Kidnapped souls : national indifference and the battle for children in the Bohemian
Lands, 1900–1948 / Tara Zahra.
      p. cm.
Includes bibliographical references and index.
ISBN 978–0–8014–4628–3 (cloth : alk. paper)
ISBN 978–0–8014–7760–7 (pbk. : alk. paper)
   1. Children and politics—Czech Republic—Bohemia—History—20th century.
   2. Children—Government policy—Czech Republic—Bohemia—History—20th century.
   3. Nationalism—Czech Republic—Bohemia—History—20th century.   4. Germans—
Czech Republic—Bohemia—Politics and government—20th century.   5. Bohemia
(Czech Republic)—Ethnic relations.   6. Bohemia (Czech Republic)—Politics and
government—20th century.   I. Title.

HQ792.C89Z34 2008
305.23094371'0904—dc22

2007033004

Cornell University Press strives to use environmentally responsible suppliers and materials to the fullest extent possible in the publishing of its books. Such materials include vegetable-based, low-VOC inks and acid-free papers that are recycled, totally chlorine-free, or partly composed of nonwood fibers. For further information, visit our website at www.cornellpress.cornell.edu.

Cloth printing   10 9 8 7 6 5 4 3 2 1
Paperback printing   10 9 8 7 6 5 4 3 2 1

To Pieter Judson

Contents

List of Figures and Maps

Preface

In 1998 I spent my first summer in Europe. I was not fortunate enough to be sent on an exchange to live with a family of German or Czech peasants as a child, and so the official purpose of this visit was to learn German so that I could apply to graduate school. During that summer, instead of backpacking through Europe's great cities, I spent several weeks in the Austrian National Library's reading room looking at the yellowed and crumbling newsletters of German nationalist associations from the fin de siècle. Some of the first words of German I learned were *Lehrer* and *Schule,* as one of my tasks was to figure out how many teachers served as leaders in German-Bohemian nationalist associations between 1896 and 1909. I quickly learned that teachers had become the heart and soul of German nationalist associations in the final decade of the Austrian Empire. Even with my limited vocabulary, it was also clear to me that Austrian nationalists spent a lot of time throwing rocks at schoolhouse windows and that they were virtually obsessed with schools and education. When it came time to choose a dissertation topic, I decided to write about these nationalists and their efforts to transform children into Czechs and Germans. I soon discovered that nationalist school conflicts were only one small part of a much broader crusade to secure the loyalties of nationally ambiguous children in the Bohemian Lands between 1900 and 1948. Czech and German nationalists built new minority schools; promoted pedagogical reform; constructed orphanages, soup kitchens, and summer camps; and finally resorted to bribery, boycotts, threats, denunciations, and new laws to classify children and their parents as Germans or Czechs, often against their will.

I began my research with the assumption that the profusion of nationalist polemics about children reflected the depth of nationalist sentiment and the intensity of nationalist conflict in the Bohemian Lands. Almost every textbook or popular representation of East European societies I had encountered reinforced a sad and singular lesson—whenever people who are different from one another share a community, bloodshed and strife are the inevitable result. Only the homogenous nation-state, in this view, could guarantee lasting democracy, peace, and prosperity. It was therefore a puzzling surprise to discover that the nationalist battle for children's loyalties was not actually driven by popular nationalism. Rather, it was propelled by the very indifference, ambivalence, and opportunism the "masses" expressed toward the nationalist movements that claimed to represent them. I believe that this national indifference ultimately offers an alternate explanation for the radicalization of nationalist politics in East Central Europe. Rather than a world in which Czechs and Germans fought for control of the streets and for political power, I discovered a world in which Czech and German nationalists fought over who was Czech and who was German.

Competing claims on children had dramatic consequences for the people and political and social institutions of the Bohemian Lands. The battle for children shaped understandings of democracy and minority rights, the development of the welfare state, and finally the dynamics of the Nazi occupation in the Bohemian Lands. Two of these issues seem particularly relevant to contemporary concerns. The first is the entanglement of democracy and nationalism as the two emerged, triumphantly locked together, in the aftermath of the First World War. The tautological argument that the Czech nation was inherently "democratic," for example, bolstered the claim that any crusade in the name of Czech nationalism was also a crusade for democracy. This historical example may shed light on subsequent efforts at "nation-building" undertaken in the name of democratization around the globe. The second is the peculiar conception of children as collective property that developed through nationalist activism in the Bohemian Lands. In telling the story of this activism, this book seeks to historicize and challenge contemporary assumptions that all state intervention into the so-called private family represents a form of antidemocratic or totalitarian politics and that current ideals of family and child rearing are universal or natural. Nationalists in the Bohemian Lands in the early twentieth century promoted a very different conception of the boundaries between children, families, and the state. Their model, moreover, had both disciplinary and progressive potential. From a feminist perspective, it seems critical to historicize contemporary ideals of the family and parent-child relations, and to consider the ways in which historically specific assertions about children's "best interests" have underpinned policies that have perpetuated gender inequality inside and outside the family.

In the course of writing this book I have myself benefited from many extraordinary pedagogical efforts. At the University of Michigan I enjoyed the generous, imaginative, and challenging intellectual guidance of Kathleen Canning, Geoff Eley, and Scott Spector. I am particularly grateful to them for encouraging me to reach beyond the traditional intellectual and geographic boundaries that structure German history. I was fortunate to receive financial support for the research and writing of this book from the Jacob Javits Fellowship, the Fulbright-Hays Fellowship, the University of Michigan History Department, the Woodrow Wilson Center's East European Studies Program, and the Milton Fund at Harvard University. I also thank the archivists and librarians at the Austrian and Czech state archives, the Austrian National Library, the National Library in Prague, and the Bundesarchiv in Bayreuth for their generous assistance. Cambridge University Press (*Central European History*) and the *American Historical Review* kindly allowed me to reprint some of the material that appears in chapters 3 and 4 of this book.

I could not have realized this project without the solidarity and cheer provided by my friends and colleagues in Ann Arbor. In particular, I thank Erika Gasser, Erik Huneke, Mia Lee, Kathrin Levitan, Marti Lybeck, Mary O'Reilly, Roberta Pergher, Nathalie Rothman, and Jessica Thurlow, whose insights helped to focus early drafts of this book. I also thank Will Mackintosh, Hervé Jezequel, and Alice Ritscherle for their friendship in Ann Arbor. Mia Lee deserves special kudos for risking life and limb during a treacherous two-day drive from Michigan to Boston. I had the good fortune to meet Erika Gasser in Somerville the summer before starting graduate school. I continue to cherish her wit, intellectual insight, and friendship.

Outside Ann Arbor, I was lucky to receive a warm welcome into the field of Central European history. Christiane Brenner, Chad Bryant, Melissa Feinberg, Eagle Glassheim, Peter Haslinger, Maureen Healy, Robert Moeller, and Nancy Wingfield all shared their knowledge of Central European history and archives with me and helped me to rethink my arguments in several sections of this book. My friends and colleagues David Gerlach, John Deak, Krista Hegburg, Melissa Martin, Heather Hess, Edith Sheffer, and Kim Strozewski kept me company in Vienna, Munich, and Prague and rescued me from occasional despair induced by a surfeit of fried cheese. I am particularly grateful to Jeremy King and Peter Bugge, who have challenged and supported me since I presented a draft of my first chapter in an idyllic setting in Skagen, Denmark. This book has benefited a great deal from their deep knowledge about all things Bohemian and from their enthusiasm for debating the finer points of my arguments.

I have been extremely privileged to spend the past two years at the Harvard Society of Fellows, where I wrote the final draft of this book. In the yellow house at 78 Mt. Auburn Street, I enjoyed more intellectual freedom, stimulating conversation, and good cheese than anyone could hope for. In particular, I thank fellow Central and East Europeanists Jonathan Bolton, Edyta Bojanowska, Debbie Coen, and Cristina Vatulescu. Daniella Doron and Francesca Trabacca helped me to begin new research and kept my spirits high in Paris and Washington, DC. I also thank Alison Frank for her friendship and collegiality and for many stimulating hours spent discussing

Central European history (and everything else) over hot chocolate in Cambridge. Melissa Mullin has been a steadfast friend in spite of the distance that has separated us over the years.

I am particularly indebted to Laura Lee Downs, whose inspired approach to the history of childhood and gender has shaped this work. She has challenged me with her intellectual insights, infected me with an enthusiasm for French history (which has enriched my understanding of Eastern Europe), and supported me with her friendship.

Finally, I could not have written this book without the love and support of my own nationally indifferent parents, Debbie and Marc Zahra. I thank them for their culinary and emotional wisdom, their imagination and sense of humor, and for encouraging me to pursue this project no matter where it took me.

I dedicate this book to Pieter Judson, whom I first met in his German history class at Swarthmore College in 1994. It is thanks to him that I discovered national hermaphrodites, Central Europe, and the excitement of being an historian. He saw a historian in me before I saw one in myself, made Austrian nationalists seem irresistibly exciting, and has supported me with tireless patience, empathy, wit, and intellectual enthusiasm ever since. Many of the arguments in this book developed through our conversations. He is a model of the scholar, teacher, and human being I strive to be.

Map 1. The Habsburg Empire, 1914.

Map 2. The Bohemian Lands, 1918–45.

List of Archives and Abbreviations

AVA   Allgemeines Verwaltungsarchiv
AdR   Archiv der Republik
AN   Archives nationales, Paris
AOK   Armeeoberkommando
BA   Bundesarchiv, Berlin
BB   Bundesarchiv, Bayreuth
ČZK   Česká zemská komise pro ochranu dítěte a péče o mládež
DLS   Deutsche Landesstelle für Kinderschutz und Jugendfürsorge
GZNB   Gemeinsames Zentralnachweisbüro des Roten Kreuzes
KA   Kriegsarchiv
KÜA   Kriegsüberwachungsamt
Kuratorium   Kuratorium pro výchovu mládeže v Čechách a na Moravě
MfKU   Ministerium für Kultus und Unterricht
MfSV   Ministerium für soziale Verwaltung
MKV/R   Ministerstvo kultu a vyučování-Vídeň
MPSP-R   Ministerstvo ochrana práce a sociální péče- repatriace
MŠ   Ministerstvo školství
MV-NR   Ministerstvo vnitra-nová registratura
MV-SR   Ministerstvo vnitra-stará registratura
MZA   Moravský zemský archiv, Brno
NA   Národní archiv, Prague
NJS   Národní jednota severočeská
NRČ   Národní rada česká
NJS   Národní jednota severočeská
NSS   Nejvyšší správní soud
ÖstA   Österreichisches Staatsarchiv
PMR   Předsednictvo ministerské rady

Sb NÚIČ	Sbírka dokumentů nacistých úřadů a institucí na území okupaného českého territoria
SdP	Sudetoněmecká strana
SSD/R	Správní soudní dvůr ve Vídni, 1898–1918
ÚPV-bez	Úřad předsednictva vlády
ÚŘP	Úřad řišského protektora
USHMMA	United States Holocaust Memorial Museum Archive
VGH	Verwaltungsgerichtshof
VÚA	Vojenský ústřední archiv
WuWf	Witwen und Waisenfond
ŽNR	Ženská národní rada, 1923–42
ZŠR	Zemská školní rada v Praze, 1918–51

Note on Places and Names

Many of the places and people referred to in this book were contested by German and Czech nationalists. Nationalist struggles have notoriously focused precisely on the power to name. Not only were geographic places known by different Czech and German names, but some of the nationally ambiguous individuals discussed in this book spelled their own names differently (using Czech or German versions of the same name) depending on the context. At the risk of burdening readers with unwieldy formulations, I have chosen to use both Czech and German place names in this book in order to avoid privileging particular nationalist claims on those places. For the same reason, I refer to Bohemia, Moravia, and Silesia as the "Bohemian Lands" rather than the "Czech Lands." In referring to persons whose names were nationally contested, I have, wherever possible, used the spellings preferred by the individuals themselves.

Kidnapped Souls

Introduction

> Czech parents! Remember that your children are not only your own property but also the property of the nation. They are the property of all of society and that society has the right to control your conduct!
>
> —*Pamphlet for parents in Brno/Brünn from the*
> *Czech National Social Party, 1899*

Long before American university students descended on Europe's capital cities in search of adventure, the children of peasants and workers became the first "exchange students" in Central Europe. Throughout much of the nineteenth and early twentieth centuries in the Bohemian Lands (the former Austrian provinces of Bohemia, Moravia, and Silesia), Czech-speaking children commonly spent their summer holidays or even a school year with German-speaking families (and vice versa) for the purpose of learning the second provincial language. As adults, most participants remembered these exchanges fondly as vehicles for linguistic and national understanding. In 1960, one German recalled that although he grew up in a village near a "language frontier" (*Sprachgrenze*) in Bohemia, a bilingual region where Czechs and Germans were supposedly locked in bitter national conflict, social and economic relations between Czechs and Germans had been quite friendly in interwar Czechoslovakia.[1] These amicable relations, he claimed, began in childhood, since many farmers had spent a school year or summer living with a family of the "other" nationality.[2] Karl Renner, the first chancellor of both the first and second Austrian Republics, recalled in his memoirs that there was hardly a day in his youth when a Czech child did not sit at the family table. These childhood friendships often lasted a lifetime: "The Czech

---

[1] On the language frontier in Habsburg Central Europe, see Pieter M. Judson, *Guardians of the Nation: Activists on the Language Frontiers of Imperial Austria* (Cambridge, MA, 2006); Mark Cornwall, "The Struggle on the Czech-German Language Border, 1880–1940," *English Historical Review* 109 (September 1994): 914–51.

[2] Anonymous, Gemeinde Neueigen/Nová Ves nad Odrou, 2, Ost Doc. 20/37, BB.

child called my parents 'Vater' and 'Mutter,' and we boys called the Czech parents 'otec' and 'matka.' . . . Our entire lives the two families and the individual exchange students remained the best of friends."[3]

Nostalgic memories of peaceful national coexistence are common in postwar German memoirs as they cloak life before Nazism with the apolitical innocence of lost youth.[4] Yet in regions where Czech speakers and German speakers had long married each other, lived, worked, traded, and socialized together, many parents were genuinely eager to see their children enjoy the potential social and cultural advantages of bilingualism. Notices in local newspapers attest to the persistence of the practice well into the twentieth century: "I offer my 13-year-old boy for exchange to a German area," advertised North Bohemian tailor Franz Vodhanil in 1907.[5] In 1934, amidst growing political tensions between Sudeten German and Czech political leaders in Czechoslovakia, an announcement in a German magazine for youth welfare advertised an annual exchange program run by the Czech organization České srdce. The advertisement boasted, "This program has wide-ranging importance for both nations. The children on exchange become accustomed to everyday language and get to know different regions as well as the lifestyles of the local residents."[6]

In an age of growing nationalist movements, however, not everyone was a fan of the so-called child exchange (*Kindertausch/handl*). German and Czech nationalist activists in the early twentieth century warned that these exchanges might result in nothing less than the complete Germanization or Czechification of the nation's children. Much to their dismay, however, nationalists could do little to prevent parents from sending their children into the schools and homes of the so-called national enemy. In 1907 the central committee of the Czech Nationalist Union of Northern Bohemia (Národní jednota severočeská) launched an aggressive propaganda campaign against the practice of exchanging children but failed to convince even the association's own local leaders that bilingualism posed a threat to their children. In a letter to the Czech National Council, a nationalist umbrella organization for Czech associations and political parties, the union lamented, "This nuisance is so widespread in the countryside that even local notables participate, and it is with a clean conscience that they sit on the leadership committees of the local National Union of Northern Bohemia, Czech School Association, and

---

[3] Karl Renner, *An der Wende zweier Zeiten: Lebenserinnerungen* (Vienna, 1946), 7, 45, 76.
[4] See Ingrid Kaiser-Kaplaner, *Tschechen und Deutsche in Böhmen und Mähren, 1920–1946* (Klagenfurt, 2002), 136, and Helmut Fielhauer, "'Kinder-Wechsel' und 'Böhmisch-Lernen': Sitte, Wirtschaft, und Kulturvermittlung im frueheren niederösterreichischen-tschechischen Grenzbereich," *Österreichische Zeitschrift für Volkskunde* 81 (Neue Serie 32) 1978: 115–48.
[5] *Allgemeine Anzeiger für Nordböhmen* (Rumburg), 28 August 1907, 7.
[6] "Fereienaustausch tschechischer gegen deutsche Kinder," *Jugendfürsorge* 18 (May 1934), 190.

other patriotic associations and send their children on exchanges to German schools. They justify it with the argument that the Germans also send their children to the Czech schools."[7]

Kindertausch is not the subject of this book, but it is a powerful metaphor for the fears that drove nationalist mobilization around children in the early twentieth century. It is also a telling example of the uneven success of nationalist activism in East Central Europe. This book traces the role of children as objects of nationalist conflict in the Bohemian Lands between 1900 and 1945. German and Czech nationalists in the Bohemian Lands feared that children "born" to their nation could literally be "exchanged," "lost," or "kidnapped" from the national community through education in the wrong national milieu or by nationally indifferent parents. Nationalists in the Bohemian Lands were hardly alone in claiming that children comprised a precious form of "national property" at the turn of the century. In an age of mass politics and nationalist demography, nationalists across Europe worried about the quantity and quality of the nation's young. They were nonetheless unique in their ability to transform their polemical claims into a legal reality. Between 1900 and 1945, German and Czech nationalists promoted a political culture in which children belonged more rightfully to national communities than to their own parents.

Children became targets of nationalist activism in part because they presented tremendous problems for nationalists. Most learned languages quickly. One such child, Heinrich Holek, was a native Czech speaker who attended a German school near Ústí nad Labem/Aussig in the late nineteenth century. At first he struggled to understand and be understood, but it was not long before the impenetrable language began to make sense to him. "By the time we learned to write the letter 'R,' I already had the German language deep inside me. I learned German, without being able to say how. By the end of the year I could speak as well as all the others," he recalled.[8] Many children did not even have to be "exchanged" for this purpose, as they became proficient in the second provincial language in the course of their daily lives in bilingual families and neighborhoods. Robert Scheu, an Austrian-German writer who traveled through Bohemia at the end of the First World War, recalled an encounter with one such "borderland" child in the town of Prachatice/Prachatitz. "One day I was brought a two-year-old little girl, clearly a clever child, who alternatively spoke German and Czech, and both completely flawlessly," he marveled. "The little child never once mixed the two languages, as if each was kept in a separate chamber of the brain. Here is a subject for the psychologists!"[9]

---

[7] Národní jednota severočeská, letter to NRČ, Č. 2212, Prague, 19 June 1907, NRČ, carton 508, NA.

[8] Heinrich Holek, *Unterwegs. Eine Selbstbiographie mit Bildnis des Verfassers* (Vienna, 1927), 44.

[9] Robert Scheu, *Wanderung durch Böhmen am Vorabend der Revolution* (Vienna, 1919), 200–201.

The assertion of essential difference between national communities is at the very heart of nationalist politics. Yet in the Bohemian Lands in the nineteenth century, as Peter Bugge has argued, little besides language use actually differentiated self-identified Germans from Czechs.[10] Children, who seemed to slip easily between linguistic and national communities, therefore threatened to expose the deepest assumptions of nationalist politics as myths. The story of nationalist activism around children also threatens to expose as a myth one of the conventional and most powerful narratives of East European history. Typically, the history of East Central Europe is written in terms of escalating nationalist conflict that culminated in the violence of ethnic cleansing. The history of nationalist activism around children in the Bohemian Lands questions the assumptions about popular loyalties underlying this narrative. As we will see, nationalist battles over children in the Bohemian Lands did not typically pit Czechs against Germans in a world of national polarization. Rather, conflicts raged over who was Czech and who was German in a world of national ambiguity.

This book treats indifference to nationalism as a central category of analysis, a driving force behind historical change in East Central Europe. I use the term "national indifference" to describe several different kinds of behavior. For some, particularly in Habsburg Austria, this indifference could entail the complete absence of national loyalties as many individuals identified more strongly with religious, class, local, regional, professional, or familial communities, or even with the Austrian dynasty, than with a single nation. They considered themselves neither Czech nor German. With the collapse of the Austrian Empire into self-declared nation-states in 1918, this blatant national agnosticism became more exceptional. The Czechoslovak government increasingly devoted itself to nationalizing citizens, if necessary, by forcibly classifying them as Czechs on the census and for the purpose of school enrollment. Indeed, nationalists themselves gleefully celebrated the demise of national indifference in the aftermath of the Revolution of 1918. Hugo Heller, a German nationalist child welfare activist in Bohemia, recalled that in 1918 nationalist enthusiasm "rushed in like a fresh spring, awakening life throughout all of German Bohemia, melting the snow and ice of national ambivalence, dispersing the clouds which had paralyzed and depressed nationalist thought, feeling, and will. . . . Those were the good times!"[11]

Much to Heller's chagrin, national ambivalence resurfaced in different forms after 1918. Some citizens remained on the fence when it came to national affiliation, particularly those who were bilingual. These individuals switched sides depending on political and social circumstances. Ironically, the nationalist battle for children's loyalties may even have encouraged

---

[10] Peter Bugge, "Czech Nation-Building, National Self-Perception and Politics, 1780–1914" (PhD diss., University of Aarhus, 1994), 26.

[11] Hugo Heller, *Die Erziehung zu deutschen Wesen* (Prague, 1936).

opportunistic side switching as Czech and German schools and welfare institutions offered parents generous welfare benefits to attract higher enrollments and expand the ranks of the nation. Many Czech speakers continued to marry German speakers and vice versa, and in these families bilingualism and fluid national loyalties were often the norm. Even more individuals may have considered themselves nominally Czechs or Germans but rejected the all-encompassing demands of nationalist politics. Nationalist activists in the early twentieth century worked tirelessly to educate citizens about the many duties that accompanied national belonging. Being a good German did not simply entail casting a ballot for nationalist politicians on election day. Loyal Germans were to shop exclusively in German-owned stores; decorate their homes with tasteful "German" furnishings; visit endangered German language frontiers on vacation; join German choral groups, fire companies, and nationalist associations (and regularly make financial contributions); speak only German at home; marry Germans; and above all, send their children exclusively to German kindergartens, day-care centers, welfare institutions, summer camps, and schools. Is it surprising that relatively few individuals embraced the exhausting demands of this nationalist lifestyle?

This indifference to nationalism was not simply a relic of a premodern age. It was itself a driving force behind escalating nationalist radicalism. It propelled nationalists to devise and impose novel and increasingly disciplinary forms of national ascription or classification as well as new "progressive" pedagogies and nationalist welfare institutions in the Bohemian Lands. An ongoing confrontation between nationalists and nationally indifferent parents also shaped changing understandings of democracy and minority rights, the dynamics of occupation and Germanization under Nazi rule, and the relationship among parents, children, and the state between 1900 and 1948. It may seem paradoxical to view indifference as an agent of change or as a cause of radical nationalism. Indifference to nationalism was rarely a memorable historical event. It was not typically recorded in newspapers, broadcast in speeches and political manifestos, memorialized through public monuments, or celebrated with festivals and songs. There was no Association for the Protection of the Nationally Indifferent, no Nonnational People's Party, and no newspaper for the promotion of national apathy, opportunism, and sideswitching. Institutions that explicitly claimed to transcend divisions of nationality or language in the Habsburg Empire, such as the Social Democratic Party, the nobility, the Catholic Church, and the Austrian army and civil service, represented diverse constituencies and interests that were unlikely to unite in defense of national indifference. Moreover, by the turn of the century these institutions were themselves increasingly nationalized, if not nationalist. National indifference therefore appears most clearly at the moments that nationalists mobilized to eliminate it.

The sources that historians typically rely upon have themselves conspired to bury indifference to nationalism. Maps and census statistics, for example, have notoriously served to obscure bilingualism and national ambiguity in

East Central Europe. In 1910, Austrian census takers registered 63.1 percent of the Bohemian population and 71.7 percent of the Moravian population as Czech speakers and 36.7 percent of Bohemians and 27.6 percent of Moravians as German speakers.[12] At the time, nationalists themselves depicted these numbers as alarming indicators of the nation's demographic strengths and weaknesses. Too often, social scientists have followed their lead, drawing ethnographic maps of the Habsburg Empire based on the false assumption that language use transparently reflected national loyalties or ethnicity.[13] In fact, the census only asked individuals to declare their "language of daily use" (*Umgangssprache/obcovácí řeč*), and deliberately refrained from questioning citizens about their nationality. Both the census and maps effaced individuals in Habsburg Central Europe who spoke more than one language (which they could not record on the census), were identified only situationally with a nation, changed nationalities over the course of their lifetimes, identified with more than one nation, or remained apathetic to nationalist politics. Bilingualism however was widespread in the Bohemian Lands. One Bohemian demographer found that in Prague in 1900, 16.6 percent of schoolchildren were bilingual. In Budějovice/Budweis, the percentage of bilingual children reached 16.2 percent, in Liberec/Reichenberg, 16.1 percent, and in Most/Brüx, 22.4 percent of children spoke both Czech and German fluently.[14]

This book builds upon a rich foundation of historical research that has highlighted the fundamental contingency and fungibility of national loyalties. Theorists such as Ernest Gellner, Benedict Anderson, Miroslav Hroch, and Eric Hobsbawm revolutionized our understanding of nationalism by demonstrating that nations are modern rather than primordial communities. Yet these scholars did little to dispel nationalists' own insistent claims that all modern men, women, and children are card-carrying members of distinct national communities. Nations may be modern, but nationalization did not unfold through an organic and inevitable process of modernization.[15] In

---

[12] Adam Wandruszka and Peter Urbanitsch, eds., *Die Habsburger Monarchie, 1848–1918*, vol. 3 (Vienna, 1980), 38–39.

[13] On the uses and abuses of the Austrian census, see Emil Brix, *Umgangssprache in Altöster-reich zwischen Agitation und Assimilation* (Vienna, 1982); Judson, *Guardians of the Nation*, 14–15, 23, 27–33, 135–39. For examples of nationalist demography, see Heinrich Rauchberg, *Der nationale Besitzstand in Böhmen* (Reichenberg, 1905); J. Zemmrich, *Sprachgrenze und Deutschtum in Böhmen* (Braunschweig, 1902).

[14] Heinrich Rauchberg, *Der nationale Besitzstand in Böhmen* (Leipzig, 1905), 435.

[15] The classics include Ernest Gellner, *Nations and Nationalism* (Ithaca, 1983); Benedict Anderson, *Imagined Communities: Reflections of the Origins and Spread of Nationalism* (London, 1983); Eric Hobsbawm, *Nations and Nationalism Since 1780: Programme, Myth, Reality* (New York, 1991); Miroslav Hroch, *Social Preconditions of National Revival in Europe* (New York, 1985); Eugen Weber, *Peasants into Frenchmen: The Modernization of Rural France, 1870–1914* (Stanford, 1976). Prasenjit Duara has warned against uncritically positioning the nation-state as the authentic "subject of History," or the apex of modernity and modernization. See Duara, *Rescuing History From the Nation: Questioning Narratives of Modern China* (Chicago, 1995). For a critical survey of literature and theories of nationalism, see Geoff Eley and Ronald Grigor Suny, eds., "Introduction," in *Becoming National: A Reader*

addition, by focusing primarily on the contested content of nationalist ideologies, remaining inside nationalists' own discursive universe, studies of nations as "imagined communities" may have inadvertently exaggerated the universality and transparency of nationalist loyalties. Historians of the Bohemian Lands have recently begun to focus on the spotty and fluid nature of national loyalties well into the twentieth century. Gary Cohen's groundbreaking study of the German-speaking community in Prague first illuminated the process by which lower-middle-class German speakers became Czechs in late-nineteenth-century Prague. Jeremy King has told the story of how "Budweisers," loyal citizens of the local Bohemian community of Budějovice/Budweis, first came to define themselves as Czechs and Germans. King's work suggests not only the importance of nonnational, local, and supranational loyalties but the extent to which nations developed out of political and social alliances rather than any kind of preexisting linguistic or "ethnic" differences. Eagle Glassheim has also shed light on how a supranational community, the Bohemian aristocracy, came to embrace nationalist politics as it adapted to the demands of mass politics. Chad Bryant's study of the Nazi occupation of the Bohemian Lands, meanwhile, demonstrates that so-called national amphibianism persisted well into the twentieth century as many individuals chose whether they would become German subjects or Czech citizens under Nazi rule. Finally, Pieter Judson has recently made national indifference itself a subject, detailing the failure and frustration faced at every turn by activists who attempted to nationalize Habsburg Central Europe's rural language frontiers.[16]

The story of nationalist activism around children from the Austrian Empire to the Nazi Empire thus contributes to a growing effort to transcend the geographical and conceptual framework of the nation-state through "transnational" approaches to history. Challenging the nationalist assumptions that shape the history and memory of Europe, however, will require more than simply seeking out institutions, identities, or processes that appear to float above or below or across the borders of nation-states (migration, trade, empire building, war and occupation, tourism, religion, localism, regionalism,

---

(New York, 1996), 3–38. For a critique of the uses of ethnicity in writing on nationalism, see Jeremy King, "The Nationalization of East Central Europe: Ethnicism, Ethnicity, and Beyond, " in *Staging the Past: The Politics of Commemoration in Habsburg Central Europe, 1848 to the Present,* ed. Maria Bucur and Nancy Wingfield, 112–53 (West Lafayette, IN, 2001).

[16] See Gary Cohen, *The Politics of Ethnic Survival: Germans in Prague, 1861–1914* (Princeton, 1981); Jeremy King, *Budweisers into Czechs and Germans: A Local History of Bohemian Politics, 1848–1948* (Princeton, 2003); Eagle Glassheim, *Noble Nationalists: The Transformation of the Bohemian Aristocracy* (Cambridge, MA, 2005); Chad Bryant, *Prague in Black: Nazi Rule and Czech Nationalism* (Cambridge, MA, 2007); Judson, *Guardians of the Nation;* Robert Luft, "Nationale Utraquisten in Böhmen: Zur Problematik nationaler Zwischenstellungen am Ende des 19. Jahrhunderts," in *Allemands, Juifs et Tchèques a Prague, 1890–1924,* ed. Maurice Godé et al., 37–54 (Montepellier, 1994); Timothy Snyder, *The Reconstruction of Nations: Poland, Ukraine, Lithuania, Belarus, 1569–1999* (New Haven, 2003); Kate Brown, *A Biography of No Place: From Ethnic Borderland to Soviet Heartland* (Cambridge, MA, 2005); Pieter Judson and Marsha Rozenblit, eds., *Constructing Nationalities in East Central Europe* (New York, 2004).

hybridity, and cosmopolitanism, to name a few). Important as they are, all these approaches are perfectly compatible with, and can even reinforce, nationalist categories and narratives. For example, at first glance, Europe's so-called borderlands and the allegedly hybrid identities of their inhabitants appear to be rich subjects for transnational historical studies.[17] Upon closer examination, however, it is clear that both the concept of the borderland and the notion of hybridity were in fact the political inventions of Eastern European nationalists. German and Czech nationalists, as we will see, both romanticized and demonized language frontiers and their populations. Scholars risk following nationalists' example by idealizing borderlands as idyllic sites of multiculturalism and cosmopolitanism or pathologizing them as settings for inevitable conflict and violence. In fact, both the concept of the hybrid and that of the borderland smell of nationalism. Both assume the mixing of two distinct parts, each of which already existed as an autonomous national community or culture. In other words, the borderland and the hybrid exist as such in the eye of the nationalist beholder.[18] My goal is therefore not to write the story of German-Czech relations "from both sides." It is rather to trace how those "sides" were first constituted. In spite of nationalists' insistent claims that children were a precious form of national property, well into the twentieth century it remained frustratingly difficult to determine which children belonged to which nation.

Challenging national categories and narratives requires us not only to think transnationally but also to reconsider the very units of analysis and agents of change that structure historical writing. Too often historians position nations as the basic subjects and agents of history, telling the story of "the Czechs," "the Germans," "the Poles," or "the Ukrainians." Instead, we might consider how historical narratives change if we assume indifference to nationalism among ordinary people. To use Rogers Brubaker's helpful formulation, we need to see nations as "perspectives on the world" rather than "things in the world."[19] National indifference, moreover, was consequential, because the parents who rebuffed nationalist demands exercised a kind of agency to which nationalists felt compelled to respond. Like class conflict,

---

[17] On the methodologies and concerns of transnational history, see Jürgen Osterhammel and Sebastian Conrad, eds., *Das Kaiserreich Transnational: Deutschland in der Welt, 1871–1914* (Göttingen, 2004); Thomas Bender, ed., *Rethinking America in a Global Age* (Berkeley, 2002); Phillip Ther, "Beyond the Nation. The Relational Basis of a Comparative History of Germany and Europe," *Central European History* 36 (2003): 45–74; Ute Frevert, "Europeanizing Germany's Twentieth Century," *History and Memory: Studies in Representation of the Past* 17 (Fall 2005): 87–116; Patricia Clavin, "Defining Transnationalism," *Contemporary European History,* 14 (2005): 421–39; David Blackbourn, "Europeanizing German History: A Comment," *Bulletin of the German Historical Institute* 36 (Spring 2005): 25–32.

[18] For critiques of the concepts of the borderland and hybridity in Eastern and Southeastern Europe, see Pamela Ballinger, *History in Exile: Memory and Identity at the Borders of the Balkans* (Princeton, 2002); Scott Spector, "Mittel-Europa? Some Afterthoughts on Prague Jews, "Hybridity," and Translation," *Bohemia* 46, no. 1 (2005), 28–38; Judson, *Guardians of the Nation,* 19–22, 25–42, 256–57.

[19] Rogers Brubaker, *Ethnicity Without Groups* (Cambridge, MA, 2004), 17.

war, technological change, or shifting understandings of gender, indifference to the nation could and did stimulate important historical transformations.

The history of the nationalist battle for children also enriches our understanding of childhood and the family. It is a common assumption of contemporary American social policy and popular culture that the nuclear family alone is the best and natural site for raising children. This assumption has not, however, been universally shared across time and space. In the Bohemian Lands between 1900 and 1945, nationalists nourished a political culture in which the health, welfare, and education of children were believed to be the responsibility of the collective rather than the family alone.[20] Beginning with the Nazi occupation, Czech and German nationalists themselves gradually began to promote education in the family rather than collective education as a strategy for protecting the nation's influence on children against the competing claims of the Nazi state. After the defeat of Nazism, however, the very idea that mass political movements could or should "own" children was typically discredited in the Cold War West. Anti-Communist activists, pedagogues, and psychoanalysts depicted the evil of totalitarianism in terms of excessive intervention into family life. They championed education in the family in the name of individualism, democratization, and de-Nazification, as well as the psychological "best interests" of children.

These imagined links between collective education and totalitarianism do not, however, do justice to the complexities of nationalist claims on children, which bristled with both progressive and disciplinary potential. As German and Czech nationalists competed for the souls of working-class and rural children, they built a nationally segregated child welfare system with few parallels in modern Europe. Local nationalists mobilized to enroll children in a vast network of German and Czech day-care centers, kindergartens, nurseries, health clinics, summer camps, and orphanages. As they sought to improve the quality and increase the quantity of the nation's children, these activists contributed to the decline of infant mortality, provided support for working mothers, and promoted new child-centered pedagogies and psychoanalytic techniques.

The nationalist battle for children also powerfully shaped the development of democracy in the Bohemian Lands. The notion of forced national or racial classification evokes some of the darkest moments in recent history: the "separate but equal" segregationist American South, apartheid in South Africa, and of course Nazism's yellow stars and identity cards. But in the Bohemian Lands, it was in the name of democracy, national self-determination, and minority rights that parents first lost the right to choose a national affiliation. Beginning in 1910, in order to prevent opportunist or nationally ambivalent parents from "Germanizing" or "Czechifying"

---

[20] For an exploration of issues of collective versus familial education in France, see Laura Lee Downs, *Childhood in the Promised Lands: Working Class Movements and the Colonies de Vacances in France, 1880–1960* (Durham, NC, 2002).

their own children, state officials increasingly resorted to new practices of national classification or ascription. On the basis of census results, language examinations, courtroom interrogations, police investigations, and anonymous denunciations, they assigned contested children and parents to a single national community based on "objective characteristics" rather than allowing individuals to choose their own national affiliation.

These practices of classification became even more widespread in interwar Czechoslovakia. Following the collapse of the nationally neutral Austrian state, Czech nationalists promoted practices of national classification with new zeal and with the power of the state on their side. In the Bohemian Lands under Habsburg rule forcible national classification had been limited to children and parents in Moravia. In Czechoslovakia in 1921 citizens of all ages and in all parts of the Bohemian Lands were subject to national ascription through new laws regulating the declaration of nationality on the census. Individuals who were found guilty of declaring a "false" national identity on a census form or who sent their children to the "wrong" school were subject to interrogations, fined, and even imprisoned. Thousands of people who professed to be Germans on the census were changed into Czechs against their will by state officials, who insisted that "the official census records controllable, objective characteristics, and not subjective opinions and personal convictions."[21] In fact, Czech and German nationalists alike promoted a vision of national democracy after 1918 that was focused more on protecting the nation's collective claims on children than on the preservation of individual rights. Yet rather than measuring interwar democracy against an ideal type that became the norm in Western Europe only after 1945 (and finding it lacking), this book attempts to understand Eastern European democracy on its own terms.

When the Nazis did march eastward, they built on native understandings of children as national property and on local practices of national ascription as they attempted to implement their racial program. Germanization in the Bohemian Lands represented far more than simply a policy applied by Reich German Nazis to Eastern *Raum,* or to a population self-evidently divided into Czechs and Germans. Rather, Germanization was a contested set of ideologies and practices whose very meanings were powerfully shaped by a fifty-year local history of nationalist mobilization around children. Czech nationalists across the political spectrum mobilized to keep Czech children ethnically Czech under Nazi rule. They understood their crusade against Nazi Germanization as a continuation of a fifty-year nationalist struggle over the souls of children. Nazi racism did not provoke Czech resistance. Rather, Czech nationalists mobilized against Nazism in the name of protecting Czech ethnic purity. In response to overwhelming Czech resistance, the

---

[21] See Oddělení spisovny 11, č. 58, podčislo 19, carton 251, MV-SR, NA.

Nazi regime eventually abandoned its ambitions to Germanize children in the Bohemian Lands. Instead, Nazi officials in organizations such as the Kuratorium for Youth Education sought to secure the loyalty of Czech youth to the Third Reich as Czechs with a policy that became known as "Reich-loyal Czech nationalism." Czech nationalists ultimately fought and won a battle with the Nazi occupiers in a shared language of defending ethnic purity—a language that had been fine-tuned through a fifty-year struggle against the alleged Germanization and Czechification of children. The Czech nationalist campaign against Germanization under Nazi rule may have succeeded in keeping Czech children Czech, but it also encouraged indifference to those outside a closed ethnic community, including Jews and antifascist Germans, and justified the violence of the postwar expulsions.

This book is therefore not concerned simply with the relationship among children, parents, and political movements but with nationalization and its failures, understandings of democracy in Eastern Europe, and the local and historical contingencies that shaped the dynamics of the Nazi occupation in the Bohemian Lands. By examining the ways in which nationalists used their claims on children to navigate the rise and fall of three very different political regimes, it may be possible to rewrite some of the grand narratives of Central European history with children at the center of the story.

Between 1900 and 1948, children in the Bohemian Lands lived under four radically different political regimes: the supranational Habsburg Monarchy, the Czechoslovak nation-state, the Nazi Protectorate of Bohemia and Moravia/Sudetenland, and finally a postwar Czechoslovak state cleansed of its German residents. Nationalists used their claims on children to navigate these revolutionary transitions. Through educational and social activism, they struggled to construct and reconstruct the boundaries of the nation and family in a time when the boundaries of the state were constantly in flux. Yet histories of the Bohemian Lands rarely traverse the traditional moments of rupture signaled by the rise and fall of states, an approach that tends to emphasize change and downplay the continuities across political regimes. The result is that even astute critics of nationalism often find themselves inadvertently writing within nationalist frameworks, positioning nations or nation-states as either the starting point or end-point of Central European history.

In addition to revealing continuities that have been obscured in previous studies, traversing four political regimes highlights striking ruptures. The most important of these is the critical role of the state in the nationalization of modern Europe. The history of the nationalist battle for children in the Bohemian Lands highlights the surprising persistence of national indifference, but a nagging question remains. How did we get from this world of national ambivalence and ambiguity in 1900 to the violent homogenization of Eastern Europe through ethnic cleansing during and after World War II? Where did all the "national amphibians" go? Focusing on the changing role of the state in national politics between 1900 and 1945 suggests some answers to this question. In the late Austrian Empire, the supranational Habsburg state typically served as a neutral umpire, adjudicating between competing nationalist claims. Far from working against the Imperial state, the German and Czech nationalist movements alike competed to demonstrate their loyalty to the Habsburg dynasty. During the First World War, Austrian officials actually turned to nationalist social welfare activists in their own hour of need as they struggled to fortify the Imperial state's legitimacy in the face of a growing social crisis. German and Czech nationalist child welfare activists became the architects of an ambitious new nationally segregated welfare state in the Bohemian Lands, which was to become a model for the Empire's other multilingual regions. In the final years of the Monarchy, nationalists therefore dramatically expanded their authority over children as the Habsburg state's own trusted agents.

Politics, everyday life, and individual loyalties transformed dramatically when the Imperial state's neutrality was abandoned in favor of the nationalizing policies of the Czechoslovak nation-state and the Nazi Empire. Fewer parents could claim to be neither Germans nor Czechs after 1918, as nationalizing regimes forced individuals into a single nation in order to exercise basic political and social rights and to be counted as citizens or subjects. Czech nationalists were more determined than ever to pin down fence-sitters and side-switchers. They mobilized against Germanization in the name of democratization itself—and they now had the full power of the state on their side.

Across four regimes, Czech nationalists claimed to embody democratic principles, to be the antithesis of their "barbaric" and antidemocratic German neighbors. It comes as no surprise that nationalist movements in the Bohemian Lands were built on such assertions of fundamental difference, on binary oppositions between Germans and Czechs, Germanness and Czechness. One does not have to dig deep beneath these claims, however, to unearth a more nuanced history of similarities and conflicts that played out in a universe of shared assumptions. Examining nationalist claims on children over the course of fifty years undermines the very claims of essential national difference at the heart of nationalist politics. Lurking beneath nationalists' polemical assertions of difference was a powerful set of shared beliefs about children, family, democracy, minority rights, and the relationship between the individual and the collective. Together, German and Czech nationalists created a unique political culture in which children were treated as national property. These nationalist claims on children profoundly shaped Central European politics and society for half a century but were largely vanquished and forgotten after 1945, when ethnic cleansing finally guaranteed that no child's soul would ever again be exchanged, lost, or kidnapped from the nation in the Bohemian Lands.

I   *"Czech Schools for Czech Children!"*

September was a busy time of the year for nationalists in the Habsburg Monarchy. By the turn of the century, nationalist agitation ranked with new shoes and teachers as a back-to-school tradition in many multilingual towns of the Bohemian Lands. While traveling through the town of Prachatice/Prachatitz in the late summer of 1918, the German writer Robert Scheu observed, "There is always a great deal of agitation during the holidays because of the schools. Both nations attempt to win students over for their schools, and not always with the most honest methods. Some families send their children alternately to the Czech school one year and the German school the next."[1] How did this nationalist battle for children's souls begin? What kind of "dishonest methods" did Scheu observe? And what were the consequences of the struggle to "win" children for the nation?

This chapter traces the origins of the nationalist campaign to eradicate national indifference and bilingualism among parents and children in the Bohemian Lands. In the eyes of Czech nationalists at the turn of the century, the very survival of the Czech nation depended on keeping as many children as possible in Czech schools. To nationally contested children and their parents, national affiliation was, however, rarely the obvious basis on which to choose a school. Although Czech nationalists actively cultivated a democratic self-image, positioning themselves as representatives of a popular rebellion against German elitism, they confronted persistent apathy and indifference to their demands among parents. Czech nationalists deployed a wide range of strategies to eradicate this indifference, beginning with a pedagogical campaign to convince parents of the moral and psychological

---

[1] Robert Scheu, *Wanderung durch Böhmen am Vorabend der Revolution* (Vienna, 1919), 200–201.

dangers of bilingualism. When pedagogy and persuasion failed, they resorted to more radical tactics, including bribery, denunciation, threats, and finally, the force of law. In the last decade of the Habsburg Monarchy, nationalist activists were increasingly successful in transforming their polemical claims that children comprised a form of precious "national property" into a legal reality.

The back-to-school nationalism discovered by Scheu was the product of a legal and political framework created by the Habsburg state itself, a system that increasingly recognized nationality in order to diffuse nationalism. Beginning in the mid-nineteenth century, Austrian liberals had attempted to relegate nationalist expression to an imagined private sphere and to preserve the supranational character of public institutions like the bureaucracy, army, and dynasty. They thereby inadvertently created an expansive and promising space for nationalist mobilization around children, education, and the family.[2] The Austrian Constitution, crafted by liberals, further galvanized nationalist activism around children and schools. Article 19 of Austria's 1867 constitution stipulated, "All national groups within the state are equal, and each one has the inviolable right to preserve and cultivate its nationality and language." To this end, each nationality was guaranteed "the necessary means for education in its language."[3] The Imperial School Law of 1869, meanwhile, obligated municipal governments to support an elementary school wherever an average of more than forty pupils (over five years) lived within four kilometers of it. These laws provided a critical constitutional and legal basis for nationalists to make aggressive claims on the Imperial state for new schools. Between 1884 and 1886, Gerald Stourzh has shown, a series of decisions by the Austrian Supreme Administrative Court (Verwaltungsgerichtshof) determined that Article 19 actually guaranteed linguistic minorities a right to state-funded elementary schools in their language. After 1886, if the parents of more than forty children demanded a school for their children in a recognized language, the municipality was required to provide one.[4]

Finally, in the early twentieth century, a series of compromises designed to alleviate national tensions in the Monarchy had the perverse effect of

---

[2] On Austrian liberalism in the 1860s, see Pieter M. Judson, *Exclusive Revolutionaries: Liberal Politics, Social Experience, and National Identity in the Austrian Empire, 1848–1914* (Ann Arbor, 1996). On the supranational character of "public" Imperial institutions see Istvan Deak, *Beyond Nationalism: A Social and Political History of the Habsburg Officer Corps, 1848–1918* (Oxford, 1990); Gerald Stourzh, *Die Gleichberechtigung der Nationalitäten in der Verfassung und Verwaltung Österreichs, 1848–1918* (Vienna, 1985); Ernst Brückmüller et. al., eds., *Bürgertum in der Habsburgermonarchie,* 9 vols. (Vienna, 1990–2000).

[3] See Gerald Stourzh, "Die Gleichberechtigung der Volkstämme als staatsbürgerliches Recht," in *Die Habsburgermonarchie, 1848–1919: Die Völker des Reiches* (Vienna, 1980), 1014, 1125.

[4] See Stourzh, "Die Gleichberechtigung der Volkstämme," 1128–47; Hannelore Burger, *Sprachenrecht und Sprachgerechtigkeit im Österreichs Unterrichtwesen, 1867–1914* (Vienna, 1995), 39, 101.

further legitimizing nationalist claims on children. In 1905, representatives of German and Czech political parties in Moravia ratified the Moravian Compromise. The Lex Perek, paragraph 20 of the Compromise, stipulated that children in Moravia were legally permitted to attend a school only if they were "proficient" in the school's language of instruction. In 1910 this law was modified so that children could attend a school even if they could not speak the language of instruction as long as they could prove that they belonged to the corresponding nation. But it was no longer enough for parents to simply declare themselves and their children Czechs or Germans, as had previously been the case. Now, in cases of conflict, local officials were empowered to conduct an investigation and assign both parents and children to a single national community based on "objective characteristics." These characteristics could include language use, reading habits, social contacts, education, census records, and descent. National affiliation, once a matter of personal choice, gradually became a matter for state investigation and classification through the nationalist battle for children. These developments all bolstered the claim that schools and schoolchildren were the property of nationalist movements and that nationality was an inherited quality rather than a political or social choice.

A Brief History of Czech and German Nationalism

A visitor to a bilingual town in the Bohemian Lands in the early nineteenth century would not have encountered many Czechs or Germans. Little separated Czech speakers from their German-speaking neighbors throughout much of the nineteenth century, and few people thought of themselves in national terms. In multilingual communities on the language frontiers of the Bohemian Lands, language use was itself highly situational. As Jeremy King has argued, the language a person spoke in 1848 did not necessarily correspond to any distinct cultural, religious, ethnic, or class affiliations, nor did it determine the national affiliation of a person's descendants two generations later.[5] Only in the mid-nineteenth century did some middle-class, urban Bohemians and Moravians begin to add a national layer to their existing mélange of local, regional, religious, professional, familial, and dynastic loyalties. These citizens began to mobilize into nationally segregated and mutually exclusive choral societies, fire brigades, gymnastics movements, and other civic associations, promoting nationalization in the name of modernity and progress. Fledging nationalist clubs and associations were particularly

---

[5] Jeremy King, "The Nationalization of East Central Europe: Ethnicism, Ethnicity, and Beyond," in *Staging the Past: the Politics of Commemoration in Habsburg Central Europe, 1848 to the Present*, ed. Maria Bucur and Nancy M. Wingfield (West Lafayette, IN, 2001), 112–53.

active wherever German speakers were found: in the regions of Northern and Southern Bohemia bordering Germany, in Prague, and sprinkled in "language islands"—that is, urban centers in Moravia such as Brno/Brünn and Jihlava/Iglau, which boasted a substantial concentration of German speakers. In the largely Czech-speaking interior and other rural areas of the Bohemian Lands, nationalists enjoyed far less success.[6]

Yet even in regions supposedly most torn by nationalist conflict, nationalism was slow to catch on among the popular classes. Only in the late nineteenth century, as nationalist movements competed for state resources, schools, political power, and cultural prestige, did they begin to energetically recruit workers and peasants for their cause. This development accompanied the more widespread rise of mass politics in the Austrian Empire. In 1879, German liberals had suffered a defeat in the Austrian parliament. New mass political parties quickly blossomed, including the Young Czech Party (founded in 1874), Austrian Social Democratic Party (founded in 1889), Karl Lueger's Christian Social Party (founded in 1893), and the Czech National Socialist Party (founded in 1898—no relation to the Nazi Party). Male suffrage also gradually expanded, culminating in the introduction of universal male suffrage for Austrian parliamentary (Reichsrat) elections in 1907. Nationalists, meanwhile, appealed to a widening constituency in expanding voluntary associations. The largest and most successful of these associations were devoted to issues of education. In 1880 German liberal nationalists formed a German School Association (Deutscher Schulverein) to support German minority schools in the Austrian Empire. Czech nationalists followed almost immediately with the Central School Foundation (Ústřední matice školská), which promoted the parallel mission of building Czech minority schools. These organizations soon ranked among the largest voluntary associations in Central and Eastern Europe. In 1902, the German School Association managed twenty-six of its own private German minority schools and provided financial support to forty-one others across the Habsburg Empire, with a budget of 4.3 million crowns. The Czech School Association, for its part, distributed 8 million crowns in 1900, thanks to contributions from thirty thousand members, and enrolled ten thousand children in its private minority schools in the Bohemian Lands.[7] Thanks largely to the activism of these associations, multilingual regions of the Bohemian Lands far outpaced

---

[6] On the geographic dimensions of the national conflict, see Mark Cornwall, "The Struggle on the Czech-German Language Border, 1880–1940," *English Historical Review* 109 (September 1994): 914–51.

[7] On the origins and politics of the School Association, see Judson, *Exclusive Revolutionaries*, 207–40, 210 for figures. The German School Association already had more than one hundred thousand members in 980 local chapters in 1885. For other statistics on the Schulverein and Matice školská see Bruce M. Garver, *The Young Czech Party 1874–1901 and the Emergence of a Multiparty System* (New Haven, 1978), 112–13.

more homogenous areas of the Habsburg Monarchy in terms of the density of schools. In 1913, for example, Moravia boasted one school per 871 inhabitants, almost twice as many schools as in neighboring Lower Austria, which had only one school per 1,701 inhabitants that year.[8]

Throughout the nineteenth century and early twentieth centuries, Czech nationalists defined the boundaries of the nation predominantly through language use. Peter Bugge has suggested that the preoccupation with the Czech language among early Czech nationalists can be attributed precisely to a lack of any significant cultural, religious, or social differences between German speakers and Czech speakers in the early nineteenth century.[9] Not surprisingly, the Czech nationalist movement expended extraordinary energy to keep Czech-speaking and bilingual children firmly bound to a Czech linguistic community in Czech schools. Czech nationalists adamantly insisted that all children who spoke Czech (even if they spoke German as well) or who were descended from Czech-speaking parents were ethnic Czechs. German nationalists, in contrast, typically promoted a more assimilationist understanding of national belonging. They considered individual self-identification as well as the possession of bourgeois cultural attributes to be the most significant criteria for membership in the German nation, even as racial ideas took hold within the movement at the turn of the twentieth century.[10] These distinctions were more of emphasis than of type. Depending on the context, both German and Czech nationalists instrumentally used a mixture of arguments based on language, descent, history, race, and culture to claim as many children as possible as Germans or Czechs. But as each national movement competed to expand its ranks, Czech nationalists typically attempted to raise the barriers to exit. By deploying a conception of the Czech nation centered on language and descent, they aimed to prevent children labeled Czech by nationalists from enrolling in German schools and becoming Germanized. German nationalists, in contrast, focused more on lowering barriers to entry, recruiting working-class and peasant families into the national community, at least until 1918. Given these competing understandings of national belonging, it was not at all uncommon for both national movements, relying on their own internal logic, to claim the same children.

---

[8] See Jiří Kořalka and R. J. Crampton, "Die Tschechen," in *Die Habsburger Monarchie, 1848–1918,* ed. Peter Urbanitsch and Adam Wandruszka, 3:520 (Vienna, 1980), 520; Gary B. Cohen, *Education and Middle Class Society in Imperial Austria* (West Lafayette, IN, 1996), 141–43; Jeremy King, *Budweisers into Czechs and Germans: A Local History of Bohemian Politics, 1848–1948* (Princeton, 2002), 104–6; *Statistik der Unterrichtsanstalten* 14, no. 3 (1912–13): 29; Burger, *Sprachenrecht,* 46.

[9] Peter Bugge, "Czech Nation-Building, National Self-Perception and Politics, 1780–1914" (PhD diss., University of Aarhus, 1994), 26.

[10] On the relationship between language and nation in the Bohemian Lands see also King, *Budweisers into Czechs and Germans,* 46, 63–65, 102, 112–13; Emil Brix, *Umgangssprache in Altösterreich zwischen Agitation und Assimilation* (Vienna, 1982), 271–74, 431.

The Czech nationalist campaign against Germanization began in an era when the path to social mobility in the Habsburg Monarchy often ran through the German schools. Since German liberals in the nineteenth century had defined their national collective in terms of middle-class attributes such as culture and property, middle-class Czech speakers often assimilated into a German-speaking social world in Austrian universities and in the Austrian civil service and military. Nineteenth-century Czech nationalists rejected this assimilationist model and began to demand opportunities for social mobility as Czech speakers, through Czech schools. They claimed to lead a popular, democratic movement of the Czech-speaking masses against the tyranny of German privilege. Yet Czech speakers' functional interests in challenging German social or linguistic hegemony are not sufficient to explain the appeal of Czech nationalism, even in the early period of the National Revival. The first Czech nationalist patriots were themselves mostly bilingual, and faced few social barriers as Czech speakers. They attempted, as Peter Bugge has argued, "to create a special Czech high culture by separating it from the Austrian high culture of which they themselves, linguistically, as well as socially, were fully integrated members."[11] As early as 1860, assimilation began to move in both directions in Bohemia and Moravia, although nationalist associations always depicted such assimilation as a one-sided loss. Working-class German speakers in cities such as Prague were likely to learn Czech and assimilate into a Czech-speaking social world, while Czech-speaking miners and workers were likely to learn German and assimilate into the German-speaking milieu in Northern Bohemia.[12]

By 1900 there were still clear advantages to be gained by Czech speakers who learned German (and for German speakers who learned Czech). However, there was actually little to be gained socially for a native Czech speaker by *becoming* a German, that is, identifying with the German nation. In fact, Czech and German nationalists were surprisingly well-matched foes in 1900. According to the 1900 census, more Czech speakers (93.7 percent) than German speakers (91.8 percent) as a whole in the Monarchy could read and write. Czech speakers had also achieved near parity in secondary and higher education. In 1900, Czech speakers, who comprised 23 percent of the Empire's total population, accounted for 26.4 percent of all students in Austria enrolled in secondary schools, 27.1 percent of students in technical

---

[11] Bugge, "Czech Nation-Building," 16–44, 34–35, 40–44, 307.

[12] On the assimilation of Prague's German speakers into Czech-speaking society in Prague see Gary B. Cohen, *The Politics of Ethnic Survival: Germans in Prague, 1861–1914* (Princeton, 1981). On nineteenth- and twentieth-century assimilation patterns in general see Jiří Kořalka, *Tschechen im Habsburgerreich und im Europa, 1815–1914* (Munich, 1991), 93–95. For a contemporary nationalist analysis of national assimilation patterns and demographics based on census data see Heinrich Rauchberg, *Der nationale Besitzstand in Böhmen* (Reichenberg, 1905).

colleges, and 20.5 percent of university students. On balance Czech-speakers' social and occupational standing did not differ significantly from that of the German-speaking population in 1900. It therefore makes little sense to speak of Germans as a "dominant" nation in turn-of-the-century Austria.[13] However, by 1900, Czech nationalists also boasted a long and arguably successful tradition of couching social demands in nationalist terms and vice versa. As we will see, long after social inequalities between German speakers and Czech speakers had diminished, Czech nationalists continued to represent their battle against the Germanization of Czech children as part of a larger struggle against alleged German social and political hegemony.

Battling Bilingualism

The Czech nationalist movement against the Germanization of children and against national indifference crystallized in Prague at the turn of the century, when the Czech National Council (Národní rada česká, NRČ) launched an ambitious campaign entitled "Czech Schools for Czech Children!" The National Council, an umbrella organization created in 1900 to represent Czech national interests, was one of the most powerful nationalist pressure groups in the Habsburg Monarchy. Every Czech political party, the Sokol (Czech Gymnastics Associations), the School Association, and five regional national protection associations were represented on the council with two members each. Together these organizations raised more money than their German counterparts in both real and relative terms.[14] In spite of its impressive resources, however, the council quickly discovered that it was far from simple to convince Czech-speaking parents that German schools and bilingualism were threatening to their children.

As Gary Cohen has demonstrated, Prague's German speakers were in rapid numerical and political decline by 1900. The German-speaking community had shrunk to a small and relatively weak minority, as working-class and lower-middle-class Germans gradually assimilated into the Czech-speaking majority. While in the Imperial Census of 1880 15.3 percent of Prague's residents had declared German to be their language of everyday use, by

[13] On literacy, see Wandruszka and Urbanitsch, eds., *Die Habsburger Monarchie*, 3:511; Adalbert Rom, "Der Bildungsgrad der Bevölkerung Österreichs und seine Entwicklung seit 1880, mit besonderer Berücksichtigung der Sudeten und Karpathenländer," *Statistische Monatsschrift* (Vienna, 1914), 622. On school attendance, see Cohen, *Education and Middle Class Society*, 275, 278–79. For official statistics on the number of Realschule and gymnasium students by language, see Burger, *Sprachenrecht*, 250–60. For occupational statistics, see Kořalka and Crampton, "Die Tschechen," 509.

[14] For more on the composition and political influence of the council, see Jaroslav Kučera, *Minderheit im Nationalstaat: Die Sprachenfrage in den tschechisch-deutsch Beziehungen, 1918–1938* (Munich, 1999), 50.

1910 German speakers made up only 7.0 percent of Prague's population. German political parties also experienced a rapid loss of municipal political power after 1880. The local government, largely in the hands of the nationalist Young Czech Party after 1890, devoted considerable energy to reducing expenditures on German schools and gaining control of the German district school board in order to keep Czech-speaking children out of German schools. The number of Czech-speaking children enrolled in German schools was therefore already shrinking by the turn of the century. But the National Council's concerns had more to do with the place of Prague in the Czech nationalist imagination, as a showcase of Czech national values and cultural achievement, than with hard numbers. Even one Czech child in a German school was too many "in the heart of the Czech crownland," council members argued in a 1908 memo.[15]

The council's campaigns against alleged Germanization typically began with an analysis of school enrollment lists. Activists scanned hundreds of German registration lists seeking out all Czech-sounding names and marked potential Czechs in red pen with a "Č."[16] In light of centuries of intermarriage the fundamental fluidity of linguistic and cultural identities in the Bohemian Lands, the use of names to determine national identity was nonsensical but reflected the National Council's ethnicized conception of national belonging. One memo conveyed the typical result: "Altogether 258 pupils attended the German school at St. Voršily in Prague in the last school year. That the majority of them are from purely Czech families can be judged from the following names: Adamec, Babka, Barabaš, Bařtipán, Beneš, Bezdek, Cmíral. . . ."[17] On the basis of this method of investigation, one Czech nationalist newspaper polemically claimed that in 1906 there were 21,038 Czech children in Prague's German schools, over 99 percent of the children enrolled.[18]

The council fully exploited its network of political and associational contacts in order to identify and discipline renegade parents. In 1909, for example, the Czech Social Democratic Party informed the National Council that the party had mobilized all its local organizations for the cause and stood fully behind the council's effort to prevent "children of Czech workers from being bullied into German schools."[19] The activism of Czech Social

---

[15] "Českým rodičům a pěstounům v Břevnově a okolí," folder Ia, České dítě do české školy, 1908, carton 509, NRČ, NA; Cohen, *The Politics of Ethnic Survival*, 110. On Czech control of the municipal government in Prague, 86–139, 143–48.

[16] These lists can be seen in folder Ia, České dítě do české školy, 1908, carton 508–509, NRČ, NA.

[17] Folder Zapisové Akce Varie. 1903–6, carton 508, NRČ, NA.

[18] Undated newspaper clipping, folder I, České dítě do české školy, 1905–7, Zapisové Akce Varie, 1903–6, carton 508, NRČ, NA.

[19] Letter from the Czechoslovak Social Democratic Party in Prague to the NRČ, 8 October 1909, folder Ia, České dítě do české školy, 1908, carton 509, NRČ, NA.

Democrats on behalf of minority schools ultimately led to open conflicts between Germans and Czechs within the Socialist Party. German Social Democrats in Austria generally supported the creation of minority schools in bilingual regions in Bohemia and Moravia but were typically less enthusiastic about the creation of Czech minority schools in Vienna and Lower Austria. Czech Social Democrats meanwhile actively campaigned for Czech minority schools in and around the Imperial capital, partly in order to compete with the more radical Czech National Socialist Party for votes. In general, German Austro-Marxists viewed the assimilation of ethnic minorities as a "natural" process inherent in capitalism and sought to encourage it while preventing what were seen to be the excesses of "forced" assimilation practiced by the German administration in Eastern Prussia.[20] Karl Renner, himself born in Moravia, advocated a pragmatic form of bilingual education for all children in mixed-language regions, writing in 1909, "Obviously bilingualism is an advantage in daily life in a mixed-language region, and the Germans themselves notoriously encourage their young: Learn Czech! It is no different among insightful Czechs. Are we really at a point that we honestly see the learning of a second language as a disadvantage or even as a disgrace?"[21]

The members of the Czech National Council were certainly less than enthusiastic about bilingual education, as were the many Czech associations that joined the campaign against Germanization. The Association of Czech Progressive Jews in Bohemia and Moravia, for example, lamented that many Jews in the Bohemian Lands had been led astray by the "false prophets" of the German nationalist movement, reporting, "Year after year we are faced with the sad fact that a great number of the Jews living in Czech surroundings send their children to German schools and thereby . . . educate their children to be enemies of the Czech nation. . . . We know that hardly any Jews here have succeeded . . . in freeing themselves from traditional circles, that they walk blindly down the well-trodden paths to their own detriment, and allow themselves to be hypnotized by false prophets."[22] The Czech Progressive Jews assured the Czech National Council that they had organized meetings of parents, distributed brochures, and personally knocked on doors to combat "false prophets" such as German nationalists and Zionists in the Jewish community.

---

[20] See Karl Renner, "Die nationalen Minderheitschulen," *Der Kampf* 2 (1909), 252; Otto Bauer, "Nationale Minderheitschulen," *Der Kampf* 2 (1909), 13–24; Ludo M. Hartmann, "Zur Frage der Minoritätenschulen," *Der Kampf* 2 (1909), 59–63. For a general analysis of Social Democratic positions on the nationality conflict, see Hans Mommsen, *Die Sozialdemokratie und die Nationalitätenfrage in Habsburgervielvölkerstaat* (Vienna, 1963), 393–96; Burger, *Sprachenrecht*, 218–19.

[21] Karl Renner, "Die nationalen Minderheitsschulen," *Der Kampf* 2 (1909), 256.

[22] Letter from the Union of Progressive Jews in Bohemia and Moravia to NRČ, 20 August 1909. carton 509, NRČ, NA.

The efforts of the Czech-Jewish movement merit further consideration, as they reflected the precarious position of the Jewish population in Bohemia as both objects and agents in the campaign against national indifference. On the one hand, Jews were frequently targeted by Czech anti-Semites for their alleged national indifference and for their association with German culture. Even as greater numbers of lower-middle-class and rural Jews in Bohemia assimilated to their Czech-speaking surroundings in the late nineteenth century, Czech anti-Semites accused Jews of aiding and abetting Germanization. These imagined links between Jews and Germanization dated back to the 1780s, when Austrian Emperor Joseph II had issued a series of reforms within the Bohemian Jewish community. In particular, a provision of the so-called *Toleranzpatent* of 1781 had established a network of secular Jewish elementary schools in Bohemia, which were supervised by the state but supported by the Jewish community. In these schools, German (rather than Yiddish or Czech) was the language of instruction. By 1885, only one-third of Jewish elementary school children attended these Jewish schools, but most of them were located in predominantly Czech-speaking regions. At the turn of the century, Czech nationalists often continued to depict these schools, and Jews more generally, as agents of Germanization in nationally contested regions.[23]

The nationalist competition for children also mitigated anti-Semitic exclusion, however, as both Czech and German nationalists eagerly mobilized to integrate Jewish children into their schools and communities. The German School Association, for example, quietly supported German-Jewish schools in the Bohemian Lands until the 1880s and recruited Jewish children to attend its minority schools and bolster census results. Jews participated actively in the German School Association and its successor in Czechoslovakia, the Kulturverband, as well as in the German nationalist Böhmerwaldbund. In Prague, Jews accounted for almost half of all German speakers in 1900 and were well integrated into the German national community. The Czech-Jewish movement meanwhile mobilized zealously to close local German-Jewish schools in the Bohemian countryside and to encourage Jewish parents to send their children to Czech schools.[24]

The National Council also exploited its connections in town hall and Prague city offices in order to secure material and logistical support for

---

[23] On Czech anti-Semitism and Germanization, see Michal Frankl, "Sonderweg of Czech Anti-Semitism? Nationalism, National Conflict and Anti-Semitism in Czech Society in the Late 19th Century," *Bohemia* 46, no. 1 (2005): 120–34; Michael Miller, "The Rise and Fall of Archbishop Kohn: Czechs, Germans and Jews in Turn-of-the-Century Moravia," *Slavic Review* 65 (Fall 2006): 446–74.

[24] On the Czech-Jewish movement to eliminate German-Jewish schools and the association of these schools with Germanization see Hillel Kieval, *Languages of Community: The Jewish Experience in the Czech Lands* (Berkeley, 2000), 135–57. On the integration of Jews into Prague's German-speaking community, see Gary B. Cohen, "Jews in German Society: Prague,

its campaign against Germanization. For example, municipal offices in the Prague districts of Vinohrady, Žižkov, and Karlín all gladly loaned out their secretaries for several weeks in order to lighten the daunting clerical burden of harassing renegade parents.[25] The annual campaign culminated in a publicity blitz in Czech-language newspapers, timed to coincide with school registrations. Almost every local and national Czech newspaper published an editorial reminding parents of their duties to their children and to the nation and of the devastation wrought on Czech children by education in German schools.[26]

Linguistically Neutral Hermaphrodites

Czech nationalists did not shy away from using parents' love for their children to make their case for Czech education. "If you really love your children, allow them to be educated only in their mother tongue!" demanded one 1909 brochure for parents in Prague.[27] Nationalists claimed that educating children exclusively in the Czech language was not merely a national and moral obligation but also a precondition for children's intellectual, spiritual, moral, and emotional development. In making this claim, turn-of-the-century Czech nationalists typically paid their first respects to seventeenth-century Moravian pedagogical reformer, theologian, and Czech national icon Jan Amos Komensky, who insisted that children should be taught in their native language rather than in Latin.[28] Pedagogical critiques of bilingualism first emerged within the romantic nationalist movements of the early nineteenth century, when nationalists began to view language as

1860–1914," *Central European History* 10, no. 1 (1977): 28–54; Dimitry Schumsky, "Introducing Intellectual and Political History to the History of Everyday Life: Multiethnic Cohabitation and Jewish Experience in Fin-de-Siècle Bohemia," *Bohemia* 46, no. 1 (2005): 39–67. On Jews in German nationalist associations and German minority schools see Pieter M. Judson, *Guardians of Nation: Activists on the Language Frontiers of Imperial Austria* (Cambridge, MA, 2006), 49–52, 164, 247.

[25] Memo from NRČ to the Prague town hall, 12 August 1909; Memo from the municipal office of Žižkov to the NRČ, č. 35049; Memo from municipal office of Karlín to NRČ, č. 16079; all in carton 509, NRČ, NA.

[26] "Školství v Praze," *Národní listy*, 5 October 1909; "Český otče, česká matko!" *Lidové noviny*, 1 September 1909; "Do které školy dáti dítě," *Lidové noviny*, Malé vydaní, 6 August 1909, 1; "Před zápisem do škol," *Český sever*, 10 September 1909, 1; *Národní politika*, notice from Ženský klub český, 7 September 1909; *Právo lidu*, 3 October 1909; "Českým rodičům v Pošumaví na uváženou!" *Šumavské proudy*, 11 September 1909, 1–2.

[27] The pamphlet is undated but filed in a folder of material from 1909. "Dejte své dětí–jestli je opravdu milujete–Vychovati jen v řeči mateřské!" carton 509, NRČ, NA.

[28] For Czech nationalist references to Komensky see unauthored pamphlet *České dítko a jazyk německý* (Prague, 1882); Jan Kapras, *Řeč mateřská orgánem školy obecné a znakem národnosti* (Prague, 1883); Národní, socialisté českým rodičům v Brně! *České dítě patří do české školy!* (Brno, 1899), 6 (unauthored pamphlet).

the embodiment of an essential national spirit. If individual character and personality were a function of language, having two mother tongues threatened to leave a child with no stable character or self at all.

These fears loomed large after the Imperial census of 1880, the first time that Austrian citizens were asked by the government to declare their "language of everyday use." In 1882, the importance of primary education in the "mother tongue" was the theme of the annual meeting of Czech teachers in Bohemia, where twelve hundred Czech educators gathered to learn about the pedagogical dangers of bilingual education.[29] A year later, Jan Kapras, a Czech gymnasium teacher in Brno/Brünn, published a pedagogical manifesto in which he claimed that the 1880 census had exposed a disturbing "Moravian specialty" in child rearing. Many Moravian parents apparently registered different languages for different children in their households, claiming that one child spoke German and another Czech if both languages were spoken at home. These parents, Kapras insisted, either "don't know what a mother tongue is or they don't know the educational principles that should be followed from a child's first breath." Learning two languages at once, he maintained, "overburdens a young person's memory and delays the pace of intellectual development." Such families ultimately produced children whose ambiguous loyalties threatened the very social order. He warned, "They educate children without any national individuality, who sway like reeds in the wind, who do not join any actual society at all, who trespass everywhere they go and are very dangerous to everyone. This is the class of linguistically neutral hermaphrodites, who sail to any wind, calling themselves Czech here, German there, and are educated to constantly go back on their word."[30] Kapras's warnings reflected the conventional wisdom among pedagogical experts in Austria in the late nineteenth century: bilingualism stunted the emotional, intellectual, and moral development of impressionable children, threatening to breed a dangerous "lack of character and hermaphroditism."[31]

This pedagogical bias against bilingualism found indirect legal support in the Austrian Constitution, in the form of the so-called *Sprachenzwangsverbot*. This constitutional provision protected Austrian citizens from being forced to learn a second language, effectively making monolingualism a civil right in the Austrian half of the Dual Monarchy. A German elementary school in Bohemia could therefore legally require students to study Latin, Greek, or French but not to study Czech.[32] In practice, however, public elementary

---

[29] *České dítko a jazyk německý.*

[30] Kapras, *Řeč mateřská*, 9–10.

[31] Burger, *Sprachenrecht*, 27–30; citation from *Encyclopädie des gesamten Erziehungs und Unterrichtswesens*, vol. 4, ed. D. Palmer (Gotha, 1881), s.v. "Muttersprache."

[32] On the *Sprachenzwangsverbot*, see Gerald Stourzh, "Die Gleichberechtigung der Volksstämme als Verfassungsprinzip, 1848–1918," in *Die Habsburgermonarchie, 1848–1919: Die Völker des Reiches* (Vienna, 1980), 1124–47; Burger, *Sprachenrecht*, 26–27; Judson, *Exclusive Revolutionaries*, 124–25.

schools with four or more classes and all middle and secondary schools offered the second provincial language as an optional subject. Private schools, military academies, and trade schools also could and did require students to learn German or Czech. In defiance of the constitution, the second provincial language was introduced as an obligatory subject in all Moravian secondary schools after 1895 and in Moravian gymnasiums after 1905.[33]

Czech nationalists' pedagogical arguments against bilingual education fused linguistic nationalism with new pedagogical ideals and theories of child development. Czech children in German schools, nationalists insisted, were doomed to become outcasts and suffer from low self-esteem because they could not keep up with their peers in foreign-language schools. The Czech child in the German school, argued Kapras, "staggers behind the others and is conscious of his weakness. He loses his self-confidence, which is at the core of any noble effort."[34] The nationalist journal *Šumavské proudy* explained to parents, "A foreign, incomprehensible language fills the child with resistance from the earliest age, and awakens in his heart the first feelings of hatred toward the school!" Children educated in a second language ultimately wasted away passively in classrooms where they received no attention from their teachers, becoming "spiritually, intellectually, and physically stunted," argued the *Šumavské proudy*. These students were doomed to become "tumors on society" and "burdens to their parents and siblings," who shirked productive labor and lacked the maturity to reach their own goals.[35] Some nationalists even made explicit links between bilingual education and adolescent delinquency. In 1910 the Young Czech Party's *Národní listy* published an editorial alleging that several young thieves and murderers had recently been acquitted because the criminals had not been educated in their native tongue. The judge, reported the newspaper, actually considered a bilingual education an extenuating circumstance, a kind of insanity defense. Even more shocking was the story of one unfortunate Czech father whose neighbor asked him why in the world he continued to send his child to a German school, given the obvious dangers. The father replied, "I want for the poor boy to have at least one extenuating circumstance!"[36]

[33] Robert Luft, "Sprache und Nationalität an Prager Gymnasien um 1900," in *Brücken nach Prag: Deutschsprachige Literatur im kulturellen Kontext der Donaumonarchie und der Tschechoslowakei*, ed. Klaas-Hinrich Ehlers et. al. (Frankfurt, 2000), 109. Luft estimates that between one-half and one-fifth of the students in Prague's German gymnasium opted not to study Czech between 1890 and 1906.

[34] Kapras, *Řeč mateřská*, 12.

[35] "Českým rodičům v Pošumaví na uváženou!" *Šumavské proudy*, 11 September 1909, 1–2.

[36] "České dítě patří do české školy," *Národní listy*, 13 August 1910. For another reference to the criminal tendencies of children subjected to bilingual education see "K zápisům do škol," *Hlas*, 6 September 1913, 1.

Czech Socialist leaders meanwhile claimed that bilingual education ruined children for the class struggle. A demonstration in Prague in August 1908 to protest the poor condition of Czech minority schools reportedly attracted eighteen thousand Czech Socialists. Socialist leaders at the rally demanded the creation of more Czech minority schools in Northern Bohemia "because we are speaking mainly of working-class children in the region, who are wasting away in schools with a language of instruction they don't understand, diminishing the consciousness of the next generation of the working class and their effectiveness in the class struggle."[37] The Czech National Socialist Party fused the class struggle with the battle against Germanization in more radical terms. Parents who educated their children to be bilingual often did so out of their desire for social mobility—the hope that their children would enjoy a career as a civil servant or in trade rather than as a worker or farmer. Czech National Socialists insisted, on pedagogical grounds, that bilingual education would have the opposite effect, transforming Czech children into deformed, passive workers without personal or political agency. In an 1899 pamphlet for parents in Brno/Brünn, the party denounced German factory owners in Brno for deliberately luring Czech children into German schools "in order to stultify Czech children in their institutions for Germanization, so that they can create an army of ignorant people out of these poor, feeble youth, and quickly and easily triumph in the capitalist battle." These devious German capitalists sought to ensure "that the Czech people emerge from German schools a generation of idiots, slaves in both social and national life," National Socialists claimed.[38]

On both sides of the national divide, nationalists warned that children educated in the "wrong" language actually grew up to be the most violent renegades, enemies of their own parents and nation. Leaders of the Czech Sokol in Nusle, a Prague suburb, forwarded a list of Czech children attending German schools to the National Council with the addendum, "In reality lessons in the German school are animated with a different spirit than in our schools. Instead of learning to love their mother tongue, they learn to hate it. Instead of learning to respect their history and monuments, they learn to laugh at them and speak of them with contempt." These children, claimed Sokol leaders, were well known to become "the nation's greatest enemies."[39] In the journal of the German School Association in 1912, nationalist school activist Emma Rösler evoked similar threats, lamenting, "We know from sad experience: when German children are forced to attend enemy schools they are torn away from the influence of their family, they become alienated

---

[37] "Obrovská manifestace ve prospěch menšinového školství," *Věstník ÚMŠ*, 9 August 1908, 15.

[38] Národní, socialisté českým rodičům v Brně! *České dítě patří do české školy!* (Brno, 1899), 4 (pamphlet).

[39] Které české dítě chodí do německých škol. Memo from Sokol in Nusle to NRČ, folder Ib České dítě do české školy, 1908–10, carton 509, NRČ, NA.

from their nation and indeed they are all too often transformed into the most bitter enemies of the nation."[40]

Czech nationalist pedagogues also attempted to convey the importance of monolingual education directly to children. Pedagogical handbooks instructed Czech teachers to educate their students about the dangers of German schools through stories, songs, and other activities in the classroom. One story in a handbook for kindergarten teachers offered a model of the strategies children might deploy at home. Five-year-old Marenka's grandmother, a shopkeeper, had promised her German customers to send the child to a German school. Marenka's Czech kindergarten teacher had however warned her pupils that in a German school they would not be able to make any friends or learn anything because they would not understand the teacher or the other children. Marenka begged her father, "Daddy, please don't send me to the German school, because I am a Czech child and Czech children belong in the Czech school!" She recited a nationalist proverb and sang him the following tune, a play on the Czech national anthem *Kde domov můj*, which she had also learned from her patriotic Czech kindergarten teacher:

> Where is my school?
> Where Czech songs are sung
> Where I am happy
> Where the Czech language rings
> I want to go to school
> Where Czech children thrive
> Czech school, home of mine!

Moved to tears, Marenka's father grasped her to his chest, kissed her, and promised to send her to Czech school as she wished.[41]

From Christmas Gifts to Coercion

Much to the dismay of nationalists, many parents were not deterred by these dire warnings. Few six-year-olds appear to have followed Marenka's heroic example. Parents continued to choose both German and Czech schools for their children based more on pragmatic considerations than nationalist loyalties. Heinrich Holek, a working-class, bilingual Bohemian, recalled in his memoir that his own had father decided to send him to a new Czech minority

---

[40] Emma Rösler, "Der Kindergarten in seiner nationalen Bedeutung," *Der getreue Eckart: Monatsschrift des deutschen Schulvereines* 10 (1912), 308.
[41] Božena Studenická, *Články pedagogické a methodické* (Prague, 1901), 114–20, 159–60.

school erected by the Czech School Association in Ladowitz/Ledvice. This decision did not, however, reflect his father's nationalist conviction, or the success of nationalist propaganda about the dangers of German education. Young Heinrich was enrolled in a Czech school because of the many benefits being offered to children at the school. He wrote, "No Czech child should attend a German school! This motto was promoted by the Czechs with great zeal. For my father, however, this propaganda was less decisive than the fact that the children of poor parents were promised clothing and shoes as Christmas gifts. Another consideration for my father was that it could also be useful for me to learn to write properly in Czech. A number of children of German parents also attended this school."[42] Parents such as Holek's father weighed heavily on the minds of Czech nationalists. They exposed the yawning gap between nationalist claims to represent the victimized masses and the reality of national indifference and opportunism among working-class and peasant parents. Even when parents did enroll their children in Czech schools, it seems that they did so for the wrong reasons, in the view of nationalists.

The example of Holek's father suggests how parents may have used the nationalist competition for children to their own advantage. Bribery, it seems, proved far more effective than pedagogical warnings in attracting children to Czech and German minority schools. This bidding war for children continuously escalated and ultimately contributed to the development of a full-fledged nationally segregated welfare system. In 1909, the Czech National Council determined that many Czech-speaking parents in Prague sent their children to German schools because these schools offered better school lunches, shoes, textbooks, clothing, and even Christmas gifts to their pupils. The council therefore successfully requested funds from the Prague City Council in order to match these benefits.[43] Even while Czech nationalists engaged in such tactics, however, they depicted parents who accepted bribes from the national enemy as victims of a devious German scheme to purchase children's souls. Brno/Brünn, with its German-controlled municipal government, was frequently the setting for such stories. A nationalist newspaper for minority school teachers, *Menšinový učitel,* reported with outrage in 1910 that German nationalist "drivers" in Brno/Brünn lurked in the streets of working-class neighborhoods during the school enrollment period in order to prey on defenseless Czech children: "A mother herself

---

[42] Heinrich Holek, *Unterwegs. Eine Selbstbiographie mit Bildnis des Verfassers* (Vienna, 1927), 146.

[43] Petition from NRČ to Prague City Council, 11 October 1909, carton 509, NRČ, NA. German nationalists also frequently accused Czech nationalists of buying German children. See Franz Perko, "Streiflichten über die nationalen und wirtschaftlichen Verhältnisse der gemischt-sprachigen Bezirke Westböhmens, mit besonderer Berücksichtigung des deutschen Schulwesens," *Der getreue Eckart* 3 (1905), 2.

reported that one driver on Špitalská street washed her child, dressed him, combed his hair, gave him a bag of candy, and according to the stupefied mother, led him away to be registered in the German school."[44]

Czech nationalists portrayed themselves as unwilling bidders in this market for children. The middle-class biases of Czech nationalist educational activists emerged sharply in these discussions. Czech nationalists had carefully cultivated a contrast between wealthy German nationalists and victimized, working-class Czech parents in order to explain the lack of nationalist discipline in their ranks. In this framework, parents who sent their children to German schools were weak, hapless victims of local German political and economic power: "Germans used their respectability and their economic power to entice our poor people with the status and value of the German language. When that didn't work, they opened their purses. The Germans began to buy children. And however we may deny it, poverty triumphed among our spiritually plain comrades, and they succeeded," commented one writer in *Menšinový učitel* in 1913. Simultaneously, however, activists worried that nationalist competition for children was breeding materialism and opportunism among parents rather than the desired nationalist loyalties. "Now we can do nothing without a parade. . . . From *voluntary* collections we've created a duty, and support for the poor has become support for notorious lazybones, self-interested parents, a *traffic in children,*" *Menšinový učitel* lamented.[45]

Middle-class nationalists increasingly suspected that parents' lack of nationalist enthusiasm was not the result of German nationalist treachery. It was rather a consequence of deficient morality and lackluster national discipline. In one Czech nationalist newspaper, a writer recounted a conversation on a train with a frustrated Czech minority school teacher from Southern Bohemia. The teacher lamented, "Our people are poorer than the Germans, and if the children don't get pens, notebooks and some kind of shoes or new pants at Christmas, some parents threaten that they are going to send their children to the German school, where the children receive everything for free, there are no school fees, and at Christmas there is always a generous gift." While the teacher had certainly encountered some children of the deserving poor, who appeared as "orderly and decent as the wealthy," he taught an equal number of "disorderly children, where alcohol is the real cause of poverty, and the children run about in tatters." Supporting these children, the teacher lamented, amounted to supporting their father's alcoholism—but withholding benefits would result in the children's being "bought" by the national enemy.[46]

---

[44] Jan Zahradecký, "Školské poměry národností na Brněnsku," *Menšinový učitel,* 1 February 1910, 72.

[45] J. Loučka, "Stíny menšin," *Menšinový učitel* 4, December 1913, 42. Emphasis in the original.

[46] "Hoské hovory," *Stráž severu: Věstník národní jednoty severočeská,* 1 July 1910, 1.

Czech educational activists constantly complained that they were forced to battle on two fronts: not only with local German nationalists but also with apathetic, indifferent, and downright selfish and amoral parents in their own ranks. These parents' "lack of character" and desire for the smallest personal advancement induced them to "sell themselves and their children" to the national enemy.[47] Shortly before the school enrollment season, the Moravian Catholic newspaper *Hlas* observed that there was a disturbing number of "Herods" among Czech parents. While chastising these "foolish mothers and fathers," however, *Hlas* continued to emphasize the role of German treachery in tempting defenseless Czech parents astray. The "hunt for Czech children," the newspapers claimed, was the saddest testimony to the barbarity of the Germans: "Even in the darkness of Africa the subcultural native sees to it that the children know their own language and learn legends about the history of the tribe." Only German nationalists would sink so low as to force Czech parents to "forget their own blood."[48]

This deep suspicion of parental loyalties ultimately justified more disciplinary strategies for harnessing children to the nation, including public denunciation and boycotts. One of Brno's major Czech-language newspapers, the Old Czech Party's *Moravská orlice,* complained in 1910 of meager gains in Czech school enrollments, blaming parental indifference: "Our national expansion in Brno has not yet nearly reached a normal, natural level. That means that the people of our nation do not possess nearly enough self-consciousness or character to perform their national duty." Czech parents, the newspaper explained, simply did not hate enough. They were not, however, to direct their hatred toward Germans but rather toward "renegades," those Czech-speaking parents who sent their children to German schools against all better judgment. "If every Czech person could double their hatred and contempt for the renegades . . . enough people would think twice before Germanizing themselves and their children," the newspaper concluded.[49]

Members of the Czech National Council agreed. It did not take long for the council to become frustrated with the unsatisfying results of their campaign against bilingualism. In a 1906 meeting in Prague's Old Town attended by representatives from fifteen Czech associations, the gathered delegates concluded, "All of the measures that have been used up until now to reduce the enrollment of Czech children in Prague's German schools have been insufficient." It was therefore necessary, they decided, "to resort to more extraordinary measures."[50] As a first step, members of the council planned to use their lists of nationally derelict parents as blacklists, expelling

[47] *Výročni zpráva národní jednoty severočeské,* 1908, 4.
[48] "K zápisům do škol," *Hlas,* 6 September 1913, 1, carton 509, NRČ, NA.
[49] "Po brněnském zápise," *Moravská orlice,* 14 September 1910, 1.
[50] Protokol schůze agitačního sboru pro Prahu I.-V., folder I, České dítě do české školy, 1905–6, carton 508, NRČ, NA.

the named parents from Czech associations and enforcing a social boycott against them. In 1909, Zeman Vojtěch, an employee at the bank Slavie, suggested that activists in Prague and its suburbs turn to even more personal forms of intervention, "as do the German-Jewish henchmen."[51] They were to "work from man to man and woman to woman completely on the sly," offering children clothing and school supplies as well as free German classes in exchange for transferring their children to Czech school. The National Council also sent a letter to the Czech Union of Landlords in Prague in 1906, urging its members to evict tenants who sent their children to German schools, a tactic adopted by German nationalists as well.[52] Finally, the Czech National Council sent personal letters to renegade parents, threatening:

> With great regret we have discovered that you send your child to a German school. We are only fulfilling our duty to those who have offended our national feelings and consciousness when we amicably inform you of the consequences of your perverted, nonsensical behavior. Your child does not understand a word his teacher says, sits passively, does not prosper, is becoming stunted, and will only curse you later for arming him so poorly for his life. Not only can your child learn nothing in a German school, but he will painfully feel his deficiencies in comparison to his happier German classmates and will lose his will to work. Therefore we call upon you one last time: If you want to be called a Czech, send your child to a Czech school! And if you don't, we will consider you a German and there will be no place for you in Czech society.[53]

There is no record of responses to these threats, but official statistics compiled by the city of Prague indicate that between 1900 and 1910, the number of Czech-speaking children attending German schools decreased from 952 to 375 children, suggesting that these tactics were at least marginally effective.[54] The Czech National Council's campaign against renegade parents soon bred a nascent culture of denunciation within nationalist circles as official denunciations encouraged denunciations of a more personal nature. One anonymous postcard sent to the Czech School Association (and passed on to the National Council) in 1907 informed nationalist leaders, "If you are concerned about securing one more Czech child for Czech schools, allow me to inform you that the daughter of the tram driver Pták has attended a school of the German School Association for 4 years. . . . The town hall should order him to send his daughter to Czech school."[55] The council also

[51] Letter from Zeman Vojtěch, April 1909, carton 508, NRČ, NA.

[52] Národní rada česká, Memo to Spolku majitelů domů, 7 September 1906, folder I, České dítě do české školy, 1905–6, carton 508, NRČ, NA.

[53] Template of letter sent to Czech parents, carton 508, NRČ, NA.

[54] Cohen, *Politics of Ethnic Survival*, 110.

[55] Anonymous postcard sent to ÚMŠ, passed on to the Czech National Council, folder II, České dítě do české školy, 1907, carton 508, NRČ, NA.

denounced renegades parents to local city officials in each of Prague's districts, requesting that officials personally intervene to save children from German schools. One such letter informed a municipal office, "We have discovered that Josef Ebr, a gatekeeper living at Motol number 5, sends his two children to the German private school in Prague 3, although he is a Czech and there are plenty of excellent Czech schools in Prague. Allow us to emphatically call your attention to the disorderly nature of this conduct from both a national and pedagogical standpoint, and to ask that you take urgent personal measures to ensure that at least next year, the named fellow citizen will enroll his children in a Czech school." The National Council records indicate that many city officials responded to this call to arms.[56]

The National Council's confrontations with nationally indifferent parents powerfully reveal the problematic contradictions between the Czech nationalist movement's populist self-image and the more tepid commitment of working-class and rural parents to the nationalist cause. While the "instrumental" behavior of these parents was surely exaggerated by nationalists for rhetorical effect, many parents continued to weigh the practical, social, and cultural benefits of bilingualism more heavily than warnings about the dire consequences of a confused national identity. Indeed, nationalist competition for children, intended to secure the loyalty of parents to the nation, may have inadvertently reinforced the very national hermaphroditism that so irked nationalists. The nationalist bidding war for children ultimately conferred a kind of agency on those parents and children who could move easily between national communities, claiming rights and privileges from both. Limiting this agency would require far more radical measures than propaganda and threats.

The Moravian Compromise and the Lex Perek

At the same time that members of the Czech National Council and Prague's municipal government were busy making house calls in Prague, Czech and German political parties sanctioned a national compromise in Moravia. The Moravian Compromise and the Lex Perek ultimately provided nationalists with a radical new set of legal tools with which to strengthen and enforce their rights to educate children. In Moravia, a territorial division of the province based on nationality or language use would have been impossible without some sort of population transfer. German speakers, who comprised 27.9 percent of the province's population in 1900, were geographically dispersed

---

[56] Letters from NRČ to municipal offices, 11 September 1906, folder I, České dítě do české školy, 1905–6, carton 508, NRČ, NA. At least fifteen such letters are on file in this folder as well as some responses from the city offices contacted.

in cities and towns like Brno/Brünn and Jihlava/Iglau. Instead of dividing territory, German and Czech political leaders in Moravia therefore agreed to divide Moravia's 2.5 million people between the two nations. The Compromise, signed on November 27, 1905, stipulated that all citizens eligible to vote in elections for the Moravian Diet, except those voting in the curia of the great landowners, would henceforth be registered to vote within one of two mutually exclusive national cadastres, each with powers of autonomous self-management over arenas such as agriculture, commerce, and education.[57]

The Moravian Compromise also had far-reaching consequences for Moravia's children. Lex Perek, paragraph 20 of the Compromise, stipulated, "As a rule children may only be accepted into an elementary school if they are proficient in the language of instruction."[58] Where persuasion and threats had failed, a law would now prevent non-German-speaking children from attending German schools. The Compromise illustrates how national indifference drove significant political, legal, and social changes in the Bohemian Lands. At the beginning of every school year, German and Czech school boards, as official representatives of the nation, were now legally empowered to "reclaim" children from the other nation's schools if they could prove that the children were not competent in the school's language of instruction. While it may not have been the intention of the lawmakers who drafted the Compromise, a series of court decisions soon rendered the national identity of children, previously a matter of parental choice, subject to state investigation and ascription.[59]

The Compromise began to institutionalize a unique form of nationalist-corporatist citizenship whereby fundamental civil rights such as the right to vote or to education were accessed through national collectives. Austrian Socialist Karl Renner saw the Moravian Compromise as a positive means through which nations could constitute themselves "as that which they are—communities of people, on the basis of the personality principle." To Renner, national cadastres represented an attractive alternative to the

[57] For background on the political negotiations leading up to the Compromise and more detailed analysis of its other provisions, see Mills Kelly, "Last Best Chance or Last Gasp? The Compromise of 1905 and Czech Politics in Moravia," *Austrian History Yearbook* 34 (2003): 279–301; Stourzh, *Die Gleichberechtigung der Nationalitäten*, 213–28; Kořalka, *Tschechen im Habsburgerreich*, 165–173; Hörst Glassl, *Nationale Autonomie im Vielvölkerstaat. Der Mährische Ausgleich* (Munich, 1977).

[58] Cited in Stourzh, *Die Gleichberechtigung der Nationalitäten*, 216. See also Richard Indra, *Zákon perkův, právní priručky pro učitelstvo* (Zabreze, 1913); Václav Perek, *Ochrana menšin národnostních dle mírových smluv a skutečné poměry v naší republice* (Prague, 1922).

[59] For a discussion of the legal and institutional debates surrounding national classification in late Imperial Austria see Jeremy King, "Group Rights in Liberal Austria: The Dilemma of Classificatory Procedure," unpublished paper, 2007. For contemporary discussions of nationality law, see Wolfgang Steinacker, *Der Begriff der Volkszugehörigkeitsbestimmung im altösterreichischen Nationalitätenrecht* (Innsbruck, 1952); Edmund Bernatzik, *Über nationale Matriken* (Vienna, 1910); Rudolf von Herrnritt, "Die Ausgestaltung des österreichischen Nationalitätenrechtes durch den Ausgleich in Mähren und der Bukowina," in *Österreichische*

territorially defined nation-state. Individuals would freely choose which nation they belonged to, and nations would be endowed with a legal "personality." In other words, under certain circumstances, national collectives (like corporations) would enjoy the legal status of individuals.[60] Yet if national cadastres institutionalized a conception of the nation as a community of individuals, they also eliminated the possibility for individuals to stand outside the national community.[61]

The Moravian Compromise, which became a model for similar agreements in Bukovina (1910) and Galicia (1914)—as well as planned compromises in Bosnia-Herzegovina, Bohemia, and the Bohemian city of Budějovice/Budweis—offers a unique historical example of both the equalizing and disciplinary potentials of identity politics, of a system of collective rights in practice.[62] The government intended these agreements to reduce or defuse the social and political effects of the nationality conflict. They did so, however, by recognizing, institutionalizing, and reifying national categories. The Moravian Compromise emerged from the fundamental principle that good fences make good neighbors. This was a misreading of the nationality conflict in that it presumed not only that ordinary Bohemians and Moravians were nationalized but also that nationalist tensions were so explosive that the only solution was an administrative separation of the two populations. In fact, the national cadastres created by the Moravian Compromise were not an organic reflection of self-evident national loyalties. Rather than ameliorating national conflict over children, the Compromise further enflamed disputes over which children belonged to which nation and to which school, over how the nation's new rights to its children should be defined and enforced in practice. These conflicts played out in countless schoolrooms, local political offices, school board meetings and courtrooms in Moravia, and ultimately plagued the highest levels of the Austrian judiciary. The Supreme Administrative Court in Vienna had the final word when German and Czech school boards made competing claims on children through the Lex Perek, and was charged with resolving the many unforseen problems that arose when local officials and nationalists attempted to put

---

Zeitschrift für offentliche Recht (Vienna, 1914), 584–618; Rudolf Laun, "Darstellung des österreichischen Nationalitätenrechtes," *Recueil des Rapports*, vol. 3 (Haag, 1917).

[60] Cited in Burger, *Sprachenrecht*, 190. Quotation originally from Rudolf Springer (Karl Renner), *Grundlagen und Entwicklungsziele der Österreichisch-ungarisch Monarchie* (Vienna, 1906), 182.

[61] The Compromise was intended, for example, to limit the disruptive potential of Socialist internationalism. See Mills Kelly, "Last Best Chance or Last Gap?," 281–82; Judson, *Exclusive Revolutionaries*, 262–63.

[62] On compromises in Bukovina and Galicia see Stourzh, *Die Gleichberechtigung der Nationalitäten*, 230. On compromise negotiations in Budweis/Budějovice and Bohemia, King, *Budweisers into Czechs and Germans*, 137–47, and Kořalka, *Tschechen im Habsburgerreich*, 165–73.

the law into practice.[63] By examining these cases, which involved the disputed "reclamations" of children, we can learn a great deal about how Czech and German nationalists defined the boundaries of the nation, how they sought to secure their claims on children, how the supranational state attempted to resolve these conflicts, and how ordinary Moravian parents and children themselves may have experienced and responded to new practices of national classification.

Austrian state officials assiduously avoided assigning citizens national identities until the final years of the Empire's existence. These principles were first clarified in the context of nineteenth-century battles over the creation of minority schools in the Bohemian Lands. Throughout the last several decades of the Habsburg Monarchy, both German and Czech-dominated localities fought tooth and nail to avoid their constitutional obligation to build schools for linguistic minorities. German officials and Czech officials nonetheless generally relied on different arguments to defend their communities against the financial responsibility and imagined national threat posed by minority schools. These defense strategies reflected different respective understandings of how the national community was constituted and established the framework within which later battles over children under the Lex Perek were fought.

In one of the first such cases, which reached the Austrian Supreme Administrative Court in 1877, Czech municipal authorities rejected a German demand for a minority school in the working-class district of Žižkov in Prague. School officials from Žižkov argued that the parents making the request, who claimed to be Germans, were actually Czechs and therefore had no right to demand an education in the German language. The Ministry of Education rejected this argument, countering that there was no legal standard for determining the nationality of children other than the "personal will of the parents, which is expressed through the enrollment of the children in the German or Czech school." The Supreme Administrative Court affirmed the ministry's conclusion. Parents had the right to decide for themselves which nationality they and their children belonged to.[64] The case marked the beginning of a long tradition of legal battles between Czech nationalist

---

[63] The Supreme Administrative Court was the highest court in Austria in cases involving disputes between various branches of state administration (for example a district school board and the Ministry for Culture and Education) or between government agencies and individuals. Reclamation cases were typically decided by a panel of seven judges, three of whom were argued by Germans to be either Czech or Czech-friendly (Pantůček, Srb, and v. Hernritt). Stourzh, *Die Gleichberechtigung der Nationalitäten,* 220; *Der getreue Eckart* 7, 1909, 283. For more on the composition and function of the Verwaltungsgerichtshof, see Edmund Bernatzik, *Die österreichischen Verfassungsgesetze mit Erläuterungen* (Vienna, 1911).

[64] Stourzh, *Die Gleichberechtigung der Nationalitäten,* 168. For a parallel case in Prague, see Adam Freiherrn von Budwinski, *Erkenntnisse des k.k. Verwaltungsgerichtshofes* 1, Decision no. 228, 9 March 1878.

authorities and parents over the right to determine the identities of children. These battles typically pitted German nationalists, who upheld individual self-identification as the primary basis for national belonging, against Czech nationalists, who claimed that ethnic descent and language use were the decisive markers of nationality.

In a 1909 case in Marianské Hory/Marienberg in Moravia, for example, local Czech authorities argued that they were not obligated to build a German minority school because the parents who petitioned for the school were actually Czechs who had been pressured by their employer, a Prussian firm, to declare themselves Germans. In their complaint, Czech officials maintained that while the fathers petitioning for the German school could speak German and professed to be Germans, they were still actually Czechs, insisting, "There is certainly a great difference between those who learn to speak German and those who belong to the German nation."[65] German officials, in contrast, typically rejected Czech demands for minority schools with the elitist claim that the Czech minorities in their midst comprised a "fluctuating population" of migrant workers, servants, or railway officials who would disappear when the jobs ran out or who had been "artificially" imported into their communities as civil servants. German officials in the Northwestern Bohemian town of Podmokly/Bodenbach, located close to the German border, refused to build a Czech school on the grounds that the Czech minority was in no way rooted in the community. Czechs, they insisted, comprised a "fluctuating collection of splinters from the nation, who are for the most part imported to Bodenbach as railway workers, and have no desire to take up permanent residence here." This Czech minority, argued town authorities, could not be compared to the "German language islands of Budweis [Bohemia], Iglau [Moravia] or Gottschee [Carniola] or the long established indigenous, German minorities in Prague and Pilsen [Bohemia] with their towering economic importance."[66]

Clearly, these arguments reflected German nationalists' own wishful thinking more than the economic or social realities of migration in the late Habsburg Empire. But between 1870 and 1905, the Supreme Administrative Court decisively rejected both Czech nationalist arguments based on national ascription and German nationalist arguments based on the supposedly transient quality of the Czech minority communities. The court consistently ruled in favor of those minority communities that demanded new

[65] Aktenbund II/28 1909, Stadtgemeinde Ortsschulrat Marienberg v. MfKU, Stižnost, 15 February 1909, AVA, VGH, carton 302, ÖstA.
[66] Beschwerde der Stadtgemeinde Bodenbach und des Ortsschulrates Bodenbach, 8 December 1910; Aktenbund II/154 1910, Stadtgemeinde Bodenbach, Ortsschulrate der Stadtgemeinde Bodenbach v. MfKU, AVA, VGH, carton 306, ÖstA. The court decisively rejected the German community's argument and the town was forced to open a Czech school. See Budwinski, *Erkenntnisse* 36, Decision no. 1022, 27 January 1912. See also Stourzh, *Die Gleichberechtigung der Nationalitäten*, 173–76.

schools and against local officials who sought to obstruct the constitutional rights of minority populations. In the 1880s, however, the Supreme Court recognized for the first time that nationality could be legally ascertained and that national belonging was the legal basis for parental claims for a new minority school. Czech parents could not simply demand a German minority school because they wanted their children to learn German, for example. They had to convincingly make the case that they belonged to the German nationality. At the same time, the court continued to affirm that individual self-identification was the decisive legal measure of national identity. In cases in which someone's national identity was contested, officials were simply to ask the individual concerned about his national affiliation and treat him "as a member of that nation to which he himself professes."[67]

Austrian officials upheld the principle that individuals had the right to choose their own nationality until the Moravian Compromise brought new conflicts to the fore. On May 14, 1907, Minister of Education Gustav Marchet, a German liberal nationalist, finally issued a heavily contested implementation ordinance for the Lex Perek. Marchet's ordinance deeply angered Czech nationalists because they believed it allowed for far too many exceptions to the law. Exceptions were permitted when a child had attended a school in the same language in the previous year, when a student was sent on an exchange (*Kindertausch*) explicitly for the purpose of learning the second provincial language, and finally, when "the parents want to send their child to a particular school for other good reasons." Proficiency in a language was also defined quite liberally: children were merely required to be able to understand their teachers well enough to follow the instruction.[68]

In December of 1910, the Supreme Administrative Court issued a critical decision that overturned Marchet's ordinance and guided the reclamation process in Moravia until the Monarchy's collapse in 1918. The case, concerning sixteen children who were reclaimed from the German public school in the town of Uherské Hradiště/Ungarisch Hradisch, radically transformed the ways in which nationality was legally defined in Moravia.[69] The decision specified that district school boards in Moravia were no longer mere state authorities in the technical sense but were now local national organs, "which are called upon to bring to bear the legal claims of their nation, such that the children who legally belong in the school of a given nationality are not withheld

---

[67] Stourzh, *Die Gleichberechtigung der Nationalitäten,* 171. For original quotation, see Budwinski, *Erkenntnisse 4,* Decision no. 130, 3 January 1881, 1163. For other examples, see Budwinski, *Erkenntnisse 5,* Decision no. 1566, 22 November 1882, as well as Budwinksi, *Erkenntnisse 7,* Decision no. 2027, 20 February 1884.

[68] Stourzh, "Die Gleichberechtigung der Volkstämme," 1174–75; Burger, *Sprachenrecht,* 193–94.

[69] Konvolut II/150 1908 z. 6727 ex 1910, carton 82, SSD/V, NA. The full text of the decision is also published in Budwinski, *Erkenntnisse 34,* Decision no. 6727, 11 December, 1910.

from it." The court thus explicitly codified an understanding of children as national property, acknowledging "the right of every nation in the province to its members." Through the creation of this collective right, the rights of parents were correspondingly limited, the court elaborated, ruling "the freedom of parental will in the choice of public schools for their children has been considerably limited to the benefit of the national collective." Parents henceforth enjoyed the right to choose between a German and Czech school in Moravia only when their children could demonstrate proficiency in both languages. The decision also clarified previously contested questions such as how linguistic "proficiency" was to be defined. Children were now required to demonstrate that they could "express their thoughts and ideas" in the language being tested. The goal of this strict standard was to ensure that children attended a school corresponding to their nationality, the intent of the Lex Perek: "Without a doubt, as a rule a child will only be able to do this in his mother tongue, in the language of his nationality, that of his parents," the decision explained.[70]

The court also explicitly eliminated previous exceptions to the Lex Perek for children sent on exchanges during the school year, a decision that provoked apprehension among at least some of the judges. In the court's private deliberations, Justice Tezner thus posed the question, "In polyglot states it goes without saying that the so-called Kindertausch proves itself practical. Is the Supreme Administrative Court therefore justified to completely eliminate this useful practice through its ruling?"[71] Ultimately the court concluded that it had no choice but to ban Kindertausch. The final decision conceded that while "a practice through which parents strive to insure that their children learn the second provincial language is certainly understandable and useful," the letter of the law allowed no exceptions.[72]

Liberal critics of the Supreme Court's 1910 decision argued that this ruling disadvantaged children of workers and peasants precisely because middle-class parents typically had the means to send their children to private language schools or to hire tutors. In the *Neue Freie Presse* in 1911, Dr. Johann Jarolim, a liberal German-Moravian representative in the Moravian Provincial Diet, argued that it was natural in a multilingual province that parents should seek to educate their children in both provincial languages. "While better-off parents have the means to provide the necessary language instruction to their children, this possibility will henceforth be eliminated for needier parents," he claimed. Through the court's decision, poor children were "doubly disinherited: materially and intellectually."[73]

---

[70] Budwinski, *Erkenntnisse* 34, Decision no. 6727, 11 December 1910, 1741.

[71] Folder II/150 1908 Beratungsprotokolle vom 22 June 1910, in causa no. 6727, Tezner, carton 82, SSD/V, NA.

[72] Budwinski, *Erkenntnisse* 34, Decision no. 6727, 11 December 1910, 1744.

[73] Johann Jarolim, "Die Mährische lex Perek, ihre Durchführungsverordnung und der Verwaltungsgerichtshof," *Neue Freie Presse*, 10 March 1911, 2, and 9 February 1911, 2–3. The

Indeed, a significant majority of the children reclaimed under Lex Perek originated from the families of workers, peasants, or small retailers, individuals who were seeking social mobility or who were interested in bilingualism so that they could deal with customers and workers in either language.

The court also introduced the possibility for children to attend a school if they were not proficient in the language of instruction but belonged to the nationality represented by the school in question. A child who spoke no German but had a German father was thereby entitled to attend a German school on the basis of his or her German nationality. In a significant departure from Austrian nationality law, however, parents' own claims to be a German or a Czech were no longer sufficient proof of national belonging. Henceforth, national identity could not be ascertained "through the simple declaration of the parents about their nationality, which would also be the nationality of the child. In conflicts over believability and truthfulness, this declaration would have to be supported with objective, concrete characteristics," the ruling stipulated.[74] With this ruling, nationalists were handed a decisive victory in their battle against nationally indifferent parents: the power to assign parents and children to a national community (and a school) against their will.

The Reclamation Ritual

The court's 1910 decision did not defuse nationalist conflict, as German nationalists themselves were eager to point out. The *Tagesbote aus Mähren und Schlesien* observed at the beginning of the 1911 school year that "precisely in the arena of education, the Compromise of 1905 has not brought the hoped-for peace. To the contrary, the battle for children burns . . . with even more heat and bitterness."[75] Between 1906 and 1918 over sixty cases reached the Supreme Administrative Court that hinged on determining the nationality of individual children. These cases represented only a fraction of the thousands of children caught up in the annual ritual of reclamations between 1906 and 1918. In the city of Brno/Brünn alone 926 children were reclaimed from German schools in September of 1913.[76] In many towns the majority of the children enrolled in the first grade at the local German school

---

vice-chair of the Supreme Administrative Court, Rudolf Ritter v. Alter, responded to Jarolim's critique in an editorial also entitled "Die Mährische lex Perek, ihre Durchführungsverordnung und der Verwaltungsgerichtshof," 21 February 1911, 2–4.

[74] Budwinski, *Erkenntnisse* 34 Decision no. 6727, 11 December 1910, 1742.

[75] "Deutscher Schulschutz und Schulschutzzentrale," *Tagesbote aus Mähren und Schlesien,* 12 September 1912, 3–4.

[76] Z. 378, Bezirksschulrat in Brünn an den böhmischen kk Bezirksschulrat für die Stadt Brünn, Brünn, 5 February 1913, carton 318, ZŠR, B22 1. část, MZA.

were reclaimed each year by Czech school authorities. In Jihlava/Iglau, for example, 22 out of 30 first-graders enrolled in one German elementary school were reclaimed in 1910, while 22 out of 30 children were successfully reclaimed from the German first-grade class in Třebič/Trebitsch that year.[77]

After the reclamations were filed, the testing began. German language exams quickly became annual spectacles, involving nine to eleven teachers and officials, sometimes including gendarmes in uniform and the town mayor. Six-year-old Anna Poschopil in Brno/Brünn, who successfully passed her German language exam, was asked the following questions to ascertain her language abilities: "Where are you? What grade are you in? What is the blackboard made of? How many fingers do you have? What is the Emperor's name? Who is our father in Heaven? What do we need milk for? What else can a person drink?"[78] The testing procedures themselves were the subject of hair-splitting disputes among parents, Czech and German school officials, and the state. Local Czech school boards insisted that German authorities were not above preparing children in advance by distributing the questions or training children with memorized responses.[79] These exams soon became the target of widespread criticism from both German nationalists and parents. In November 1911, Friedrich Papirnik wrote a letter of complaint to the district school board in Jihlava/Iglau to protest his son's exam. The child had been tested by a commission consisting of several teachers from the German school, the Imperial school inspector, the chairmen of the German and Czech provincial school boards, and a government representative in uniform. In the face of the assembled crowd, Papirnik claimed that his child was "so frightened that he also didn't speak in Czech, which is no wonder with a small six-year-old child, since it is not uncommon that even grown men accustomed to speaking in public can't produce a correct sentence in the presence of higher-ranking individuals."[80] In response, the district school board defended the results of the examination, alleging that his child had answered the question "What is your father's name?" with gibberish and that when the teacher asked him about some body parts and grabbed him by the ear, the boy answered, "That are shoes."[81]

[77] Böhmische Ortsschulrat in Trebitsch v. MfKU, z. 9987, Aktenbund II/96 1910; Böhmische Ortsschulrat in Trebitsch v. MfKU, Beschwerde z. 9985, Aktenbund II/105 1910; Böhmische Ortsschulrat in Hussowitz, Beschwerde z. 840, Aktenbund 11/130 1910; all in Carton 305, VGH, AVA, ÖstA.

[78] Z. 487, carton 318, ZŠR, B22 1. část, MZA.

[79] For Czech complaints about testing irregularities, see Böhmische Ortsschulrat in Unter Kolnitz v. MfKU, Aktenbund II/153 1912; Beschwerde des Böhmischer Ortsschulrat in Wall. Meseritsch v. MfKU; Böhmische Ortsschulrat in Schreibendorf gegen die Entscheidung des MfKU vom 20 February 1912, z. 7648, 28 December 1912, Aktenbund II/68, 1912; all in carton 311, VGH, AVA, ÖstA.

[80] Memo to District school board in Iglau from Friedrich Papirnik, 16 November 1911, carton 329, ZŠR, B22 1. část, MZA.

[81] Übersetzung z. 982–11, carton 329, ZŠR, B22 1. část, MZA.

Meanwhile, in a bitterly contested 4–3 decision, the Supreme Court ruled in 1911 that Lex Perek did not apply to private schools. Private German schools could therefore still legally accept children who were not proficient in the German language.[82] Czech nationalists furiously depicted this ruling as a backhanded strategy to continue Germanizing Czech children. Local Czech school boards unsuccessfully attempted to reclaim children from German private schools several times between 1906 and 1914 in order to eliminate this loophole. The Czech school board's complaint in the 1911 case asserted that in Brno alone, German associations supported forty-five German private kindergartens in order to seduce "poor Czech children" into German schools. There were also six private German schools in Brno/Brünn, "established in the worker's quarters on the periphery of the city," which were "filled with healthy Czech children from Brno and the surrounding areas who cannot go to public German schools because of their lack of knowledge of the German language. In these private schools 240–300 children of the Czech nationality are denationalized yearly."[83] Against such accusations, German school officials and nationalists defended German private schools in the name of parental rights. The lawyer representing parents in the Brno case argued, "It can no longer be denied that the principles of the Lex Perek have limited the legal rights of citizens of both nationalities in Moravia. Nationality has been to a certain extent degraded to a coerced community, and all of society, Germans and Czechs, stand face to face with this law of coercion. If a father wants to send his child to a different school according to his conviction . . . he exercises a certain emergency right when he sends the child to a private school. . ."[84]

Until the end of the First World War private schools retained the right to accept children who did not speak German. German nationalists eagerly took advantage of the loophole. Associational literature even suggested that poor children who were not proficient in German should be offered scholarships to private German schools and kindergartens, which they could attend until they had learned enough German to enroll in a public school.[85] In its propaganda the Czech School Association angrily denounced these kindergartens as "secret and insidious backdoors" to German schools. While healthy and happy Czech kindergarten students spent their summers with their mothers, listening to fairy tales, singing songs, and playing outside in the sunshine, the children sent to German

[82] Böhmische Ortsschulrat Komein v. MfKU, Erkenntnis, 4 May 1912, z. 5591, Aktenbund II/115 1911, carton 310, VGH, AVA, ÖstA.

[83] Böhmische Ortsschulrat Komein v. MfKU, Erkenntnis, 4 May 1912, Stížnost z. 1875, Aktenbund II/115 1911, carton 310, VGH, AVA, ÖstA.

[84] Böhmische Ortsschulrat Komein v. MfKU, Erkenntnis, 4 May 1912, Verhandlungsprotokoll, Aktenbund II/115 1911, carton 310, VGH, AVA, ÖstA.

[85] *Der getreue Eckart* 7, 1909, 284–85.

kindergartens by their unenlightened parents were "subjected to their employers like workhorses, without even fresh air. Day after day they are forced to spend their joyful vacation dragging the strange handcart of German enlightenment."[86]

Parents who wished to evade the Lex Perek thus took liberal advantage of their children's ability to learn German quickly. The Supreme Court threw these parents another bone in 1910 by ruling that while children were contested and their cases made their way through a complicated bureaucracy, they could remain in the schools chosen by their parents. Czech nationalists bitterly contested this ruling, arguing that it essentially nullified Lex Perek, since it enabled children to stay in German schools until they could pass the required language test easily.[87] These defeats forced Czech nationalists to confront the practical limits of defining nationality based on language use. In spite of nationalists' own dramatic claims that bilingual education would stunt children for life, many children easily learned German between one year and the next. The Austrian Supreme Administrative Court explicitly allowed children who failed the language test in one year to enroll in a German school the following year if they successfully passed the required German test. In the school district of Třebíč/Trebitsch near Iglau, for example, 93 out of the 128 children reclaimed at the start of the 1911–12 school year had been successfully reclaimed for Czech schools in the previous year but reenrolled in a German school again in 1911 after brushing up on their German.[88] While the Lex Perek had seriously limited parental rights, the use of language as a measure of national identity kept the door open for many parents to choose a bilingual education for their children.

Parents Talk Back

Passing a German test offered one route into German schools under the Lex Perek, but for children who couldn't speak German at all, nationality provided another. The Supreme Court's 1910 decision allowed parents to enroll their children in German schools if the child's father could prove on the basis of objective characteristics that he was a member of the German

---

[86] "Oplatky," *Věstník ÚMŠ*, nos. 6–7 (1909): 190. See also Richard Indra, "Návod, jak reklamovati české dítky z německých škol," in *Zákon perkův, právní příručky pro učitelstvo* (Zábřeh, 1913), 49–50.

[87] *Die Schülereinschreibung in Mähren und die Lex Perek* (Brno, 1913), 14–15; Böhmische Ortsschulrat in Königsfeld, Stížnost, Aktenbund II/108 1910, carton 305, VGH, AVA, ÖstA.

[88] Böhmische Ortsschulrat in Seelowitz v. MfKU, Erkenntnis Z. 1814, Aktenbund II/45 1910, carton 304, VGH, AVA, ÖstA; Z. 10881, Schülereinschreibung, 1911–12, Brünn, 17 April 1912, carton 329, ZŠR, B22 1. část, MZA.

nation. This provision gave rise to a flood of nationality trials in Moravia as Czech school boards contested such claims as a matter of routine. Civil servants in the office of the district captain, the chief official representing the Austrian state in each local district, were empowered to conduct lengthy investigations into parents' lives in order to ensure that their children were assigned to the proper national community and school. A 1913 guide for Czech teachers and schools specified that officials in charge of these investigations were to gather testimony "about the family, origins, language of everyday use at home and in private and public life, knowledge of the German language, inclinations, education, knowledge of songs, literature, magazines, national history and ideas, and other similar markers of national belonging."[89]

In practice, as a first step, the parents of a contested child were typically required to fill out a survey. Parents' responses reveal that many of the nationally contested children came from mixed marriages, grew up in bilingual families, or had parents who lived for many years in Vienna or Lower Austria.[90] These questionnaires presumed both that social commitments measured identity and that every individual belonged to one national community or the other. The surveys' biases toward national voices reflected, at a local level, a larger transformation in the Habsburg state. As Jeremy King has suggested, the nonnational or supranational state increasingly became multinational after the turn of the century, institutionalizing nationality in its attempts to prevent national conflict.[91] In this case the state's job was not to encourage nonnational loyalties but rather to determine whether parents had honestly declared which community they belonged to.

The surveys began by asking "to which nationality do you profess?" but quickly moved on to descent, demanding the names, language abilities, nationality, and residence of the contested child's grandparents. Parents were questioned about whether they had attended German or Czech schools and which language they used "in family circles and which in social life" as children and adults. Next parents were required to provide information about "official" markers of nationality, including which language they had declared in the census of 1910, in which voting cadastre they were registered, and whether any of their other children had ever been reclaimed from German schools. These questions reflected the extent to which most Moravian citizens had acquired some sort of official track record of nationality by 1905, which they could not easily escape. Finally, the surveys asked parents to reveal their social, associational, and political commitments, whether

[89] Richard Indra, "Návod," 43.

[90] See surveys of Franz Raus, Franz Roček, Josef Tours, Karl Vojaček, Josef Vostál, Franz Rous, carton 329, ZŠR, B22 1. část, MZA.

[91] King, *Budweisers into Czechs and Germans,* 114–52.

they belonged to German or Czech associations, whether they were "otherwise active in public life in national relationships," and "in which direction" such activity took place.

We rarely get to hear the voices of the parents caught up in the processes of national ascription set in motion by Lex Perek. These surveys nonetheless provide at least some glimpse of how parents talked about their own linguistic and national affiliations. Parents' responses reveal that even in 1911, the concept of a single and unchanging national identity was foreign to many Moravian citizens. For example, in response to the simple question, "What was the nationality of your parents?" many parents in Jihlava/ Iglau were evasive. Franz Rous responded that he couldn't say much about his parents' national loyalties. He considered himself a German and spoke mostly German at home but had declared Czech as his language of daily use in the 1910 census and had been registered on the Czech voting list. Josef Vostál insisted, "I don't profess to any nationality" and claimed that his parents were neither Czechs nor Germans. Franz Raus, who considered himself German, claimed that his parents had belonged to the Catholic nationality. Parents of contested children typically proved to be a bundle of national contradictions and reveal the extent to which the objective characteristics sought by authorities were frustratingly unhelpful in their quest to assign individuals to the "correct" national community. Too often, the objective characteristics recorded by the surveys conflicted, undermining a binary understanding of national identity. Josef Tours, for example, reported that his parents were Czech, that both German and Czech were spoken in his home, that he had listed German as his language in the census of 1910 but voted in the Czech cadastre in 1911, that his wife was German, and that he considered himself German.[92] These parents' testimony also suggests just how new the concept of national identity was for many Moravian citizens, even in the last decade of the Habsburg Monarchy, when historians typically claim the Empire was torn asunder by nationalism.

Occasionally, individual parents actively protested a child's reclamation. When Josef Hubaček's daughter was reclaimed from a German school in Zábřeh/Hohenstadt in 1912, he responded with an angry letter to the Supreme Court, writing, "I consider the interference of the Czech School Board . . . to be an infringement on my free discretionary rights over my child, which appears to have no legal justification whatsoever."[93] Johann Lehar also appealed his daughter's exclusion from a German school in Hohenstadt in 1911. Lehar had enrolled his daughter Anna in the German

[92] Deutscher Bezirksschulrat in Iglau an Bezirkshauptmannschaft in Trebitsch, 28 April 1911, z. 3896, carton 329, ZŠR, B22 1. část, MZA.
[93] Beschwerde, Josef Hubaček, Hausbesitzers in Hohenstadt, 14 June 1912, 3, folder II/84 1912, with II/114 1912. SSD/V, carton 89, NA.

school solely on the basis of his claim to belong to the German nation, as the child could not speak German well enough to pass the language exam. She was reclaimed along with twenty other children at the beginning of the 1910 school year, and his claim to be German was disputed by the Czech school board. During the investigation that followed, the local district captain determined that Lehar had registered German as his language of daily use in the 1910 census and was a member of the nationalist Association of Germans in Northern Moravia and the local German fire company. But he had also been registered in the Czech voting curia, declared himself a Czech speaker in the 1900 census, and confessed to being a Czech under interrogation by the head of the local Czech school board. The district captain therefore decided that he was actually a Czech, along with his daughter Anna.

In his appeal, Lehar insisted that he had been wrongly classified, writing, "I adamantly dispute that I belong to the Czech nation and that the assessment of my nationality is correct." He explained that he had only declared himself Czech under the pressure of interrogation. Moreover, he questioned the very legitimacy of national classification in a linguistic borderland like Zábřeh/Hohenstadt. German speakers and Czech speakers had lived together for generations, he explained, and it was now impossible to objectively determine who descended from which nation. "Along the language frontier, it is common for many families of purely German descent to have become Czech, and for many families of purely Czech descent to have become German over time, and to have joined the German nation," he explained. "It is completely impossible to determine whether my ancestors were of Germanic or Slavic origins. The various professions of nationality made by my ancestors as well as their various linguistic competencies, would in any case have been different at different points in time. . . . Feelings alone are decisive in measuring belonging to one or the other nation, and these cannot be determined through the procedures of a court." The court, however, disagreed and affirmed the district captain's conclusion that Lehar was a Czech and that his daughter belonged in the Czech school.[94] Lehar's letter of protest may have been exceptional, but his case powerfully illustrates the distance traveled by the courts in the final years of the Habsburg Monarchy. National ascription had been explicitly rejected by the Austrian Supreme Court in 1909. By 1912 forcible classification was a legitimate legal means of transforming nationally indifferent Bohemians and Moravians into Czechs and Germans.

While it became increasingly difficult to evade national classification in the late Austrian Empire, parents were not completely without agency.

---

[94] The full original text of this appeal is published in Stourzh, *Die Gleichberechtigung der Nationalitäten*, app. 8, 311–16. The original document can be found in folder II/84 1912, with II/114 1912, carton 89, SSD/V, NA.

As we have seen, until the collapse of the Habsburg Empire, the parents of children who were genuinely bilingual retained the right to choose a German or Czech school. Children who failed the German language test could brush up on German and try again the next year. Parents with the financial means could send their children to private German schools regardless of their language skills or nationality and could also enroll their children in German nursery schools and kindergartens. Czech nationalists responded to these perceived loopholes in Lex Perek by deploying more disciplinary strategies to reclaim children for the Czech nation. In a round of negotiations over the implementation of Lex Perek in 1911, a Czech parliamentary deputy argued, "Parental rights are really only a pretense used by German employers to exercise force over Czech parents."[95] If granting individual choice to parents only enabled their victimization by German overlords, the solution was to eliminate choice altogether. The purpose of the Moravian Compromise, argued the Czech school board in Třebič/Trebitsch, had been to "prevent the absorption of one tribe by the second." Achieving this goal required that national identity no longer be left to individuals to decide for themselves. The school board maintained, "One can stop members of this or that nationality, as a basis and condition of national preservation and development, from changing their nationality according to impulse at any moment. National belonging must be decided through consideration of the actual conditions and all relevant circumstances, and a very wide surveillance of both individuals and government offices must be permitted [for this purpose]."[96]

Even while language proficiency remained the clear legal basis for reclamations, Czech school boards increasingly attempted to reclaim children on the grounds that they were Czech by descent, regardless of how well they spoke German. In one 1913 case, the Czech school board in Valašské Meziříčí/Wall-Meseritsch reclaimed five children in spite of the fact that they had successfully passed the required German language test. The children's ability to speak German was irrelevant, according to the school board's interpretation of Lex Perek: "According to the law, the circumstance of whether a child speaks German or not is not decisive, because the right of a nation to educate its children in their maternal language cannot be obstructed simply because the child masters a second language."[97] Between 1910 and 1913, Czech school boards repeatedly reclaimed children who had passed the German language exam. The verdict was always the same, as the Supreme Court rejected attempts to reclaim children who were bilingual

[95] Protokoll über die am 20 Juli 1911 im Statthaltereigebäude in Brünn abgehaltene Beratung betreffend die Regelung der Aufnahme der Kinder in die öffentlichen Volksschulen, z. 33621, sig. 18a 1909, carton 4625, Unterricht, Mähren in genere, AVA, ÖstA.
[96] Beschwerde z. 9985, Aktenbund II/105 1910, carton 305, VGH, AVA, ÖstA.
[97] Z. 7916, Aktenbund II 87/1912, carton 311, VGH, AVA, ÖstA.

purely on the basis of their alleged Czech descent.[98] These cases illustrate the limits to the Habsburg state's embrace of forcible national classification. The Austrian Supreme Administrative Court refused to distinguish between a first, second, or third language: children who were proficient in German had the unambiguous right to attend a German school, regardless of when or how they had learned the language. No Moravian citizen could escape national categorization after the Moravian Compromise, but the courts provided at least one possibility for children to escape the national community into which they were legally born.

Political theorist Will Kymlicka has distinguished between two different kinds of collective rights for ethnic and national minorities: "external protections," which aim to protect a group from larger social inequalities, exclusion, or domination by other groups or the state, and "internal restrictions," which empower a collective to limit the freedom of its own members in the name of group solidarity. Kymlicka argues that liberal, multicultural societies can and should guarantee the first kind of "group-differentiated" right while prohibiting the second kind. Yet this framework wrongly assumes that national groups or ethnic minorities are preconstituted and that the two kinds of rights can be easily distinguished.[99] The story of the nationalist movement to keep Czech children in Czech schools offers one example of how easily collective rights justified as external protections ultimately enabled internal restrictions. Advocates of the Lex Perek claimed to uphold the rights of parents to express their nationality by guaranteeing all Moravian children an education in their native language and by protecting parents from local social, economic, and political pressures to assimilate to the culture of the national majority. Yet precisely because it was not self-evident which children belonged to which national group (or that they belonged to any national collective at all), the Lex Perek was instead used by nationalists to first constitute the national collective.

The practices of national ascription authorized by Lex Perek were but one manifestation of larger trend toward identity ascription in modern European societies, as states attempted to render populations legible with censuses, passports, identity papers, and other forms of surveillance.[100] These trends

---

[98] See, for example, z. 765, Böhmische Ortsschule in Unterkanitz v. MfKU; z. 9546, Beschwerde des böhmischen Ortsschulrates in Unter Kanitz/Dol. Kounice; z. 8150, Beschwerde des böhmischen Ortsschulrates in Königsfeld gegen die Entscheidung des MfKU vom 13 February 1912; z. 2679, Wegen Aufnahme zweier Kinder in die deutsche Volksschule, 1910–11 and 1911–12; all in carton 92, SSD/V, NA.

[99] An example of an "external protection" could be affirmative action or bilingual education. An "internal restriction" might restrict the right of Amish parents to remove their children from school at age twelve or prohibit female genital mutilation. Will Kymlicka, *Multicultural Citizenship: A Liberal Theory of Minority Rights* (Oxford, 1995), chaps. 3–5.

[100] See Jane Caplan and John Torpey, eds., *Documenting Individual Identity: The Development of State Practices in the Modern World* (Princeton, 2001); Götz Aly and Karl Heinrich Roth,

seemed ominous to some contemporary observers. Edmund Bernatzik, rector and legal scholar at the University of Vienna, warned in 1910, "There loom trials all too reminiscent of the tribunals of the Inquisition. At stake here, after all, is the ascertainment of convictions! A person could be sentenced by an authority or a court to belong or not to belong to a particular nation. That is absurd, and would be even more absurd if there were to be several mutually contradictory judgments—which is entirely possible."[101] In the multinational Habsburg Empire, however, the driving force behind this movement to categorize was not the state itself, which remained ambivalent about national ascription. It was rather popular nationalist movements, which sought to inscribe their collective claims on children in the law.

In fact, the very qualities of the nationalist campaign to secure their claims on children through Lex Perek calls into question conventional images of late Habsburg Austria as a thoroughly nationalized landscape. Nationalists in late Imperial Austria claimed to speak on behalf of the masses but used the collective rights they won to first constitute distinct national communities. Many parents themselves were not easily persuaded that bilingualism was dangerous, that assimilation was threatening, or that national hermaphroditism would do more harm than good to their children. This indifference to nationalism, far more than nationalist polarization, inspired the denunciatory tactics of the Czech National Council and the new practices of national classification introduced by the Lex Perek. It would take the collapse of the Habsburg Monarchy, however, to transform many of Bernatzik's predictions into a legal reality. Without the moderating influence of the supranational Habsburg state, nationalists were free to pursue their campaign to eradicate national indifference with more radical efficiency. If Czechs could reclaim children from Germans and Germans could reclaim children from Czechs, after 1918 it would become even more difficult for parents to reclaim their children from nationalists.

Die restlose Erfassung: Volkszählen, Identifizieren, Aussondern im Nationalsozialismus (Berlin, 1984); James C. Scott, *Seeing Like a State: How Certain Schemes to Improve the Human Condition Have Failed* (New Haven, 1998); Gerald Stourzh, "Ethnic Attribution in Late Imperial Austria: Good Intentions, Evil Consequences," in *The Habsburg Legacy: National Identity in Historical Perspective,* ed. Ritchie Robertson and Edward Timms, 67–83 (Edinburgh, 1994); Sheila Fitzpatrick, *Tear off the Masks! Identity and Imposture in Twentieth-Century Russia* (Princeton, 2005), 3–27.

[101] Bernatzik, *Über nationale Matriken*, 30.

2 · *Teachers, Orphans, and Social Workers*

In Joseph Roth's novel *The Radetzky March,* District Captain Herr von Trotta, an aging Austrian civil servant posted to a small Bohemian town, laments the shrinking number of Habsburg loyalists at the turn of the twentieth century. He links this disturbing decline in Austrian, Imperial loyalties with the growth of new mass nationalist movements.

> The district captain felt as if the whole world were suddenly made up of Czechs—a people he viewed as unruly, hardheaded, and stupid as the inventors of the very concept of "nation." A lot of people might exist, but no nations. . . . He even thought he noticed that they were multiplying unnaturally, in a way that was not suitable for human beings. It had become quite clear to the district captain that the "loyal elements" were growing less and less fertile and bearing fewer and fewer children, as proved by the census statistics, which he sometimes leafed through. He could no longer squelch the dreadful thought that Providence itself was displeased with the Monarchy.[1]

At the turn of the century in the Bohemian Lands, the power of the nation was measured in numbers. Nationalists obsessively counted and compared the number of Czech speakers and German speakers recorded in the census, the number of children enrolled in Czech and German schools, and the number of children "lost" to the nation each year through alleged denationalization or infant mortality. The Austrian Imperial Census of 1880 was largely to blame. That year, for the first time, the census asked all Austrian citizens to record their "language of everyday use." Although the census deliberately asked citizens only about language use, not nationality, this did not stop

---

[1] Joseph Roth, *The Radetzky March,* trans. Joachim Neugroschel (New York, 2002), 228.

nationalists from depicting the census as a measure of the nation's demographic health, or from identifying language use with national belonging.[2]

This turn toward quantifying the nation and the general rise of mass politics were foreboding trends for German nationalists. In the nineteenth century German liberals and nationalists had typically based their claims to political power not on numerical strength but on the alleged transcendent value of German culture. Although the 1880 census showed that German speakers comprised a majority of the population of the Austrian Empire as a whole, they were outnumbered almost two to one in the Bohemian Lands. The radical German nationalist association *Südmark* was acutely aware of these challenges. In 1914 the association reported the founding of a new German Austrian Society for the Promotion of Social Welfare in Vienna. The organization's mission statement proclaimed, "The standing of Austrian Germandom is based on its historical accomplishment, economic power and culture. The decline in its political influence is largely the fault of the democratic movements of our times, which lay a great deal of weight on numbers. If the Germans in Austria have up until now been able to maintain their relative proportion of the total population, that is solely thanks to the fact that they were always in a position to Germanize foreign elements. That we face ever greater difficulties here requires no further discussion."[3]

As German nationalists confronted the challenges of mass politics, they were no less frustrated than their Czech peers with the national indifference of parents and no less creative as they sought to expand the ranks of the nation. Czech nationalists, as we have seen, increasingly defined national belonging primarily on the basis of ethnicity and descent in order to prevent Czech-speaking children from slipping across national lines in German schools. German nationalists meanwhile were finding it increasingly difficult to secure the numbers required for a mass political movement by assimilating upwardly mobile speakers of Czech, Slovene, Italian, or Polish into the German nation. Confronted with the flood of reclamations in Moravia and an increasingly militant Czech nationalist movement, German nationalists in the Bohemian Lands also began to define the German nation in terms of language use and descent. In the realm of child welfare, this entailed improving the quality and increasing the quantity of German children within an ethnically bound community. The children of peasants and workers once would have been excluded from the German national community on the

[2] Pieter Judson, *Exclusive Revolutionaries: Liberal Politics, Social Experience, and National Identity in the Austrian Empire, 1848–1914* (Ann Arbor, 1996), 204–5. See also Emil Brix, *Umgangssprache in Altösterreich zwischen Agitation und Assimilation* (Vienna, 1982); Z. A. B. Zeman, "The Four Austrian Censuses and Their Political Consequences," in *The Last Years of Austria-Hungary*, ed. Mark Cornwall, 31–41 (Exeter, 1990).

[3] "Gründung einer deutschösterreichische Beratungsstelle für Volkswohlfahrt," *Mitteilungen des Vereines Südmark* 9,1914, 9.

basis of their inferior cultural and class status. Now these children were targeted for inclusion in an expanding German nation by virtue of their common German language or even "blood."[4]

Two parallel nationalist movements sought to transform the children of the popular classes into Germans at the turn of the century: a nationalist pedagogical reform movement and a nationalist child welfare movement. While these two movements overlapped considerably at the local level in the Habsburg Monarchy, they would eventually harden into two competing camps in interwar Czechoslovakia, promoting different pedagogical methods and social reforms that reflected their diverging relationships to the Czechoslovak state and to Nazi Germany. The German nationalist school reform movement attempted to use the space provided by a nationally segregated school system to expand the national community through an internal civilizing mission. While Czech nationalists sought to reconcile tensions between their populist self-image and the reality of parental apathy to nationalism, German nationalists struggled to integrate German-speaking workers and peasants into the national community without threatening their elite self-image as *Kulturträger* (culture bearers) in Central Europe. Through progressive pedagogical movements such as *Heimat* (homeland) education, art education, physical education, and child-centered pedagogy, nationalist school reformers strove to civilize and nationalize German workers and peasants at the same time, expanding the boundaries of the nation through pedagogical uplift in the rural Heimat.[5]

Simultaneously a new nationalist social welfare movement responded to the demographic challenges confronting the German nationalist movement by making claims on children that extended well beyond the schoolhouse walls. In 1908, nationalist activists founded the German and Czech Provincial Commissions for Child Welfare. Local branches of these commissions competed to enroll children in a vast network of nationally segregated health clinics, day-care centers, kindergartens, nurseries, soup kitchens, summer camps, and orphanages. German nationalists in particular focused their efforts on decreasing alarming rates of infant mortality in the industrial borderlands of the Bohemian Lands, offering material assistance and child-care services to working mothers. Within a framework created by the Austrian state itself, German and Czech nationalists constructed a nationally segregated welfare system that may have been unique in modern Europe.

---

[4] "Hinweg mit den Kastengeist!" *Mitteilungen des Vereines Südmark* 4, 1909, 1–3. On this shift in German nationalism, see Judson, *Exclusive Revolutionaries*, 193–272.

[5] Heimat education was not always antiurban. Jennifer Jenkins has recently analyzed the connections between Heimatkunde and progressive school reform in turn-of-the-century Hamburg, where liberal educators explicitly embraced an urban ideal of Heimat. See Jennifer Jenkins, *Provincial Modernity: Local Culture and Liberal Politics in Fin-de-Siécle Hamburg* (Ithaca, 2003), 146–77.

Both the school reform movement and the German nationalist child welfare movement promoted paradoxical views regarding the role of women
and mothers in the national community. Like nationalist movements across
Europe, nationalists in Austria represented women as the guardians of national culture in the home.[6] Mothers were to encourage German nationalist loyalties and habits in their children by speaking only German, singing
German songs, cooking German foods, upholding "German" standards of
cleanliness, thriftiness, and good taste, and sending their children to German
schools. This nationalist ideal of Germanness as a set of rules for good
housekeeping had parallels in German colonial settings, especially after
1918, when popular imperialist associations in Weimar Germany emphasized a gendered, cultural "civilizing" mission in the East in lieu of military
occupation overseas.[7]

In Austria's borderlands, however, nationalists never fully trusted German mothers to cultivate their children's national loyalties. The nationalist
school reform movement and the child welfare movement, like the Lex Perek,
were animated by fundamental suspicions of parental loyalties. In the multinational Habsburg Empire, the state did not serve as a nationalizing force of
last resort, as in nation-states such as Germany and France. Nationalist movements therefore increasingly sought to supersede the authority of parents
in realms of education and social welfare, to ensure that children were not
"lost" to the national community because of parents' persistent indifference
to nationalist priorities in the home. In this spirit, nationalists constructed
a network of institutions for collective education that supported working
mothers and challenged the very ideal of the family as the preferred setting
for the education and socialization of children.

Teachers Civilize the Language Frontier

Who were the nationalist activists who spent so much time worrying
about the loyalties of children? What motivated them to spend their time
mobilizing against the perceived menace of denationalization? It is hardly

---

[6] On nationalist women in late Imperial Austria see Heidrun Zettelbauer "*Die Liebe sei
Euer Heldentum*": *Geschlecht und Nation in völkischen Vereinen der Habsburgermonarchie*
(Frankfurt, 2005); Pieter M. Judson, "The Gendered Politics of German Nationalism in Austria,"
in *Austrian Women in the Nineteenth and Twentieth Centuries: Cross-Disciplinary Perspectives*,
ed. David F. Good, Margaret Grandner, and Mary Jo Maynes, 1–17 (Oxford, 1996); Katherine
David, "Czech Feminists and Nationalism in the Late Habsburg Monarchy: The First in Austria,"
Journal of Women's History 3, no. 2 (1991): 26–45. On the relationship between gender and
nationalism more broadly, see Nira Yuval-Davis, *Gender and Nation* (London, 1997).

[7] Lora Wildenthal, *German Women for Empire, 1884–1945* (Durham, NC, 2001); Elizabeth
Harvey, *Women and the Nazi East: Agents and Witnesses of Germanization* (New Haven, 2003);
Nancy Reagin, "The Imagined Hausfrau: National Identity, Domesticity, and Colonialism in
Imperial Germany," *Journal of Modern History* 73 (March 2001): 54–86.

surprising that a growing cadre of nationalist teachers stood at the vanguard of nationalist movements in turn-of-the-century Austria. In 1909 the
German-Moravian Teachers' Association boasted, "At the Conference of
the [nationalist] Association of Germans in Northern Moravia, the teachers had such a majority over the other classes, and were so numerous in
the Main Assembly that one participant remarked 'one might think he was
at a teacher's conference.' "[8] While in 1896 teachers and schools officials
made up only 5 percent of the local branch secretaries of the nationalist
Bund der Deutschen in Böhmen, by 1909 30 percent of the secretaries of the
same association were teachers and school officials.[9] Czech teachers were
equally prominent in Czech nationalist associational life. In 1900 Czech
teacher and writer František Joklík reported that "in the countryside teachers alone organize all the nationalist collections. Close to 1,000 from their
ranks belong to the Central School Association, and the local branches of
our national unions owe their existence in the countryside mainly to the activity of teachers. . . . Teachers work in every way possible for the national
awakening of the indifferent countryside."[10]

Teachers moved to the forefront of nationalist movements as the Austrian
education system rapidly expanded in the late nineteenth century. In 1869
a new liberal school law had been ratified in Austria. The law required
eight years of primary schooling for both boys and girls starting at age six
and wrested primary education from the hands of the Catholic Church by
creating a universal system of free, secular education. It also required that
municipal authorities support an elementary school wherever an average of
forty pupils over five years lived within four kilometers of the school. These
reforms resulted in an explosion of new schools, and new schools required
new teachers. Since teachers were now accorded the status of civil servants,
many young people from peasant or lower-middle-class backgrounds saw
the profession as a path to social mobility and social prestige. Meanwhile,
teachers deployed to Austria's rural and provincial outposts increasingly
saw themselves as agents of modernization and progress, with a mission to
simultaneously nationalize and civilize the peasantry.[11]

---

[8] "Die nationale Tätigkeit der Lehrerschaft," *Deutsch-Mährische Schulblatt* 13, 1910, 234.
[9] *Bericht über die Tätigkeit des Bundes der Deutschen in Böhmen*, 1896, 52–81; "Die
Bezirksverbände und Ortsgruppen," *Bericht über die Tätigkeit des Bundes der Deutschen in
Böhmen*, 1909.
[10] František Joklík, *O poměrech českého národního školství a učitelstva v království Českém*
(Prague, 1900), 129. Joklík claimed that the National Unions of the Bohemian Woods and
Northern Bohemia each boasted at least five hundred teachers in 1900.
[11] Karl G. Hugelmann, ed., *Das Nationalitätenrecht des alten Österreich* (Vienna, 1934),
371; Hannelore Burger, *Sprachenrecht und Sprachgerechtigkeit im Österreichs Unterrichtwesen,
1867–1914* (Vienna, 1995), 39–43. For statistics for the Empire as a whole, see Gary B. Cohen,
Education and Middle Class Society in Imperial Austria (West Lafayette, IN, 1996), 56, 65. On
the nationalizing and civilizing mission of teachers in rural France, see Eugen Weber, *Peasants
into Frenchmen: The Modernization of Rural France, 1871–1914* (Stanford, 1976), 195–241.

Several German nationalist schoolteachers soon built successful careers as nationalist pedagogical "experts," traveling the countryside in the Bohemian Lands in order to enlighten parents, teachers, and concerned citizens about the need for change in German schools. These teachers published widely on pedagogical topics such as Heimat education, a curriculum based on the student's immediate surroundings in his or her local or regional homeland (Joseph Blau and Emil Lehmann), "natural" education (Ewald Haufe), art education, and rural education (Ernst Heywang). Nationalist teachers were also regular contributors to the magazines of nationalist associations such as the Bund der Deutschen in Böhmen, the German School Association, and the Südmark. They published extensively in the Austrian school reform publication *Schaffende Arbeit und Kunst in der Schule,* as well as in a new Moravian school reform magazine, the *Deutsche Schulwart.* The *Schulwart,* which was devoted exclusively to promoting nationalist pedagogical reform, appeared monthly beginning in 1906, soon after the Moravian Compromise divided the provincial school boards in Moravia into Czech and German sections, each with significant control over its own "national" curriculum.

Teachers thus shouldered a heavy burden in the development and expansion of growing nationalist movements. Their motivations and concerns are crucial to untangling the alliance between nationalism and progressive school reform in the Monarchy and to understanding the forces generating nationalist enthusiasm more broadly at the turn of the century. What, then, explains teachers' zealous investment in the nationalist cause? Above all, nationalist activism provided an alluring platform for teachers as they sought to increase their own status at the local and national level. The symbolic importance of children to the nation-building project offered teachers a direct route to higher levels of political and cultural influence. At a 1909 conference on school reform, heavily attended by both teachers and nationalist associations from across the Austrian Empire, one representative of the Moravian-German teachers' association thus celebrated the importance of teachers in educating the nation's youth, proclaiming, "Our profession will finally no longer play the shameful role of the Cinderella of the educated classes."[12]

In the context of the school reform movement, teachers were encouraged to envision themselves as missionaries, as anthropologists, and as artists, privileged by their intimate knowledge of the "misery of the wide masses."[13] Although teachers were typically outsiders in the communities in which they taught, their presumed expertise about local communities formed the basis

---

[12] "Die nationale Tätigkeit der Lehrerschaft," *Deutsch-Mährische Schulblatt* 13, 1910, 234. See also "Die Würde des Standes," *Deutscher Schulwart: Monatsschrift zur Wahrung deutscher Schul-, Erziehungs- und Volksbelangen* 7, 1912, 241.

[13] "Die soziale Frage und ihrer Bedeutung für Jugenderziehung und Jugendfürsorge," *Deutsch-Mährische Schulblatt* 11, 1908, 221.

for their claims to authority within nationalist movements. One German nationalist school reformer explained in 1908, "The teacher who lives in the middle of the Volk proves to have a full understanding of the activity and motivations of the Volk, which he has investigated through his research activities."[14] Articles in reform publications advised teachers on how best to exploit their relationships with locals for the nationalist cause. Ewald Haufe, in an article entitled "How I Live with the Peasant," even suggested that teachers earn peasants' trust by offering free medical advice. "Then it is easy to do some good when the matter at hand is a spiritual or social-economic question," he counseled.[15] These teacher-anthropologists were to visit the homes of each and every student, in order to gain a firsthand appreciation of the child's individual strengths and weaknesses. Through these visits, activists maintained, "The teacher gains deep insight into the soul of the Volk and learns a great deal of folklore. . . . The knowledge of popular viewpoints, especially in moral arenas, provides him with a starting point for his work."[16]

While the nationalist school reform movement sought to elevate teachers' social standing, it also demanded greater professionalism and nationalist self-discipline. If teachers were to transform peasants into Germans, their own professional and cultural respectability had to be in order. Teachers' publications therefore frequently exhorted young teachers to adhere to middle-class, "German" standards of hygiene and culture. Nationalist pedagogical reformer Ernst Heywang reserved particular ire for teachers who insisted on continuing their extracurricular farming activities, insisting, "The peasant class and the teachers' class are so fundamentally different in the qualities of their knowledge, their activities, their character, their required appearances, that they cannot be one and the same. And when a teacher farms, he must become a peasant [*verbauern*]. He then ceases being a teacher, and no flattery or kind words can help."[17] Heywang urged older teachers to police the behavior of their younger colleagues, particularly in their choice of a spouse, lamenting, "Young teachers have long not been selective enough in their choice of wives. The teachers so, so seldom strive upward with their choices."[18] Teachers' wives were the object of intense scrutiny precisely because the bourgeois respectability—indeed, the "Germanness" so coveted by these reformers—was produced and displayed in the home. The teacher's own household was to serve as a model of ideal

---

[14] "Für die deutsche Heimat," *Deutsch-Mährische Schulblatt* 11, 1908, 94.

[15] Ewald Haufe, "Wie ich mit dem Bauer Lebe," *Deutscher Schulwart* 3, December 1909, 87–88.

[16] Joseph Blau, *Der Lehrer als Heimatforscher. Eine Anleitung zu heimatkundlicher Arbeit* (Prague, 1915), 40.

[17] Ernst Heywang, *Landschulprobleme und Landlehrerfragen* (Prague, 1916), 90.

[18] Ibid., 91.

"German" housekeeping, hygiene, taste, and culture for members of his or her community. The complaints of nationalist school reformers suggest, however, that it was an uphill battle to convince teachers to conform to these "German" ideals. One Austrian reformer complained in 1911, "In the teaching profession there are certainly difficulties to overcome. Many of its members come from the peasant class or those social circles that offer youth few opportunities to become accustomed to finer lifestyles."[19]

The story of teachers in the school reform project is useful for understanding the broader dynamics of nationalist activism and its civilizing dimensions in the Habsburg Monarchy. This was a process through which anxieties about the nationalist and cultural credentials of German adults were projected onto children. For teachers, nationalist movements made concrete many of the possibilities that were offered more abstractly to the children, peasants, and workers who were objects of nationalist pedagogy. Through this movement teachers, as well as peasants and workers, were offered integration and even higher status in the German national community. This integration reflected German nationalists' determination to succeed in the world of mass politics. It nevertheless took place on terms clearly inherited from a more elitist German liberal tradition.

A Pedagogy for Mass Politics

At the turn of the century, the German nationalist movement, animated by teachers, turned to progressive pedagogical reform in the hopes of redefining citizenship for mass politics in the Austrian Empire. Most of their ideas were appropriated from a fairly stable repertoire of progressive pedagogical methods gaining popularity across Europe and America through the writings of educators such as Ellen Key (Sweden), Maria Montessori (Italy), Celestin Freinet (France), Anton Makarenko (Soviet Union), and John Dewey (United States). These pedagogical reformers demanded that students no longer be treated as passive objects, subject to rote memorization and authoritarian discipline. They promoted a curriculum that seemed especially appropriate to working-class children, grounded in the students' immediate experiences, aimed at fostering self-sufficiency, creativity, and the individual personality of the child. Across Europe, groups that perceived themselves to be excluded from the existing political order appropriated these experimental pedagogies for diverse causes. In France, for example, Catholics (who were excluded from control of, or even participation in the republican school system) and some Socialists became partisans of pedagogical reform; in England and Germany Socialists led the progressive school reform movement. In each of

---

[19] "Die Würdigung der Lehrerarbeit," *Österreichische Schulbote* 61, 1911, 302.

these national settings, outsiders to the political mainstream construed progressive pedagogy's emphasis on active learning and independent thinking as preparation for a lifetime of adversarial political engagement.[20] In Austria, Social Democrats such as Otto Glöckel famously championed pedagogical reform, especially the creation of unified elementary and middle schools for children of all social classes. He was not, however, alone, in demanding abolishment of authoritarian and hierarchical schools. The school reform movements' emphasis on cultivating children's agency also appealed to German nationalists, who felt such agency was necessary if Germans were to overcome their embattled position in the nationalist struggle. Writing in the *Deutscher Schulwart*, German nationalist school reformers proclaimed in 1909, "We can only prevail when we overcome all of the difficult disadvantages in the outside world through the building of inner power. . . . And to this end, the persistent improvement of the elementary school, which is attended by no less than 95 percent of our male youth, is indispensable."[21]

The above-mentioned "disadvantages" seemed to loom larger for Germans in the last several decades of the Monarchy as Czech nationalists made more successful claims on the Austrian state, especially in the realms of school politics and language politics. Not only were local German nationalists faced with the yearly raid on German schools through Lex Perek in Moravia, but laws such as the Stremayr Language Ordinance (1880) and Badeni Decrees (1897) threatened the privileged position of German as the language of the state, expanding the use of the Czech language within the civil service in the Bohemian Lands. Nationalists insisted that "un-German weakness" had facilitated these defeats, which symbolized no less than "the possibility of total conquest" for Germans in bilingual regions.[22] Nationalist pedagogical reformers understood that if they wanted to compete successfully for the loyalties of workers and peasants, they would have to abandon, or at least repackage, the elitism associated with liberal nationalism. In a populist voice, they therefore rejected many of the prevailing liberal ideals of education. Although the nationalist school reform movement relied heavily on new scientific and expert medical ideas about child development, for example, it also insisted that schools were no longer the exclusive turf of bureaucrats and technical experts. "The school should belong to the people who created it, who need it like bread and clothing in order to live, and

---

[20] On turn-of-the-century reform pedagogies see Laura Lee Downs, *Childhood in the Promised Land: Working-Class Movements and the Colonies de Vacances in France, 1880–1960* (Durham, NC, 2002); Marjorie Lamberti, *The Politics of Education: Teachers and School Reform in Weimar Germany* (New York, 2002); Carolyn Steedman, *Childhood, Culture, and Class in Britain: Margaret McMillan: 1860–1931* (London, 1990); Jenkins, *Provincial Modernity*, 115–146.

[21] "Wir deutsche, unsere Bildungsnot und unser Lehrerstand," *Deutsch-Mährisches Schulblatt* 15, 1912, 327.

[22] *Deutscher Schulwart* 1, September 1906, 1.

therefore not to the powerful in the state and the Church," argued writers in the *Deutscher Schulwart*.[23] School reformers depicted their enemies as fiends not only to children and the German nation but to democratization and progress itself. Among the "dark forces" threatening to destroy the German school, Heimat activist Joseph Blau named "the rulers' cowardly fear of the Enlightenment of the lower classes; militarism, the enemy of culture, which saps away the fruits of the citizen's work; the power of political influences . . . the atrocious payment of the teaching profession . . . in general, the force of poverty and the lack of all consideration for justice and freedom."[24]

In an expression of this populism, nationalists also rejected many of the time-honored methods of classical liberal education. In the place of Greek, Latin, passive drill, and rote memorization, they demanded a pedagogy that would cultivate active bodies, minds, and ultimately, active citizens. Children's bodies had long held a central place in the nationalist programs promoted by Czech and German gymnastics associations.[25] Now nationalist education reformers also promoted physical education, active classrooms, handicrafts, and outdoor education in the name of the moral and physical regeneration of the nation. A preoccupation with practical work, physical education, and active schoolrooms was common in progressive reform movements across Europe, but German nationalists in the Habsburg Monarchy specifically linked liberal overreliance on "book knowledge" to tangible national weaknesses and defeats. A senseless preoccupation with "dead letters" had prevented national revitalization and kept Germans from breaking free from the old liberal parties, the Church, and the "priests of the red and gold International," argued writers in the *Deutscher Schulwart* in 1910. Only through "powerful self-help, which is achieved through an intensive strengthening of the body and spirit, can we again free ourselves from these shackles."[26] Taking this logic to an extreme, one school reformer even argued that the development of language skills was dependent on vigorous movement of the right arm, literally contesting the mind/body distinction. "The language center is first found inside the movement center of the right arm, and is only later differentiated. Since every movement of the arm is nothing less than an intellectual function projected outwards, it follows that there is no fundamental difference between intellectual and physical

[23] "Natürliche Erziehung," *Deutscher Schulwart* 2, February 1907, 123.

[24] Joseph Blau, *Heimat und Volkstum: Gedanken und Vorschläge zur Erneuerung unseres Schulwesens. Beihefte zur Zeitschrift Schaffende Arbeit und Kunst in der Schule*, no. 88 (Prague, 1915), 1.

[25] These organizations clearly promoted physical education as the basis of nationalist pedagogy beginning in the mid-nineteenth century. On the Sokol see Clare Nolte, *The Sokol in the Czech Lands to 1914: Training for the Nation* (New York, 2002).

[26] "Die soziale und nationale Seite der Schulreform," *Deutscher Schulwart* 5, September 1910, 5; "Bausteine zu neuer deutscher Volkspolitik," *Deutscher Schulwart* 2, 1907, 7, 17.

work. Mental and hand labor are one and the same," he insisted in a plea for physical education.[27]

Nationalists also praised progressive pedagogy and physical education as an antidote to the perceived moral and medical risks posed by urban life. In one issue of the *Deutscher Schulwart*, nationalist pedagogue Ewald Haufe tells the story of Olga, a German child who had been "fresh and healthy" when she lived on her parents' farm in the countryside. She played outside in the garden and in the fields, and at nine years old, "she was as strong as a twelve-year-old in the city." That is, until her parents, infected by a short-sighted lust for social status, sent her off to be educated in Berlin. "In place of meadows and creeks, the woods and the hills of the free golden days, came the poisoned air of sunless factory barracks." Olga sat all day in the school and at night on the train and became "round and fat." Only return-ing to the countryside and a simpler lifestyle ultimately cured her. Haufe concluded with the moralizing assertion that the liberal-bourgeois notion of a "cultured" education was an illusion that could not compete against a healthy upbringing in the rural provinces.[28]

"Personality" took on an analogous role in redefining German nation-alism for the needs of mass politics. Like the cultivation of active bodies, educating children with strong personalities promised to strengthen the nation by training future citizens to break free from the restraining politi-cal traditions of the nineteenth century. Discussions of personality also led to debates about the role of nature and nurture in child development as nationalist school reformers disagreed about the extent to which children's personality traits were innate or the product of their environment. Typi-cally, in a Lamarckian spirit, nationalist reformers promoted education as a way of cultivating and developing innate qualities. In 1917, Heimat activist Emil Lehmann explained to members of the Bund der Deutschen, "The *Volkstum* lies within each individual from the outset, and requires outer encouragement and national pedagogical methods only so that it is brought out and developed."[29] Other nationalists, however, were so confident in the power of blood to shape children's personalities that they declared education obsolete. One reformer argued in *Deutscher Schulwart* in 1913, "We often do our children an injustice when we want to educate them with specific moral characteristics that already reside within the tribe to which they belong. . . . When for example, the tribe to which the child belongs is truth-loving, what is the need for special measures for inculcat-ing the love of truth, when it is entirely certain that this trait will surface even without school and education! It is entirely unnecessary to force the

[27] G. Schmiedl, "Der darstellende Unterricht," *Die Schulreform* 4, January 1910, 1.

[28] Ewald Haufe, "Olga's höhere Erziehung," *Deutscher Schulwart* 2, March 1907, 172.

[29] Emil Lehmann, "Erziehungsgedanken von der Sprachgrenze," *Mitteilungen des Bundes der Deutschen in Böhmen* 11, 1917, 110.

German child in a direction that is already well known to be found in German blood."[30]

Nationalist education reformers ultimately used the notion of personality to carve out a tenuous space between the disciplined national unity required for mass politics and liberal individualism. German children were to become political agents, capable of withstanding the temptation of Socialism, the power of the Catholic Church, and the pressures of local Czech nationalists. In this sense, personality stood for a kind of political agency and autonomy within a world defined by mass politics. But this agency was to be firmly directed toward the German national good. Nationalists simultaneously demanded that citizens use their "strong personalities" to contribute to nationalist goals in both politics and daily life so that individualism would not slip into the dangerous realm of Socialist materialism or "one-sided Americanism."[31] In spite of a growing populist emphasis on challenging liberal ideals of education, moreover, nationalist school reformers were not without their own anxieties about the democratization of the national community. These anxieties were most clearly expressed in their plans to bring art and Heimat education to the masses, a civilizing mission in the name of national integration.

Creating the Tasteful Heimat

Even while reaching out to the popular classes, nationalist school reformers did not abandon liberal notions of Germans as the Kulturträger of Central and Eastern Europe. Nationalists therefore faced a serious dilemma as they sought to integrate workers and peasants into the national community. What should they do with the "ignorant" peasant or the "pleasure-seeking" worker, whose German blood was now a ticket into the German community but whose bad taste or poor hygiene threatened the ideal of the German Kulturträger? Pedagogical reform became one tool for dealing with these anxieties, a civilizing mission that would transform German peasants and workers into Kulturträger and expand the ranks of the German nation.

Nationalist pedagogical reformers typically expressed their fears about the democratization of the German nation by preaching on the harmful potential influences of mass culture, consumption, urban lifestyles, and Socialist politics.[32] Mass culture, they warned, would destroy the "inner power"

[30] "Die völkische als eine wahre natürliche Erziehung," *Deutscher Schulwart* 7, June 1913, 226.

[31] Heywang, *Landschulprobleme und Landlehrerfragen*, 27, 37.

[32] On German nation building and taste reform see Jennifer Jenkins, "The Kitsch Collections and the Spirit in the Furniture: Cultural Reform and National Culture in Germany," *Social History* 21 (May 1996): 123–41. On French nation building and taste, see Leora Auslander, *Taste and Power: Furnishing Modern France* (Berkeley, 1996).

and self-control of Germans, allowing the nation to sink into a "worthless, chaotic mass."[33] German teachers, nationalists lamented, were frequently forced to stand by with a heavy heart as the students they had so lovingly educated were "seen marching in the ranks of the Social Democrats, even with Czech workers, only a few weeks after graduation from school."[34] Nationalists also invoked the dangers of urban life and mass culture to define Germanness in opposition to other races and nations. German teachers, argued school reformers in a newspaper for Moravian teachers, needed to lead a "heroic fight" against the powerful efforts to bring Germans down to a lower culture, which "unfortunately seems to be the taste of an important percentage of the other nations of Austria."[35] To "sink into the swamp" of sensational romance novels, detective fantasies, and clerical publications was literally to renounce one's Germanness, reformers warned: "Pretty soon we will all lie here dreaming, just like the Chinese, who slept through a century, during which the other nations actively pushed forward into their jobs. . . . No, I think that this Chinese ideal should not be allowed to become the ideal for German men and women."[36]

Not surprisingly, nationalists also depicted mass culture as a threat to German masculinity. In their battle against mass consumption school reformers made ample use of the classic association of frivolous, consuming women with an irrational and emotional mass.[37] Pedagogical reformers in Moravia warned in 1909, "Nourished by foreign-racial elements, a new spirit has emerged, especially in city circles . . . Pleasure! . . . Pleasure at any price, even if it means that one allows his better power to be stuck somewhere in the swamp of sensuality and exchanges it for an unmanly, sleepy, female essence."[38] These nationalists simultaneously blamed female consumption for the alleged downfall of the nation, for "running a thousand fathers to the ground and a hundred thousand children alongwith him with their eternal fashions and needs." Nationalist educators therefore urged women, as guardians of national culture in the home, to choose simplicity, harmony, and old-fashioned German goods: "Show that the apple means more to us than the orange, the potato more than the artichoke!"[39]

A contradictory vision of women permeated the nationalist reform movement. At the same time that nationalists elevated the role of women

[33] "Über die Erziehung zur inneren Kraft," *Deutscher Schulwart* 2, 1908, 123.

[34] "Im gefährlichen Alter," *Deutscher Schulwart* 1, October 1906, 37.

[35] "Erziehung zur Minderwertigkeit," *Deutsch-Mährische Schulblatt* 12, 1909, 79.

[36] "Volksbildungsarbeit," *Deutsch-Mährische Schulblatt* 12, 1909, 3.

[37] On the gendering of mass consumption in modern Europe, see Victoria de Grazia, ed. *The Sex of Things: Gender and Consumption in Historical Perspective* (Berkeley, 1996); Auslander, *Taste and Power.*

[38] "Über die Erziehung zur inneren Kraft," *Deutscher Schulwart* 2, 1908, 124.

[39] "Mütter, seid natürlich!" *Deutscher Schulwart* 7, January 1912, 114.

as guardians of the nation in the home, they harbored a deeper suspicion of parental inadequacy that drove the internal civilizing mission. As a result, they promoted collective forms of education outside the home and family in order to guarantee that children received a nationalist education. For example, nationalist pedagogical reformers demanded kindergartens and nurseries to fill the gaps left by absent or insufficiently German mothers, to ensure that "dependence and linguistic confusion" were not "established in children's hearts in their earliest youth."[40] These activists revealed that they were not always confident that the immediate surroundings of the home and Heimat provided an ideal setting for a nationalist upbringing. Nor was every German mother or small-town teacher qualified to raise German children with a nationalist spirit. German School Association activist Emma Rösler described the qualities that distinguished nationalist kindergarten teachers from the average German woman in 1906, explaining, "It is certainly not everyone's thing to affirm her national feelings loudly and openly. . . . The majority shrink away from such battles and would rather not deal with the unavoidable tensions. Therefore, not every kindergarten teacher is called to the language frontier. If they don't feel the great, selfless, and I must say holy drive within themselves to make the national cause the highest master of their feelings, then they are better off staying away and choosing calmer sites for their work. Feelings of weakness can not be indulged."[41] This image of German kindergarten teachers as an elite cadre of tough, resilient, nationalist soldiers found echoes in later Nazi appeals to women to serve the Third Reich in the German kindergartens of the conquered Eastern territory.[42]

Nationalist anxieties about parents' national loyalties and their cultural capital fed logically into a pedagogical mission that sought to civilize the popular classes and nationalize them at the same time. These goals were concretely expressed in nationalist demands for art education and Heimat education. "The Heimat has long been the most important source of our curriculum and of nourishment for our schools; she can and should be the middle point of all teaching and learning activity," argued Joseph Blau in a 1919 pedagogical handbook for teachers. Heimat pedagogy reflected the larger tensions within the German nationalist movement itself, the challenges of building a disciplined mass political movement out of middle-class associational politics. On the one hand nationalists extolled the virtues of an authentic German education based on "experience" and "nature" in the local Heimat and home. At the same time they clearly feared that the local rural Heimat looked like anything but a German nationalist paradise.

---

[40] "Der deutsche Kindergarten," *Deutscher Schulwart* 1, November 1906, 66.

[41] Emma Rösler, "Der Kindergarten in seiner nationalen Bedeutung," *Der getreue Eckart: Monatsschrift des deutschen Schulvereines* 11, 1912, 308–10.

[42] See Harvey, *Women and the Nazi East.*

Nationalist advocates of art and Heimat education continuously bemoaned peasant taste at the same time that they extolled the national authenticity and high moral value of rural life. One of the most outspoken advocates of (nationalist) art education was Ernst Heywang, who wrote two handbooks for teachers on rural education, one focused explicitly on the role of art in the rural German school. Although Heywang was an enthusiastic proponent of Heimat education, he found much to criticize in the rural Heimats he served. In both handbooks he took the reader on a critical tour through the peasant household, beginning with the remark: "One would often almost like to wish that there were no furnishings there at all."[43] Alongside inadequacies in taste, Heywang and others lamented the sorry state of rural hygiene, complaining that cleanliness was not yet a natural instinct for the peasant. He speculated critically, "How many peasants bathe? How many peasant families especially in winter? In which peasant families have all the members of the family actually brushed their teeth? Whoever can answer these questions based on his personal experiences will know how difficult it is to achieve victories on this ground."[44]

Heywang called upon teachers to remedy these deficiencies in taste and hygiene. He promoted a pedagogy that rendered Germanness concrete in household objects, above all in furniture and decor. The most widespread reform was the introduction of drawing and singing instruction in German public schools. Nationalists linked these arts to the cultivation of taste, the struggle against (Socialist) materialism, and the training of skilled workers and craftsmen. Heywang demanded that the schoolroom itself set the first example of good taste for German students, arguing, "The children should learn from the beautiful wall decorations in the school that there are nicer paintings than those that they see daily in their homes. They should gain a true dislike for ugly, marionette-like pictures, which can never offer us a noble, lasting joy."[45] At the same time that he fiercely denounced "mass-produced" furniture and art, however, Heywang was confident that good taste could be ordered out of a catalog with a teacher's careful guidance. Children, he suggested, "should learn that the teacher is at any time readily prepared to lend out the catalogs of the most important firms, and even to handle the ordering, when one perhaps doesn't want to take the trouble or doesn't have the ability on one's own."[46]

Reformers also praised the benefits of evening lectures and parent-teacher conferences, through which they hoped to extend the positive effects of nationalist pedagogy to adults. In his guidebooks Heywang instructed his

[43] Ernst Heywang, *Landschule und Landlehrer in Dienst der bildenden Künste* (Prague, 1920), 10–30; quotation, 10.
[44] Ibid., 11.
[45] Heywang, *Landschulprobleme und Landlehrerfragen*, 30.
[46] Ibid.

colleagues on how to attract parents and villagers to evening lectures, advising them that the lectures should not be "too difficult in expression or form," should avoid technical terms and foreign vocabulary, last no more than half an hour, and by all means include pictures. The list of suggested topics included "Furniture," "The Colors in our Home," and "How we Dress Ourselves."[47] Parent-teacher conferences also provided a precious opportunity for teachers to offer the Volk guidance on how to raise their children. Nationalist school reformers proclaimed in 1906, "Parent-teacher conferences have proven themselves to be the ideal realm in which everything can be discussed that, in the interest of children, the nation should promote: the appropriate nutrition of the child; movement games; swimming; bathing; dental hygiene; the prevention of sexual aberration; the choice of profession; preservation of folk songs; character building; the importance of school attendance; the fight against alcoholism; and animal and plant care."[48]

School reformers also enthusiastically promoted Heimat museums, which collected and displayed artifacts from everyday life to document local history and culture. They saw these museums as both a tool for cultivating pride in local German culture and an opportunity to provide peasants with lessons in interior decorating. By creating artifacts for Heimat museums, school reformers hoped that children would develop respect for "authentic" German art and subscribe to a higher level of taste and culture: "The peasant should again, as in the old times, build, nail, whittle, paint, and garden. . . . Girls should lay fashion journals to one side and compete with each other from self-developed embroidery patterns."[49] During the First World War another nationalist pedagogical journal proposed a "school museum for home furnishing" that would display both worthy and unworthy models of home furnishing in order to demonstrate the difference between "pure and bad, practical and unpractical products, taste and tastelessness." Nationalists specifically hoped to reach working-class German girls with these lessons in interior design. Educators speculated that because of their future roles as housewives, girls "are interested their entire lives in bedroom and kitchen furniture, cooking and table dishes, clothing, and washing materials."[50]

As nationalists in the late Austrian Empire competed to claim children for their national communities, they produced a unique vision of Heimat, or homeland in Central Europe. In Germany, historians have analyzed how the

[47] A. Pehersdorfer, "Der Schmuck des Schulzimmers, ein Faktor zur Kunsterziehung," *Schaffende Arbeit und Kunst in der Schule: Zeitschrift für die praktische Ausgestaltung der Arbeitsschule und der Kunsterziehung* 1, 1913, 22.

[48] "Elternkonferenzen," *Österreichische Schulbote* 56, 1906, 91–92.

[49] "Die Heimatkunst und ihre Belebung im Volk," *Deutsch-Mährische Schulblatt* 14, 1911, 221.

[50] Ludwig Praehauser, "Ein Schulmuseum für Heimaustattung," *Jahrbuch der Gesellschaft Lehrmittel-Zentrale in Wien*, 1918, 98, 101.

concept of Heimat served to reconcile tensions between local and national political cultures.[51] In the Bohemian Lands, Heimat activism addressed the peculiar tensions that plagued German nationalist movements in East Central Europe: between ethnic and cultural understandings of the German nation, between liberal and mass politics, and between an idealized nationalist vision of the language frontier and the more ambiguous social relations that characterized those communities.

In 1911 many of the educational reforms proposed by nationalist reformers were officially recognized and institutionalized in the state-sanctioned curriculum for German elementary schools in Bohemia. This curriculum emphasized the need to "place appropriate emphasis on the hands as a means for education and expression" and "to set the self-directed activity of the student in the service of education." The curriculum also institutionalized the central place of Heimat, unifying all branches of social studies instruction from grades three to five under the banner of what was called *Heimatkunde*.[52] The nationalist school reform magazine *Schaffende Arbeit und Kunst in der Schule* praised the new curriculum as a milestone in the reform movement, arguing, "The basis on which the new curriculum is built can withstand all criticism. They are the principles of creative work, of art education, the concentration of all subjects around knowledge of the Heimat, etc. The teachers of Bohemia have every reason to be proud of this curriculum, which came into being through their activism."[53] It is difficult to say how widely the guidelines were translated into practice, but nationalist school reformers appear to have successfully claimed the right to set the agenda for German schools in the Bohemian Lands. Their pedagogical methods were not, however, the only means by which German nationalists attempted to expand the ranks of the nation. At the same time that Blau, Heywang, and Haufe promoted German culture in the rural Heimat, other nationalist activists were looking outside the schoolhouse walls. In the emerging fields of child welfare, public hygiene, and social work, they discovered ambitious new strategies to consolidate national loyalties.

Nationalizing Child Welfare

In 1913, Hugo Heller, the leader of the German Provincial Commission for Child Welfare in Bohemia, reflected on the flourishing new child welfare

---

[51] See Celia Applegate, *A Nation of Provincials: The German Idea of Heimat* (Berkeley, 1990); Alon Confino, *The Nation as a Local Metaphor: Württemberg, Imperial Germany, and National Memory, 1871–1918* (Chapel Hill, NC, 1997), 8; Jenkins, *Provincial Modernity*.

[52] *Lehrplan für Volksschulen mit deutscher Unterrichtsprache in Böhmen* (Prague, 1911), 1–4.

[53] Anton Herget, "Dem neuen Jahrgange zum Geleit," *Schaffende Arbeit und Kunst in der Schule* 2, 1914, 1.

movement in the Bohemian Lands. "The deepest and most powerful driving forces behind the youth welfare movement are precisely national in nature," he claimed. Nationalists "wish not only to improve the inner diligence of the nation and to promote its economic interests but above all to maintain the nation's numerical strength and its ability to uphold its cultural values, its quest for the improvement of the self and of humanity."[54]

Denunciations, threats, and national classification were clearly not the only outcomes of the nationalist battle for numbers. As Czech and German nationalists in the Austrian Empire competed to fill their schoolrooms and expand the ranks of the nation, welfare programs became one of their most successful tools. The shoes, lunches, clothing, and Christmas gifts that lured parents to enroll their children in minority schools soon inspired far more ambitious social programs. By the outbreak of the First World War, nationalists in the Bohemian Lands had become the foremost experts in child welfare in Habsburg Austria and presided over an expansive nationally segregated child welfare system which ultimately became a model for other multilingual regions of the Habsburg Monarchy.

The first major social welfare initiatives in Austria took effect in the 1880s, when a conservative coalition of provincial landowners, social Catholics, and Czech and Polish nationalists led by Count Eduard Taaffe (the so-called Iron Ring) introduced reforms targeting industrial workers, including protective legislation that restricted the working hours of children, youth, and women. These laws were considerably more restrictive than protective legislation in Germany and France at the time. In 1888, inspired by Bismarck's example in Germany, the Iron Ring also created a comprehensive health and accident insurance program for industrial workers.[55] The social welfare programs created by nationalists after the turn of the century differed qualitatively from these state-sponsored initiatives. Because the legislation of the 1880s was the brainchild of an antiliberal coalition of landowners, Catholic conservatives, and Slavic nationalists (in an era when most industry was in German hands), it mainly targeted urban, working-class families while families in rural areas were hardly affected. Nationalist child welfare activists, in contrast, focused as much on rural children and lower-middle-class children as the children of workers. Nationalist child welfare programs, moreover, often targeted children directly, rather than their parents, and were built around specific pedagogical ideals.

The nationally segregated child welfare system that developed in the Bohemian Lands was not typical of all regions of the Habsburg Monarchy. Thanks to the competitive activism of nationalists, social work was actually

---

[54] Hugo Heller, *Jugendland. Eine Einführung in die Aufgaben der deutschen Jugendfürsorge in Böhmen* (Prague, 1913), 34.

[55] William Jenks, *Austria under the Iron Ring, 1879–1893* (Charlottesville, VA, 1965), 179–95, 196–220. See also Margarete Grandner, "Special Labor Protection for Women in Austria, 1860–1918," in *Protecting Women: Labor Legislation in Europe, the United States, and Australia, 1880–1920*, ed. Ulla Wikander et. al., 150–87 (Chicago, 1995).

far more developed in the Bohemian Lands than in any other part of the Dual Monarchy by the eve of the First World War, including urban Vienna and Budapest.[56] In Bohemia in 1914, ninety-five professional social workers supervised 2,510 children, while in Moravia, fifty-four social workers cared for 3,599 children. Most of these social workers were employees of the ČZK or DLS, which set up frequent professionalization courses to recruit and train them. Lower Austria, which included urban Vienna, lagged far behind with only seventeen social workers in 1914.[57]

Political theorists and sociologists commonly suggest that a unified national culture is an essential basis for a developing welfare state. Will Kymlicka argues, for example, that "the sort of solidarity essential for a welfare state requires that citizens have a strong sense of common identity and common membership, so they will make sacrifices for each other, and this common identity is assumed to require (or at least be facilitated by) a common language and history."[58] Such claims, however, presume the preexistence of national communities. Rather than seeing social solidarity as the product of a shared identity, we might consider how in multilingual regions of Europe, national communities were first constituted through social assistance. Middle-class nationalists justified the national segregation of social welfare institutions by arguing that they possessed unique empathy for and expertise about their clients. Within this logic, only Czech social workers and guardians could fully understand the problems of Czech families, and only German social workers could address the needs of German children. These were highly polemical claims. The emerging nationally segregated welfare state in the Bohemian Lands was not a reflection or product of preexisting nationalist loyalties or social differences. Rather, like the Lex Perek, it was a nationalist strategy for claiming ever more children as Czechs and Germans. Thanks to burgeoning nationalist pedagogical and child welfare movements, national affiliation would soon determine not only where children attended school but how they spent the summers, preschool years, and after-school hours, and who they turned to for a cup of soup or a medical exam in times of need.

Orphans Save the Day

At the beginning of the 1909–10 school year, the German School Association received disturbing news from the director of the German minority

---

[56] On Budapest and Vienna see Susan Zimmermann, *Prächtige Arbeit. Fürsorge, Kinderschutz und Sozialreform in Budapest. Das "sozialpolitische Laboratorium" der Doppelmonarchie im Vergleich zu Wien, 1873–1914* (Sigmaringen, 1997), 154–57, 300–317, 384–90, 398–410.

[57] Generalvormundschaft, carton 433, Justizministerium, sig. I, AVA, ÖstA.

[58] Will Kymlicka, *Multicultural Citizenship: A Liberal Theory of Minority Rights* (Oxford, 1995), 77; Peter Baldwin, *The Politics of Social Solidarity: Class Bases of the European Welfare State, 1875–1975* (New York, 1990), 33.

school in the village of Pavlov/Pawlow in Moravia. The tiny German population in the town appeared to be in steady decline, and the number of children enrolled in the school had slipped dangerously below the critical mass (forty pupils) required to retain state funding. Thanks in part to Lex Perek, German schools in Moravia could no longer easily recruit Czech-speaking children to boost their sagging enrollments. The German School Association was quick to the rescue: the association decided to save the threatened school by colonizing the town with German orphans. "On the 14th of October a colony of 10 children was created in Pawlow and placed under the oversight of our school directors, thereby securing the existence of the school," the School Association triumphantly reported.[59] Orphans, probably "rescued" from predominantly Czech-run municipal orphanages in cities such as Prague, had saved the day.

Orphans seemed to offer the ideal raw material for nationalist movements in the Austrian Empire. Orphanages and orphan "colonies," which typically consisted of ten to fifteen children with a pair of guardians, served multiple goals in the nationalist struggle. First, nationalists hoped that by raising children in their own institutions, they could save children from the perceived threat of denationalization in public orphanages or in the foster homes of the national enemy. In one 1913 appeal to build new orphanages, Czech nationalists lamented, "Every day children are lost to us in orphanages, where they are given a piece of bread with one hand and robbed of their mother tongue with the other."[60] Second, orphans could be settled wherever and whenever the nation needed them. Since they typically attended the local public schools, nationalist organizations carefully placed their colonies and children's homes in nationally contested regions, especially where local minority schools appeared to be threatened by declining enrollments. Best of all, orphans did not have nationally indifferent parents to interfere with nationalist pedagogical goals. Although the number of children who grew up in nationalist orphanages was relatively modest, orphan welfare programs figured prominently in the propaganda arsenal of early-twentieth-century nationalist associations and ultimately emboldened nationalists to develop far more expansive child welfare programs.

The Bund der Deutschen in Böhmen established the first German orphan colony in the fiercely contested village of Třebenice/Trebnitz in Bohemia in 1898. Other nationalist associations soon jumped on the bandwagon. On the eve of World War I nationalists had established forty-five orphan colonies altogether in Moravia, twenty-nine Czech colonies with 397 children, and sixteen German colonies with 252 children. In Bohemia, meanwhile, German nationalist organizations cared for at least 1,367 children in eight

---

[59] "Die Kinderbesiedlungen des Deutschen Schulvereines," *Der getreue Eckart* 11, 1913, 7.

[60] "O dětech národu," *Ludmila: Časopis věnovaný ochraně opuštěných dětí a sirotků vůbec a zvláště na Ostravsku* 1 (1913): 4.

colonies and nine institutions in 1913, while Czech nationalists raised 574 children in their orphanages and homes in that year.[61] The driving force behind these efforts was himself a nationalist orphan. In 1908 Hugo Heller, raised in the St. John the Baptist orphanage in Prague, was just embarking on what would become a long and impressive career as a nationalist child welfare activist. With financial support from the orphanage, Heller attended Charles University in Prague, became a gymnasium teacher, and eventually earned a Ph.D. in philosophy and pedagogy. As a member of the Bund der Deutschen in Böhmen, he quickly became the association's foremost expert on child welfare. In 1906 Heller founded the German Central Commission for Orphan and Youth Welfare (Zentralstelle für deutschen Waisenpflege und Jugendfürsorge in Böhmen) under the auspices of the German Casino in Prague. Following the First Imperial Austrian Child Welfare conference in 1907, the Zentralstelle changed its name to the German Provincial Commission for Child Protection and Youth Welfare in Bohemia (Deutsche Landesstelle für Kinderschutz und Jugendfürsorge, DLS), and a parallel Czech organization was established (Česká zemská komise pro ochranu dítěte a péče o mládeže, ČZK). They were quickly followed by German and Czech commissions in Moravia and Silesia.[62] These institutions would profoundly shape the development of the welfare state in Bohemia and Moravia over the next half century, becoming the most important and wide-reaching child welfare institutions in the Bohemian Lands. Heller himself remained at the helm of the German Provincial Commission in Bohemia until he retired in late 1937, shortly before the Nazi annexation of the Sudetenland.

Through its orphanages and orphan colonies, nationalist organizations literally brought minority school politics, pedagogical reform, population policy, and new forms of nationalist social work together under one roof. These themes converged in the opening ceremonies for a new Bund der Deutschen orphanage in 1908. At 8:00 a.m. on October 11, a warm fall day, a festive crowd assembled for a celebratory march to the town square of Dolní Třešňovec/Nieder-Johnsdorf in Bohemia. The gathered merrymakers included a German nationalist delegate to the Austrian parliament, the mayor, representatives from the Pan-German League in Berlin, nationalist

---

[61] Jugendfürsorge: Bericht über die erste deutsch-böhmische Jugendfürsorge-Konferenz zu Prag, 23 and 24 February 1907, 13–14, carton 425, Justizministerium, AVA, ÖstA; "Die Kinderbesiedlungen des Deutschen Schulvereines," *Der getreue Eckart* 11, 1913, 6; "Sirotci kolonie a sirotci spolky," *Ochrana dítěte: Časopis české zemské komise pro ochranu dítek a péči o mládež v Markrabství moravském* 3, 25 June 1914; Jahresbericht der deutschen Landeskommission für Kinderschutz und Jugendfürsorge in Böhmen für das Geschäftsjahr 1913; A. Tůma, "Zpráva o činnosti české zemské komise pro ochranu dítek a péči o mládež v. král. českém v roce 1913." *Ochrana mládeže: Časopis pro veřejnou a soukromou péči o mládež v Království českém* 4, 1914, 55–62.

[62] On the founding of the provincial commissions in Moravia, see *Ochrana dítěte* 1, 15 November 1911, 1, and *Dr. Margarete Roller und die Deutsche Landeskommission für Kinderschütz und Jugendfürsorge in Mähren* (Brno, 1970).

fraternities, choral groups, women's associations, military associations, and gymnastics clubs, along with teachers, children, and firefighters from four neighboring towns. The cause for celebration was the grand opening of the Bund der Deutschen's new Dr. Karl Schücker Orphanage, the first explicitly nationalist home for orphans in the Bohemian Lands. In his remarks at the grand opening celebration, local village official and Bund der Deutschen leader Adolf Hübl lamented that previously German orphans in the Bohemian Lands had faced a sad fate, which he blamed on popular indifference to the nation's least fortunate children. "We should never tire of remembering how German villages mercilessly sold their orphans off to Czech villages," he lectured, describing "how children were left with broken limbs, how others had to wander from farmer to farmer in order to beg for their daily bread or a place to sleep in a horse stall, how children lacked sufficient nourishment or dental hygiene, and others entered our care with lice, bruises, and open wounds. And we demanded from such children love for humanity, love for the nation!"[63]

The new orphanage, Hübl explained, would not only offer these children the most modern facilities and flawless care but also contribute to the gradual transformation of Bohemia's national demography. To this end, Hübl hoped that the institution would ultimately expand into a "small village" of orphans composed of ten homes, each housing twenty children. The Bund der Deutschen orphans, all boys, attended the local German public school, where they inflated enrollments and guaranteed the school's existence. They simultaneously helped to increase the town's German-speaking population from 706 to 789 between 1900 and 1910.[64] After graduation the Bund planned to apprentice its wards to German shopkeepers, artisans, and farmers in nationally threatened regions of Bohemia. They were to settle, prosper, and reproduce, all part of a broader scheme "to gradually replace the dangerous Czech civil servants with hard-working Germans," Hübl explained. The orphanage was not simply a home for boys, he concluded. It was nothing less than a "powerful wall against which the Czech onslaught will ricochet helplessly, with a foundation so strong that no Czech flood can wash it away."[65]

The Bund der Deutschen's orphanages acutely reflected the extreme frustration of middle-class nationalists with the apathy and national indifference of the citizens they claimed to represent. Since the turn of the century German nationalists had actively campaigned to save orphans for the nation by matching German-speaking orphans with suitable German foster

---

[63] "Dr. Karl Schücker Waisenheim des Bundes der Deutschen in Böhmen," *Jahrbuch der Deutschen Jugendfürsorge in Böhmen* 2, 1909, 12.

[64] *Gemeindelexikon von Böhmen*, vol. 9 (Vienna, 1904); *Spezialortsrepertorium von Böhmen* (Vienna, 1915).

[65] "Dr. Karl Schücker Waisenheim," 1–3, 10, 12.

Fig. 1. The wards of the Bund der Deutschen's Dr. Karl Schücker orphanage, 1909.
Das Dr. Karl Schücker-Waisenheim des Bundes der Deutschen zu Nieder-Johnsdorf bei Landskron (Prague, 1909).

parents. In 1911, a leading Austrian official for public health, Theodor Altschul, proposed that the German Provincial Commission recruit "trustworthy women" to take in German foundlings from the industrial regions of Northern Bohemia and Prague in order to prevent the "frequent denationalization of foundlings with German mothers through the emergency accommodation of children of German descent with Czech foster parents."[66] The problem was that such trustworthy women were in short supply. Before sending children to their new homes, the DLS issued foster parents the following stern instructions: "Raise the child to possess an inner, self-sacrificing love of their nation! Naturally you yourself must feel this same burning love for our nation. If you are not in a position to make our child into a loyal, true German comrade, who is proud to be a German, then you are not called upon to raise our foster child. You would bitterly disappoint us and our benefactors if you did not fulfill your duty to raise the child to be German to the core!"[67] Apparently very few parents lived up to these

[66] "Vortrag, gehalten am I. Delegiertentage von K.K. Obersanitätsrat MUDr. Theodor Altschul," *Jahrbuch der deutschen Jugendfürsorge in Böhmen* 4, 1911, 147.
[67] Hugo Heller, "Leitordnung der Zentralstelle für deutsche Waisenpflege und Jugendfürsorge in Böhmen für die Waisenerziehung in Pflegefamilien," *Jahrbuch der deutschen Jugendfürsorge in Böhmen* 2, 1909, 227.

lofty expectations. Some German-speaking foster parents even contributed to the denationalization of orphans, German nationalists complained. The Bund der Deutschen lamented: "Where could we find the degree of understanding that we required when a strictly national upbringing was a near miracle even among our own erstwhile national comrades?"[68] Activists in the German nationalist association Südmark shared these concerns. Foster parents, they argued, "often fail for the national purpose, or are at the very least insufficient. And it is around this end that all of child rearing should be oriented." Nationalist child welfare activists therefore came to see collective education in orphanages and orphan colonies as an attractive alternative to family placement. The Südmark concluded in 1918, "Institutions that can take in a greater number of heads and be run in a unified nationalist spirit are necessary so that *völkisch* concerns are not neglected."[69]

The pedagogical principles deployed in Bund der Deutschen orphanages drew from the recommendations of the school reform movement. The directors shared Heimat activists' concerns about the harmful influences of the big city on the nation's young. "To the greatest extent possible in our homes, we want to combat flight from the land. Our homes are in a position to awaken love for the sacred ground of Heimat and for simple lifestyles," they explained.[70] In practical terms this meant that the children were constantly outdoors as the orphanage was a working farm. They were also carefully educated according to the principles of progressive pedagogy. House rules affirmed that children should be allowed to chatter freely at mealtimes, for example: "Mealtimes should not be ruled by dead silence. The children should be encouraged to speak freshly and freely from their hearts." These nationalists also rejected corporal punishment, encouraging caregivers in the orphanage to appeal to the "mind and reason" of their wards. Through an education aimed at "increasing joy in life and self-consciousness," nationalist social workers hoped that the German nation itself could substitute for their wards' lost parents—and that the orphans would express their gratitude by devoting their lives to their new national family.[71] In the early twentieth century, German and Czech nationalists alike dreamed of colonizing the Czech-German language frontier with orphans. The scope of these schemes was limited, but orphaned children were among the first participants in early nationalist attempts to alter the national demography of East Central Europe through resettlement. These colonies reflected growing ambitions among nationalists to "fortify" the nation by moving and improving human material.[72]

---

[68] "Dr. Karl Schücker Waisenheim," 21.

[69] "Deutschvölkische Waisenhäuser und Kriegswaisenfürsorge," *Mitteilungen des Vereines Südmark* 13, 1918, 156.

[70] "Dr. Karl Schücker Waisenheim," 37.

[71] Ibid., 49.

[72] On the origins of twentieth-century population transfers in Eastern Europe, see Norman Naimark, *Fires of Hatred: Ethnic Cleansing in Twentieth Century Europe* (Cambridge,

The Origins of the Nationally Segregated Welfare State

Bolstered by the apparent success of orphan welfare programs, nationalists soon set out to make more ambitious claims on children with living
parents. At the first German-Bohemian youth welfare conference in Prague
in 1907, Franz Vollgrüber, a delegate to the Bohemian Diet, argued that nationalists should not limit their attention to orphans and children of single
mothers but rather target "children in general," and "especially the school-
aged children of workers."[73] Through the provincial commissions, nationalists in the Bohemian Lands soon assumed responsibilities for children that
were typically taken on by the state or private charities in nation-states such
as Germany, France, and England. Social welfare activists were particularly
concerned with improving the quantity and quality of the nation's children
by decreasing infant mortality rates and providing child-care support for
working mothers in industrial regions.

It was no coincidence that activists pioneered this nationally segregated
child welfare system in the wake of the Moravian Compromise and Lex
Perek. The Compromise offered social workers and nationalist activists an
attractive model for asserting national ownership of children by dividing
entire populations into national cadastres. On the basis of this model, the
German and Czech Provincial Commissions now set out to divide all of
Bohemia and Moravia's needy families and children between a segregated
network of Czech and German welfare agencies. In 1910 the German and
Czech Provincial Commissions in Bohemia together submitted a proposal to
the Austrian Ministry of the Interior in Vienna, demanding the division of all
child welfare institutions in the Austrian Empire along national lines. Like
the Moravian Compromise, the plan required that every child be classified
as either a Czech or a German: "The nationality of the child would have to
be determined in each individual case, such that assignment to the appropriate commission would follow. Hereby the principle must be upheld that
a child who is not proficient in the language of the Commission cannot be
successfully raised by that Commission."[74] This reference to language ability, clearly inspired by the Lex Perek, was all the more remarkable given that
many of the children were themselves infants who could not yet speak.

MA, 2001); Eagle Glassheim, "National Mythologies and Ethnic Cleansing: The Expulsion
of Czechoslovak Germans in 1945," *Central European History* 33, no. 4 (1999): 463–75.
For analysis of other nationalist resettlement programs in the Habsburg Monarchy see Pieter
M. Judson, *Guardians of the Nation: Activists on the Language Frontiers of Imperial Austria*
(Cambridge, MA, 2006), 100–141.

[73] Jugendfürsorge: Bericht über die erste deutsch-böhmische Jugendfürsorge-Konferenz zu
Prag, 23 and 24 February 1907, carton 425, Justizministerium, AVA, ÖstA.

[74] Wohltätigkeitsaustalten, memo from the Landesausschusses des Königreich Böhmen, betreffend die gesetzliche Regelung der Fürsorgeerziehung, 11. z. 42991, 1910, carton 2759,
Ministerium von Innern, AVA, ÖstA.

Nationalist child welfare activists promoted the national segregation of social welfare institutions in the Habsburg Monarchy on the basis of the claim that national differences permeated deep into family life. If the nascent Austrian welfare system was to be democratic and effective, nationalists claimed, it had to allow each nation the greatest possible autonomy to address its allegedly unique social needs. In a 1909 memo to the Ministry of the Interior, the ČZK outlined its democratic ambition "to escape a purely official role, and to secure the popular support of the broadest classes of the population." Achieving these goals required that the state acknowledge the "differences in the cultural development, economic relationships, and social composition" of each nation. The entire welfare system had to be based on strict national segregation "if one nation is not to hinder the other in the development of its youth's welfare," the memo concluded.[75]

Nationalist claims about the "unique" social needs of German and Czech families gained currency through a series of turn-of-the-century studies that uncovered substantial differences in rates of single motherhood, female employment, and infant mortality between districts with a German-speaking majority and those with a Czech-speaking majority in the Bohemian Lands. According to the 1900 census, women in Bohemia accounted for 38.5 percent of the total workforce, and 38.2 percent of women worked outside the home. While German and Czech women were equally represented among working women, German-speaking women were almost twice as likely to be employed in industry as Czech speakers, who were far more likely to perform agricultural labor.[76] As social workers and demographers studied rates of female employment, they also began to compare infant mortality rates in German-speaking and Czech-speaking regions of Bohemia. The results provoked serious alarm among German nationalists. Heinrich Rauchberg, a rabid German nationalist, professor at Charles University, and well-known demographer, drew a direct link between high rates of female industrial employment in German-speaking regions of Bohemia and the infant mortality rate among German-speaking women. In 1900, for every thousand children born in districts in Bohemia with a German-speaking majority, 28.1 percent died within one year and 35.8 percent died within five years. In Czech-speaking districts the numbers were only slightly less appalling: 23.7 percent of children did not reach their first birthday, and 32 percent did not survive five years. In Europe, only Russia had higher infant mortality rates.[77]

[75] Memo, Böhmische Landeskommission für Kinderschutz und Jugendfürsorge in Prag, betreffend die Verwendung der Kaiser Jubiläumsfonds "Das Kind," 15 November 1909, carton 2757, Ministerium von Innern, AVA, ÖstA.

[76] Peter Urbanitsch and Adam Wandruszka, eds., *Die Habsburger Monarchie, 1848–1918*, vol. 3 (Vienna, 1980), 38, table 1, and Heinrich Rauchberg, *Der nationale Besitzstand in Böhmen* (Leipzig, 1905), 336, 586.

[77] Rauchberg, *Der nationale Besitzstand*, 586. Infant mortality rates in the Bohemian Lands were higher than those for the Monarchy as a whole. In Austria-Hungary as a whole, 23.8

Some nationalists blamed high infant mortality rates among German speakers on the German mothers' reluctance to breast-feed. In a 1910 memo to German teachers, Alois Epstein, a professor of pediatrics at the German University in Prague, demanded the national segregation of all welfare institutions in the Bohemian Lands on the basis of this alleged German peculiarity:

> The requirements for child protection in the German districts in various respects are of a different character than in the Czech districts and therefore demand different means and methods. . . . Just as individual nations have in the course of their development adopted certain tendencies and character traits that exercise a great influence on the type and activity of their entire economic life, there is also national individuality with respect to attitudes and practices in family life. This cultural condition is not learned on the school bench and has nothing to do with so-called education. The traits that are meant here . . . are passed on through tradition from family to family, generation to generation, and have become unique to the concerned nation.[78]

In the Bohemian Lands, he claimed, Germans and Czechs had "lived next to one another for centuries . . . both equipped with high cultural characteristics, but sharply physically separated by a language frontier, and thereby different not only with respect to language but also customs, social character and in economic life." The fact that German women were less likely to breast-feed was not a simple matter of employment patterns, class, or convenience, Epstein insisted. Rather, the two nations had completely different conceptions of "the instinctive feelings of the female, a mother's love, and the ethical form as well as the practical fulfillment of maternal duty."[79]

German social welfare activists explicitly understood their battle against infant mortality as a response to mass politics, a strategy for expanding the nation's numerical power without assimilating Slavs. Writing for the magazine of the Bund der Deutschen in 1913, Marianne Tuma von Walkampf reminded readers that numbers were more important than ever in the nationalist struggle, thanks to growing Czech cultural and economic power. "While among nations of unequal cultural quality the number of activists is not as important as their intellectual and moral strength, the more equal the enemies, the more important relative numerical power," she explained in an appeal to combat infant mortality.[80] It was also no coincidence that

---

infants out of 100 in 1895 and 19.2 infants per 100 in 1910 died in the first year of life. See Wilhelm Hecke, *Die Verschiedenheit der deutschen und slawischen Volksvermehrung in Österreich* (Stuttgart, 1916), 7.

[78] Alois Epstein, *An die deutsche Lehrerschaft in Mähren-Kinderschutz und Volksvermehrung mit besonderer Beachtung der Verhältnisse in Böhmen* (Vienna, 1910), 21.

[79] Ibid., 25.

[80] Marianna Tuma von Waldkampf, "Kindersterblichkeit und nationaler Besitzstand," *Mitteilungen des Bundes der Deutschen in Böhmen* 7, 1913, 129.

nationalists focused on decreasing infant mortality rather than increasing the birthrate. German nationalists explicitly rejected pronatalism on eugenic grounds. In 1910 the German School Association identified pronatalist policies designed to increase the birthrate with "uncontrolled exploitation, debilitation, exhaustion," while decreasing the infant mortality rate supposedly represented "efficient economic production, the improvement of parental material, the maintenance of national power." The children produced for the nation through pronatalist campaigns "originate from increasingly degenerating and weak maternal sources," the School Association maintained, while lives saved by combating infant mortality allegedly sprang from "wombs that retain and even save or contain power."[81] Hugo Heller agreed, arguing in 1913 that since large families were common among the "lowest classes of the population, who have in no way retained any exploitable power to refresh our blood," pronatalism could only lead to a disastrous "racial degeneration" rather than the sought-after national regeneration.[82]

Wherever the Home Fails (A Nationalist Day Care Succeeds)

While nationalists such as Epstein pressured women to breast-feed, other child welfare activists stressed the material conditions that threatened children's survival. Hugo Heller blamed infant mortality on "bad housing conditions, insufficient income, the largest part of which goes toward rent, so that spending on food is limited, and incorrect, insufficient nutrition and care."[83] In Moravia, German nationalists sought to address infant mortality through a network of local mother-counseling stations, which dispensed medical supplies and treatment, breast-feeding advice, and basic necessities such as sanitized infant formula, food and clothing, all aimed toward "protecting the children from the hygienic dangers that gnaw at the nation's roots."[84] The DLS also established day-care centers, summer camps, soup kitchens, and nursing stations in industrial regions. The nationalist campaign to decrease infant mortality, led by the German and Czech Provincial Commissions, thereby represented a strategy for integrating working-class and peasant families into the nation that differed from the one promoted by Joseph Blau, Haufe, and other members of the school reform movement. While DLS social workers shared Heimat activists' concerns about the harmful hygienic and moral effects of urban life, they promoted material assistance rather than an idyllic vision of Heimat to address this crisis.

---

[81] "Leben und Schutz unseren Säuglingen!" *Der getreue Eckart* 8, 1910, 49–50. See also Tuma von Waldkampf, "Kindersterblichkeit und nationaler Besitzstand," 1.

[82] Heller, *Jugendland*, 34.

[83] Jugendfürsorge: Bericht über die erste deutsch-böhmische Jugendfürsorge-Konferenz zu Prag, 23 and 24 February 1907, 6, carton 425, Justizministerium, AVA, ÖstA.

[84] *An die deutsche Lehrerschaft in Mähren* (Brno, 1912), 1.

Working mothers were a particular source of concern to nationalist welfare activists, but nationalists rarely condemned female employment outside the home. Indeed, working mothers afforded nationalists an irresistible opportunity to expand the nation's primary pedagogical influence on children. Women were forced to work by economic circumstances, explained the DLS in 1909, and "our bleak economic condition will hardly change in the foreseeable future." The Commission insisted that in light of this economic reality, "the public has the duty to take youth welfare in its own hands."[85] Likewise, the Czech nationalist newspaper *Stráž severu* argued in 1909 that it was a nationalist duty to create new day-care centers in industrial regions, "where children of those parents who are called outside the home by their employment . . . are provided with a place to spend the day with appropriate supervision."[86] In 1912 Heller elaborated that nationalist child welfare organizations should share the burden of child rearing with the working mother, who "should be helped in her difficult situation, to pursue paid employment in order to earn a living, to run a household and to become a mother or simply to be a mother."[87]

In 1913 one enthusiastic local nationalist, Albin Dimter, described how nationalists in the Bohemian industrial town of Broumov/Braunau had put the commission's ideals into practice. It was an economic necessity in this town, he explained, for both fathers and mothers to seek out paid employment in the factories. Too often their children were left to the care of older siblings, sick and frail older relatives, or simply their own devices. The local branch of the DLS endeavored to offer "morally flawless supervision and stimulating activities for those poor children whose parents must earn their bread, in day cares, nurseries, soup kitchens, student workshops, and homes for girls." Through "play and healthy, rational sports like sledding, iceskating, rowing, and swimming, through field trips, garden work, and similar activities," he elaborated, "the poor child's missing parental home should be replaced as much as possible, so as to raise a new generation that finds joy in work, that is competitive and happy."[88]

By the eve of the First World War competition between the German and Czech Provincial Commissions in the Bohemian Lands had contributed to the development of an expansive network of social welfare institutions. The DLS in Bohemia boasted 90 district branches, encompassing almost every German school district in Bohemia, while the ČZK in Bohemia had already

[85] Wilhelmine Wiechowski, "Mädchenfürsorge," *Jahrbuch der deutschen Jugendfürsorge in Böhmen* 2, 1909, 98.
[86] "Školství menšinové a ochrana mládéže," *Stráž severu: Věstník národní jednoty severočeská,* 31 December 1909, 2.
[87] Heller, *Jugendland,* 26–34.
[88] Albin Dimter, *Die Deutsche Landeskommission für Kinderschutz und Jugendfürsorge* (Branau, 1913).

formed 104 local branches.[89] As we have seen, social workers justified the segregation of these welfare institutions by claiming that German and Czech families had unique social needs. In reality, however, it appears that parents in bilingual regions rarely chose welfare institutions according to their nationalist loyalties. In 1909, for example, the DLS lamented that it was difficult to maintain the desired level of national segregation in its day-care centers in Prague. The organization had established five nurseries for German preschool children in Prague, all "created through German initiative and largely maintained by German money." But activists had to concede in frustration that these institutions "almost exclusively benefited the children of the Czech working classes."[90] Such complaints suggest the practical limits of segregating social welfare institutions and organizations at the local level. Families in need probably based their choices of day-care centers, soup kitchens, and nurseries far more on the generosity of the organizations and the facilities' geographical proximity than on nationalist convictions.

Nationalist pedagogy and social work contained both emancipatory and disciplinary potential. These activists imposed nationalist worldviews and middle-class ideals about proper "German" or "Czech" child rearing and culture at the same time that they sought to cultivate children's political agency, support working mothers, and shrink infant mortality rates. Indeed, the nationalist child welfare movement in the Bohemian Lands was propelled by a fundamental spirit of solidarity. Competition between Czech and German nationalists to fill schools, inflate census results, and create expanding mass political movements fostered a culture in which no child could be left behind. By the end of the Habsburg Monarchy, parents no longer enjoyed unlimited "rights" to educate or govern their children as they pleased. Instead, they enjoyed the right to a national education for their children and to certain social services also provided by the national community. In return, both parents and children owed the national community the duty of political allegiance. Confronted with a universe in which nationalist loyalties and identities were far from self-evident, nationalists built legal, institutional, and social structures that made nationality the basis not only for education but also for meeting basic social needs in times of crisis. These nationalist social welfare initiatives would have profound effects on both family life and politics during the social crisis of the First World War.

---

[89] In 1909 the provincial commissions in Bohemia supported 270 German and 114 Czech kindergartens, 21 German and 61 Czech day-care centers, 720 German and 927 Czech soup kitchens, 237 German and 559 Czech playgrounds, 24 German and 15 Czech summer camps, and 1,012 German and 1,065 Czech Christmas collections. *Jahrbuch für deutschen Jugendfürsorge in Böhmen* 3, 1910, xiii. For another comparison of day-care centers, soup kitchens, etc. by nationality, see *Jahresbericht des k.k. Landesschulrates in Böhmen* (Prague, 1909), 74–78. For a report of Czech Provincial Commission activities in 1914, see A. Tůma, "Zpráva o činnosti české zemské komise pro ochranu dítek a péči o mládež v. král. českém v roce 1913," *Ochrana mládeže* 4, 1914, 55–62.
[90] Wiechowski, "Mädchenfürsorge," 98–99.

3   Warfare, Welfare, and the End of Empire

In the fall of 1917, Franziszka Pollabrek, a Czech factory worker, was at her wit's end. In a scathing letter to the Austrian Ministry of Education in Vienna, she demanded that the state do something about her increasingly incorrigible teenage sons. Pollabrek expressed her frustration with the state's inaction in the face of what she perceived to be a disturbing wartime collapse of the family. Discipline and order had all but disappeared from her town and family along with all the fathers and male teachers, she claimed. "My boys will become nothing but thieves, liars, and murderers, if you, dear Sirs, don't intervene soon," she complained. "The fathers are in the military, the male teachers are mobilized, and I work in the factory. You want to do nothing, so where should I begin? Since you have taken away their father, why don't you take the children as well, let the boys be locked up or shot, so that I don't have to see them anymore."[1]

Pollabrek was not alone. Across Europe during the First World War, citizens depicted the social upheaval of war through stories of broken families, absent fathers, negligent mothers, and delinquent children.[2] Several related anxieties about children and youth spanned the continent, transforming children's health and welfare into matters of dire national interest. First, European states were under widespread pressure to provide for the

[1] Z. 8.500, Vienna, 15 October 1917, carton 2483, MfSV, Jugendfürsorge, AVA, ÖstA. See also F. V. Vykoukal, "Na ochranu mladého pokolení," *Česká osvěta* 13, 1917, 93–96.

[2] For examples of similar demands, see Stimmung und wirtschaftliche Lage der österreichische Bevölkerung im Hinterland, carton 3751, AOK, KA, GZNB, ÖstA. On Austria, see Maureen Healy, *Vienna and the Fall of the Habsburg Monarchy* (Cambridge, 2004), 211–300. On Germany, see Edward Ross Dickinson, *The Politics of German Child Welfare from the Empire to the Federal Republic* (Cambridge, MA, 1996), 113–18; on the "moral panic" over endangered youth after World War I in Germany, see Richard Bessel, *Germany after the First World War* (Oxford, 1993), and Elizabeth Harvey, *Youth and the Welfare State in Weimar Germany* (Oxford, 1994).

dependents of the men who had been called up for military service. Second, the war intensified a panic about declining birthrates, now directly linked to military strength. Nationalist anxieties about shrinking populations only intensified with rising death tolls.[3] Finally, citizens, state officials, and child welfare activists expressed growing concerns about the physical, educational, and moral welfare of the nation's young as fathers departed for the front, mothers were mobilized in war factories, and, in Central Europe, rations shrank to starvation levels. As Pollabrek's letter suggests, fears about youth delinquency and neglect often rested on gendered understandings of parental roles as many observers blamed the perceived epidemic of youth delinquency on an absence of male authority in the home.[4] These concerns provoked popular demands for state action. The ability of the state to provide for the material, educational, and moral welfare of children during the First World War was directly linked to the legitimacy of the state, the development of interwar welfare states, and new, gendered understandings of citizenship.[5] Maureen Healy and Belinda Davis have convincingly argued that the failure of the state in Central Europe to fulfill its social promises during World War I contributed significantly to the fall of the Habsburg and German Empires in 1918.[6]

In the Bohemian Lands, German and Czech nationalist child welfare activists took the initiative in responding to these demands. By 1914, nationalists had already established an impressive network of private, nationally segregated institutions for child welfare, through the Czech and German Provincial Commissions for Child Welfare. Frightened by the seemingly contagious potential of the Russian Revolution in 1917, the supranational Austrian

[3] On war, nationalism, and pronatalism see Dickinson, *The Politics of German Child Welfare*, 118–24; Cornelie Usborne, "Pregnancy Is the Woman's Active Service: Pronatalism in Germany During the First World War," in *The Upheaval of War: Family, Work, and Welfare in Europe*, ed. Richard Wall and Jay Winter, 392–93 (Cambridge, 1988); Nicoletta Gullace, "*The Blood of Our Sons": Men, Women, and the Renegotiation of British Citizenship During the Great War* (New York, 2001), 53–72; Karen Offen, "Depopulation, Nationalism, and Feminism in Fin-de-siècle France," *American Historical Review* 89 (1984): 648–70.

[4] On parallel concerns in World War II France see Sarah Fishman, *The Battle for Children: World War II, Youth, and Juvenile Justice in Twentieth Century France* (Cambridge, MA, 2002), chaps. 1–2.

[5] On gender, family, and citizenship during the First World War in Europe, see Maureen Healy, "Becoming Austrian: Women, the State, and Citizenship in World War I," *Central European History* 35, no. 1 (2002): 1–35. Belinda Davis, *Home Fires Burning: Food, Politics, and Everyday Life in WWI Berlin* (Chapel Hill, 2000); Susan Pederson, *Family, Dependence, and the Origins of the Welfare State: Britain and France, 1914–1945* (Cambridge, MA, 1993), 79–133; Laura Lee Downs, *Manufacturing Inequality: Gender Division in the French and British Metalworking Industries, 1914–1939* (Ithaca, 1995), 119–47; Susan Grayzel, *Women's Identities at War: Gender, Motherhood, and Politics in Britain and France During the Great War* (Chapel Hill, 1999).

[6] Davis, *Home Fires Burning*, esp. 190–218; Healy, *Vienna*, esp. 1–30. On state legitimacy and welfare provision during the First World War, see also Richard Wall and Jay Winter, eds., *The Upheaval of War: Family, Work, and Welfare in Europe, 1914–1918* (Cambridge, 1988).

state turned specifically to these private, nationalist child welfare organizations to build and manage an ambitious new Ministry for Social Welfare (k.k. Ministerium für soziale Fürsorge) in 1917–18. As the acknowledged pioneers in the realm of child welfare, nationalist activists easily claimed to have the scientific expertise, infrastructure, and popular legitimacy necessary to provide for Bohemian and Moravian children. By harnessing an existing nationalist child welfare system to the Austrian state, the new ministry hoped to repair the war-damaged bodies and morale of Austrian citizens and to boost the state's own flagging legitimacy. German and Czech nationalists dramatically expanded their authority over children during the First World War as the trusted agents of the multinational Austrian state.

Contemporary observers and historians since 1918 have typically blamed the dramatic collapse of the Austrian Empire on the Habsburg state's failure to establish democratic legitimacy in the face of competing nationalist claims and a growing social crisis. Nationalism, in this view, was a lethal force directed against the Austrian state.[7] But what was the actual relationship between nationalists and the Habsburg state at the moment of the Empire's collapse? In fact, far from working against the Austrian state, German and Czech nationalist welfare organizations became the architects of a new Imperial welfare state in the Bohemian Lands during the First World War.[8] By bringing nationalists into the state, Austrian officials themselves helped to transform a potential social revolution into the national revolutions that precipitated the Empire's collapse.

When Austrian state officials entrusted private nationalist welfare organizations in the Bohemian Lands with the management of the state's most ambitious social programs to date, they simultaneously empowered nationalists to define social questions in nationalist terms. The revolutions of 1918–19 did not, therefore, represent the revolt of the nationalized masses against a state doomed to collapse. Far from passively slipping into the twilight, Austrian government officials responded to citizens' claims with a significant

[7] For examples of narratives about the inevitable collapse of the Monarchy, see Solomon-Wank, "The Habsburg Empire," in *After Empire: Multiethnic Societies and Nation-Building: The Soviet Union, and the Russian, Ottoman, and Habsburg Empires,* ed. Karen Barkey and Mark von Hagen, 45–58 (Boulder, CO, 1997); Robert Kann, *The Multinational Empire: Nationalism and National Reform in the Habsburg Monarchy,* 2 vols. (New York, 1970); for a revisionist perspective, see Gary B. Cohen, "Neither Absolutism nor Anarchy: New Narratives on Society and Government in Late Imperial Austria," *Austrian History Yearbook* 29, pt. 1 (1998), 37–61.

[8] For other work that emphasizes the state's own role in exacerbating nationalism during the war see John W. Boyer, "Silent War and Bitter Peace: The Revolution of 1918 in Austria," *Austrian History Yearbook* 35 (2003), 12; Mark Mazower, *Dark Continent: Europe's Twentieth Century* (New York, 1999), 46; Mark Cornwall, "The Dissolution of Austria-Hungary," in *The Last Years of Austria-Hungary: A Multi-national Experiment in Early Twentieth Century Europe* ed. Mark Cornwall (Exeter, 2002); Jeremy King, *Budweisers into Czechs and Germans: A Local History of Bohemian Politics, 1848–1948* (Princeton, 2002).

attempt at reform in 1916–18. Although these last-ditch efforts failed to save the monarchy, the creation of a separate but equal wartime welfare state did contribute to an escalating trend toward the national segregation of public institutions in the Austrian Empire, setting the stage for the revolutions that would carve the map of East Central Europe into nation-states.

Even Small Children Can Save a Regiment!

Not long after they mobilized men for the battlefields and women for the armaments factories in 1914, Europe's Great Powers mobilized children for the First World War.[9] "No child is too young to help!" argued Austrian school reformer and teacher Dora Siegl. "Students of all ages can contribute to a considerable degree."[10] In Britain, France, Germany, and Russia, as well as in the Habsburg Monarchy, state officials and nationalist activists demanded that children rally for war. Girls and boys soon spent their afternoons knocking on doors and collecting money, old paper, tea bags, metal, coal, winter clothes, books, wool, and bones for the war effort. Education officials quickly introduced a sharply gendered war pedagogy in Austrian schools, preparing boys for their future in the military and encouraging girls to knit and sew to keep soldiers warm and boost their morale. Nationalist pedagogues demanded that young girls in particular devote themselves to what they called *Liebestätigkeit* (love activity) in the schools.[11] Ernst Heywang reminded schoolteachers in 1915, "Girls must sew without pause during their handiwork lessons for our brave soldiers, so that they do not become cold."[12] Through this so-called labor of love, frivolous girls were to mature magically into patriotic and self-sacrificing women. Resi Berndt, a pedagogical reformer in Liberec/Reichenberg, observed proudly, "How industrially and with what love and patience they [schoolgirls] knitted this year, while in other years they blundered about half asleep while knitting stockings. These times have made our children more mature. Out of their own free will they gave up games and pleasure and worked for the Red Cross."[13]

---

[9] On war pedagogy in Austria see Healy, *Vienna*, 211–40; Christa Hämmerle, "Diese Schatten über unserer Kindheit gelegen: Historische Anmerkung zu einem unerforschten Thema," in *Kindheit im Ersten Weltkrieg* (Vienna, 1993), 265–335. On war pedagogy in France, see Stéphane Audoin-Rouzeau, *La guerre des enfants. Essai d'histoire culturelle* (Paris, 1993).

[10] Dora Siegl, "Der Krieg und die Jugend," *Schaffende Arbeit und Kunst in der Schule: Zeitschrift für die praktische Ausgestaltung der Arbeitsschule und der Kunsterziehung*, 5, 1917, 67.

[11] On the gendering of war pedagogy see Hämmerle, "Diese Schatten über unserer Kindheit gelegen," 265–335.

[12] Ernst Heywang, "Schule und Lehrerschaft im Völkerringen," *Schaffende Arbeit und Kunst in der Schule*, 3, 1915, 44.

[13] Resi Berndt, "Der Handarbeitsuntrreicht im Zeichen des Krieges," *Schaffende Arbeit und Kunst in der Schule*, 3, 1915, 367.

The war was good news for nationalist school reformers in Austria. Heimat activists quickly moved to the forefront of the movement to mobilize children for war. These reformers transformed progressive pedagogical methods such as Heimat education, art education, child-centered education, and experience-based education into the foundation of a new nationalist war pedagogy. While most voluntary associations and publications suffered heavily during the war, due to shortages of labor, funds, and supplies, the Heimat movement thrived. Anton Herget, Bohemian editor of the German nationalist reform publication *Schaffende Arbeit und Kunst in der Schule,* attributed the Heimat movement's growing popularity to the war. He contended in 1916, "The war has powerfully bolstered love of Heimat, and precisely this circumstance has worked to the advantage of our movement."[14] Science teacher Heinrich Kinzelmann affirmed that the war had won many converts to Heimat education. "In some schools, where there was previously little understanding for the simplification of the curriculum through Heimat education, the curriculum has now acquired more support. Through the great experiences of the war, a heartfelt exchange of ideas has replaced mechanical exercises," he enthused.[15] Learning through "active experience" in the local Heimat soon took on a whole new meaning as Heimat reformers presented war itself as a great pedagogical experience. "Let children witness the war!" demanded Ernst Heywang in 1915. "It is possible for even schoolchildren to save regiments, and thereby to defeat the enemy."[16]

German nationalists were not alone in promoting the war as a beneficial pedagogical experience. In 1915, a Czech provincial judge and child welfare activist, Franz Mézl, published a pamphlet in which he urged Czech educators, "Each teacher . . . must impress children's hearts with the great duties being performed by his national brothers on the battlefield for his homeland. The teacher must, when he speaks of the enemy, introduce a drop of hatred into the child's soul."[17] While nationalists across Europe praised the pedagogical and patriotic value of "hatred" in 1915, these words generated an

[14] "Dem fünften Jahrgange zum Geleit," *Schaffende Arbeit und Kunst in der Schule,* 5, 1917, 1. See also Ernst Heywang, "Die Pädagogik des Krieges," *Schaffende Arbeit und Kunst in der Schule,* 3, 1915, 337–40; Otto Tumlirz, "Psychologisch-Pädagogisch aus dem Schützengraben," *Schaffende Arbeit und Kunst in der Schule,* 3, 1915, 83–87; Joseph Blau, "Die Kriegschronik auch ein Stück schaffender Arbeit," *Schaffende Arbeit und Kunst in der Schule,* 3, 1915, 88; Alois Kunzfeld, "Krieg und Jugendkunst," *Schaffende Arbeit und Kunst in der Schule,* 3, 1915, 153–55; Br. Clemenz, "Krieg, Schule, Heimatschutz," *Schaffende Arbeit und Kunst in der Schule,* 5, 1917, 4–15; W. Ratthey, "Krieg-Heimat-Zukunftsschule," *Schaffende Arbeit und Kunst in der Schule,* 5, 1917, 117, 165; Walter Thielemann, "Die Zukunft unseres Volkes liegt in der Heimat," *Schaffende Arbeit und Kunst in der Schule,* 5, 1917, 453–56.

[15] Heinrich Kinzelmann, "Naturkunde in der Kriegszeit," *Beiblatt zur Zeitschrift Schaffende Arbeit und Kunst in der Schule,* September 1915, 306.

[16] Ernst Heywang, "Schule und Lehrerschaft im Völkerringen," *Schaffende Arbeit und Kunst in der Schule* 3, 1915, 44.

[17] F. Mézl, *Rada zemského soudu, válka světová a naše péče o dorost* (Brno, 1915), 9, sig. IEI/3, 1900–1918, carton 433, Justizministerium, AVA, ÖStA.

Fig. 2. Mobilizing children for war, 1917. *Schaffende Arbeit und Kunst in der Schule: Zeitschrift für die praktische Ausgestaltung der Arbeitsschule und der Kunsterziehung* 2, no. 6 (1915).

unusual amount of controversy among Austrian civil servants. The mobilization of children for war in Austria clearly created anxieties for the Austrian state that did not burden officials in neighboring nation-states. Universal primary education had long been a primary strategy through which nation-states such as Great Britain, Germany, and France sought to cultivate the patriotic loyalties of the next generation. In the Bohemian Lands, however, primary schools were firmly in the hands of nationalists by 1914. For decades, Czech and German nationalists in the Bohemian Lands had competed to show their patriotic loyalty to the Habsburg dynasty. With the outbreak of war, however, German nationalists seized the opportunity to depict Czechs as subversive traitors. German officials in Moravia perceived a threat to Imperial loyalties in Mézl's pedagogical tract. Czech teachers, they contended, "cannot be expected to encourage hatred against Russians and Serbs."[18]

As the Austrian state initially mobilized the home front in 1914, few officials raised concerns about the patriotic loyalty of Czech speakers to

[18] Report of the OLG Abteilung 5 to z. 22058/15, sig. IEl/3, 1900–1918, carton 433, Justizministerium, AVA, ÖstA. In a study of Austrian state censorship of soldiers' letters, Alon Rachamimov has demonstrated that while nationalist sentiments in letters written by Magyar,

the Imperial state or to the war effort. The myth of Czech opposition to the Austrian state and to the war, which continues to shape Czech collective memory of the Great War, was largely invented by German nationalists. Ironically, Czech nationalists later appropriated this narrative as a founding myth of the Czechoslovak nation-state.[19] Franz Kafka remarked in his diary that as the newly mobilized troops marched along Prague's na Příkopě, they were greeted by Czechs with nothing less than "flowers, shouts of hurrah, and *nazdar!* [hooray]"[20] Reports from the Bohemian governor's office and from local informants at the outset of the war confirmed that officials encountered little resistance as they mobilized Czech citizens.[21] In his study of wartime censorship of POW correspondence in Austria, Alon Rachamimov has also demonstrated that Czech prisoners of war frequently expressed their loyalty to the Empire and were no more likely to criticize the war or the Imperial state than their German-speaking comrades-in-arms.[22]

Until at least early 1917, many Czech nationalists hoped to use their record of patriotic service during the war to lobby for concessions from the Austrian state when the war ended. In January of 1917, for example, the editors of *Národní politika*, the newspaper of the Czech National Social party, insisted that the image of disloyal Czechs was the invention of German nationalists, who were determined to prevent Czechs from claiming their just reward for willing wartime sacrifice: "The Czech nation has up until now perfectly performed its duties to the Empire, full of initiative, capably, and with the highest level of courage in the face of the many sacrifices demanded from every branch of the nation," the editors declared. "This inner loyalty of ours, the realization that we have capably performed our duties to the Empire and the dynasty, must strengthen our firm, unshakable faith in future justice, even if it is inconvenient to a few German nationalists!"[23]

Germans, and Polish soldiers were judged to be compatible with loyalty to the Habsburg Empire, any hint of Czech or Slovak nationalism was deemed irreconcilable with Imperial loyalties. Alon Rachamimov, "Arbiters of Allegiance: Austro-Hungarian Censors during World War I," in *Constructing Nationalities in East Central Europe*, ed. Pieter Judson and Marsha Rozenblit, 21 (New York, 2004).

[19] For an overview of Czech and German responses to the outbreak of World War I, see Jan Křen, *Die Konfliktgemeinschaft. Tschechen und Deutschen 1780–1918* (Munich, 1996), 303–400; Rachamimov, *POWs and the Great War: Captivity on the Eastern Front* (New York, 2002); Hans Mommsen et al, eds., *Der erste Weltkrieg und die Beziehungen zwischen Tschechen, Slowaken, und Deutschen* (Essen, 2001).

[20] Cited in Mark Cornwall, *The Undermining of Austria-Hungary: The Battle for Hearts and Minds* (New York, 2000), 16, from Franz Kafka, *The Diaries of Franz Kafka 1910–1923*, ed. Max Brod (New York, 1972), 301.

[21] See Kolektiv prácovníků NA, *Soupis dokumentů k vnitřnímu vývoji v českých zemích za 1. světové války 1914–1918*, 4 vols. (Prague, 1993–1997), 1:87–89 (doc. 33) and 2:39–40 (doc. 10).

[22] Rachamimov, "Arbiters of Allegiance," 21.

[23] "K vnitřím experimentům není doba vhodné," *Národní politika*, 6 January 1917, 4–5. see also "Vnitropolitické otázky za války," *Národní listy*, 20 January 1915, 1; "Národní souručenství,"

In spite of considerable evidence of Czech patriotism, however, the Austrian state began to suppress Czech nationalism almost immediately following the outbreak of the war. The Bohemian Diet had already been dissolved in 1913. In 1914, Francis Joseph did not reconvene the Austrian parliament. Instead, the government converted the parliament building into a hospital and suspended constitutional civil rights. State persecution of Czech citizens intensified after the Austrian army's 1915 defeats on the Eastern front. Myths and rumors began to circulate, asserting that Czech soldiers had actually surrendered to the Russians without a fight in an expression of pan-Slavic solidarity with the Russian and Serbian enemy. The Austrian state abandoned its traditional position of impartiality in nationalist affairs and increasingly treated Czech citizens as a dangerous fifth column, arresting Czech nationalist leaders and censoring the nationalist press. As the military's influence on domestic affairs intensified in 1915, so did the persecution of Czech-speaking citizens by the government. A newly established War Surveillance Office (Kriegsüberwachungsamt) was quickly flooded with tales of renegade Czech educators, who appeared to threaten the state whether armed with chalk or machine guns.[24]

In the Bohemian town of Benešov/Beneschau in 1916, for example, a district captain wrote a lengthy report depicting massive treason in the state's Czech schools. The report, which was forwarded to the Ministry of Education and Ministry of the Interior in Vienna, reflected the state's fears that Imperial loyalties would be undermined by Czech nationalist pedagogy. This German official insisted, "In our town the Czech teachers are the propagators of all separatist, autonomist, and constitutionalist ideas. . . . The cancer in the public life of the Czech nation is to be found in the school and among the teachers."[25] As teachers moved from the schoolhouse to the battlefield, officials perceived even more ominous threats to the state. Anonymous denunciations accused Czech teachers of shunning combat through feigned illnesses and forged doctor's notes. A German military officer received a rash of threatening letters in Czech and concluded, "Since most of them were written out in strong, neat, and pretty handwriting, they were certainly written by teachers."[26] These denunciations were nothing new in local

Národní politika, 14 November 1915, 4; "Skvělá jednota a kázeň českého národa," *Lidový deník,* 3 December 1914, 1.

[24] Z. 43438, 1915, KÜA, KA, ÖstA; on the Habsburg state's anti-Czech politics during the First World War see Jan Havránek, "Politische Repression und Versorgungsengpässe in den böhmischen Ländern 1914 bis 1918," in *Der erste Weltkrieg,* 47–67; Křen, *Die Konfliktgemeinschaft,* 303–400. On denunciations of Czech citizens in Vienna during the First World War see Healy, *Vienna,* 122–59.

[25] Statthaltereipraesidium in Böhmen an MfKU in Wien, Einsichtsbogen, betreffend Pflege des österreichischen Staatsgedankens in der böhmischen Bevölkerung, Prague, 12 June 1916, carton 7, Národnosti 1911–18, z. 13 669, MKV/R, NA.

[26] Tschechische Lehrer, Erhebungen, Böhm, Leipa, 19 August 1915, z. 38000, 1915, KÜA, KA, ÖstA.

nationalist politics. Now, however, the state took flimsy nationalist accusations seriously, using them as grounds for persecution of Czech speakers.

Czech-speaking teachers in Bohemia quickly denied all accusations of disloyalty. In August of 1915 the four major Czech teachers' associations in Bohemia released an official "profession of loyalty of all Czech teachers and pupils," which was published throughout the province. The statement praised Czech teachers' and students' patriotic activities and proclaimed their hopes for victory and their loyalty to the Habsburg dynasty.[27] In spite of such gestures, however, Bohemian governor Max Coudenhove heeded the warnings of local German nationalists, as well as increasing pressures from the military to crack down on suspected subversion. He ordered a thorough purge of all Czech schools to eliminate alleged nationalist subterfuge. Superficial accommodation wouldn't do: "Heart, mind, and reason must be equally saturated with Austrian patriotism," demanded Coudenhove. In 1915 and 1916 German nationalists attempted to use the war as an opportunity to "resolve" the nationalist school conflicts of the Monarchy to their advantage once and for all, using the power of the state. Musing on the sins of the past, Coudenhove reflected, "It occurs to me that although the Czech teachers were often openly politically active in a radical-national direction before the war, too little action was taken against such elements."[28] Now that the tides had turned, he ordered that Czech nationalist teachers be supervised, transferred, or fired. German nationalists, confident that victory in the war would produce a powerful German-dominated *Mitteleuropa*, meanwhile intensified their demands upon the state for favorable reforms, including administrative autonomy for "German Bohemia" and limitations on Czech linguistic rights. For a short time it appeared that these demands might actually be satisfied by the state.[29]

The persecution of Czech nationalists by the Austrian state during the war had significant consequences for post-World War I nation building as well as for the daily lives of Czech speakers. The Austrian state's attacks on Czech schools, "where every nation must feel it most deeply, where the greatest bitterness must arise," held a special place in the founding myths of interwar Czechoslovakia.[30] While the demonization of Czech teachers in official wartime propaganda ran deep, however, it is worth considering how Czech nationalists responded to wartime conditions on the home front. The logic of Czech interwar nation building placed a high premium on tales of national

---

[27] "Imposantní projevy loyality českého učitelstva a žactva," *Škola městanská*, 18 August 1915, 271–73.

[28] Runderlass an die Herren Vorstände der k.k. Bezirkshauptmannschaften und politischen Exposituren in böhmischen und gemischtsprachigen Bezirken, Prague, 12 June 1916, carton 7, Národnosti 1911–18, z. 13 669, MKV/R, NA.

[29] Křen, *Die Konfliktgemeinschaft*, 325. See the petition of the Deutsche Volksrat in Böhmen, "An das deutsche Volk in Böhmen!" *Prager Tagblatt*, 22 July 1917, 1.

[30] Haus der Abgeordneten 13, Sitzung der XXII Session, 3 July 1917, "Anfrage des Abgeordneten Franz Stanek, Dr. Zdenek Tobolka und Genossen an Seine Excellenz den Herrn

victimization under the alleged bondage of Habsburg rule, reinforcing an image of Czechs as a subject population rather than equal citizens in Austria. This bias may have at least partially obscured the genuine indeterminacy of the final years of World War I and the complexity of the relationship between nationalists and the Austrian state up until the Empire's collapse.

Parents Take the Blame

The demonization of Czech educators led censors' gaze to the children in their care, those ostensibly most threatened by the "cancer" of Czech nationalism. Children's behavior became a topic of heated political debate, as the state, teachers, parents, and nationalists offered competing interpretations of the underlying causes of wartime youth delinquency. Schools and state officials were forced to contend with troubling questions: to what extent were children capable of political behavior, and to what extent were their teachers or their parents at fault for children's delinquent and potentially seditious actions?

On September 9, 1915, Oberleutenant Eduard Eller was strolling with his girlfriend in a vegetable garden in a small Bohemian town when he was accosted with the insult "German dog!" from behind a fence. Officials soon apprehended three Czech-speaking children. Two six-year-old boys immediately confessed to the crime, whereas the third, seven-year-old Martha Kavalek, denied calling the lieutenant "German dog" but admitted that she had called him "German ass" on several other occasions.[31] Such incidents became cause for serious state investigation and harsh punishment during the First World War. By July 1917, tables compiled by the provincial school board named seventy-five Czech-speaking children from Bohemia between the ages of six and sixteen who had been accused of treason, lèse-majesté, or disloyal or unpatriotic behavior since 1914.[32] Czech-speaking children were apprehended for participating in food riots, buying cigarettes for Serbian prisoners of war, throwing stones at trains, and writing letters about the unsanitary conditions in Hungarian hospitals. The elementary school student Wenzel Hauk received four weeks' detention and a failing grade in citizenship and was corporally punished for poking out the Emperor's eyes on a classroom poster.[33]

The Imperial state demanded explanations from Czech school authorities for such behavior. The nationalist movements of the late Habsburg

Ministerpräsidenten, betreffend das Verhalten der Regierungskreise während des Krieges gegenüber der böhmischen Nation," carton 7, MKV/R, präs. NA.

[31] Z. 34161, 1 November 1915, sig. 18 D2 1915–18, carton 4506, Böhmen in Genere, MfKU, AVA, ÖstA.

[32] Politisch beanständete Kinder der Volks und Bürgerschulen mit böhmischer Unterrichtssprache in Böhmen, 13 July 1917, sig. 18 D2 1915–18, Böhmen in Genere, carton 4506, AVA, MfKU, ÖstA.

[33] Z. 12936, 14 June 1916, sig. 18 D2 1915–18, Böhmen in Genere, carton 4506, AVA, MfKU, ÖstA.

Monarchy had actively and successfully promoted the claim that schools were national property and that the nation was responsible for the children in its care. As a result, Czech schools and teachers were initially held guilty until proven innocent for these lapses in Imperial patriotism, even when they occurred outside the school. Nationalists' hard-fought collective "rights" to children were thus accompanied by collective responsibilities for children's patriotic loyalties during the First World War. Educators took these wartime responsibilities seriously. In Kolín/Kolin, for example, after "small children, women, and rabble" held a demonstration outside the district captain's office on May Day in 1917, Czech teachers were deputized by the local police. They patrolled the streets after 8:00 p.m. to enforce the curfew for three weeks. Eventually they caught and punished twenty-one children for participating in the demonstration, which the children had attended with their mothers. While German-speaking pupils attended demonstrations in equal numbers, it was rare for them to be apprehended for similar crimes.[34]

In spite of such biases, Czech school officials were not wholly without means to defend themselves and their charges. School authorities typically shifted the blame to neglectful parents in order to depoliticize the troublesome wartime behavior of Czech children. Mothers worked in war factories and fathers were mobilized. The school days had been shortened, and children were sent into the streets to search for food and coal or accompanied their parents to demonstrations.[35] Czech school officials cited such conditions to throw the question back at the state: could they truly be held responsible under such circumstances if children didn't obey their patriotic teachers? In one case, a teacher overheard ten-year-old Pravoslav Vebr criticizing the patriotic postcards on sale in his classroom with the remark, "Such dumb pictures, the best thing to do with them is wipe your ass." He was arrested, brought before the district court, spent eight days in detention, and was expelled from school. Yet after a thorough investigation, the final governor's report concluded, "The behavior of the above boy can be traced back solely to the neglectful upbringing of the child, in that the father of the apprehended, Gottlieb Vebr, currently active in the XX/75 *Wachkompagnie* in Pilsen, is an anarchist and atheist, as is the entire family."[36]

The popular Austrian concept of national *Gesinnung,* or orientation, contributed to these accusations of subterfuge by Czech children. Gesinnung was used by officials to determine one's likely national identity as well as loyalty to the state; it was an ambiguously defined emotional/biological orientation,

---

[34] Z. 577, Okresní školní rada v Kolíně, 21 May 1917, Z. 1567, sig. IV 13u-2 1917, carton 2588, ZŠR, NA.

[35] Demonstration in Chrast anlässlich der Getreiderequisition, sig. IV 13u-2 1918, carton 2588, ZŠR, NA.

[36] Abschrift zur z. 49.472 präs, Ai 1915, k.k. Bezirkshauptmannschaft, Prague, carton 4506, 4 December 1915, MfKU, AVA, ÖstA.

much like sexuality in contemporary discourse, that could be read through social and familial affiliations but was rooted within. Maureen Healy has argued that Gesinnung passed like a germ from male heads of household to their wives and children, rendering entire families guilty by association.[37] The idea of national Gesinnung as a family-bound trait may have developed precisely through such contests between Czech school authorities and the state over responsibility for children's patriotic delinquency. Czech school officials used the assumption that disloyal Gesinnung passed from father to son to shift the blame for unruly youth behavior from nationalist teachers to rotten parents. In spite of significant discursive mobilization against "disloyal" Czech teachers in 1915–17, deviant parents, poverty, and social upheaval generally took the blame for children's political outbursts. The case of Stanislaus Prusha in Pohoř/Pohor, accused of lèse-majesté, was typical. The district school inspector interviewed teachers, pupils, and local school officials and assured officials in the Ministry of Education, "It is certain that the teachers in Pohor are not at all to blame for the behavior of Stanislaus Prusha. Education in the school leaves nothing to be desired in either a moral or patriotic respect. Love of the fatherland is always promoted, and the children are brought up to be loyal citizens who love the dynasty. The criminal confusion of the boy is the result of insufficient household oversight."[38]

By the war's end, it seemed, irresponsible and neglectful parenting had left school officials helpless in the battle against Czech children's delinquency, at least according to the reports of local Czech authorities. After a rash of particularly violent food demonstrations around Pilsen in 1918, the Czech school board reported with exasperation to the provincial school board in Prague: "The school is totally powerless. Parents manage their children absolutely inconsistently. In deliberate opposition to the school and the attempts of the teachers to prevent it, they send their children precisely where the school forbids them to go. They evade the school and the teachers in any way possible and threaten the school and teachers with resistance if they undermine the effects of this parental 'upbringing.'"[39]

In conceding such impotence, had Czech nationalist teachers and social workers finally surrendered their long-fought claims to educate Czech-speaking children? By 1918, Czech nationalist activists themselves certainly noted a shift in nationalist priorities. The fundraising efforts of the Czech School Association (Matice školská) were suffering, reported *Ochrana*

---

[37] On Gesinnung see Gerald Stourzh, "Ethnic Attribution in Late Imperial Austria: Good Intentions, Evil Consequences," in *The Habsburg Legacy: National Identity in Historical Perspective*, ed. Ritchie Robertson and Edward Timms, 71 (Edinburgh, 1994), and Healy, "Becoming Austrian," 19.

[38] Z. 4733, Stanislaus Prusha, Majestätsbeleidigung, 3 February 1916, sig. 18 D2 1915–18, carton 4506, Böhmen in Genere, MfKU, AVA, ÖstA.

[39] Demonstration in Chrast anlässlich der Getreiderequisition, sig. IV13u-2 1918, carton 2588, ZŠR, NA.

mládeže, the journal of the Czech Provincial Commission in Bohemia. The School Association was 25 million crowns in debt. Czechs had only themselves to blame for this sorry state of affairs: national minority schools were no longer "in fashion," the ČZK lamented. The writer chastised readers, "What a painful and sad impression it makes, that we don't have the means for the protection of Czech children in minority schools, when we have plenty of money for other things!"[40] In fact, the ČZK could afford to encourage Czech speakers to give to the struggling School Association. While nationalist support for minority schools diminished during World War I, the ČZK was thriving financially. The budget of the ČZK in Bohemia quadrupled during the war, from 186,578 crowns in 1913 to 917,901 crowns in 1916, a significant sum even given inflation.[41] If the Austrian state and a shift in popular concerns had closed down one path for Czech nationalist activists, a new path had opened in the realm of social welfare.

A peculiar cycle soon developed. While nationalists had justified their educational claims on children in the late Austrian Empire in order to protect them from nationally indifferent and neglectful parents, those schoolchildren who had best internalized the lessons of Czech nationalist pedagogy now risked being branded traitors to the state. Czech school officials attempted to explain the nationalist behavior of children in depoliticized terms during World War I. Using the new language of the child welfare movement, they shifted the blame for children's behavior from nationalist teachers to bad parents. At the same time, nationalist organizations were well prepared to propose solutions to the wartime epidemic of delinquency by expanding institutions for collective education outside the school and home. As the wartime social crisis intensified, these solutions became increasingly attractive to the Austrian state. Even as Austrian officials suppressed Czech nationalism with paranoid zeal, the war ultimately provided both Czech and German nationalists alike an unprecedented opportunity to assume new parental powers over children in the Bohemian Lands through expanding social welfare activism.

The Tip of the Volcano

The war began in the Bohemian Lands with a chorus of nationalist declarations about the pedagogical benefits of war, but it did not take long for more pessimistic voices to prevail. Across Europe the experience of the First

---

[40] "Věc, která nestrpí odkladu," *Ochrana dítěte: Časopis české zemské komise pro ochranu dítek a péči o mládež v Markrabství* 8, 20 August 1918. Contributions to the German School Association declined dramatically during the war as well. See "Němci nechtějí nic dát šulfrajnu," *Národní politika,* 3 August 1917, 1.

[41] "Činnost hospodářská," *Ochrana mládeže: Časopis pro veřejnou a soukromou péči o mládež v Království českém* 7, 1917, 135.

World War challenged idealized, liberal views of the family as harmonious and self-sufficient and helped to produce a political culture ripe for state intervention. As early as 1916, reports from across the Bohemian Lands warned of a menacing crisis of youth. Children of both nations allegedly roamed the streets aimlessly, patronized bordellos and cabarets, stole food and provisions, threw rocks at store windows, and begged in railway stations. Those teenagers who found employment in war factories had plenty of money but nothing to spend it on, since food and other necessities were rarely available. Instead, claimed officials in the Austrian Defense Ministry, they developed adult vices as "a lack of oversight and parental instruction encourages the imitation of bad adult habits." The Defense Ministry was particularly concerned about the perceived outbreak of delinquency among youth, which officials argued threatened the state's military capacity: "This office can toss aside these disturbing facts all the less, in that it concerns the physical deterioration and moral degeneration of that human material out of which the state should rejuvenate its defensive power."[42] The Bohemian governor's office attempted to counter this perceived epidemic of youth delinquency in 1916, restricting smoking, drinking, attending variety shows, and gambling, and instituting a 9:00 p.m. curfew for youth under 16.[43]

These disciplinary measures hardly sufficed to counter the growing social crisis. By 1917 the Austrian population was starving.[44] As food shortages became more frequent and poverty consumed even the middle classes, observers in the state and nationalist circles began to fear that the love of mothers for their children was itself at risk. In 1917 one state censor reported that as mothers were heard talking of killing themselves along with their children, the "destruction of family life and the burial of motherly instincts" was proceeding apace.[45] In the same year the DLS in Bohemia reinforced popular fears about the destruction of familial bonds: "The war has revealed the sad truth, that the pretty picture of the family as a force of social education has been destroyed by hard economic realities, and a certain wildness has emerged in its place. Feelings of parental duty are considerably stunted."[46] A 1917 state censor's report cited the letter of the Czech teenager Stefanie Pěkná to her father stationed in Italy to illustrate the social crisis brewing on the home front. "We are here alone without our father, and perhaps we will soon be without a mother as well, as our mother doesn't want to and

---

[42] Ministerium für Landesverteidigung an das Ministerium des Innern, Jugendfürsorge in Krieg, Vienna, 20 November 1916, carton 2475, Jugendfürsorge 1918, MfSV, AdR, ÖstA.

[43] Massnahmen Gegen die Verwahrlosung der Jugend, 31 December 1917, carton 2475, MfSV, AdR, ÖstA.

[44] Between 1915 and 1918, food rations allocated to the average consumer in Vienna declined from 1,300 to 830 calories per day. On the crisis of provisioning in wartime Austria, see Healy, *Vienna*, 31–86; for statistics, 45.

[45] Z. 4766, July 1917, carton 3752, AOK, GZNB, KA, ÖstA.

[46] Auszug aus dem Tätigkeitsbericht der Deutschen Landeskommission für Kinderschutz und Jugendfürsorge in Böhmen für das Jahr 1917, carton 2475, Jugendfürsorge 1918, MfSV, AdR, ÖstA.

cannot support us," Pěkná reported. "Every day she goes without breakfast and at lunch we have only black coffee. At night she comes home totally exhausted, cries from hunger and we cry with her. When she goes to work we stay home hungry and with no one to watch us."[47]

Meanwhile, nationalists in the Bohemian Lands painstakingly interpreted the social crisis in nationalist terms, building on claims that they had made before the war. Since the 1860s, when the Austrian Constitution was drafted and ratified, the supranational Austrian state had attempted to relegate nationalist expression to an imagined "private" and "social" sphere while preserving the "universal" and supranational quality of state/public institutions such as the dynasty, army, church, and bureaucracy.[48] In constructing this public/private divide in the nineteenth century and relegating nationalism to an imagined private realm, Austrian liberals could not have anticipated that state legitimacy would one day hinge precisely on such social questions as the health, welfare, and bad behavior of children. Nationalist movements flourished by focusing their attention on children and families and by defining social issues as questions of national survival. During the First World War, Czech and German nationalists were in a prime position to shape popular understandings of social conflict as well as influence social policy. Austrian officials had no choice but to create new institutions to address growing wartime social concerns, but it was too late to reconstruct child welfare as a supranational domain in the Bohemian Lands. The state was dependent on the infrastructure that nationalists had already built through the strictly nationalized provincial commissions.

The most threatening food riots and the longest strikes came from bilingual border regions of the Bohemian Lands, where economic despair was also most extreme. In 1917 alone 252 hunger demonstrations were held in Bohemia, and in 1918 citizens took to the streets to protest provisioning at least 232 times. Several of these riots culminated in the plundering of Jewish stores and violence against Jews.[49] German nationalists blamed Czechs for the food crisis, arguing that Czech farmers refused to surrender

---

[47] Bemerkenswertennachrichten zur Verpflegungsfrage in der Monarchie, carton 3752, AOK, GZNB, KA, ÖstA.

[48] On Austrian liberalism in the 1860s, see Pieter M. Judson, *Exclusive Revolutionaries: Liberal Politics, Social Experience and National Identity in the Austrian Empire* (Ann Ar bor,1996), 69–165. On the supranational character of "public," Imperial institutions, see Istvan Deak, *Beyond Nationalism: A Social and Political History of the Habsburg Officer Corps, 1848–1918* (Oxford, 1990); Gerald Stourzh, *Die Gleichberechtigung der Nationalitäten in der Verfassung und Verwaltung Österreichs, 1848–1918* (Vienna, 1985); Daniel Unowsky, "Reasserting Empire: Habsburg Imperial Celebrations after the Revolutions of 1848–49," in *Staging the Past: The Politics of Commemoration in Habsburg Central Europe*, ed. Maria Bucur and Nancy Wingfield, 13–46 (West Lafayette, IN, 2001).

[49] Z. 4647, Stimmung und wirtschaftliche Lage der österreichischen Bevölkerung im Hinterland, carton 3751, AOK, GZNB, KA, ÖstA. See also Peter Heumos, "Kartoffeln her oder es gibt eine Revolution: Hungerkrawalle, Streiks, und Massenproteste in den böhmischen Ländern, 1914–1918," in *Der erste Weltkrieg*, 255–87, for a survey of popular protests in the Bohemian lands.

requisitioned crops, while Czech nationalists replied that all the food was being sent to the German Reich.[50] As soldiers returned from the Russian front in 1918, censors reported fearfully that they brought new revolutionary ideas with them and did not hesitate to compare the situation at home with that in the "free Russian state." The condition of their families did not lead to favorable conclusions and appeared to prepare the ground for social revolution: "Contributing to the disappointment that has seized the demobilized soldiers is the physical and spiritual state of many of the women and children who meet them at home," Austrian censors observed.[51] Austrian officials were compelled to respond to these grievances, which appeared to threaten the state's very legitimacy. An informant's report from June of 1917 conveyed these words of warning from an intercepted letter by Socialist-feminist Amalie Seidel: "I have the feeling that we are sitting here on a volcano which is rumbling and boiling inside. The only thing missing is the igniting spark."[52] The threatening popular mood, coupled with the shadow of the Russian Revolution, propelled a genuine change of course for the Austrian government in early 1917. Emperor Karl, who assumed the throne after Francis Joseph's death in November of 1916, reconvened the Austrian parliament, pronounced a general amnesty, releasing most Czech political prisoners, and secretly negotiated to take Austria out of the war.[53]

In this spirit of last-ditch reform, Austrian authorities established a new Imperial Ministry for Social Welfare in August of 1917. Not surprisingly, the ministry opened its doors to face a flood of nationalist demands. Czech delegates to the Austrian parliament initially rejected the new centralized ministry altogether, fearing a challenge to their well-established rights to educate Czech children. The influential Czech liberal magazine *Naše doba* reported that Antonín Kalina, representing the Czech National Socialist Party in the Austrian parliament, protested that the new central agency would "disturbingly intervene into each and every Czech person's life, requisitioning for itself the last scrap of Czech autonomy in the realm of social welfare." Czech delegates were explicitly concerned that private nationalist institutions such as nursery schools, day-care centers, and orphanages "could pass from the autonomous national sphere" into the hands of an overpowering central state, "which could cause great damage, especially . . . in the realm of

[50] Z. 4837, Beilage 6 zum Monatsbericht pro Sept 1917, carton 3753, AOK, GZNB, KA, ÖstA.

[51] Stimmung und wirtschaftliche Lage der österreichischen Bevölkerung im Hinterland, June 1918, carton 3759, AOK, Evidenzbüro, KA, ÖstA.

[52] Stimmung und wirtschaftliche Lage der österreichischen Bevölkerung im Hinterland, June 1917. Carton 3752, AOK, GZNB, KA, ÖstA.

[53] Křen, *Die Konfliktgemeinschaft*, 348–50. For statements by Czech nationalist leaders in the fall of 1917, see *Národní listy*, 21 October 1917, 1, articles by Karel Kramář and Alois Rašín. On attempts by the Austrian government to liberalize and strengthen its popular legitimacy in 1917–18, see Joseph Redlich, *Österreichische Regierung und Verwaltung im Weltkriege* (New Haven, 1925), 262–63.

national education."[54] Bitter that their own more radical demands for state reforms in their favor were rejected in 1917, German nationalists also approached the new ministry with skepticism, warning officials, "It would be as incomprehensible for us as it would be unbearable if . . . an Austrian government should again attempt to place German Bohemia under the rule of common Czech authorities, and to force us into a community that we are determined to reject."[55]

"Each Nation Cares Only for Its Own"

It did not seem like a fortuitous beginning. In fact, however, nationalists should not have been so concerned about the state's usurping their authority as officials in the new ministry planned the national segregation of its regional and local offices from the outset. During the parliamentary debates surrounding the ministry's creation, newly appointed minister Heinrich Mataja declared, "The new Ministry for Social Welfare will strive to be national/popular [*volkstümlich*]. It will be open and accessible to everyone and will in particular strive to attract the enthusiastic cooperation of private associations and autonomous organizations."[56] He was true to his word. In the Bohemian Lands, state welfare programs were built to expand an infrastructure that nationalist activists in the Bohemian Lands had already created from the bottom up. Nationalists from the private provincial commissions were immediately appointed as advisers, judges, and officials in the new ministry. The state hoped to harness the private, nationally segregated child welfare system to achieve its own goals in 1917–18. Above all, Austrian officials aimed to take advantage of a claimed reservoir of trust between nationalists and local populations in order to reinforce the legitimacy of the war-battered Austrian state.

In 1917 the ministry convened a Youth Council (Jugendbeirat), which was charged with developing a new centralized Imperial youth welfare policy. This council was designed explicitly with the goal of facilitating national representation and included Czech, Polish, Italian, Croat, and Jewish delegates, many of whom represented private nationalist social welfare institutions in their respective crown lands.[57] In one of the council's first and only official sessions, Jona Kimmel, a Jewish social welfare activist from Galicia, requested state funding for Jewish kindergartens and

[54] "Věci sociální," *Naše doba*, 20 January 1918, 19–20; see also *Bohemia*, 21 November 1917, 2.
[55] Z. 98, 7 January 1918, carton 45, Praes. 1918, MfSV, AdR, ÖstA.
[56] "Fortsetzung des Sitzungsberichtes, Wien, 20 November, Abgeordnetenhaus," *Prager Tagblatt*, 21 November 1917, 2. Mataja was a prominent Christian Socialist from Vienna.
[57] Jugendbeirat, I. Band, carton 2475, Jugendfürsorge 1918, MfSV, AdR, ÖstA.

welfare organizations. His proposal reflected the extent to which the national segregation of Austrian welfare programs was a foregone conclusion. Anticipating the nationalization of educational and social institutions across Habsburg Central Europe, Kimmel suggested that Jewish commissions for social welfare be erected next to those of other nationalities in all mixed-language regions of Austria. "Considering the fact that public life in Austria will certainly sooner or later be oriented according to purely national perspectives, I consider it a given that the time will come in which each nation cares only for its own," he speculated. "The Jewish population will then be receptive to the idea of a pan-Austrian organization for the care of school-age Jewish youth, which could arrange its own Jewish kindergartens in every community."[58]

As negotiations surrounding the creation of the new ministry continued, nationalist child welfare activists successfully depicted their expertise as far more than the sum of knowledge, labor, and experience. "Expertise" now implied an intimate, emotional understanding of the local populations being served, an ability to connect with, mobilize, and earn the trust of the client. The empathy of nationalist social workers, based on national solidarity, supposedly bred popular legitimacy, distinguishing the nationalized welfare system from both liberal paternalism and cold bureaucracy. In a 1917 memo by Anton Tůma, submitted on behalf of the Czech Provincial Commissions, Czech nationalists asserted, "Our deep understanding of practical life has convinced the ČZK, that . . . what actually can be successfully achieved through a law can only be hoped for from a law written in a national spirit, which can count on the inner understanding and eager cooperation of the widest masses."[59]

Nationalist rhetoric powerfully linked national autonomy with popular legitimacy in 1917–18. Drawing on long-standing assertions about the nationally circumscribed social needs of German and Czech families, child welfare activists called upon the new ministry to segregate social welfare institutions in the name of democracy itself. Austrian officials were obligated to create a nationally segregated welfare system in order to "reinforce the recent tendency of individual nations to express their national individuality in public services as well as the trend toward the widespread democratization of government," Tůma insisted.[60] The ČZK also invoked this alleged nationally exclusive empathy and expertise to lobby for the appointment of new Czech judges during the war. Soon after the new ministry was formed, the ČZK in

---

[58] Protokoll über die erste konstituierende Sitzung des Jugendbeirates am 17 Juni 1918, Beilage 3, z. 1807/18, carton 2475, Jugendfürsorge 1918, MfSV, AdR, ÖstA. On Jews and Jewish identity during World War I in Austria, see Marsha Rozenblit, *Reconstructing a National Identity: The Jews of Habsburg Vienna during WWI* (Oxford, 2001).

[59] Anton Tůma, Beilage 1, Protokoll über die erste konstituierende Sitzung des Jugendbeirates am 17 Juni 1918, z. 1807/18, 35–39, 14 June 1918, carton 2475, Jugendfürsorge 1918, MfSV, AdR, ÖstA.

[60] Ibid.

Moravia successfully demanded the appointment of a senior Czech judge in the Moravian family court, insisting, "A German judge has neither the necessary understanding nor emotional sympathy for the claims and rights of Czech children!"[61]

If Czech nationalists were expecting a fight from their German colleagues or the Austrian state, they were sorely disappointed. Margarete Roller, representing the DLS in Moravia, agreed in 1917 that wartime social welfare programs "will only be executed in the spirit of the population and find support in the population if the provincial youth offices are fully nationally separated."[62] By August 1918 the Austrian state was prepared to concede far more than nationalists themselves might have envisioned, putting the local administration of critical state welfare programs directly into nationalist hands. Activists in the formerly private provincial commissions were not unaware of their role in rescuing a state overwhelmed by the social demands of its citizens. The DLS in Bohemia boasted in 1918, "As a private union we actually had to take the place of a government authority, because nothing was undertaken from the side of the government or the provincial bureaucracy to relieve the misery of youth in our time."[63] The state threw in its lot with nationalists not only because the two shared concerns about youth delinquency and social unrest during the war but because nationalists were simply ahead of the state in the development of welfare programs. Officials in the Justice Ministry and Ministry of Interior affirmed in 1914, "The national segregation of the guardian councils is not to be undone in Bohemia and Moravia. All of youth welfare is built on this foundation there, as the planned child welfare laws already acknowledge."[64] Out of desperation or choice, the state relied on the private, nationalist welfare system to achieve its own goals.

Through the tireless wartime work of professional social workers, nationalists' self-congratulatory claims to possess "exclusive" popular legitimacy seemed to become a self-fulfilling prophecy. As the social needs of families grew during the war, so too did nationalists' own sense of self-importance about their influence in local communities. German nationalist social worker Anton Vrbčka boasted in early 1916, "From day to day I felt more and more how the DLS was anchored in the Volk, how the people's trust for the commission grew stronger and stronger, since the people often came from far away and from foreign districts and with every possible malady. Nothing

[61] Berufung eines böhmischen Richters in das Ministerium für soziale Fürsorge, z. 323 1918, 1 January 1918, carton 46, Praes. 1918, MfSV, AdR, ÖstA.

[62] Protokoll über die erste konstituierende Sitzung des Jugendbeirates am 17 Juni 1918, z. 1807/18, carton 2475, Jugendfürsorge 1918, MfSV, AdR, ÖstA.

[63] Auszug aus dem Tätigkeitsbericht der Deutschen Landeskommission für Kinderschutz und Jugendfürsorge in Böhmen für das Jahr 1917, z. 5524, carton 2475, Jugendfürsorge MfSV, AdR, ÖstA.

[64] Entwurf einer Verordnung über Vormundschaftsräte, z. 37.299, 23 October 1914, carton 433, sig. I Generalvormundschaft, Justizministerium, AVA, ÖstA.

seemed too minor, for every pain I sought a remedy, and I found one too."[65] If the misery and delinquency of children seemed almost impossible to overcome, these pioneers took minimal comfort in knowing that their charges degenerated less than those of the national enemy. Czech Social worker Josef Petr thus concluded a 1917 report: "The corruption and immorality of the children is to a large degree a result of their indigence, which is enormous in this area: the children are hungry, they soon begin begging, then they steal and before long they have become complete criminals. The only small gratification is that children of German nationality, and a great many of them too, are just as morally delinquent."[66]

The provincial commissions, not surprisingly, enjoyed tremendous financial and organizational growth during the war. By 1918, the ČZK in Bohemia boasted 130 district offices, while the DLS in Bohemia had established 95 branches. Hardly an inch of territory in the Bohemian Lands was unaccounted for. In 1917 the DLS in Bohemia distributed 773,619k, up from 27,539k in 1908, while the ČZK in Bohemia reported a budget of 558,368k in 1916.[67] DLS activists boasted in their 1917 annual report, "We don't want to neglect to emphasize that the mentioned payments flowed almost exclusively into German districts, and of course only to the benefit of German children."[68] These impressive numbers, raised through private contributions, only begin to measure the vast sums of money that actually passed through local branches of the nationally segregated commissions en route to Austrian children. The organizational and financial fusion of the welfare state in the Bohemian Lands with the provincial commissions was most powerfully consolidated when the state officially entrusted the administration of the Imperial Widow and Orphan Fund (k.k. Witwen und Waisenfond, WuWf) to the DLS and ČZK. By 1917, the WuWf had given out over 30 million crowns empirewide, employed over ten thousand civil servants, and mobilized one hundred thousand women in its women's

---

[65] Berufsmundes in der Kriegszeit, z. 1452 1918, carton 50, MfSV, AdR, ÖstA.

[66] Josef Petr, "Zpráva pana Josefa Petra, poruc̆ níka z povolání," *Ochrana mládeže* 8, 1918, 151.

[67] For German statistics, see "Auszug aus dem Tätigkeitsbericht." For Czech statistics see z. 8504, 25 October 1917, both in carton 2475; Jugendfürsorge 1918, MfSV, AdR, ÖstA; and *Ochrana dítěte*, 15 November 1915; 31 May 1917. The German Provincial Commission in Bohemia distributed several hundred thousand more crowns than the Czech Provincial Commission, although the Czech Provincial Commission would have served a larger population. While most state subsidies were allocated proportionally according to the percentages of German and Czech speakers in the 1910 census, these disparities reflected differences in the private fund-raising success of the two organizations as privately raised funds accounted for the vast majority of the respective budgets. The Czech Provincial Commission in Moravia complained in 1917 that certain subsidies (such as those from the Red Cross) were divided evenly between the Czech and German Commissions, even though the ČZK served more children. See "K naší péči o mládež za války," *Ochrana dítěte: Časopis české zemské komise pro ochranu dítek a péči o mládež v Markrabství moravském* 6, 15 March 1917.

[68] "Auszug aus dem Tätigkeitsbericht."

auxiliaries, becoming the Monarchy's largest wartime welfare fund.[69] In the Bohemian Lands these funds were distributed exclusively through local branches of the provincial commissions.

Familiar reasoning motivated the state to join forces with the nationalists. The state faced financial collapse and a crisis of legitimacy, and the DLS and ČZK offered a final chance to meet the frustrated expectations of an agitated population. In a 1918 memo, Ministry of Social Welfare officials claimed that the provincial commissions offered individualized care, an efficient means of distribution, and scientific expertise.[70] The nationalist commissions now best represented the values the state itself wanted to appropriate. The funds from the WuWf flowed through the district offices of the provincial commissions in Bohemia beginning in June 1915, and a year later the success of this arrangement encouraged the WuWf to extend the program to other crown lands.[71] The financial dependence of the state on these half-private organizations is striking. Much of what was officially called "state support" during World War I was in fact money raised for the state by private charities. The Monarchy's largest welfare fund thus relied heavily on the generosity and patriotism of Austrian citizens. The ČZK in Bohemia alone raised 514,000k for the WuWf in 1915–16.[72] The state could not compete with the impressive fund-raising efforts and expertise of local nationalists and recognized that the best strategy was to harness this formidable power to its own emerging social welfare apparatus.

Officials responsible for the WuWf believed that individuals were more inclined to generosity when guaranteed that their money would be used within their locality and would exclusively benefit members of their own nation. The agreement they created with the DLS and ČZK therefore specified that 75 percent of any funds raised by a local office would benefit national comrades in their own local district. Equally important, the state recognized that its social goals could be realized only through another kind of financial contribution—namely, the efforts of voluntary (female) labor. "The fund will do best not to create new organizations, which especially in smaller places could only be staffed by the same people and therefore create unnecessary complications or otherwise lead to clearly undesirable rivalries and tensions," officials in the WuWf argued in August 1916.[73] The leader of the Youth Office of the Ministry for Social Welfare, Eduard Prinz

---

[69] "Hinterbliebenen und Jugendfürsorge," 11 May 1918, carton 2481, Jugendfürsorge, MfSV, AdR, ÖstA.

[70] Memo from 5 December 1917 to the Ministries of Finance and Social Welfare, z. 1262, z. 1246, carton 49, Praesidium, MfSV, AdR, ÖstA.

[71] "Zemská úřadovna c.k. fondu pro vdovy a sirotky po rakouských vojínech," *Ochrana dítěte* 6, 15 March 1917, 1.

[72] "Činnost hospodářská," *Ochrana mládeže* 7, 1917, 138.

[73] K.k. Österreichischer Militär Witwen und Waisenfond, z. 3645, 2 August 1916, carton 2479, Jugendfürsorge 1918, MfSV, AdR, ÖstA.

Fig. 3. An Austrian official places children under the guardianship of the Czech Provincial Commission for Child Welfare in Bohemia. *Ochrana Mládeže: Časopis pro veřejnou a soukromou péči o mládež v Království českém* 5 (1915).

von Liechtenstein, applauded cooperation between the state and the provincial commissions until the war's end, also stressing efficiency. In a widely published lecture given in May 1918, he praised the merger of the DLS, ČZK, and WuWf, which "puts the advertisement of its ideals and also the people who are available for this branch of work in the service of the common cause—and so both win out."[74]

The financial justifications for the state's contract with nationalists remind us of the extent to which "nationalization" in the Habsburg Monarchy was a consequence of middle-class activism. The state was certainly intent on revitalizing its popular legitimacy, but that legitimacy depended on the adequate provision of welfare services. Provision of services, in turn, hinged on the financial generosity and volunteer labor of middle-class individuals and organizations, those most likely to be nationalist.[75] The decision to embrace a nationally segregated welfare state may have ultimately reflected the nationalist loyalties of charitable middle-class women much more than the nationalist demands of the working-class and peasant clients of welfare organizations, in spite of nationalist claims to represent the popular will.

By 1918, Austrian nationalists held a firm mandate to realize some of their most ambitious ideals with regard to youth. German and Czech nationalist welfare activists and social workers stood at the vanguard of a broader movement toward the establishment of a nationally divided social welfare system throughout Habsburg Central Europe. By 1916, nationalist social welfare activists had demanded nationally segregated guardianship councils in cities such as Graz (Styria), Ljubljana/Laibach (Krain), and Cracow (Galicia) and in Austrian Silesia, all based on the precedents set by child welfare activists in the Bohemian Lands.[76] In 1917 policymakers in Vienna officially adopted the system established in the Bohemian Lands, whereby each nation managed its own public social welfare institutions, as the model for an expanding public child welfare system in all multilingual regions of Habsburg Austria, including Galicia, the Bukovina, Southern Styria, and Silesia. In each of these regions, government officials in the new Ministry for Social Welfare planned to create nationally segregated city and regional youth welfare offices, guardian councils, and provincial commissions to care for the physical and moral welfare of the Empire's children and youth.[77]

[74] Hinterbliebenen und Jugendfürsorge," z. 6731, 11 May 1918, carton 2481, Jugendfürsorge 1918, MfSV, AdR, ÖstA.

[75] On the Austrian state's wartime dependence on the voluntary labor and financial support of middle-class citizens, see Joseph Redlich, *Österreichische Regierung und Verwaltung im Weltkriege* (New Haven, 1925), 153–56.

[76] Note des Ministerium des Innerns, betreffend die Generalvormundschaft, z. 13739, 20 April 1916, carton 433, sig. I, Generalvormundschaft, Justizministerium, AVA, ÖstA.

[77] On Silesia, see z. 14915, June 16, 1918, k.k. Landesregierung in Troppau, carton 2477, Jugendfürsorge 1918, MfSV, AdR, ÖstA. On plans for the national segregation of welfare

In the Bohemian Lands, meanwhile, German and Czech social welfare activists were united in the self-congratulatory rhetoric with which they advertised their role as the local arms of the Austrian state. Czech nationalists in Moravia boasted proudly in March 1918 of their significant power as mediators between the state and Czech-speaking children. The ČZK assured its supporters that it had achieved "the greatest influence in all practical matters. Every single application from the Czech side must first go through the orphan councils and the ČZK."[78] Even the most extreme German nationalists indulged in this spirit of self-congratulation. In a June 1918 article in the nationalist *Deutsche Volkszeitung,* nationalists informed citizens in Liberec/ Reichenberg that every German was nothing less than a democratic shareholder in the new Austrian welfare state. "One often encounters the claim that the care of war widows and orphans is not the responsibility of private charity, but is solely the task of the state. This view is fundamentally correct," the editorialists claimed. "Only—who is the state in the final analysis? In fact it is only us, in that directly or indirectly, we must provide the state with the means that will enable it to fulfill its duties." Thanks to the fusion of the WuWf with the DLS, nationalist activism became coterminous with patriotic support for the Austrian Empire. The *Volkszeitung* concluded, "Everything that the Imperial Widow and Orphan Fund collects through its commissions . . . will be painstakingly nationally managed so that it is absolutely impossible that Czech war victims will be provided for with German money or Germans with Czech money. The efforts of the Fund deserve our strongest support, because everything that we do for the WuWf, we are only doing for ourselves."[79]

In 1915, Austrian authorities had mobilized zealously against Czech nationalism in the schools. Only three years later they were singing a different tune. The war ultimately offered rich opportunities to German and Czech nationalists alike to "become father and mother" to unprecedented numbers of children in the Bohemian Lands.[80] "More than ever we must step in for the ideal of the family," urged teacher and DLS activist Karl Theimer in 1918.[81] Children, nationalists hoped, would respond to their new "families" with all the loyalty they owed their biological parents. Thanks to their role in addressing the perceived crisis of the family during the First World War, nationalist

---

institutions in other crown lands of the Monarchy, see Skizze zu Richtlinien für ein Gesetz über die öffentliche Erziehung, 1 November 1917, carton 43, Praesidium 1917, MfSV, AdR, ÖstA.

[78] Zpráva o sedmém roce činnosti české zemské komise pro ochranu dětí a péči o mládež v Markrabství moravském, z. 2498, carton 2476, Jugendfürsorge 1918, MfSV, AdR, ÖstA.

[79] "Der k.k. Österr. Militär-Witwen und Waisenfond, seine Bedeutung und sein Aufgaben," *Reichenberger Deutsche Volkszeitung,* 16 June 1918, 1–2, carton 2481, Jugendfürsorge 1918, MfSV, AdR, ÖstA.

[80] Aufruf, Bund der Deutschen in Böhmen, sig. 13u-1 1917, carton 2587, ZŠR, NA.

[81] Bericht über die Errichtung der Frauenkriegsbeisteuergruppen durch die Deutsche Landeskommission für Kinderschutz und Jugendfürsorge, z. 7873–18, carton 2476, Jugendfürsorge 1918, MfSV, AdR, ÖstA.

movements in the Bohemian Lands were well positioned to speak in the name of popular legitimacy at the end of the Great War. In spite of their paranoid suspicions about the loyalty of Czech citizens, Austrian authorities willingly entrusted the state's most ambitious social welfare programs to local nationalists in an attempt to avoid the fate of the Russian Empire. If citizens increasingly expressed their social grievances in nationalist terms, this was no accident (or error) of history. The state's own reliance on nationalists contributed heavily to the nationalization of citizenship and the national segregation of public institutions in Imperial Austria. The national revolutions of 1918–19 therefore did not simply reflect a misplaced expression of social demands as nationalist demands, the climactic result of Czech émigré maneuvering, or the revolt of the masses against the tottering Austrian state. These revolutions were coproduced by dissatisfied Czech and German citizens, a state in fear of social revolution, and the prescient idealism and opportunism of nationalist social welfare movements, which eagerly offered the state a leg on which to stand.

In the Bohemian Lands, as elsewhere in Europe, the First World War represented a turning point in the expansion of the welfare state. The welfare of children was intimately linked to the legitimacy of the state and the nation's future demographic, military, and political strength. In the Austrian Empire, however, nation and state were not coterminous. When Austrian officials entrusted private nationalist associations with the management of the wartime welfare programs, German and Czech nationalists significantly expanded their influence on children and families. The expansion of the welfare state during World War I did not, however, represent a radical abrogation of parental rights or a disciplinary "invasion" of a previously apolitical private sphere.[82] In the Bohemian Lands, children already occupied a different place on the imagined frontiers between public and private, nation, state, and family before 1914. Well before the outbreak of war, children "belonged" to the nation as nationalists had successfully advanced the claim that the family alone was ill equipped to protect children's moral, social, and national well-being.

Even in Western Europe, a view of emerging welfare states as a novel and dangerous form of state interference in the family is based in part on ahistorical assumptions about the family before 1914. Autonomous, harmonious families, sanctified parental rights, and strict divisions between public and private may have represented the liberal ideal in Western Europe in the nineteenth century, but realities for working-class and rural families looked quite different. Children worked in factories and on farms, lived and played in the streets, and were cared for by wet nurses and relatives. Parents themselves were subject to the control of churches, local communities

---

[82] For an expanded version of this argument, see Tara Zahra, "Each nation only cares for its own": Empire, Nation, and Child Welfare in the Bohemian Lands, 1900–1918," *American Historical Review* 111 (December 2006), 1378–1402.

and governments, and relatives. Well before the First World War, childhood and child rearing had been politicized by Europe's growing mass political movements and by nationalizing states, which articulated new pedagogical ideals in correspondence with their political visions. When states did take on new responsibilities for children's health and welfare in Western Europe, they often built on preexisting local, municipal, and private initiatives. Across Europe, wartime states often relied on the legitimacy, expertise, personnel, and financial resources of private organizations, creating hybrid welfare structures in which the lines between public and private were far from clear. The state itself was not a unified and homogenous entity, and "intervention" did not simply emerge from the top down. Expanding child welfare programs were a product of popular demands and concerns as well as state and middle-class activism. State officials and welfare organizations such as the nationalist provincial commissions explicitly sought to cultivate and claim popular legitimacy through child welfare initiatives, however polemical these claims may have been.[83]

For German nationalists, the First World War represented a fleeting moment of empowerment. In the fall of 1918, the DLS continued to appeal to the German-Austrian Ministry for Social Welfare even after the Emperor had abdicated the throne and the Monarchy dissolved. In late November 1918, a request from Silesia for funding from the Austrian state begged for "consideration of the German character of the city of Fulnek," arguing that as a "German-Moravian city," Fulnek would surely be "handed to the administrative realm of the German-Austrian authorities."[84] Instead, Czech troops occupied German towns, and the allies ignored German declarations of national self-determination. German nationalist demands for a German-Bohemian nation-state or for annexation to the German Austrian rump state were effectively suppressed by March 1919, when the Czechoslovak army

---

[83] For examples of how welfare-state structures were built from and/or shaped by private activism and social work organizations and municipal or regional initiatives in Western Europe and the United States, see Kathleen Canning, *Languages of Labor and Gender: Female Factory Work in Germany, 1850–1914* (Ithaca, 1996), 126–217; Laura Lee Downs, *Childhood in the Promised Land: Working-class Movements and the Colonies de Vacances in France, 1880–1960* (Durham, NC, 2002); Edward Ross Dickinson, *The Politics of German Child Welfare from the Empire to the Federal Republic* (Cambridge, MA, 1996); Seth Koven, "Borderlands: Women, Voluntary Action, and Child Welfare in Britain, 1840–1914, in *Mothers of a New World: Maternalist Politics and the Origins of Welfare States,* ed. Seth Koven and Sonya Michel, 94–127 (New York, 1993); Theda Skocpol, *Protecting Soldiers and Mothers: The Politics of Social Provision in the United States* (Cambridge, MA, 1992); Pat Thane, "Women in the British Labor Party and the Construction of State Welfare, 1906–1939," in *Mothers of a New World,* 343–72; Young-Sun Hong, "Neither Singular nor Alternative: Narratives of Modernity and Welfare in Germany, 1870–1945," *Social History* 30, no. 2 (2005), 133–53.

[84] Memo from the Schlesische Landesregierung, Troppau to the Deutschösterreichisches Staatsamt für soziale Fürsorge, 15 November 1918, z. 918, carton 50, MfSV-praesidium, AdR, ÖstA.

killed over fifty German demonstrators who had gathered to protest their exclusion from the new Austrian parliament.[85]

In the course of the revolution, Hugo Heller, head of the DLS in Bohemia, was placed under Czech military guard.[86] At the same time, Anton Tůma, head of the ČZK in Bohemia, received a promotion. As the freshly appointed Minister of Youth Welfare in the new Czechoslovak Ministry for Social Welfare, he joined Anton Miřička, his replacement at the ČZK, and Alice Masaryk, the daughter of Czech president Thomas Garrigue Masaryk, to organize a massive new child welfare organization. In 1919–20, the district offices of the DLS and ČZK, under the direction of the new charity "Czechoslovak Child Welfare," distributed the reconstruction gift of one multiethnic nation-state to another—6 million American dollars to feed and clothe the children of a new democracy.[87]

[85] For an account of the political negotiations that doomed German Bohemian claims to "self-determination" and demands to be annexed to Austria, see Boyer, "Silent War and Bitter Peace," 27–33.

[86] See *American Relief Administration a československá péče o dítě v Republice československé, 1919–20* (Prague, 1920).

[87] American Relief Administration—European Children's Fund, Československá péče o dítě v roce 1919, carton 145, Ministerstvo sociální péče (MSP), NA.

4 Reclaiming Children for the Nation

In 1918, newly elected Czechoslovak president Thomas Garrigue Masaryk consigned the Austrian Empire to the dustbin of history in the name of democracy's triumph. "On the whole, great multinational Empires are an institution of the past, of a time when material force was held high and the principle of nationality had not yet been recognized, because democracy had not been recognized," he declared.[1] As Czech nationalists assumed state power in 1918, they knit democratic principles, national self-determination, and ethnic character into a tightly woven tautology. Both Czech and German nationalists demanded national "rights" to children in the name of values such as minority rights, national self-determination, and democracy in interwar Czechoslovakia. Czech nationalists mobilized these new doctrines of minority rights and the power of the nationalizing state in a radical campaign to eliminate national indifference by assigning contested families to national communities based on "objective" characteristics.

Practices of national classification in interwar Czechoslovakia built on precedents established in the Austrian Empire, but dramatic changes accompanied the collapse of the Habsburg Empire. In the Bohemian Lands before the First World War, only Moravian children and parents had been subject to forcible national classification through the Lex Perek. In interwar Czechoslovakia, all citizens lost the right to freely choose their own national affiliation through new laws regulating the choice of a nationality on the decennial census. Census takers and state officials were accorded the right to "correct" a person's declaration of nationality on the census if they believed this declaration did not correspond to the person's objective characteristics.

---

[1] Thomas Garrigue Masaryk, "The Problem of Small Nations and States," in *We Were and We Shall Be: The Czechoslovak Spirit through the Centuries*, 153, ed. Zdenka and Jan Muzner (New York, 1941).

Thousands of citizens who professed to be Germans on the census of 1921 were subject to interrogations, fines, and imprisonment for illegally declaring a "false" nationality.

Through the Lex Perek and the creation of a nationally segregated welfare system, nationalists in Imperial Austria had gradually succeeded in appropriating state power, nationalizing public institutions and anchoring nationalist claims on children in law. The Habsburg state, however, had never become the political instrument of a single nation. The Imperial state behaved rather like an umpire, adjudicating claims between competing nationalist movements. Austria's courts had preserved some leeway for bilingual parents to choose schools and national affiliations for their children. In interwar Czechoslovakia, Czech nationalists promoted the battle against Germanization with new fervor, but now these nationalists had the full power of the new nation-state at their disposal.

The history of Czechoslovak educational policy confirms that the minority rights created at Versailles and St. Germain were understood by European contemporaries as collective rather than individual or human rights. As Hannah Arendt incisively observed in *The Origins of Totalitarianism*, interwar democracies were founded on a particularist, nationalist understanding of rights dressed in a universalist guise, with tragic consequences for European Jews. "The conception of human rights," she insisted, "based on the presumed existence of human beings as such, broke down at the very moment when those who professed to believe in it were for the first time confronted with those who had indeed lost all other qualities and specific relationships—except that they were human."[2] In interwar Czechoslovakia, new doctrines of minority rights and national self-determination safeguarded the collective rights of the nation to educate its children rather than the rights of individuals to freely determine their own national affiliation. The nation itself became the privileged liberal subject. Czech nationalists, moreover, continued to portray themselves as a victimized minority in their own nation-state. In their view, it was Czechs in predominantly German-speaking regions, rather than Germans, who required new minority rights protections. Václav Perek himself, author of the Lex Perek, insisted in 1922, "In reality [the German minorities] don't require the protection of the peace treaties for their development, because they have retained the greater power and greater rights. On the other hand . . . the Czech minority must be brought under state protection if it is not to be destroyed or denationalized."[3]

---

[2] Hannah Arendt, *Origins of Totalitarianism* (New York, 1951), 299. On national democracy in interwar Europe, see Mark Mazower, *Dark Continent: Europe's Twentieth Century* (New York, 1999), 41–138; Rogers Brubaker, *Nationalism Reframed: Nationhood and the National Question in the New Europe* (New York, 1996), 79–179.

[3] Václav Perek, *Ochrana menšin národnostních dle mírových smluv a skutečné poměry v naší republice* (Prague, 1922), 17.

Under these new circumstances, individuals responded to the initiatives of the Czechoslovak state by articulating their own identities and interests in nationalist terms. When nationality became something ascribed rather than chosen, they appealed to the state for justice. Yet these citizens, many of whom would have frustrated nationalist educators and social workers with their national ambivalence during the Habsburg Monarchy, increasingly acknowledged the nation's preeminent claims on their children. Rather than invoking their rights as parents to choose a school for their children, they demanded the right to a German education as Germans.

Alone in Central Europe

Historians' accounts of democratization in interwar Eastern Europe have centered largely around a single question: how well did states such as interwar Czechoslovakia, Poland, Romania, and Yugoslavia conform to an ideal type of democracy, defined by a commitment to liberal individualism? The question itself is anachronistic, since it makes little sense to compare Czechoslovakia in 1918 to the United States in the late twentieth century. Most Western democracies, including France, Britain, Germany, and the United States, themselves hardly conformed to this ideal type in the interwar period. The pressing question, therefore, is not whether any state deserves to be classified as an authentic democracy. It is far more helpful to ask what democracy actually meant to Czechoslovak citizens between the wars. How did state officials, parents, and local nationalists practice democracy and understand the minority rights they had pledged to uphold? In interwar Czechoslovakia, practices such as national ascription and denunciation did not reflect economic or political backwardness, antidemocratic leanings, or the inevitability of the state's ultimate collapse. They rather reflected a specific conception of national democracy, rooted in the Habsburg past, and expressed through local activism and law in interwar Czechoslovakia.

Until recently, questions of continuity across the caesuras of 1918 and 1939 were rarely posed in studies of the Bohemian Lands, precisely because Czechoslovakia has so often been seen as the poster child for East European democracy.[4] Czechoslovakia's claim to democratic exceptionalism was typically based on the assumption that both 1918 and 1939 represented zero hours in Czechoslovak history. This framework obscured the many legacies of Austrian political culture that shaped Czechoslovak democracy,

---

[4] Recent studies that have fruitfully traced continuities across regimes include Jeremy King, *Budweisers into Czechs and Germans: A Local History of Bohemian Politics, 1848–1948* (Princeton, 2002); Eagle Glassheim, *Noble Nationalists: The Transformation of the Bohemian Aristocracy* (Cambridge, MA, 2005); Melissa Feinberg, *Elusive Equality: Gender, Citizenship, and the Limits of Democracy in Czechoslovakia, 1918–1950* (Pittsburgh, 2006).

as well as the interwar institutions and conflicts that informed life under Nazi rule. The claim that Czechs had a special affinity for democracy was not the invention of twentieth-century historians. This notion was carefully nurtured by nineteenth-century Czech nationalists themselves and played an important role in bolstering the legitimacy of the new Czechoslovak nation-state after 1918. Long before the Nazis ranked the Czechs at the top of an imagined racial pyramid in Eastern Europe, Czechs enjoyed a certain international status as "honorary" Westerners. At the Paris Peace Conferences in 1918, where the victors of the First World War gathered to carve out a new map of East Central Europe, the Czech delegation traded heavily on their alleged democratic exceptionalism to legitimate their territorial demands. In the view of French and British diplomats, writes Margaret MacMillan, "The Poles were, of course, dashing and brave but quite unreasonable, the Romanians charming and clever, but sadly devious, the Yugoslavs, well, rather Balkan. The Czechs were refreshingly Western. . . . Beneš and Masaryk were unfailingly cooperative, reasonable and persuasive as they stressed the Czechs' deep-seated democratic traditions and their aversion to militarism, oligarchy, high finance, indeed all that the old Germany and Austria-Hungary had stood for."[5]

Czech nationalists also promoted the notion of democratic exceptionalism at the local level. Nationalists consistently answered complaints about Czechoslovak school policy by reminding Germans how lucky they were not to live in Poland, Italy, or even Germany. In 1930 the Czech National Socialist Party newspaper *Národní politika* chastised the German community: "Considering how Italy, Poland and others settled the score with their national minorities, and how Germany behaved and still behaves toward its Slavic and Danish minorities, . . . the Germans should be happy that we treated them so generously after the revolution."[6] These narratives of democratic exceptionalism enjoyed a revival after the fall of Communism in Czechoslovakia, as the reemerging democracy sought a usable past in the democratic traditions of the First Republic.[7] In this framework, practices of denunciation,

---

[5] Margaret Macmillan, *Peacemakers: the Paris Conference of 1919 and Its Attempt to End War* (London, 2001), 241, 246. On constructions of a humanitarian Czech "national character" in interwar Czechoslovakia see Andrew Lass, "What Are We Like? National Character and the Aesthetics of Distinction in Interwar Czechoslovakia," in *National Character and National Ideology in Interwar Eastern Europe*, ed. Katherine Verdery and Ivo Banac, 39–65 (New Haven, 1995).

[6] "Německá škola bez dětí," *Příloha Národní politiky*, 13 March 1930, 1.

[7] On Czechoslovak democratic exceptionalism see Vera Olivová, *Dějiny první republiky* (Prague, 2000), 7; Eva Broklová, *Československá demokracie—Politický systém 1918–1938* (Prague, 1992); Jaroslav Krejči and Pavel Machonin, *Czechoslovakia 1918–1992, A Laboratory for Social Change* (Oxford, 1992); Václav Kural, *Konflikt anstatt Gemeinschaft? Tschechen und Deutschen im Tschechoslowakischen Staat, 1918–1938* (Prague, 2001); Victor Mamatey and Radomír Luža, eds., *A History of the Czechoslovak Republic 1918–1948* (Princeton, 1973); Josef Rothschild, *East Central Europe between the Two World Wars* (Seattle, 1974).

the considerable history of collaboration in Czechoslovakia under Nazi rule, the violence accompanying the expulsion of the Germans in 1945, and the excesses of the Communist regime after 1945 were typically explained so as to minimize the importance of domestic political culture. So-called undemocratic habits and practices were germs, quite literally introduced to Czech society by foreign invaders, through "imitation" of German neighbors and Nazi oppressors during the war.[8] The collapse of Czechoslovak democracy, in these accounts, was a consequence of Allied weakness at Munich and the barbarity of the Nazi regime. Czech historian Václav Kural has argued, "To tell the truth, the negation of Masaryk's conception of the ČSR was forced by the defeat in Munich and the merciless pressure of the Nazis. Only under these conditions was the democracy that was defended and protected by the Czechoslovak Republic alone in all of Central and Southeastern Europe ultimately discredited and buried!"[9]

Historians have since underlined the fissures and structural weaknesses in Czechoslovak democracy, including gaps between constitutional promises and political practice in the realm of gender equality, a lack of commitment to formal democratic procedures among elites, a deliberately weak parliament, and Masaryk's own willingness to resort to corrupt means to protect humanist values.[10] Others have explored the destabilizing effects of Czech nationalist pressure groups on interwar political culture, particularly in the realms of language policy, school politics, and land reform.[11] Czech nationalism need not, however, be counted as a strike against Czech democracy.

---

[8] Eagle Glassheim situates the expulsions in long-term nationalist ambitions. See Glassheim, "National Mythologies and Ethnic Cleansing: The Expulsion of Czechoslovak Germans in 1945," *Central European History* 33 (2000): 463–75. The assumption that the expulsions represented an "imitation" of Nazi politics rather than an outgrowth of native Czech nationalist politics nonetheless remains widespread. See Jan Havránek, "Das Tragische Jahrzehnt in Mitteleuropa," in *Nationale Frage und Vertreibung in der Tschechoslowakei und Ungarn, 1938–1948*, ed. Richard G. Plaschka et al., xiii–xvii (Vienna, 1997); Hans Lemberg, "Die Entwicklung der Pläne für die Aussiedlung der Deutschen aus der Tschechoslowakei," in *Der Weg in die Katastrophe. Deutsch-Tschechoslowakische Beziehungen, 1938–1947*, ed. Detlef Brandes and Václav Kural, 77–92 (Essen, 1994); Tomáš Staněk, *Verfolgung 1945: Die Stellung der Deutschen in Böhmen, Mähren und Schlesien* (Vienna, 2002), 222–28.

[9] Václav Kural, *Statt Gemeinschaft ein Auseinandergehen! Tschechen und Deutsche im Grossdeutschen Reich und der Weg zum Abschub, 1938–1945* (Prague, 2002), 101.

[10] Antonín Klimek, *Boj o hrad*, vol. 1, *Hrad a pětka: Vnitropolitický vývoj Československa 1918–1926 na pudorysů zápasu o prezidentské nástupnictví* (Prague, 1996); Antonín Klimek, *Boj o hrad*, vol. 2, *Kdo po Masarykovi: Vnitropolitický vývoj Československa 1926–1935 na pudorysů zápasu o prezidentské nástupnictví* (Prague, 1998); Peter Bugge, "Czech Democracy 1918–1938: Paragon or Parody?" in *Phasen und Formen der Transformation in der Tschechoslowakei, 1918–1993*, ed. Christiane Brenner and Stephanie Weiss (Munich, forthcoming). See also Zdeněk Kárník, *České země v éře první republiky, 1918–38*, 3 vols. (Prague, 2000–2003); Peter Heumos, "Konfliktregelung und soziale Integration: Zur Struktur der Ersten Tschechoslowakischen Republik," *Bohemia* 30 (1989): 52–70; Feinberg, *Elusive Equality*.

[11] Mark Cornwall, "The Struggle on the Czech-German Language Border, 1880–1940," *English Historical Review* 109 (September 1994): 914–51; Jaroslav Kučera, *Minderheit im Nationalstaat: Die Sprachenfrage in den tschechisch-deutschen Beziehungen 1918–1938* (Munich,

Local activism around schools and children, in particular, was consonant with an explicitly nationalist conception of democracy, in which liberal individualism was not the paramount value. If we seek to understand Czech democracy on its own terms, it becomes clearer that the widespread practices of national ascription and denunciation in interwar Czechoslovakia grew logically from a conception of minority rights and democracy built around collective rights, and especially around nationalist claims on children.

Spoils of Democracy

The winners of a democratic nation-state are the recipients of a great deal of mail. Soon after Czech officials took control of the new Czechoslovak state in the fall of 1918, they were flooded with advice about what to do with it. In the revolutionary fervor of 1918–23, countless local national committees, mayors, school boards, and associations demanded reforms from the new Czechoslovak state. In the name of democracy and the minority rights promised by the Treaties of Versailles and St. Germain, many Czech citizens demanded that the state use its power to defend their children from the threat of Germanization, which ostensibly continued to plague them even in their new nation-state.

In August of 1919, a petition signed by the "Czech minority" in Moravská Třebová/Mährsich Trübau reached officials in the new Czechoslovak Ministry for Social Welfare. The few Czech residents in this small Moravian town claimed that they would soon succumb completely to their German surroundings if not immediately fortified by the state. Czech parents had been browbeaten for decades by their German landlords and employers into sending their children to German schools, the petition claimed. These children were now dangerously close to becoming "national turncoats." While the entire region of Moravská Třebová/Mährsich Trübau was currently German, even a cursory glance at the "names of the residents, areas, topographical designations, hills, brooks, and tracts of land" offered "ample proof that the region was once totally Czech," the Czech minority insisted. These local nationalists therefore demanded that the state quickly dedicate its resources to re-Czechifying the region.[12]

The Czech minority of Moravská Třebová/Mährsich Trübau proposed an ambitious plan to achieve their aims. Too many Czechs, particularly children and war widows, lived in disgraceful poverty, in desperate need of

---

1999); Glassheim, *Noble Nationalists;* Daniel Miller, "Colonizing the German and Hungarian Border Areas during the Czechoslovak Land Reform, 1918–1938," *Austrian History Yearbook* 34 (2003): 303–19.

[12] Memorandum from Czech Minority in Moravská Třebová, 15 August 1919, MSP, carton 145, NA.

shelter, food, and work. In response to the social crisis, they proposed to erect a vast, state-supported rural commune in their town, exclusively for single Czech mothers and their children, on the grounds of a former refugee camp. Mothers were to share the burdens of household chores, child care, and farm labor, while their children were educated in brand-new Czech schools. Most important, the colony, conveniently erected on lands expropriated from a German noble, would provide the town with a rapid infusion of Czechness. Nationalists hoped that the children would ultimately settle down in the region as farmers and artisans and raise their own Czech families, shifting the demographic balance in the region.

The German residents of the town naturally had other ideas. They hoped to use the abandoned refugee camp to expand the overcrowded German schools in town. But the Czech minority countered that the "the success of the Republic" itself was dependent on defeating this "Germanizing" agenda. The petition demanded that "German resistance be broken at its foundations" in order to protect the Czech minority, which petitioners claimed was otherwise "defenseless against the vengeance of the German residents." This would entail opening new Czech schools in the town, closing all German schools, and erecting the proposed settlement colony "without delay."[13] These plans were partly realized. In 1921 the former refugee camp in Moravská Třebová/Mährsich Trübau was transformed into an orphanage for sixty Czech foster children and sixty orphaned children of Czech legionnaires. In the summer of 1920 the barracks also served as a summer camp for 1100 Czech children from Vienna, who were sent to Moravia for several months of fresh air and Czech nationalist pedagogy.[14] Accordingly, the 1921 census results showed that the German-speaking population declined from 7,048 in 1910 to 6,090 in 1921, while the Czech-speaking population grew from 154 to 596.[15]

In interwar Czechoslovakia, Czech nationalists finally enjoyed the opportunity to realize nationalist fantasies unchecked by the moderating interference of a neutral state. The creation of the Czechoslovak Republic affirmed the long-standing conviction of many Czech nationalists that they had a unique democratic mission in Central Europe. These activists therefore depicted German opposition to Czech nationalist programs as a threat to democracy itself. Although Czech nationalist associations were largely shunned by Czech political parties and elites at the level of national politics, nationalist pressure groups exercised considerable influence at the local level, especially in the realms of local school and language politics.

---

[13] Ibid.

[14] Bývalý uprchlický tábor v Mor. Třebové, č. 8835/21, 11 March 1921, carton 3373, PMR.

[15] *Das Deutschtum in der Tschechoslowakei zwischen beiden Weltkriegen*, vol. 1 (Vienna, 1986); *Orientierungs-Lexikon der Tschechoslowakischen Republik*, ed. Ernst Pohl (Reichenberg, 1931), 347.

Membership in Czech nationalist borderland associations, such as the National Union of the Bohemian Woods and the Union of Southern Bohemia, actually increased rather than decreased after 1918.[16] Between 1918 and 1921, local Czech nationalist associations flooded the government with petitions urging the state to eliminate German schools and repress the rights of German citizens in the name of protecting both Czech ethnicity and democracy.

In November of 1920, the Czech Provincial Commission for Youth Welfare in Brno/Brünn, an agency now dominated by Socialists, submitted a memo to the new Ministry of Education that was typical of these appeals. The memo, written by an organization that had eagerly worked within the Habsburg state only two years earlier, linked Germans' "subversiveness" and their alleged hostility to democracy to their essential nature, asserting, "The Germans don't care about official orders, they ignore laws and behave precisely as the subversive nature of the German element dictates. For this reason we appeal to our government to finally recognize these aggressive offenses and crush the German rebellious spirit, which works for the legal and economic destruction of our Republic."[17]

Similar petitions flooded the Ministry of Education from other mixed-language regions across Czechoslovakia. These petitions typically elevated nationalist myths and memories of "Germanization" and "colonization" in the Habsburg Monarchy to the basis of educational and social policy. The Federation of National Unions cautioned education officials in 1922, "Many members of the Czechoslovak nationality have reasons to be dissatisfied, because it has not been possible in the short time since the revolution to eliminate all of the injuries and inequalities inflicted against our nation by Austria-Hungary."[18] The National Union of Northern Bohemia couched its appeal in more dramatic terms: "No small number of our brothers still suffer under the rule of foreign colonists!"[19] In Pilsen in 1921, representatives of the Club for Representatives of Czechoslovak National Democracy also claimed that many Czech citizens' expectations of their new democracy remained unfulfilled and urged the state to intensify repressive measures against German schools in order to make good on the Republic's democratic promise. The petition warned, "The Czech people in German regions are impatiently waiting for their government to finally step up and defend their civil rights. . . . It is necessary to see

---

[16]Kučera, *Minderheit im Nationalstaat,* 49–50, 309–10; Cornwall, "The Struggle on the Czech-German Language Border," 925, 929.

[17]Ústřední výbor péče o mládež, Brno, 4 November 1920, sig. 17D1, carton 368, Ministerstvo školství (MŠ), NA.

[18]Pamětní spis, O nápravě poměrů v místech národnostě smíšených, Prague, 20 September 1922, carton 376, MŠ, NA.

[19]Národní hnutí, Provolání, 8 November 1921, carton 9, Národní jednota severočeská (NJS), NA. See also memo to Ministry of Education, December 1921, carton 13, NJS, NA.

to it as quickly as possible that the approved Czech schools are opened, and to protect Czech parents from the exterminating advance of the Germans."[20]

These claims of victimization were not themselves novel, as they were developed and actively deployed by Czech nationalists in the Austrian Empire. They were nonetheless far more consequential in interwar Czechoslovakia because the Czech "victims" actually had the state's power at their disposal. The newspaper *Národní politika* summed up the prevailing nationalist consensus in 1920. The state hadn't done nearly enough to stop German "barbarians," an editorial claimed. Even German parliamentary representatives weren't above lurking around schoolhouses in bilingual regions, attempting to kidnap children's souls. German teachers "participate in demonstrations only in order to bully us, silence us, and ultimately destroy us," the newspaper proclaimed. "We ask ourselves, are we living in the Czechoslovak Republic, or somewhere in Africa among beasts, where this hunt for Czechs is allowed?"[21]

The state was not immune to the petitions and denunciations of local Czech school boards and nationalist associations. To start, Czech leaders drastically reconfigured the state after 1918 in order to reduce the potential influence of German nationalists at the local level. The historic provinces of Bohemia and Moravia were abolished, and the power of local communes to control economic and cultural life was sharply curtailed. Czech nationalists and local officials tore down German street signs and replaced them with Czech signs, and they replaced public monuments associated with Germans or the Habsburg Monarchy with monuments to Czech national heroes.[22] The transition was particularly dramatic in the realm of school politics. A memo written by officials in the Ministry of Education in June of 1919 outlined the state's official position that it was necessary to eliminate many "unnecessary" German schools and further stipulated, "It is totally out of the question that Germans themselves could participate in this decision-making process."[23]

German nationalists and the state were soon embroiled in a fierce statistical battle over school closings, which continued through the Nazi occupation and echoed on in historical writing.[24] The Czech Ministry of Education insisted

---

[20] Poměry ve smíšeném území v Čechách, č. 108/21, 31 January 1921, carton 376, MŠ, NA.

[21] *Národní politika*, č. 250, 10 September 1920, carton 4, Zemská školní rada (ZŠR), NA.

[22] Rothschild, *East Central Europe*, 112–13. Wingfield, "Conflicting Constructions of Memory: Attacks on Statues of Joseph II in the Bohemian Lands After the Great War," in *Austrian History Yearbook* 28 (1997): 147–71; Elizabeth Wiskemann, *Czechs and Germans: A Study of the Struggles in the Historic Provinces of Bohemia and Moravia* (London, 1938), 158.

[23] Memo, Ministerstvo školství a národní osvěty, k č. 3112, Prague, 26 June 1919, k č. 3112, carton 377, MŠ, NA.

[24] See, for example, Karel Řeháček, "Školství v okrese Žlutice v letech 1938–1945," *Historie okupovaného pohraničí, 1938–1945*, vol. 2 (Ústí nad Labem, 1998); Jiří Doležal, *Česká kultura za Protektorátu: Školství, písemnictví, kinematographie* (Prague, 1996); Ladislav Pallas,

that it had reduced the proportion of German schools to just below their "due" percentage based on census statistics, compensating for undeserved privileges enjoyed by the Germans during the Austrian Empire. According to statistics from the Ministry of Education, German was the language of instruction in 21.4 percent of elementary schools in Czechoslovakia in 1926, while Germans accounted for 22.3 percent of the state's total population. Although these statistics do not suggest a gross inequity, German nationalists were far more concerned about their relative losses. While German had been the language of instruction in 43 percent of secondary schools in the Bohemian Lands in 1919, by 1937 only 21 percent of the schools were in German hands.[25] Battles over school closings raged on throughout the interwar period and ultimately reached an international audience through (ineffective) German complaints to the League of Nations.[26]

Local German nationalists reserved their greatest animosity for new Czech schools supported by the Czechoslovak state in villages with small Czech-speaking minorities. These schools, they claimed, were erected in new, modern "school palaces," while German children were relegated to outdated and unhygienic facilities.[27] In a 1923 memo to the League of Nations, Germans claimed that the state supported seven hundred Czech minority schools in Czechoslovakia but only two German minority schools (other German minority schools were still financed privately by the German Kulturverband, the successor to the German School Association in Czechoslovakia).[28] Twenty years after the Nazis marched into the Sudetenland, German expellees still bitterly remembered these new Czech schools as an assault on their national property, a strategy to "Czechify" and "colonize" their children and villages.[29] Rudolf Tasler claimed that a new Czech minority school in the town of Kunštát/Kronstadt sat empty for half a year, "since the purely German village had no Czech children." Soon enough, however, a Czech accountant with several children was imported to the village and the school was opened. "Then the kidnapping of souls began, as German parents were promised jobs . . . and were offered generous donations of clothing and groceries."[30] The Czechoslovak government publicly denied all allegations of "colonization,"

"České školství v severozápadočeské oblasti v letech 1938–1945," *Slezský sborník* 89, no. 3 (1991): 181–98; Theo Keil, *Die deutsche Schule in den Sudetenländern* (Munich, 1967).

[25] *Činnost ministerstva školství a národní osvěty za prvé desítiletí* (Prague, 1928). For 1937 statistics see Č. 6524, 24 January 1938; for 1919 state statistics on secondary schools, see Č. 311, 26 June 1919; both in carton 366, MŠ, NA.

[26] Les préjudices causés aux minorités de la République tchèchoslovaque, carton 376, MŠ, NA; *Unsere deutsche Schulen und das Vernichtungsgesetz* (Eger, 1920).

[27] "Wie tschechisiert wird," *Südböhmische Volkszeitung*, 8 October 1922, 9.

[28] Les préjudices causés aux minorités de la République tchèchoslovaque, carton 376, MŠ, NA; Počet mateřských škol a opatroven, 31 October 1936, carton 366, MŠ, NA.

[29] Ost Doc. 20/37, Josef Hobler, Stadt Liebau, 8 December 1960, BB.

[30] Ost Doc. 20/40 1u2, Rudolf Tasler, Kronstadt in Adlergebirge, undated, BB.

but an internal memo of the Czechoslovak Ministerial Council in 1920 did urge state agencies to deliberately assign Czech civil servants with large families to posts in nationally contested regions. State officials explained that these Czech bureaucrats "would not only strengthen Czech existence, but would be effective as voters, send their children to Czech schools, and in the event of conflicts, defend the interests of the Republic."[31]

State education officials often made their decisions about which schools to close and which teachers to fire based on popular denunciations by nationalist pressure groups and local officials. In Prachatice/Prachatitz, for example, a longtime site of nationalist conflict over schools, local government officials declared that the German pupils at the local middle school "provoke the Czech population on the streets" and had become a dangerous "source of German irredentism who threaten the existence of the state."[32] Nationalists simultaneously lobbied vigorously for the erection of new Czech middle schools. The district captain in Prachatice/Prachatitz suggested that if all the German middle schools in the region were eliminated, "even the German citizens would be forced to send their children to Sušice [to the new Czech school], which would only further the assimilation of the population."[33] In the name of "bolstering our independence and compensating for the violence of the Austrian-Hungarian Empire," the local National Council (Národní výbor) in Prachatice/Prachatitz joined the campaign to rid the town of German schools.[34] Nationalist pressure ultimately prevailed, and two new Czech middle schools were opened in the 1920–21 school year, while the "subversive" German middle schools in both Prachatice/Prachatitz and Kašperské Hory/Bergreichenstein were closed.[35]

German teachers were particularly vulnerable to local denunciations and accusations of disloyalty, just as Czech teachers had been the targets of denunciations during the First World War. In one such case, a teacher and Bund der Deutschen leader in Vrchlabí/Hohenelbe, Josef Fischer, found himself at the mercy of an old nationalist foe after the Revolution. In 1913, Fischer had given a speech in which he urged Germans to defend their children against the activity of the Czech teacher Turka. In 1918 the very same Turka was named chair of the local National Council and had Fischer promptly transferred to Karlovy Vary/Karlsbad.[36] When Fischer and other

---

[31] České poměry v Lovosicích, 4 January 1920, Carton 377, MŠ, NA.

[32] Otázka středních škol, Okresní politická správa v Prachaticích, 1 March 1920, carton 2, ZŠR, NA.

[33] Memo from district captain's office in Prachatice to provincial school board in Prague, 3 July 1919, carton 2, ZŠR, NA.

[34] Memo from National Council in Prachatice to provincial school council, 20 March 1920, carton 2, ZŠR, NA.

[35] Č. 50094, 12 August 1920, carton 2, ZŠR, NA.

[36] Memo from Turka to the district captain's office, Vrchlabí, 31 July 1920, carton 2, ZŠR, NA.

local Germans protested the transfer, the state duly launched an investigation, sending questionnaires to local notables and Fischer's colleagues to assess his loyalty to the state. These surveys inquired about Fischer's party affiliation before the war, his role in nationalist associations, and his speeches and publications and concluded with the question, "Can you with good knowledge and conscience affirm that Professor Fischer did not speak against the Czech nation with enmity, that he never persecuted the Czech minority in Vrchlabí/Hohenelbe for national reasons, and in particular that he never pressured German factory owners and employers to fire workers of the Czech nationality who sent their children to the Czech schools?"[37] Fischer himself naturally denied these accusations and testified to his martyrdom, insisting, "As a man who . . . protects German rights with full respect and acknowledgment of the rights and property of other nations, I was dangerous for Mr. Turka. If I had to be punished because I professed to my own nation, that punishment has been more than sufficiently administered through the hard-pressing hunger and misery I have endured since the middle of February."[38]

The files of the provincial school board in Prague indicate that other German teachers with a history of nationalist activism suffered similar fates. One of the most notorious victims of the purge was Dr. Emil Lehmann, a gymnasium professor in Lanškron/Landskron. The Czech National Union of Northern Bohemia accused Lehmann of being an "organizer of extensive actions against the Czechoslovak state," and he was dismissed from his position in March 1919.[39] The mayor of Lanškron/Landskron protested the decision, arguing that his dismissal was "irreconcilable with the democratic foundations of a modern state" and that Lehmann had merely supported "the right to national self-determination and [Woodrow] Wilson's Fourteen Points, to which all of Germandom in Bohemia, Moravia, and Silesia adhere."[40] Emil Lehmann's career as a nationalist educational activist hardly suffered. He joined the ranks of the Nazi Party in the 1920s, when he traveled throughout Northern and Eastern Bohemia as a party speaker. He was eventually reinstated as a gymnasium professor but was transferred to Teplice/Teplitz in 1923, where he kept his post until 1928. In 1919 he also turned his energy and considerable financial resources toward a new nationalist school reform magazine called *Heimatbildung,* which he founded with teacher Joseph Blau, one of the most active proponents of Heimat education in the Habsburg Monarchy. The Heimat education movement quickly moved to the center of the German nationalist movement in the interwar

[37] Surveys, carton 2, ZŠR, NA.
[38] Fischer's testimony, 18 December 1918, carton 2, ZŠR, NA.
[39] Emil Lehmann, Politická agitace, č. 12515, 29 March 1919, carton 2, ZŠR, NA.
[40] Letter from Mayor Neugebauer of Landskron, č. 12515, 14 May 1919, carton 2, ZŠR, NA.

period, bringing together school reformers from the Habsburg Monarchy with the nationalist educators and activists who would lead the Nazi educational system in Bohemian Lands after 1938.[41]

The Czechoslovak Census: Making Germans into Czechs

Whereas Czech-speaking parents might once have sent their children to German schools with dreams of social mobility, the tables turned dramatically after 1918. Thousands of German-speaking civil servants and workers transferred their children from German schools into new Czech schools in 1919–20. Czech nationalists explained this flow of children into Czech schools as proof of their "liberation" from German oppression in the Austrian Empire. Authentic Czechs who had been forced to send their children to German schools in the Empire were supposedly now free to express their underlying Czech loyalties. German nationalists, meanwhile, denounced German-speaking parents who sent their children to Czech schools as "traitors" to the nation who betrayed their own children's best interests, arguing, "The parents don't realize that they don't serve their children in this way, but that they certainly seriously damage their nation and thereby work for its extinction. . . . This is the result of a lack of *völkisch* feeling, national indifference that should be a punishable offense."[42]

Long after the end of the Second World War, German expellees continued to remember German-speaking parents who sent their children to Czech schools in interwar Czechoslovakia as shameless opportunists and/or victims of political and economic pressure. These explanations built on long-standing liberal views of workers and children as dependent and immature populations requiring protection and supervision. The trope of the dependent, amoral, nationally indifferent parent further justified practices of national classification. Some citizens, in this view, were incapable of honestly declaring their true national affiliation (or of choosing a school for their child). These decisions, therefore, were best entrusted to more rational and objective "experts." Anton David, a former Sudeten German Party leader in Lázně Kynžvart/Bad Königswart recalled in his 1958 report that a Czech minority school had been erected in his town in 1927. Half of the children who attended the school were German, he insisted, "and came partly from asocial families or supporters of Communism. The

---

[41] For a discussion of Lehmann's career under and after Nazism see Eva Hahnová, *Sudetoněmecké vzpomínání a zapomínání* (Prague, 2002), 151–55. For a de-Nazifying eulogy of Lehmann's life's work see Rudolf Lochner, "Emil Lehmann: Ein Volkserzieher im deutschen Außengrenzland," *Bohemia* 6 (1965): 508–14. See also Hans Krebs, "Emil Lehmann, ein nationalsozialistischer Grenzland und Heimatkämpfer," in *Aus dem Sudetengau. Emil Lehmann, der Volksforscher und Volksbildner* (Reichenberg, 1940).

[42] *Unsere deutsche Schulen und das Vernichtungsgesetz* (Eger, 1920), 7.

children were extravagantly provided for by the Czechs, got all their school supplies for free, clothing and a big Christmas gift. Since the parents also got financial support, more and more children registered, until there were twenty."[43] Johann Herzog likewise claimed that most of the parents who sent their children to the Czech minority school in his Southern Bohemian town of Dlouhá Stropnice/Lang-Strobnitz were "in financial crisis." These parents, he elaborated, were "despised" by fellow Germans in the village. When a father sent his child to the Czech school, "no one trusted him anymore. The benefits that the minority school provided to the parents and the children, we called that Judas's wage."[44] Others described parents who sent their children to Czech schools as hapless victims whose financial desperation made them easy prey for Czech nationalists, especially during the Depression. In České Petrovice/Böhmisch Petersdorf, Ferdinand Pacher claimed, "German children were secured by any means. Above all the poorer classes, with seductive gifts. Especially at Christmas time, the children carried home entire mountains of clothing and food."[45] Through these stories German nationalists repeatedly explained nonnationalist behavior as a consequence not only of the Czechoslovak state's policies but of weak moral character and economic dependence. They conferred an authentic German identity on parents and children who might not have identified themselves as Germans and rendered illegitimate any genuine indifference to national identity or the parents' genuine interests in bilingual education.

In 1921 the worst fears of German nationalists were confirmed when Czechoslovak census takers counted 420,000 fewer Germans in the Bohemian Lands than had been counted by Habsburg authorities only ten years earlier. In some bilingual towns such as Budějovice/Budweis, the number of Germans counted shrank by 50 percent. These census results were fiercely contested throughout the interwar period. The state instituted several new policies designed to boost Czech numbers through the census in 1921. First, Czechs and Slovaks were counted together as members of the "Czechoslovak" nationality. This device created a 66 percent "Czechoslovak" majority (compared with 23 percent Germans, 5.6 percent Hungarians, 3 percent Ruthenians, and 1 percent Jews) and helped to affirm Czechoslovakia's legitimacy as a nation-state. Another factor that contributed to the disappearance of Germans was a new policy allowing Jews to register in the census as members of the Jewish nation (rather than Germans or Czechs). This tactic was successful. In 1900, out of 44,255 Jews in Moravia, 34,261 (72.42 percent) had declared themselves to be German speakers. In 1921 in Moravia and Silesia, 13,623 (30.7 percent) registered as Germans, and 18,955 (41.84 percent)

[43] Ost Doc. 20/29, Anton David, Bad Königswart, 1 August 1960, BB.
[44] Ost Doc. 20/58, Johann Herzog, Langstrobnitz, 7 April 1958, BB.
[45] Ost Doc. 20/40 1u2, Ferdinand Pacher, Böhmisch Petersdorf, 3 October 1958, BB.

declared themselves Jews. The number of "German" Jews thereby decreased by 42 percent.[46]

The decline in the number of Jews identifying as Germans was not just a product of the state's demographic maneuvers but also a result of Jewish nationalist activism. In the early twentieth century, a flourishing Zionist movement in the Bohemian Lands encouraged Jews to see themselves as members of a separate Jewish nation and to mobilize politically for Jewish minority rights. Czech-Jewish activists, meanwhile, entreated Jews to assimilate into the Czech population and send their children to Czech schools. As Tatjana Liechtenstein has argued, both movements promised to eradicate alleged national indifference among Jews, transforming them into a stable national community of loyal Czechoslovak citizens. In fact, the two movements actively denounced each other for encouraging the diseases of national hermaphroditism and opportunism among Jews. The Czech-Jewish association Kapper thus lamented in 1926, "The main impediments to the Czech-Jewish movement are the indifference of the public to its efforts, as well as anti-Semitism. . . . An additional impediment is Zionism. . . . The Zionist position is neither just nor truthful and its own disciples don't live as a separate Jewish nationality, but are actually Czechs or Germans or amphibians."[47] František Friedmann, a leader of the Zionist movement in Czechoslovakia, countered that the Czech-Jewish movement was itself guilty of fostering "indifference and a lack of respect toward Jewishness" among Czechoslovak Jews. Friedmann maintained that of the 46.7 percent of Jews in Bohemia who declared themselves to be Czechs in the 1921 census, a full one-third actually sent their children to German schools. Assimilation to the Czech nation, in his view, represented a morally bankrupt form of opportunism. "Now more than ever it is necessary to awaken morality and fight against opportunism," he insisted. "Opportunism is when, while standing on the boundary between two nations . . . you choose the ideal nation—the one that is culturally rich in every way, which you can exploit without giving anything in return."[48] These Jewish campaigns against national indifference suggest that Jews in the Bohemian Lands should not be seen as authentic specimens of the nationally indifferent population or as mere victims of anti-Semitic allegations of national indifference. Rather, Jewish politicians were themselves active participants in the campaign to eradicate the scourge of national lability in interwar Czechoslovakia.[49]

[46] František Friedmann, *Mravnost či oportunita? Několik poznámek k anketě acad. spolku "Kapper" a českožidovství a sionismu* (Prague, 1927), 24–26, 36.

[47] Ibid., 4.

[48] Ibid., 27, 34, 88.

[49] Tatjana Liechtenstein, "'Heja, Heja. Hagibor!'" Jewish Sports, Politics, and Nationalism in Czechoslovakia 1923–30," in *Leipziger Beiträge zur judischen Geschichte und Kultur*, ed. Dan Diner, 2:208 (Leipzig, 2004), 208; Tatjana Liechtenstein, "Making Jews at Home: Zionism and the Construction of Jewish Nationality in Inter-war Czechoslovakia," *East European*

Finally, not all of the four hundred thousand individuals who disappeared from the German nation in 1921 switched sides voluntarily. Thousands of self-declared Germans were simply forcibly classified as Czechs by Czechoslovak census takers. Forcible national ascription in the Bohemian Lands under Habsburg rule had been limited to children in Moravia. In interwar Czechoslovakia, national ascription was applied to citizens of all ages and in all corners of the Republic through new laws regulating the decennial census. When the first census in the new Czechoslovak state was held on February 15, 1921, all citizens were officially obliged to report their "correct" nationality based strictly on "objective traits." A law passed in October of 1920 specified, "Statements about nationality must be made with full cognizance and strictly based on the truth." If a person declared that he or she had two nationalities, or no nationality at all, census takers were required to register a single nationality for that person based on his or her "maternal language."[50]

In the event that the census taker had doubts about the truthfulness of a person's claim to be German, he was entitled to "correct" it on the spot with the agreement of the individual concerned. And if a nationally contested citizen refused to have his or her nationality corrected, local political authorities were empowered to hold hearings and interrogate witnesses in order to classify that person on the basis of objective characteristics within fourteen days. Moreover, anyone found guilty of having "consciously" declared a false nationality on the census was subject to a fine ranging from twenty to ten thousand crowns and up to three months' imprisonment. Typically, these fines ranged from fifty to three hundred crowns, which amounted to almost a week's salary for some workers. Adolf Adámek from Hlučín/Hultschin, for example, was fined three hundred crowns for declaring himself German after local officials had concluded that he was objectively a Czech. He appealed to the Ministry of Interior for leniency, since he earned only forty-nine crowns per day as a miner and had children to support. The punishment was accordingly reduced to fifty crowns or two days' imprisonment.[51]

It is hardly surprising that in all the cases in which individuals were fined or imprisoned for declaring a false nationality, self-declared Germans were changed into Czechs. These corrections were widespread—in the small town of Bruntál/Freudenthal, for example, fifty-two people were

Jewish Affairs 36 (June 2006): 49–71. On competition between the Czech-Jewish and Zionist movements, see also Katerina Čapková, "Czechs, Germans, Jews—Where Is the Difference? The Complexity of National Identities of Bohemian Jews, 1918–38," *Bohemia*, vol. 46, no. 1 (2005): 7–14.

[50] See Vládní nařizení, č. 256/1920, 8 April 1920, and č. 592/1920, 20 October 1920, in *Sbírka zákonů a nařizení státu československu* (Prague, 1920), 1503–6.

[51] Oddělení spisovny 11, č. 57, podčislo 15, carton 251, Ministerstvo vnitra—Stará registratura (MV-SR), NA.

summoned for investigations under suspicion of having declared a false nationality.[52] The procedure for correcting a person's national affiliation, moreover, directly followed a model that had been fine-tuned through the Lex Perek in the Austrian Empire. In the town of Brawin/Bravín in Silesia, for example, Sophie Broßmann, a thirty-eight-year-old woman, declared herself a German on census day in 1921. The census taker objected that she was really a Czech, but Broßmann refused to accept the change. As a result, she was invited to the municipal office in Bílovec/Wagstadt for further investigation. Over the course of three interrogations, she answered questions about her language use, origins, education, family, social life, and other so-called objective markers of nationality. While Czech officials insisted that Frau Broßmann had been born in a Czech village, attended a Czech elementary school, and had Czech parents and that her sisters had declared themselves Czechs on the census, Broßmann countered that she had been born in a bilingual town, that her father's German nationality was proven by his German last name (Schindler), that she had always been educated in German, and that the nationality of her sisters was irrelevant. Agitated, she finally declared that she "always was and always will be German," and stormed out of the office. Shortly thereafter she was notified in writing that she had been changed to a Czech on the census anyway and was subject to a fine of fifty crowns and two days' imprisonment for having declared a false nationality on the census and for her impertinent behavior during the interrogations.[53]

At least a thousand citizens whose nationalities were changed from German to Czech against their will in 1921 appealed their respective fines and prison sentences all the way to the Ministry of the Interior, and many appealed all the way to the Supreme Administrative Court. These cases probably represent only a small fraction of the individuals whose nationalities were changed, since many others surely agreed to have their nationality corrected without mounting a time-consuming legal appeal. These appeals reveal that many Czechoslovak citizens were shocked to learn that they no longer enjoyed the right to freely choose a nationality in Czechoslovakia. Some citizens even cited familiar rulings from the Austrian Supreme Court, assuming that they would continue to enjoy the individual freedoms that had been guaranteed in the Monarchy. In one such appeal, Osvald Benek from Bohuslavice/Bohuslawitz confidently asserted "that it was fully his right to profess to the German nationality, because he attended a German school for eight years . . . cannot read or write in Czech, and the Supreme Administrative Court has already ruled many times that personal feelings are decisive in the declaration of a nationality."[54] In Litovel/Littau, Terezie

[52] Oddělení spisovny 11, č. 58, podčislo 4, carton 251, MV-SR, NA.
[53] Ibid., podčislo 7, carton 251, MV-SR, NA.
[54] Ibid., podčislo 64, carton 251, MV-SR, NA.

Bürglová was also furious about the correction of her nationality. She not only protested in the name of individual rights and freedom but also challenged the ethnic conception of the nation on which the census law was based. Although she admitted that her mother had been a Czech, she maintained that she "thinks, feels, and conducts herself as a German," insisting that "no regulation . . . stipulates that nationality should be decided based on racial belonging rather than the personal will of an independent individual." Her classification as a Czech by the state, she protested, represented nothing less than an "unjustified infringement of the personal liberty of the individual."[55] Emmanuel Biskup, a store clerk, agreed that nationality was a matter of conviction. "The decision about nationality is an individual right, and ancestry and race are irrelevant. . . . Children do not have to have the same nationality as their parents, they can profess to the nationality that corresponds to their education and calling, even if they decide that they are English, French, or Hottentots," he insisted.[56]

These plaintiffs were sorely mistaken. The Ministry of the Interior formulaically rejected each appeal, instructing the plaintiffs that their own "subjective" feelings about their national affiliation were irrelevant in the eyes of the Czechoslovak state. In the case of Magdalena Brhlehová, for example, the ministry responded, "The plaintiff here believes that she can declare any incorrect nationality that pleases her, but the official census records controllable, objective characteristics, and not subjective opinions and personal convictions." Ludvík Beneš's claim to be German was likewise dismissed, with the firm admonishment that "it is completely irrelevant what the plaintiff wishes or feels."[57]

Much of this conflict occurred because the 1920 census law contained no clear definition of "nationality." In 1923 the Czechoslovak Supreme Administrative Court therefore intervened in a new attempt to clarify the procedure for classifying nationally contested individuals. Henceforth, the court ruled, "in doubtful cases, nationality is to be determined based on various objective characteristics, and not only based on maternal language, which may not be the only objective sign of nationality. These traits may include the language which a person uses in daily relations, the environment in which he lives during the moment nationality is determined, ethnic descent, the language of a spouse and other members of the family, manner of raising children, membership in associations, political convictions, the place of long-term residence etc."[58] This decision did little, however, to protect the rights of individual citizens to choose their own national affiliation.

[55] Ibid., podčislo 38, carton 251, MV-SR, NA.
[56] Ibid., podčislo 44, carton 251, MV-SR, NA.
[57] See ibid., podčislo 19, podčislo 17, podčislo 28, podčislo 38, all in carton 251, MV-SR, NA.
[58] Nejvšší správní soud, Decision from 10 February 1923, č. 10967/22, Oddělení spisovny 8, čislo 113, podčislo 4, carton 1238, MV-SR, NA.

Local officials were now obliged to consider multiple "objective traits" in their quest to reclassify dubious Germans, but they were ultimately free to decide for themselves which traits were the most important badges of national belonging.

In 1930, lawmakers returned to the drawing board and attempted to define nationality with even more precision. In an unusual concession to the nationally indifferent population, the Czechoslovak State Statistical Office even proposed that citizens be permitted to declare themselves "without nationality" (*bez národnosti*) or "nationality unknown" (*národnost neznáma*), just as it was possible to register a lack of religious affiliation on the census by declaring oneself "without a religious denomination." "Not all people have national feelings or consciousness, or the desire to belong to a specific national community," officials in the Statistical Office explained. This view was harshly rejected by activists in the Czech National Council. Allowing citizens to opt out of the nation on the census would "make it impossible to obtain a clear overview of the national composition of the state, wearing away at its borders—and not only its borders," the National Council warned. "The subjective declaration 'I don't know' may not stem from a true lack of national identity, but of a conscious denial of authentic national consciousness, in connection with radical internationalist theories, eventually strengthening Communist agitation among individuals whose actual nationality is objectively completely unambiguous."[59]

The Council's activism was successful, and the nationally indifferent population lost its chance to be counted in 1930. The census law finally ratified in June 1930 not only required all citizens to declare a single nationality, but included the most precise legal guidance to date to aid anyone with lingering doubts about their national affiliation. "Nationality is determined based on maternal language. A different nationality, other than that which corresponds to an individual's maternal language, may be declared only in cases in which the person counted does not speak his maternal language with his family or in his household and is also completely fluent in the language of the declared nationality," the law stipulated. The 1930 census law also attempted to forestall conflicts over children, specifying that the nationality of children under the age of fourteen followed that of their parents. If the parents were of different nationalities, children were to be assigned "the nationality of the parent who takes care of them." If the parents shared childrearing duties, "and in contested cases," children received their father's nationality, except for those children born out of wedlock, who carried their mother's nationality.[60] This law did not put a stop to conflicts over national

<hr>

[59] Sčítání lidu 1930, Memo from the NRČ to the State Statistical Office and the Presidium of the Council of Ministers, 16 May 1930, carton 183, NRČ, NA.

[60] Vládní nařízení ze dne 26 června 1930 o sčítání lidu v roce 1930, *Sbírka zákonů a nařízení státu československého* (Prague, 1930), 480.

classification, but it did establish clearer rules, which local officials quickly applied as they once again set out to change dubious Germans into Czechs. In Brno, for example, Josef Miček was summoned for an investigation when he refused to allow the census taker to correct his nationality on the 1930 census. Shortly after the interrogation, an official letter informed Miček that his appeal had been rejected. He had been reclassified as Czech based on the definition of nationality encoded in the new census law. The letter explained:

> Your father was called Miček, and he was of Czech origins, as his name demonstrates. Your mother Antonie was born Carblová. Based on her name, she was also certainly of Czech origins. According to the testimony of the witness Josef Tyleček, your mother was a Czech and didn't speak German. You admit that you speak Czech fluently. Since you attended the German schools in Frýdek, the only logical conclusion is that you learned Czech from your parents, therefore your maternal language is Czech. That is not changed by the fact that you now belong to a Communist organization and are also currently a member of the German organization *Volksbund deutscher Katholiken* and other German Catholic organizations, as you claim in your appeal. Your wife also testified that you speak mostly German with her at home. That does not, however, override the fact that you also speak Czech in your household.[61]

Miček had plenty of company. In Brno/Brünn in 1930, a total of 3,718 individuals were reclassified by census officials. Of this number, 2,438 individuals were changed from Germans into Czechs, and 653 were changed from Germans to Jews. These high numbers aroused the suspicion of government officials in the State Statistical Office, who hired a handwriting expert to scrutinize the entire city's handwritten census forms in 1933. The handwriting expert was forced to conclude that the census in Brno/Brünn had been systematically corrupted by four agitators, most likely officials in Brno's city statistical office. These four culprits had illegally changed 1,145 Germans into Czechs or Jews by forging their signatures and the signatures of census takers. Another 2,377 individuals were illegally reclassified by census takers themselves, who changed nationally ambiguous citizens into Czechs or Jews without the required consent or investigations. These numbers were not inconsequential. The Czechoslovak Ministry of Interior concluded, "On the basis of this investigation there is reason to believe that the census in Brno was intentionally and systematically manipulated, with the goal of reducing the German minority to below 20 percent of the population." Adding the 1,145 Germans who had been wiped from the census rolls by the forgers increased the percentage of Germans in Brno from

---

[61] Memo to Josef Mičkov in Frýdek, Odděleni spisovny 8, č. 247, podčislo 19, carton 2995, MV-SR, NA.

19.36 percent to 20.36 percent—just above the threshold of 20 percent, which entitled German-speakers to a host of minority-rights protections, such as the right to use their language in public offices and courts.[62]

Reclaiming Children for the Nation: The Lex Perek after 1918

In spite of these very real pressures to abandon national indifference, to become Czech, and to enroll one's children in Czech schools after 1918, many Czech-speaking and bilingual parents clearly continued to see themselves as Germans and to send their children to German-language schools. The Czechoslovak state also tightened its grip on these parental renegades through a reinterpretation of the Lex Perek. In interwar Moravia reclamations continued, but the rules of the game changed dramatically. In a strange expression of Czechoslovak legalism, Czech lawmakers annulled the 1905 Moravian Compromise itself, but they left a revised form of the Lex Perek on the books without extending it to Bohemia (although Bohemian parents were subject to national classification through the census). As in the Habsburg Monarchy, the Supreme Administrative Court was charged with adjudicating conflicts over reclaimed children.[63] One of the first cases to reach the court concerned the reclamation of eight children from Moravský Krumlov/Mährisch Kromau. The children's parents asserted that their children belonged to the German nation and were fluent in the German language. These children were nonetheless deemed Czech by the state and were removed from the school in the fall of 1919 with the help of local gendarmes. The Supreme Court used this case to outline the legal principles that would guide reclamations for the next twenty years. In its pathbreaking decision the court sanctioned the reclamation of these eight children in the name of guaranteeing minority rights and human rights and enforcing the laws against illegal denationalization laid out in the Czechoslovak Constitution and the Treaty of St. Germain. Citing the constitution and the relevant passages from the minority protection treaties, the court concluded, "Constitutional and human rights regulations require that when circumstances permit, a child is to be educated in the language of his nationality."[64]

---

[62] Odděleni spisovny 8, č. 249, podčislo 16, carton 2996, MV-SR, NA.

[63] The first paragraph of the new April 1919 school law in Czechoslovakia stipulated that children were to attend only schools where the "language of instruction is the same as the maternal language of the child concerned," but the court later ruled that this phrasing did not imply an expansion of Lex Perek to Bohemia. Zákon ze dne 3 dubna 1919, in *Sbírka zákonů a nařízení státu Československého*, 1919, 263; see z. 13.315/27 Podersdam/Podbořan, carton 858, NSS, NA, for a case in which a German school board in Bohemia attempted unsuccessfully to prevent an allegedly German child from transferring to a Czech school on the basis of this 1919 law.

[64] Z. 6962/22 Wolframitz/Olbramovice, carton 857, NSS, NA.

Before 1918 Lex Perek had merely specified that children could not attend a public school if they were not proficient in the language of instruction. Until the Monarchy's collapse, parents of children who were truly bilingual retained the right to choose either a German or a Czech school for their children. After 1918, however, children who wished to enroll in any German school in Moravia were required to prove they belonged to the German nation rather than that they were simply fluent German speakers. The justifying rationale changed as well. Although Czech nationalists had long insisted that children would be intellectually and spiritually destroyed by education in a second language, the court now ruled that a child's mastery of German, or even Czech, was of little importance. In the case of seven-year-old Franz Vojtěch, for example, the court concluded, "The fact that the child has not mastered the Czech language due to the influence of a German upbringing by his mother is not decisive in this matter" and ordered him to transfer immediately to a Czech school on the basis of his Czech nationality.[65] Czech nationalists had learned an important lesson: they could not easily prevent children from becoming bilingual. They could, however, change the way they defined the boundaries of the national community. In Czechoslovakia, the Supreme Administrative Court therefore decisively shifted away from an earlier focus on language as the essential mark of national identity and toward a definition of nationality centered around less mutable "objective qualities" such as descent.

In this spirit, the Supreme Administrative Court ruled that a parent's or child's own declaration of national affiliation was insufficient proof of national belonging. As in contested census cases, when a child's nationality was contested, local political authorities were to launch a thorough investigation in order to determine each child's true nationality based on "objective qualities." "The subjective declaration of the child or his legal representative about his nationality is in itself not sufficient," judges affirmed in 1922. "Besides language abilities, objective qualities include the local origins of the child and his family, mother tongue and language of everyday life, behavior in everyday life, customs, relationships, etc."[66] For the parents and children in Moravský Krumlov/Mährisch Kromau these new procedures did not bode well. Local investigators from the provincial school board concluded, "As artisans or workers the parents are materially dependent on the rich German peasants, and the Czech descent of the children is notorious in the entire region."[67] The local Czech school board concurred, asserting, "The parents of these children claim to be Germans simply out of stubbornness and lack of self-consciousness."[68]

---

[65] Z. 18098; see also z. 19.594/33; both in carton 858 NSS, NA; z. 3220/23, 6962/22, 9106/22, 3221/23. NSS, carton 857, NA.
[66] Z. 6962/22, carton 857, NSS, NA.
[67] Ibid.
[68] Ibid.

Through the census and the Lex Perek, state investigations to determine the nationality of contested children and parents became commonplace in interwar Czechoslovakia. Local officials enlisted the services of police, gendarmes, neighbors, long-lost relatives, landlords, schoolteachers, butchers, bakers, and census takers to testify about the origins, child rearing practices, social contacts, family relations, character, and reading habits of thousands of contested parents and children. Hearings about nationally contested children and adults required Czech citizens to inform on their neighbors on a massive scale as local, popular practices of nationalist denunciation were elevated to a legal, state-sponsored ritual. The widespread denunciations in Czech society during and after the Nazi occupation may thus have been fostered in the name of protecting minority rights during the Austrian and interwar period as citizens were encouraged to inform on nationally indifferent neighbors.

As in the Habsburg Empire, the overwhelming majority of contested children came from working-class, lower-middle-class, or peasant families, and a significant majority (around 70 percent) came from so-called mixed marriages.[69] The parents of these children typically sought to give their children the social advantages of bilingualism. Parents of contested children frequently expressed their hopes for social mobility in their testimony during reclamation trials. For example, Josef Maša, a coach driver in Moravský Krumlov/Mährisch Krumau, asserted bluntly, "I enrolled my daughter Viléma in the German school solely for the reason that I want her to learn German. It is my opinion that she will advance further in the world than I was able to without German."[70] Other parents chose German schools for financial or pragmatic reasons. Johann Dušek testified in 1924 that he sent his daughters, Marie and Theresie, to the German school because the Czech school was far away from his home. He could not afford to buy the clothing or shoes his daughters would need to make such an arduous journey in winter. The children spoke only German with other local children, and he feared that his children would not properly learn German or Czech if he sent them to the Czech school.[71] The parents of Ernst Tomška in Brno/Brünn, meanwhile, chose a private German Protestant school for their son because there was no Czech evangelical school in Brno/Brünn at the time.[72] These justifications, based on parents' pragmatic needs, pedagogical and social concerns, or religious faith, were always rejected by the Supreme Administrative Court, since the nation's right to its children superseded such individualist considerations.

---

[69] These statistics come from my own survey of one hundred random reclamation cases. See the files in cartons 857, 858, and 859, NSS, NA.

[70] Z. 10736/24, carton 857, NSS, NA.

[71] Z. 7992/24. carton 857, NSS, NA.

[72] Z. 15405/35, carton 859, NSS, NA. See also z. 7167/28, carton 858, for a similar case.

Children in interwar Czechoslovakia, as in the Habsburg Monarchy, were born with their father's nationality unless their parents were unmarried. The court permitted two important exceptions to this rule. First, it was possible for parents to claim that their child's father had changed his nationality in the course of his own lifetime, that a man with Czech parents had become a German and was therefore entitled to pass his German nationality on to his children.[73] Second, the court accepted the claim that under certain circumstances the nationality of a child could differ from that of his or her father. Until the 1930s this claim was typically successful only if the child's father was dead or had abandoned the family.[74] It did not take long for Moravian parents to learn these rules. While many did not privilege nationalist priorities as they chose schools for their children, they did gradually learn to articulate their own interests and identities using the national categories and scripts promoted by school officials and the state. Parents from Czech-speaking regions or with Czech-speaking ancestors increasingly described themselves as Germanized Czechs, rather than as individuals without clear national loyalties, in order to secure the right to send their children to a German school. They acknowledged the nation's claims on their children by invoking their right to a German education as Germans, rather than demanding the right to chose a school based on parental rights. These parents thereby affirmed a binary understanding of national identity even when it contradicted the social realities in which they lived.

Parental testimony from reclamation trials in the small Moravian town of Valtice/Feldsburg illustrates how many nationally ambiguous individuals began to narrate their identities in terms more amenable to nationalists in the 1920s. Valtice/Feldsberg, on the border of Lower Austria, was first incorporated into Moravia after the First World War. Seventeen children from the town were reclaimed from the German elementary school in the fall of 1919. Parents offered diverse justifications for their decisions to send their children to the German school. Anton Mrázek, a security guard and the father of Agnes und Marie, testified that though he had spoken Czech as a child, he was now a German, had married a German woman, and hoped to send his girls to Austria for their secondary education. Josef Juřička, the father of three children, was a pensioned railway worker who had also grown up speaking Czech. He claimed that he was now a German and wanted his children to attend German schools because the Czechoslovak state had forced him into early retirement. Josef Urbanek, a tablemaker, was a self-described side switcher. He declared that he had been born a Czech but had become a German because local Czechs did not support his furniture

---

[73] This principle was elaborated in the following early decisions: z. 3220/23, z. 14445/23, z. 22210/23, z. 2078/24, z. 17.227/22; all in carton 857, NSS, NA.
[74] See, for example, z. 12703/22, carton 857, NSS, NA.

business. Josef Fialka, a shoemaker married to a German woman, had considered himself a German since 1899 and spoke only German at home. He had enrolled his daughter Marie in a German school "so that she learns at least one language properly." In the cases of Urbanek and Juřicka the Supreme Administrative Court upheld the decision of local officials that the families were Czech, and the children were forced to transfer to the Czech school. In the cases of Mrázek and Fialka, however, the court ruled that local authorities "had satisfied themselves with merely proving the Czech origins of the fathers" and had not offered sufficient evidence to refute these parents' claims that they had become Germans over time. These bilingual men in mixed marriages successfully thwarted the reclamation of their children by speaking in nationalist terms, describing themselves as Germanized Czechs, and offering what the court considered objective proof of their new German affiliation.[75]

Other contested parents attempted to prove their Germanness by joining associations, subscribing to German newspapers, and joining German political parties. They, too, spoke back to nationalists in nationalist terms by attempting to demonstrate that they possessed the objective traits that could be considered legal proof of a German identity in Czechoslovakia. Eduard Jedelsky, an office worker in a factory in Skalice/Skalitz in Southern Moravia, contested the reclamation of his child in 1925 by describing his record of participation in the German fire brigade and a local branch of the Bund der Deutschen. In fact, he had been elected to the local town council as a representative of Czechoslovakia's German Nazi Party.[76] This strategy sometimes backfired. In 1934, Franz Blahota also attempted to prove his German loyalties by joining the local branch of the nationalist Deutscher Kulturverband in Branišovice/Frainspitz, but investigators discovered that he had actually been a member of the local Czech Nationalist Union until his daughter had been reclaimed from the German school.[77]

It was, however, no simple task for a "born" Czech to prove that he had become a German in interwar Czechoslovakia. In 1928 Franz Kocourek was reclaimed from his German school in Olomouc/Olmütz. The child's father, an artisan, had attended German schools all his life and for fourteen years had lived in Vienna, where he married a German woman. The court nonetheless ruled, "In view of the child's father's Czech descent, of his earliest Czech education in the family, and in view of the fact that he associates with members of both nationalities in public, it has been proven that he still belongs to the Czech nationality, in which the reclaimed child Franz follows him."[78]

---

[75] All parental testimony and decisions from z. 5518/24, Valtice/Feldsberg, carton 857, NSS, NA.
[76] Z. 22539/25, carton 857, NSS, NA.
[77] Z. 3146/34, carton 859, NSS, NA.
[78] Z. 27893/28, carton 858, NSS, NA.

In a similar case in 1935, Christine and Karl Sláma's claim to have become German was rejected after officials determined that the child's father, Karl, "doesn't exclusively use the German language in his own household, and the only newspaper he reads is the *Moravské noviny.*"[79] In its determination to prevent the Germanization of Czech children, the Czechoslovak state imagined extraordinary social and cultural boundaries between the German and Czech populations in the Bohemian Lands. State officials required that those parents who claimed to have become Germans over time demonstrate that they had completely renounced their Czech families, the Czech language, Czech culture, and Czech society. They demanded that these parents actually live in an autonomous, segregated German universe that truly existed only in the fantasies of the most extreme nationalists.

In many of these cases officials mobilized old nationalist myths from the Habsburg Monarchy to dismiss parents' claims about their national affiliations as a kind of false consciousness. In order to rectify an alleged history of forced Germanization in the Habsburg Monarchy, school officials insisted that they had to lend more weight to any trace of Czech descent than to self-identification or cultural factors. In 1929, for example, Rudolf Vyroubal was reclaimed by Czech school authorities from his German elementary school in Brno/Brünn. His father, a shoemaker, testified that he was a member of the German Social Democratic Party, had attended German schools, participated in German associations, and felt German. But a police investigation also revealed that the contested child's grandparents were born "in purely Czech villages" and that the child's father continued to speak Czech with workers in his shoe factory. The Ministry of Education soon concluded that the entire family remained Czech because the father's "undisputedly Czech" origins would have remained unchanged if it had not been impossible before 1918 in Brno "to defend individual Czech residents who were Czech by descent and conviction from denationalization by the local authorities."[80] The Czech nationalist presumption that Czech parents declared themselves German only under the influence of undemocratic pressures thus enabled the court to systematically dismiss parents' individual claims about their own identities in the name of social justice.

Czech school officials and the courts also relied on imagined gendered binaries between the public and private spheres as they sought to ascertain an individual's "authentic" national identity and expose opportunists. In the public sphere, nationally unreliable and financially dependent parents allegedly adopted a false national consciousness due to undemocratic German pressures. Not surprisingly, officials never acknowledged that the Czechoslovak state itself exerted a "public" influence on parents' choices or

---

[79] Z. 16512/35; carton 859, NSS, NA.
[80] Z. 5707/29, carton 858, NSS, NA.

identities. Nationalists meanwhile depicted the domestic sphere, ostensibly free of conflict, interests, or ulterior motives, as the realm in which a family's national identity was authentically revealed. Parents' own testimony, however, sharply revealed the limits of this romantic ideology. National identity was frequently contested within households as family members contradicted one another and testified against each other.

František Šnajnar, a carpenter in Židlochovice/Großseelowitz, therefore declared to investigators in 1924 that he and his wife were both Czechs, in spite of his wife's insistent claims to be German. He had agreed to enroll his daughter Julie in the German school, he explained, only because "my wife is anti-Czech, and I can't argue with her if I want to have peace at home."[81] There was also disagreement in the Třejba household over the family's national loyalties. While the contested child's mother professed to the German nationality, her own sister testified against her that the whole family was Czech and that she "denied her Czech origins because she is hoping to receive support from the Germans in the event of an emergency."[82] In a more unusual case in the 1930s, Franz Sochorec's divided family effectively confounded authorities' attempts to assign them a nationality. Sochorec stubbornly declared himself a "Brünner" (resident of Brno/Brünn) when interrogated about his national affiliation. School officials therefore set out to prove that his dead father (the contested child's grandfather) had been a Czech. But there was considerable disagreement within the family about their nationality. Officials interviewed Sochorec's four siblings, two of whom maintained that their father had been a Czech, while the other two claimed he had been German. The court was forced to rule that the investigation had been inconclusive, and the child was permitted to remain in the German school.[83]

Officials nonetheless invoked the public/private division to declare a Polish Jew a Czech in 1937 even after he himself confessed that he had only once registered as a Czech in the census because he thought it might improve his chances of receiving Czechoslovak citizenship. Wilhelm's Trattner's two oldest daughters testified about their father, "Given his Polish nationality and Jewish descent it is actually difficult to say if he is a German or a Czech. He has no defined nationality at all." The investigation meanwhile produced four German witnesses who declared Trattner a German and two Czech neighbors and community members who claimed him as a Czech. Faced with this contradictory evidence, the court concluded, "The testimony of Wilhelm Trattner himself can be accorded no validity because of his countless contradictions and repeated retractions." Yet if Trattner and his family

[81] Z. 20928/24, carton 857, NSS, NA. In census interrogations, parents frequently testified against their children. See, for example, Oddělení spisovny 11, č. 57, podčíslo 9, carton 251, MV-SR, NA.
[82] Z. 7645/25, carton 857, NSS, NA.
[83] Z. 12384/35, carton 859, NSS, NA.

members offered no clues as to his true national identity, the court affirmed that state officials had been correct to lend more credence to the testimony of the Czech witnesses, who had "spoken about the Trattner's familial relationships, where national inclinations are much more genuinely and honestly revealed, since they are not influenced by various public considerations." Never mind that Trattner himself had explicitly testified that such "public" considerations—namely, his desire to acquire citizenship—had motivated him to register as a Czech in the 1930 census.[84]

Trattner's case is interesting because it reveals the Supreme Administrative Court's (and the Czechoslovak state's) contradictory stance toward Jewish children. In interwar Czechoslovakia, many more Jewish children continued to attend German schools than Czech schools. Out of the 2,426 Jewish children enrolled in Moravian elementary schools in 1921–22, only 712 (30 percent) attended Czech schools.[85] Trattner's Jewish child was successfully reclaimed from a German school on the basis of her alleged Czech nationality. Six years earlier, however, in a similar case, German school authorities in Brno/Brünn had unsuccessfully attempted to reclaim seven-year-old Franz Fried from Czech schools because of the child's alleged German nationality. The Supreme Administrative Court was not convinced in this case, countering that Jews constituted a separate nationality in Czechoslovakia and could therefore not be reclaimed from Czech schools as Germans.[86] In dealing with Jewish children reclaimed from German or Czech schools, Czechoslovak authorities thus revealed their instrumentalist approach to national classification. Jewish children who could easily be classified as Czechs based on objective characteristics were eagerly reclaimed for Czech schools and the Czech nation. Jewish children reclaimed as Germans, however, were classified as "Jews" and thereby exempted from the Lex Perek. These cases also suggest the potentially inclusive dynamic of the nationalist battle for children. Well into the 1930s, local German and Czech school boards in the Bohemian Lands fought tooth and nail to enroll Jewish children in their schools—if necessary by court order. Ironically, it was Czech nationalists, rather than German nationalists, who sought to exclude Jewish children from the German nation.

In Defense of the Republic

Following Hitler's 1933 seizure of power in Germany, the campaign against the Germanization of children in Czechoslovakia took on new

---

[84] Z. 13270/37, carton 859, NSS, NA. See also z. 1269/34, Beschwerde an das Oberste Verwaltungsgerichtshof, 30 March 1934, carton 233, NSS, NA.

[85] Friedmann, *Mravnost či oportunita*, 39, 27. The percentage of Jewish children attending Czech elementary schools in interwar Bohemia was 32.7 percent in 1921–22.

[86] Z. 16046/29, carton 858, NSS, NA.

urgency. The Nazi threat reinvigorated Czech nationalist activism at the local level, and membership in nationalist associations surged.[87] In the name of the struggle against Nazism, local Czech nationalists sent multiple petitions to government agencies, denouncing German teachers as Nazis, chiding the state for not repressing German schools more aggressively, and demanding further state action to prevent the Germanization of Czech children. In a typical petition, the National Union for Northwestern Moravia in Brno/Brünn responded to the Nazi threat in 1933 by pressing for more reclamations: "We demand that the Lex Perek be strictly and thoroughly enforced, that Czech children go to Czech schools, that the reclamation of Czech children from German schools take place quickly and unconditionally in the spirit of Lex Perek. There can be no exceptions." The pressure group simultaneously insisted that the state fire all German nationalist teachers and fill administrative posts with "loyal civil servants of the Czech nationality, who have neither family nor social justifications for maintaining any kind of close relationships with individuals of the other nationality."[88]

The National Union of Northern Bohemia provided the state with a starting point for a purge in the form of a five-page blacklist that denounced dozens of German teachers for undermining the Republic in their classrooms: "They work secretly of course, but effectively. Right below the state flag, pictures of the president, and state symbols, teachers can brandish the ideas of the Third Reich to their students, introduce them to the program of Hitler's party, above all where the eye of the school inspector is less than vigilant." In Podmokly/Bodenbach almost all the teachers were secretly Nazis, the memo claimed. In Velké Březno/Großpriesen, pupils allegedly sang Nazi songs during recess with impunity. The National Union had also ascertained that a teacher in Nová Ves/Gebirgs-Neudorf was actively agitating against the state but lamented that it could not furnish concrete proof of his treachery because he was "outwardly cautious and clever."[89]

Soon the Ministry of Education began to compile lengthy blacklists of teachers suspected of antistate activity. In the fall of 1934, the provincial school board in Prague reported that it had fired eighty subversive teachers in Bohemia in the past year.[90] In a post–World War II report, Sudeten

---

[87] Peter Haslinger, "Imagined territories? Nation und Territorium in tschechischen politischen Diskurs 1890–1938," Habilitationsschrift, Albert-Ludwigs-Universität Freiburg, 2005.

[88] Resoluce, přijatá na valné hromadě národní jednoty pro jihozápadní Moravu, Brno, 12 May 1935, carton 9, NJS, NA; Z valné hromady národní jednoty pro jihozápadní Moravu, Brno, 25 June 1933, carton 366, MŠ, NA.

[89] Report on Nazi antistate movement, addendum 1, 1933, carton 9, NJS, NA.

[90] Presidium zemské školní rady v Praze, č. 6999, 21 November 1934, carton 369, MŠ, NA; Učitelé činní ve straně německé národně socialistické, 28 April 1933, carton 26, ZŠR, NA; Celkový přehled opatření, učiněných od počátku školní roku 1932–33 z důvodů politických-protistátního chování, carton 369, MŠ, NA.

German expellee Kurt Jesser, a former official in the Opava/Troppau city government, claimed that eight hundred teachers in Moravia and Silesia faced disciplinary sanctions for their affiliation or alleged affiliation with the banned German National and Nazi Parties in 1933–34. Many of these actions against German teachers were surely justified, as both German and Czech teachers had long been avid nationalists, and many German teachers did become loyal supporters of the right-wing German National Party, Nazi Party, or the Sudeten German Party.[91]

Since the state's measures against teachers were often based on denunciations by local Czech nationalists, however, they had the potential to backfire and further discredit the state in the eyes of potentially loyal German speakers. In Liberec/Reichenberg in 1934, for example, František Jeřábek was wandering down the street one afternoon when he passed the open window of the local German gymnasium. There he claimed to have observed a group of students rising in unison to perform a Nazi salute.[92] Within hours, the local Czech newspaper got word of the students' treacherous behavior and published a virulent denunciation of German teachers and schools, demanding state action. But the police investigation that followed revealed that the students had not been welcoming their teacher with the Hitler salute but had actually been holding their noses. The incident took place in a physics classroom, and shortly before the teacher entered the room a student had opened a jar of butyric acid, releasing a foul smell into the air.[93]

In another case, ten-year-old Werner Böhnke received a postcard from a friend in Berlin in 1934. This friend relayed his adventures in a Protestant scouting organization, which had recently been absorbed into the Hitler Youth. Böhnke, who had moved from Germany to Czechoslovakia the previous year, passed the card around among his school friends, boasting that he would soon return to Berlin and join this group himself. In consultation with local government authorities, school officials decided to expel Böhnke on the basis of "his behavior, his political orientation and his statements to his roommates, which according to the opinion of the leader of the dormitory make him a danger to the other students."[94] A week later Böhnke's stepfather, Otto Ziegler, responded with an angry letter of protest to the school and local officials. The child was a half-Jew according to Nazi racial laws, although he had been raised as a Protestant. In 1933 Ziegler had been dismissed from his position as head of a bank in Berlin because of his Jewish ancestry, and the entire family emigrated to Czechoslovakia. Werner

[91] Ost Doc. 21/14 fol. 1, Schulpolitik in Mähren/Schlesien vor und nach 1938, 8, BB.
[92] Protokol, testimony of František Jeřábek, ZŠR, carton 26, NA.
[93] "Studenti libereckého něm. gymnasia zdraví po hitlerovsku," 14 March 1934, 1, carton 26, ZŠR, NA; Protokol sepsaný u policejního ředitelství v Liberci, 19 March 1934, carton 26, ZŠR, NA.
[94] Státní reálné gymnasium v Plané, č. 1140, 7 December 1934, carton 26, ZŠR, NA.

was homesick and had no way of knowing that the scouting group he had belonged to in Berlin was now a part of the Hitler Youth.[95]

School officials and the courts also rallied to the defense of the Republic in the late 1930s by reinvigorating the crusade to rescue Czech children from German schools. In the 1930s, Czech nationalists liberally interpreted the court's stipulation that a child's nationality could differ from that of his or her father in order to reclaim children with Czech mothers and German fathers from German schools.[96] Until the 1930s the court had adhered to a strict patrilineal model. Unless a child's father was truly dead or out of contact, nationality generally passed from father to child. In the 1930s, however, Czech school districts increasingly reclaimed children of mixed marriages even when their German fathers lived at home, using the argument that these fathers actually exercised no influence whatsoever on their children's upbringing because they worked outside the home and left child-rearing responsibilities to their Czech wives.

In 1936 the Supreme Administrative Court therefore ruled that Karl Reich was a Czech, although his father was a Reich German who lived at home. Because Karl's German father "was occupied with his business all day" and admitted to entrusting child-rearing responsibilities mostly to his Czech wife, Czech authorities insisted that he had "no influence on the upbringing of the child."[97] In a similar case, Czech authorities invoked the gendered division of labor to declare Richard Hänsel a Czech even though the child's father was German and his mother was Polish. The provincial school board ruled that since the child's German father "fully entrusts child rearing to the mother, as he himself admits," he had no influence on Richard's national identity. Although Richard's mother herself was not Czech, the court affirmed the provincial school board's opinion that "as a member of a Slavic nation she raises her child in a Czech spirit."[98] Under no circumstances was this logic endorsed when the roles were reversed. In the late 1930s the Supreme Administrative Court repeatedly affirmed that working Czech fathers firmly exercised a Czech influence on their children at night and on the weekends, while German fathers who worked outside the home were said to have no influence on their children's national loyalties.[99]

Thanks to denunciations by local Czech school boards, several private German nursery schools and kindergartens in Prague were closed by the state for accepting Czech children between 1935 and 1938, although the

---

[95] Dr. Othmar Ziegler: Einspruch gegen den Konferenzbeschluss und das Verfahren, betr. den Schüler der III aKl. Werner Böhnke, č. 1154, 10 December 1934, carton 26, ZŠR, NA.

[96] There were at least five such cases in 1935–37: z. 16580/35, z. 16.321/36, z. 13181/37, z. 13.179/37, and z. 15409/35, all in NSS, carton 859, NA.

[97] Z. 16.321/36, carton 859, NSS, NA.

[98] Z. 3834/29, NSS, carton 858, NA.

[99] Z. 15.406/35, NSS, carton 859, NA. See also z. 13269/37, Beschwerde z. 1249/34, carton 233, NSS, NA.

Lex Perek had no legal status in Bohemia.[100] Růžena Ehrmann, the director of a private German nursery school in Prague, attempted to defend her policy of accepting Czech children in a letter to the provincial school board. Her school had actually suffered a serious decline in enrollment in the previous few years as many Czechoslovak Jews boycotted German schools while other Germans in Prague decided to change their nationality or send their children to Czech schools in protest of the Nazi seizure of power. The Czech academic and bureaucratic elite in Prague, however, still sought out bilingual education for their children. Her school served these parents. There was little danger of denationalization in her classrooms, Ehrmann insisted, pleading, "The complete loyalty of the pupils to the Czech nationality is fully guaranteed. . . . The fact is we are talking about a tiny school in the capital of the state, where other misgivings truly can be dismissed that might be relevant to the German part of the borderlands. It is also worth considering that only an exclusive circle of children attend the school, with the full voluntary support of their parents. As already proven, these are parents who belong to the most nationally conscientious and intelligent circles."[101]

By referring to the elite status of the parents who sent their children to her school, Ehrmann attempted to counter the traditional nationalist claim that only "dependent," morally questionable, working-class Czechs were forced to choose German schools for their children because of undemocratic pressure from employers or landlords. The parents of her students were rational, independent, and nationally conscious middle-class citizens who had chosen her school freely. They were in no danger of being Germanized and in no need of state protection, she insisted. Included in the file was a letter of support from the Czech painter Josef Čapek, brother of the writer Karel Čapek. Josef Čapek was a fierce opponent of Nazism who would die in the concentration camp at Belsen in 1945. He had nonetheless sent his daughter to Ehrmann's German kindergarten. He testified to the state that his daughter had most certainly not been Germanized in Ehrmann's school: "When in 1927–1928 I sent my five-year-old daughter to your kindergarten, which is truly exemplary in pedagogical and hygienic respects, I didn't see it as some kind of institution for the denationalization of children from any possible perspective," he insisted.[102] Čapek explained that he merely wanted his daughter to learn German so that she would have the opportunity to later attend a German university and enjoy the social and cultural benefits of bilingualism. These appeals fell on deaf ears, and the school was closed.

[100] Městský školní výbor v Praze, č. 52463, April 1936; Městský školní výbor v Praze, č. 19064-VI-38, 18 May 1938; Městský školní výbor v Praze, č. 44.787 VI 38, 18 May 1938, letter to the management of the private German kindergarten in Prague XI, Jičinska 20, 22 October 1937; all in carton 38, ZŠR, NA.

[101] Letter from Růžena Ehrmannova, 6 November 1937, carton 38, ZŠR, NA.

[102] Letter from Josef Čapek, 3 November 1937, carton 38, ZŠR, NA.

By 1937, protecting the Republic from Nazi values seemed to require that even the children of a Čapek be rescued from their parents' poor judgment and from the growing and overriding threat of Germanization.

The fate of Čapek's children reflected the crystallization of a particular understanding of democracy shared by German and Czech nationalists alike, centered more on the national community's collective rights than on individual rights. This nationalist conception of democracy and the practices of national classification it justified were not unique features of the exotic or "backward" reaches of Eastern Europe. The provinces of Alsace and Lorraine after 1918 offer a useful comparison in the West. Alsace and Lorraine had belonged to the French state until 1871, when they were ceded to German Empire after France's defeat in the Franco-Prussian War. Following the German defeat in 1918, the so-called lost provinces were reannexed to France. Beginning in February of 1919, French officials classified the entire adult population of Alsace-Lorraine into four ethnic categories. The Carte A was reserved for Alsatians who were born in Alsace and whose parents or grandparents had carried French citizenship before 1870. The Carte B was assigned to individuals of so-called mixed heritage, those with one parent or grandparent who had been a French citizen. The Carte C was issued to foreigners from allied states. Finally, the Carte D was conferred on individuals who were born in Germany or whose parents or grandparents were born in Germany. The 28 percent of Alsatians and Lorrainers assigned the lowly D card and the 10 percent assigned the B card exchanged currency at a lower rate, were restricted in their freedom of movement, and were sometimes fired from their jobs or expelled from the university. Thousands of Alsatians were brought before "triage commissions" after the war and prosecuted for harboring pro-German loyalties. Over two hundred thousand individuals were also expelled to Germany in an early (and mostly forgotten) episode of ethnic cleansing.[103]

At first glance, the dramatic wave of expulsions, purges, classification schemes, and denunciations in Europe's interwar borderlands seems to reflect a deep history of nationalist hostility and conflict in these regions. But across Europe it was typically the very ambiguity of national loyalties that underpinned policies of national classification. In nation-states in which basic social and political rights were dependent on national belonging, it was more important than ever that every individual belong to a single nation.

---

[103] On Alsace see Laird Boswell, "From Liberation to Purge Trials in the 'Mythic Provinces': Recasting French Identities in Alsace and Lorraine, 1918–1920," *French Historical Studies* 23, no. 1 (2000): 129–62; Christopher Fischer, "Alsace to the Alsatians? Visions and Divisions of Alsatian Regionalism, 1890–1930," *Bulletin of the German Historical Institute* 36 (Spring 2005): 55–62; David Allen Harvey, *Constructing Class and Nationality in Alsace, 1830–1945* (DeKalb, IL, 2001); Steven L. Harp, *Learning to Be Loyal: Primary Schooling as Nation-Building in Alsace and Lorraine, 1850–1940* (DeKalb, IL, 1998).

In Alsace-Lorraine, for example, the Francophile Alsatian exile and former senator Émile Wetterlé insisted on the need to use local experts to distinguish between authentic French-Alsatians and German "impostors" after World War I, arguing, "Too often the Austro-Germans, who don't shy away from any disloyal maneuver in order to assure their own impunity, have attempted to pass for locals. . . . Those of us who have a great deal of practical experience with the two populations of our provinces, we can recognize the true German and the true Alsatian or Lorrainer of old stock at first glance and after an interview of a few minutes. We sniff out the Teuton like a hunting dog sniffs its prey, and I assure you that with a little practice it is not difficult, because the odor is so particular and so strong."[104]

The examples of Alsace-Lorraine and the Bohemian Lands reflected a broader trend in Europe's interwar borderlands. In many regions, national classification followed closely on the recognition of new international principles of minority rights, as citizens and states clashed over who belonged to the protected "minorities" and were entitled to claim those rights. For example, a 1922 agreement between Poland and Germany regarding Upper Silesia specified that German children were to enjoy the "minority right" to attend German-language elementary schools. But which children were German and which were Polish? In 1926 Polish authorities launched an investigation to determine whether the children enrolled in German minority schools in Silesia were "really" Germans. They insisted that 7,114 of the children attending German schools were actually Poles and ordered their parents to immediately transfer their children to Polish schools. In many cases the parents refused, stubbornly contending that they were Germans, and were punished accordingly with police warnings and fines. The Deutscher Volksbund für polnisch Oberschlesien filed a petition with the Polish Minorities Office in Katowice and appealed all the way to the newly established Court of International Justice at the League of Nations. Now the League itself was to decide whether individual Silesian children were Polish or German.

In March of 1927, the Council of the League of Nations adopted a resolution stipulating that any child who understood German enough to profit from a German education should be admitted to the German elementary schools in Silesia. "Doubtful" cases were turned over to a League of Nations commission headed by a Swiss pedagogical expert, who administered language tests to the children. But there was continued disgruntlement on both sides when the tests continued in 1927–28, 1928–29, and 1929–30.[105] The

---

[104] Émile Wetterlé, *Ce qu'était l'Alsace-Lorraine et ce qu'elle sera* (Paris, 1915), 305.

[105] For the details of the case see Manley O. Hudson, ed., *World Court Reports: A Collection of the Judgments, Orders and Opinions of the Permanent Court of International Justice*, vol. 2, 1927–32 (Washington, 1935), 268–320, 690–91.

problem in Silesia, as in Czechoslovakia's bilingual regions and in Alsace-Lorraine,was that neither nationality nor language abilities were transparent facts. In Silesia, many children spoke neither literary German nor literary Polish but a local dialect or several languages, and many children were born of so-called mixed marriages. While Polish officials claimed that these children were "Germanized" Poles, German minority rights activists held that they were "Polonized" Germans. World Court judges recognized the pitfalls of national classification and ultimately upheld the right of individuals to decide their own nationality (and that of their children), ruling, "There is reason to believe that, in the conditions which exist in Upper Silesia, a multitude of cases occur in which the question whether a person belongs to a minority . . . does not clearly appear from the facts."[106]

The World Court defended the right of Silesian parents to choose their nationality, but Czechoslovakia and France were not bound by the same treaties. Nor were citizens protected from forcible national classification in Yugoslavia after 1918. Particularly in Southern Styria, Yugoslav authorities asserted that many individuals who identified themselves as Germans were actually "Germanized Slovenes." While German children technically enjoyed a minority right to attend German elementary schools in Yugoslavia, local authorities were empowered to investigate and dispute any individual's claim to be a German. Consequently, children with Slovene-sounding family names were often forced to attend Slovene schools, regardless of their identification as Germans.[107]

Practices commonly associated with Europe's "totalitarian" states, such as mandatory national classification, denunciation, and ethnic cleansing, emerged in the heart of republican democracies as interwar nation-states confronted so-called ethnic minorities, immigrants, refugees, and the populations of former German territories. The drive to classify was not rooted in the peculiarities of the East but in several nationalist assumptions that crystallized across Europe in 1918. In particular, new practices of identity ascription reflected an imagined link between democracy, the nation-state, and collective rights expressed in Wilson's Fourteen Points. As Hannah Arendt observed in *The Origins of Totalitarianism*, in 1918 the world stood convinced "that true freedom, true emancipation, and true popular sovereignty could be attained only with full national emancipation, that people without their own national government were deprived of human rights."[108] The presumed link between the nation-state and democracy in 1918 enabled

[106] Hudson, *World Court Reports*, 2:292.

[107] See Hans-Ulrich Wehler, *Nationalitätenpolitik in Jugoslawien: Die deutsche Minderheit, 1918–1978* (Göttingen, 1980), 23. Soviet authorities also deployed new practices of identity ascription in the aftermath of the Russian Revolution. See Sheila Fitzpatrick, *Tear Off the Masks: Identity and Imposture in Twentieth Century Russia* (Princeton, 2005), 5–9.

[108] Arendt, *Origins of Totalitarianism*, 152.

interwar states to pursue nationalizing agendas in the name of democratic values. The Czechoslovak nation-state, in particular, was founded on claims of a binary opposition between the innate democratic values and character of the Czech people and the presumed authoritarian and aggressive nature of the German minority. Under the extreme circumstances of the Nazi occupation, Czech opposition to the "Germanization" of ethnically Czech children would produce a rallying cry that transcended traditional left-right divisions and dramatically shaped the dynamics of Nazi rule.

5 Freudian Nationalists and Heimat Activists

On the morning of October 8, 1920, German schools in Czechoslovakia remained empty. The cause of this unexpected holiday was a strike—not of teachers but of schoolchildren. The previous day German newspapers throughout Czechoslovakia had published bold ads urging German parents to keep their children home from school. "In spite of all its promises and guarantees to our representatives, the Czech government continues to close German schools and classes and to expropriate German schools, built with our money and for our children, often with force, in order to open Czech minority schools, mostly for only a few Czech children," the ads proclaimed. "Through these means, the . . . German nation, which until now could be proud of its schools of all kind, is to be spiritually gagged."[1] The "school strike" was endorsed by all the German parties except the German Socialists, including the Agrarian Party and the Christian Social Party.[2] Through this demonstration, German political parties hoped to call international attention to the Czechoslovak state's alleged failure to respect the minority rights guaranteed in the 1918 Treaty of St. Germain and in the Czechoslovak constitution.

Like their Czech peers, interwar German nationalists defined concepts such as minority rights and national self-determination around collective rights to educate the nation's children. At a demonstration on the day of the Czechoslovak parliament's opening, German protesters declared, "To all the protectors and promoters of culture in the whole world! The right to self-determination in national affairs demands that every nation, no matter what language it speaks, manages and cares for its own cultural

---

[1] "Allgemeiner Schulstreik," *Deutsche Bepauer Zeitung,* 7 October 1920, 1, carton 4, ZŠR, NA.
[2] Telegrams and reports from German Schools, carton 4, ZŠR, NA.

riches, and above all its schools."[3] These protests did little to win the sympathy of the Allies or to reverse the course of Czechoslovakia's nationalist school policies. The demonstrations nonetheless reflected a rare and fleeting moment of national consensus and self-consciousness among German speakers immediately after the First World War. Across the political spectrum, German nationalists responded to their new position as a national minority in interwar Czechoslovakia by striving for radical national unity and as much national autonomy as the new political realities would allow.

Not surprisingly, the unity expressed through the school strikes proved ephemeral. Bitter divisions soon erupted among interwar German nationalists about the best strategies to achieve their goals. Two nationalist pedagogical traditions came to express these differences. Both movements had roots in the Habsburg Monarchy and had enjoyed expanding authority and influence over children during the First World War. The Heimat education movement, led by Joseph Blau and Emil Lehmann, developed from progressive pedagogical reform movements of the fin de siècle and promoted national regeneration in a utopian German Heimat as the solution to German woes. Heimat activists soon became leaders in the so-called negativist German parties, such as the German National Party, the Nazi Party, and the Sudeten German Party. These anti-Socialist, right-wing parties typically rejected the very existence of the Czechoslovak state. In the late 1930s they began to actively work toward its destruction with the help of the Third Reich. A second movement, meanwhile, focused on nationalist social work and developed within the German Provincial Commission for Child Welfare (DLS). In the interwar period the DLS championed new psychoanalytic techniques to rehabilitate German children and families from the social crisis of the First World War. DLS activists worked with and within the Czechoslovak state, and many became members of the German "activist" parties, such as the German Social Democrats. These activist parties began to work for reform by cooperating with Czech political authorities and parties in the mid-to-late 1920s. While the Heimat movement and the DLS shared common goals of achieving German national unity and autonomy, they promoted different pedagogies that reflected their distinct relationships to the state and competing ideological visions. The ultimate triumph of the Heimat movement marked the simultaneous victory of the Sudeten German Party's antistate, fascist politics over the German Social Democrats' commitment to working for reform within the Czechoslovak state.

---

[3] *Unsere deutsche Schulen und das Vernichtungsgesetz* (Eger, 1920), 14. For the Czech state's response, see Ministry of Education, z. 4780, 13 October 1920, carton 4, ZŠR, NA.

DLS Activism

For German nationalists, the collapse of the Habsburg Monarchy represented a moment of severe psychological turmoil and material loss.[4] Once the dust settled, however, many German speakers in Czechoslovakia made peace with their new situation. Although the post-WWI division of East Central Europe into nation-states forced more Bohemians and Moravians to identify as Czechs and Germans, war-weary citizens on both sides of the national divide were also eager for peace, stability, and economic recovery. In 1924 the spiraling economic crisis in the Weimar Republic gave Germans in Czechoslovakia a reason to be grateful that they lived in a "victor" state. The 1925 Treaty of Locarno ushered in a broader spirit of reconciliation, bringing Germany into the League of Nations. In 1926, the German Agrarian and German Christian Social parties joined a government coalition in the Czechoslovak parliament and were followed three years later by the German Social Democrats.[5] Moderate, middle-class Czech and German parties welcomed a chance to form a united front against the Communist Party, which had emerged as the second-largest party in Czechoslovakia in the parliamentary elections of 1925.[6] Czech Socialists, meanwhile, embraced the opportunity to collaborate with German Social Democrats on social issues. By 1930 these German "activist" parties enjoyed the support of a full 75 percent of the German population, leaving only a minority of Germans allied with the German National and Nazi parties, which rejected the legitimacy of the Czechoslovak state.[7]

In the realm of social welfare activism, the DLS best embodied the activist spirit in the interwar period as it worked within the Czechoslovak state to achieve gradual social reform. The organization's political trajectory was largely determined by the remarkable authority and responsibility it had

---

[4]See Karl Bahm, "The Inconveniences of Nationality: German Bohemians, the Disintegration of the Habsburg Monarchy, and the Attempt to Create a 'Sudeten German' Identity," *Nationalities Papers* 27 (1999): 375–406; Istvan Deak, "The Habsburg Empire," in *After Empire: Multiethnic Societies and Nation-Building: The Soviet Union and the Russian, Ottoman, and Habsburg Empires*, ed. Mark von Hagen and Karen Barkey, 129–42 (Boulder, CO, 1997); Jeremy King, *Budweisers into Czechs and Germans: A Local History of Bohemian Politics* (Princeton, 2002), 153–68.

[5]On German activist politics in interwar Czechoslovakia see Jorg Kracik, *Die Politik des deutschen Aktivismus in der Tschechoslowakei, 1920–1938* (Frankfurt, 1999); Wolfgang Mitter, "Das deutschsprachige Schulwesen in der Tschechoslowakei im Spannungsfeld zwischen Staat und Volksgruppe," in *Bildungsgeschichte, Bevölkerungsgeschichte, Gesellschaftsgeschichte in den böhmischen Ländern und in Europa*, ed. Hans Lemberg, 82–94 (Vienna, 1988).

[6]Joseph Rothschild, *East Central Europe between the Two World Wars* (Seattle, 1974), 109.

[7]Jaroslav Krejčí and Pavel Machonin, *Czechoslovakia 1918–1992: A Laboratory for Social Change* (New York, 1996), 14–15. This figure does not include those German speakers who voted for the Communists.

achieved within the Austrian state during the First World War. Between 1907 and 1918, the DLS had transformed itself from a private social welfare organization to the very foundation of a new Habsburg welfare state. After 1918 the DLS remained attached to and dependent on the Czechoslovak state and was accountable for the health and welfare of thousands of German children. Hugo Heller, who led the DLS in Bohemia from 1907 to 1937, was himself a radical nationalist, anti-Socialist, anti-Semite, and member of the Bund der Deutschen. The DLS nonetheless remained officially "apolitical," and at the local level many branches were in the hands of German Social Democrats, particularly in Moravia. Ludwig Czech, a Jew and the chair of the German Socialist Party, actually served briefly as president of the DLS in Moravia and as leader of the German Reichsverband for Child Welfare, an umbrella organization which brought together the three German Provincial Commissions (in Bohemia, Moravia, and Silesia) in interwar Czechoslovakia. He was later appointed Minister for Social Welfare in 1929, after the German Social Democrats joined the governing coalition in the Czechoslovak parliament. In a 1933 retrospective, the DLS presented an overwhelmingly positive view of the organization's relationship with the Ministry for Social Welfare and the Czechoslovak state. Writing on Ludwig Czech, Margarete Roller reflected, "Even in the most difficult times . . . he never lost sight of the goals of DLS: securing the care and education of our German children in the realm of national self-management. We thank him in large part for the respected position that the DLS enjoys today in the Republic."[8]

Ludwig Czech's Ministry for Social Welfare, working with the DLS and Social Democrats in parliament, achieved several significant victories for German "autonomy" in the late 1920s, gaining complete control over foster care for the DLS's local branches in 1930. Branches of the DLS were empowered to supervise the care of all German foster children and orphans and were given the exclusive right to appoint public guardians to all German children born out of wedlock—a right they had demanded since before the First World War. The law also required that children be assigned guardians of the same nationality and established a legal means for filing complaints in the event that the provision was violated.[9] DLS activists attributed these

[8]Margarete Roller, "Herrn Minister Dr. Ludwig Czech zu seinem 60. Geburtstag," *Jugendfürsorge: Mitteilung der Deutschen Landeskommission für Kinderschutz und Jugendfürsorge* 14, January 1930, 76–78 (hereafter *Jugendfürsorge*). See also "Dringende Arbeiten der nächsten Zeit," *Jugendfürsorge* 14, December 1930, 5; Ludwig Czech, *Soziale Arbeit in ernster Zeit. Exposé des Ministers für Soziale Fürsorge Dr. Ludwig Czech* (Prague, 1930), 17.

[9]See "Gesetze 256 aus dem Jahre 1921 über den Schutz der in fremder Pflege stehenden und der unehelichen Kinder," "25 Jahre Deutsche Fürsorge in Böhmen," *Jugendfürsorge* 17, August–September 1933, 356; "Vládní nařízení ze dne 14. března 1930, jímž se provádí zákon o ochraně dětí v cizí péči a dětí nemanželských," in *Sbírka zákonů a nařízení státu československého* (Prague, 1930), 99–106.

successes to the commission's warm relationship with the Ministry for Social Welfare and bragged of their more general role as mediators between state and nation. They used this position to secure as much autonomous control as possible over the education and welfare of German children, boasting, "We stand in the center between the official state and lawmaking efforts, which create the necessary minimal basis for organized youth welfare, and an autonomous German society, which has up until now dedicated itself to taking youth culture in its own hands."[10] These words reflected the ongoing commitment of the DLS to the activist strategy of struggling for greater cultural autonomy within the legal framework of the Czechoslovak state. As Jorg Kracik has argued, through democratic means, German activists hoped to gradually transform Czechoslovakia from a nation-state to a multinational state.[11]

German nationalist demands for autonomy in interwar Czechoslovakia centered precisely around control of educational and child welfare institutions. But the social welfare activists in the DLS understood autonomy as far more than a mere right to bureaucratic self-administration. For Heller, this spirit of autonomy was to pervade the family itself, and he demanded an end to mixed-marriages and bilingual upbringing among Czechoslovakia's German speakers. Autonomy could not be achieved in a world in which individuals still wavered indecisively or opportunistically between national communities, Heller insisted. He therefore called for nothing less than a full purge of the German educational and social work community so that only nationally uncompromised individuals would be entrusted to raise German youth. He demanded, "We must exclude from any kind of participation in German education those miserable, impoverished *Sprachgrenze* souls . . . those for whom German blood rules in one half of the heart and Czech blood in the other, who take no sides but wherever possible take both . . . in short, pitiful people who should be pilloried in a widely visible place."[12]

Freudian Nationalists

German nationalist preoccupations with achieving autonomy and unity, alongside the new realities of more limited economic and political power, encouraged nationalist child welfare activists to seek out new pedagogical

---

[10]*Erziehungsrat phil. Dr. Hugo Heller und die deutsche Landeskommission für Kinderschutz u Jugendfürsorge in Böhmen* (Prague, 1937), 12; "Das Verhältnis des Staates zur freiwilligen gesellschaftlichen Jugendfürsorge," *Jugendfürsorge* 7, July 1923, 117.

[11]Kracik, *Die Politik des deutschen Aktivismus*, 8–9, 70, 434; Johann Brügel, *Tschechen und Deutsche, 1918–1938* (Munich, 1967), 190–95; Mitter, "Das deutschsprachige Schulwesen," 82–94.

[12]Hugo Heller, *Die Erziehung zu deutschen Wesen* (Prague, 1936), 22.

methods. In the Habsburg Monarchy, social and educational activists had struggled to unify the national community through policies designed to integrate working-class and rural children into the national community. Through nationalist orphanages, progressive pedagogy, and programs to decrease alarming rates of infant mortality, nationalists sought to rescue poor children from material and spiritual deprivation and simultaneously from the overriding threat of Germanization or Czechification. World War I, however, seemed to universalize the poverty and dysfunction of the working-class family, at least in the eyes of nationalist observers and state officials. After the war, nationalist social workers continued to expand their activism to include children of the middle classes. "It is a sad fact that we now find shattered relationships not only in workers' families. The families of the middle classes, the lower civil servants, and the artisan have also begun to rot," lamented DLS activists in 1931.[13]

While the DLS never abandoned its commitment to traditional forms of public health activism, such as encouraging breast-feeding, providing medical assistance and food to working-class families, and offering courses on infant hygiene, German child welfare activists turned increasingly to preventative methods that targeted "healthy" children and middle-class families as much as poor families. In 1922 social worker Karl Theimer, who led a local branch of the DLS, reflected on the more universalist aims of post-WWI nationalist social work, writing, "The war . . . opened up new paths for social welfare. While one was previously content to save single individuals and in particular to offer the needy material support, social welfare is now charged with the task of reaching out to all youth and raising them to the highest possible level of physical, intellectual and moral perfection."[14] Hugo Heller went further, maintaining that after the Revolution, the only hope for the German nation was a new conception of youth welfare, tailored to the needs of the middle classes. The war had destroyed family life to an extent never seen before, creating an unprecedented "shortage of good mothers and fathers as educators" he lamented. Only once salvageable middle-class children had been rehabilitated from the effects of wartime social disruption would a stronger German nation (and DLS) be in a position to offer the youth of the lower classes protection and help. "It is one of the biggest mistakes of any kind of social policy to orient itself toward the deepest social evils, complete impoverishment, total breakdown," Heller claimed. "The starting point must lie in the middle classes. . . . Only from here outward can the world of misery be uplifted."[15]

[13]Elizabeth Queisser, "Meine Erfahrungen bei der Erziehung gefährdeter Mädchen," *Jugendfürsorge* 15, 1931, 239.

[14]Karl Theimer, "Praktische Jugendfürsorge," *Jugendfürsorge* 7, February 1922, 25.

[15]Hugo Heller, "Pestalozzi und die moderne Jugendfürsorge," *Jugendfürsorge* 4, 1919, 134–40.

The blossoming fields of child psychology and psychoanalytic pedagogy offered the commission's social workers radical new tools with which to both expand their influence on middle-class families and cultivate national autonomy. These methods were well suited to the universalist aims of interwar social work as they linked national and familial dysfunction to the emotional dynamics between parents and children rather than to social conditions.[16] The Viennese, mostly Jewish founders of psychoanalytic pedagogy (especially Anna Freud, August Aichhorn, Siegfried Bernfeld, and Melanie Klein) would all have been political opponents of German nationalists. Yet like nationalists, psychoanalytic pedagogues ascribed mythic importance to the family as the source of individual identity while critiquing actual parents as the source of individual and social dysfunction. They also shared a concern with educating "asocial" youth to function in a larger community.[17]

Before the Second World War, moreover, both German nationalists and psychoanalytic pedagogues embraced collective forms of education outside the home to repair the damage inflicted on children by a flawed parental upbringing. The First World War had offered nationalists and psychoanalytic pedagogues alike unprecedented opportunities to test out experimental pedagogies as they put their ideas into practice in summer camps, orphanages, and homes for war-damaged or delinquent youth. Bernfeld, a Socialist and Zionist, even shared nationalist views on the utopian potential of orphans to regenerate the nation, using the language of psychoanalysis. "Because they are orphaned from cozy attachments to the family, they will be ready for stronger, higher attachments," he reasoned. "Orphaned youth adapt themselves well into the wider and more meaningful national community. Robbed of their parents, they are more deeply and unconditionally devoted to their nearest relatives. And perhaps the education of orphans should anchor such fleeting emotions to a plan. . . . We should elevate the feelings of a lonely boy into a will to build a youth community."[18]

Leaders and social workers in the interwar DLS were particularly indebted to the theories of August Aichhorn. Aichhorn, one of the first Central European educators to embrace Freud's theories and methods, was recognized in 1918 by the Austrian Ministry of Defense for his valuable services in the field of patriotic and military education during the First World War. After the war he created a center for experimental pedagogy in Hollabrünn,

[16]On the importance of the First World War in the development and popularization of psychoanalysis see especially Paul Lerner, *Hysterical Men: War, Psychiatry, and the Politics of Trauma in Germany, 1890–1930* (Ithaca, 2003); Laurence A. Rickels, *Nazi Psychoanalysis*, vol. 1 (Minneapolis, 2002).

[17]Cultural historians have traditionally described psychoanalysis as either a reaction to or the liberal antithesis of the mass political movements that shook the Austrian Empire in the early twentieth century. Carl Schorske, *Fin de siècle Vienna: Politics and Culture* (New York, 1981), 5–6, 185; Peter Gay, *Freud, Jews, and Other Germans* (New York, 1978), 33.

[18]Siegfried Bernfeld, *Kinderheim Baumgarten* (Berlin, 1921), 11.

outside Vienna, where he focused on rehabilitating war-damaged "wayward" youth. He also worked with youth and their parents in the child guidance clinics operated by Vienna's Socialist-controlled Youth Welfare Agency.[19] While Aichhorn himself had little direct contact with German nationalists in the Bohemian Lands after World War I, his ideas and methods caught on in pedagogical circles and were well suited to the concerns of the interwar DLS. In his most well-known work, "Wayward Youth" (1925), Aichhorn sought the roots of youth delinquency in the psychoanalytic dramas of early childhood identification. He promoted the use of psychoanalytic techniques to help children navigate the treacherous path (parallel to that of human civilization itself) from an unreal infantile world ruled by libidinal desire into the realities of the adult "civilized society."[20] Aichhorn explicitly rejected the standpoint that material deprivation was the primary cause of youth delinquency. Social conditions could certainly trigger asocial behavior, in his view, but were never at the root of delinquency. He elaborated, "When I ask parents how they account for the dissocial behavior of their children, I usually receive the answer that it is a result of bad company and running around on the streets. To a certain extent this is true, but thousands of other children grow up under the same unfavorable conditions and still are not delinquent. There must be something in the child himself that the environment brings out in the form of delinquency."[21] Aichhorn relied heavily on Freud's concept of transference. Delinquent behavior, he argued, was caused by the failure of children to properly identify with their parents in the earliest years of life, which derailed them from a "normal" developmental path. In therapy, youth homes, or summer camps, nationalists hoped that endangered youth would learn to identify with nationalist analysts and social workers, who were to use their authority as substitute parents to correct a flawed upbringing.[22] Psychoanalytic approaches thus reinforced the importance of nationalist educators as direct mediators between children and a larger national or social community.

The practical outgrowth of the movement was an explosion of child-rearing advice in interwar Czechoslovakia, aimed at working-class and middle-class parents alike. The number of "Mother Counseling Centers" managed by the German Provincial Commission in Bohemia increased from 252

[19] For Aichhorn's own early reflections on patriotic education, see August Aichhorn, "Die erziehliche Handarbeit in Knabenhorten im Dienst der staatsbürgerlichen Erziehung," in *Jahresbericht des Zentralvereines zur Errichtung und Erhaltung von Knabenhorten in Wien* (Vienna, 1913). After World War II Aichhorn assumed Freud's former position as head of the Wiener Psychoanalytische Vereinigung.

[20] August Aichhorn, *Verwahrloste Jugend: Psychoanalyse in der Fürsorgeerziehung* (Vienna, 1925), 14. For background on Aichhorn's career and pedagogy, see Erik Adam, ed., *Die österreichische Reformpädagogik, 1918–1938. Symposiumsdokumentation* (Vienna, 1981).

[21] Aichhorn, *Verwahrloste Jugend*, 64.

[22] Ibid., 257.

to 534 between 1925 and 1937 and then increased to over 800 by 1938.[23] In 1937 alone 32,438 German women attended courses on mothering in Czechoslovakia, which were organized by the DLS in 782 different villages. In early 1938 the German Provincial School Board in Bohemia ordered that every girl attend a DLS course on mothering before graduating from high school. The Czech Provincial Commission, meanwhile, boasted in 1933 that 43 percent of newborn infants passed through its nationalist maternal welfare centers.[24]

Before the First World War these centers and courses had focused primarily on the public health goals of urging working-class mothers to breast-feed and supplying infants with medical care in order to combat high infant mortality rates. Social workers did not abandon these hygienic goals in interwar Czechoslovakia, but they increasingly devoted themselves to peddling child-rearing advice as child mortality rates actually declined significantly with the relative prosperity of the late twenties.[25] Nationalist social workers in the 1920s and 1930s instructed German mothers on a wide range of topics related to their children's emotional and psychological development. They lectured on "the influence of the environment on the child" and trained mothers to use games, toys, fairy tales, and picture books to stimulate their children's imagination. Young mothers were also warned about "unconscious educational influences" on their children and instructed on the important role of fantasies in the emotional life of the child. DLS social workers trained mothers to observe their children at play, explored the psychological dynamics of children's friendships, and discussed how to handle children's questions and lies. Mothers were also armed with the latest psychological theories on the effects of punishments, threats and promises on their children and, finally, were reminded of the overriding value of "education for self-sufficiency."[26]

[23] "Deutsche Jugendfürsorge," Beilage zur Frauenschaftsweisung, 15 September 1937, carton 22, SdP, NA; "Was wir alle wissen sollten," *Deutsche Jugendfürsorge Nachrichten-dienst*, 28 April 1938, carton 83, SdP, NA. The explosion of advice and interest in child psychology and development was also evident in the DLS's tremendous interwar interest in career counseling and forays into handwriting analysis.

[24] Eduard Rohn, "30 Jahre Deutsche Landeskommission für Kinderschutz und Jugend-fürsorge in Böhmen," *Jugendfürsorge* 22, August 1938, 294; "Schule und Jugendfürsorge," *Deutsche Jugendfürsorge Nachrichtendienst*, 28 January 1938, carton 83, SdP, NA; "V celé republice nápadný pokles porodnosti," Česká zemská péče o mládež v Brně, č. 6, 1933, carton 9, NJS, NA.

[25] "V celé republice nápadný pokles porodnosti," česká zemská péče o mládež v Brně, č. 6, 1933, carton 9, NJS, NA. On infant mortality in the Habsburg Monarchy see Heinrich Rauchberg, *Der nationale Besitzstand in Böhmen* (Reichenberg, 1905), 586; Wilhelm Hecke, *Die Verschiedenheit der deutschen und slawischen Volksvermehrung in Österreich* (Stuttgart, 1916), 7. For an overview of infant mortality rates in Czechoslovakia from 1919 to 1937 see *Statistisches Jahrbuch für das Protektorat Böhmen und Mähren* (Prague, 1941), 148.

[26] Karl Theimer, "Vermehrte erziehliche Fürsorge für die Kleinkinder," *Jugendfürsorge* 18, April 1934, 137.

In 1926 the DLS even established a new Department for Child Rearing. In a report on this promising new field of activism, social workers complained about the many parental flaws they were forced to combat in their daily work, ranging "from idiocy and ineptitude to maliciousness and squalidness. On closer examination of all these cases one often asks oneself: What is actually more necessary here? The education of the children or that of the parents?"[27] To counter these parental defects, nationalist social workers created a network of new child guidance clinics (*Erziehungsberatungsstelle/dětské poradny*). These clinics were inspired in part by Vienna's municipal child guidance clinics, which were often staffed by psychoanalytically trained professionals (including August Aichhorn himself). In 1933 the Czechoslovak Ministry for Public Health and Physical Education counted 1,757 child guidance clinics in Czechoslovakia, the majority of which (1,597) were founded and managed by local branches of the Czech and German Provincial Commissions. The clinics, staffed mostly by paid social workers and doctors, had provided counseling to 262,470 children by 1933. The DLS, moreover, ran 783, or 45 percent, of the child guidance clinics in Czechoslovakia, even though Germans made up less than one-third of the state's total population.[28] By 1933 the organization was optimistic about its progress. Counseling centers would soon offer every German family good advice "when possible behavioral disturbances become noticeable in their children," DLS social workers boasted.[29]

It would be easy to criticize these programs as yet another example of middle-class efforts to discipline unruly working-class parents and children. DLS pedagogues and social workers, however, found fault with middle-class and working-class parents in almost equal measure. Aichhorn had elaborated in 1925 that "excessively affectionate relationships with parents or siblings early on can later lead to delinquency." German nationalist social workers accordingly pointed their fingers at middle-class mothers, who allegedly smothered and spoiled their children with excessive love and attention. Working-class parents, meanwhile, were considered more likely to contribute to their children's delinquency through an excessively strict, brutal, or loveless upbringing, or by schizophrenically alternating between excessive pampering and affection (by the mother) and violent abuse (by the father).[30] Only a year after

[27]Heinrich Runtsch, "Abteilung für Erziehungsfürsorge, " *Jugendfürsorge* 11, January–February 1927, 35.

[28]"Dětské poradenství v r. 1933," *Statistická ročenka Republiky československé* (Prague, 1936), 194. See also "Erziehungsberatungsstelle," *Deutsche Jugendfürsorge Nachrichtendienst*, 23 February 1938, carton 83, SdP, NA.

[29]Heinrich Schubert, "Über die Notwendigkeit einer planmäßigen freien Jugendberatung," *Jugendfürsorge* 14, February 1930, 102–5. See also Richard Lux, "Tagung der Jugendgerichtshilfe in Troppau." *Jugendfürsorge* 9, January 1925, 29; Grete Swoboda, "Seelenkundige Erziehung in frühkindlichen Leben," *Jugendfürsorge* 14, April–May 1930, 200–203.

[30]Aichhorn, *Verwahrloste Jugend*, 75, 251.

the publication of "Wayward Youth," the DLS published proposals for a new "Counseling Center for Difficult Children" in Brno/Brünn (*Beratungsstelle für schwererziehbare Kinder*), where social workers put Aichhorn's insights into practice. DLS social workers in Brno/Brünn (mostly Social Democrats) had long been aware that while "children are often now free of error in terms of physical health, there has been little progress in their upbringing." The article went on to demonstrate how defective identification between parent and child could breed delinquency, with examples corresponding to Aichhorn's various "types" of wayward youth (and wayward parents). One child's mother treated her son "sometimes with roughness, sometimes with a monkey's love. . . . What we learn from this example is the damaging effects of an inconsistent upbringing that wavers between the extremes of pampering and excessive harshness." In another case, concerning an only child, social workers determined, "Excessive pampering has above all had the effect on the child of suffocating any bud of self-sufficient behavior. It is not necessary for the child to strive in his own tasks when the father always helps him with everything."[31]

In the late 1930s the DLS increasingly focused on the supposed psychological and pedagogical dangers of small families. Because of their isolation from other children, nationalist social workers reasoned, only children were condemned to a life of stunted social relationships and rarely made functional members of the national community. "They fail when they need to submit to others . . . when they should order themselves in a community. The upbringing of only children, who are so common today, has therefore become a burning problem, not only from a pedagogical perspective but also from a social point of view," the DLS cautioned in 1936.[32] This turn toward pronatalism marked a distinct shift away from the policies espoused by nationalists in the Habsburg Monarchy. Before World War I nationalist social workers had largely rejected pronatalism, striving to increase the German population by decreasing infant mortality rates rather than by promoting additional births. At the height of the Depression in Czechoslovakia, nationalists now advertised the supposed pedagogical advantages of large families. In a radio discussion on "Mother Education and German Child Welfare" in early 1938, experts from the DLS urged parents to have at least three or four children in order to secure the maximum psychological benefits for their offspring, insisting, "In a healthy large family the children actually learn from the first day onward to submit themselves to a larger community when necessary, without any grand educational methods. . . . It never seems

---

[31] "Beratungstelle für Schwererziehbare Kinder," *Jugendfürsorge* 10, January–February 1926, 55–58.

[32] Theodor Heller, "Die abwegige und sittlich defekte Kind," *Jugendfürsorge* 20, January 1936, 9.

all that difficult for them to learn what every upstanding human being must learn sooner or later, especially in today's fateful times: to defer to a more important cause, to be able to deny oneself something pleasant and enjoyable for the sake of a duty."[33]

Parents who refused to follow this expert advice were duty-bound "at the very least to find a suitable replacement" for a big family by sending their children to day cares, youth groups, and summer camps. Fortunately, nationalist pedagogues and activists in the DLS had been busy creating precisely such institutions for collective education. During World War I the DLS had sent approximately thirty thousand Bohemian German children to live with peasant families in the countryside in the hopes of rehabilitating undernourished and tuberculosis-prone city children with fresh air and hearty meals.[34] Since accommodation with peasant families "left much to be desired," and children were too often used as a kind of temporary farm labor by peasants, the commission ceased placing children directly with families by the mid-1920s. With the economic prosperity of the late twenties, DLS summer camps shifted their attention to more expansive nationalist pedagogical goals—namely, achieving "spiritual influence through a capable leader" and promoting "the value of communal living in the colony itself."[35] By 1934, over 134,198 children had attended ČZK summer colonies, for which the Ministry for Social Welfare paid a third of the cost. In the same year children in the Bohemian Lands attended 365 DLS summer camps.[36] The DLS hoped to reform its charges in these camps by isolating them from damaging (or insufficiently nationalized) family environments. "The successes are often attributable alone to the transfer of a child from an unfavorable milieu at home into the favorable environment of a holiday home," social workers boasted. In place of brutality, harsh discipline, conflict-ridden, loveless homes, daily fear and worry, and/or the smothering affection of overbearing mothers, children were to experience "peace and order, friendly reception, a carefree atmosphere, and understanding attention to personal, physical or emotional complaints" in DLS summer camps.[37]

---

[33]Kat Baierl and Uli Simon, "Erziehung in der Familie," *Jugendfürsorge* 22, June 1938, 272.

[34]Hugo Heller, "Die Stellung der Deutschen Jugendfürsorge innerhalb der Sudetendeutschen Volksgemeinschaft," *Jugendfürsorge* 22, May 1938, 193.

[35]"Bericht über die Aktion Kinder aufs Land in Jahre 1925," *Jugendfürsorge* 10, December–January 1926, 59. On the parallel path taken from hygienic rehabilitation in peasant families to pedagogical intervention in communal colonies in France's *Colonies de vacances*, see Laura Lee Downs, *Childhood in the Promised Land: Working-Class Movements and the Colonies de vacances in France, 1880–1960* (Durham, NC, 2002).

[36]"V dětech je národ věčný. Zpráva o činnosti, zemského ústředí péče v Čechách, 1934," carton 668, NRČ, NA; "Spolky, ústavy a zařízení pro péči o mládež ochrany potřebnou a pro péči o chudé v r. 1934," *Statistická ročenka Republiky československé* (Prague, 1936), 222.

[37]Ernst Slawik, "Die seelische Betreuung der Kinder in Erholungsheime," *Jugendfürsorge* 17, December 1933, 509. For other discussions of child psychology see Paula Mehoffer,

Eugenics offered interwar social workers another set of tempting solutions to social problems.[38] There was, however, considerable disagreement within the DLS about the degree to which heredity determined a child's destiny. The psychological turn of the mid-1920s may have shifted attention away from material deprivation and toward psychological dynamics within the family, but it also convinced some social workers that they had actually overestimated the role of heredity in triggering child delinquency. In 1926 the DLS in Bohemia optimistically speculated: "Science has now learned to minimize the concern over heredity to a proper level, and in turn to appreciate the determinant role of the outer environment on humans."[39] Other nationalist social workers agreed that psychological and psychoanalytic theories had largely discredited purely genetic theories of child development. In 1930, DLS activist and doctor Greta Swoboda insisted, "All of the difficulties of child raising can be traced back to mistakes and negligence made in the upbringing of the infant. Isn't it at least in the realm of possibility, that almost nothing is determined by heredity, and that the entire child development process is dependent on the type of upbringing?"[40] In 1933, Theodor Gruschka, a DLS activist from Ústí nad Labem/Aussig, attacked the pseudoscience behind new Nazi sterilization laws, defending a commitment to old-fashioned social programs. He warned, "Today one all too often hears attacks against social welfare built on solidarist assistance. . . . The uneducated layperson is taught that social welfare can be rendered superfluous by surgery. The rejection of environmental influences in the treatment of diseases has already taken on grotesque forms under the influence of these warped teachers."[41]

Detlev Peukert and others have linked the economic crisis of the 1930s in Germany to a shift from inclusionary to exclusionary (and ultimately murderous) social welfare policies, as the Nazi state sought to eliminate adults and youth with supposed hereditary defects. Activists in the DLS in Czechoslovakia, however, were not so eager to distinguish between "educable" and "uneducable" youth and to exclude the "uneducable" from the

---

"Charaktereigenschaften und Seelenleben der Kinder," *Jugendfürsorge*10, November–December 1926, 437; Hugo Heller, "Behandlung kindlicher Unwahrhaftigkeit," *Jugendfürsorge* 10, April 1926, 134.

[38]On eugenics in Weimar Germany, see Atina Grossmann, *Reforming Sex: The German Movement for Birth Control and Abortion Reform, 1920–1950* (Oxford, 1995); on eugenics in interwar Romania see Maria Bucur, *Eugenics and Modernization in Interwar Romania* (Pittsburgh, 2002).

[39]"Beratungsstelle für schwererziehbare Kinder," *Jugendfürsorge* 10, January–February 1926, 56.

[40]Grete Swoboda, "Seelenkundige Erziehung in frühkindlichen Leben," *Jugendfürsorge* 14, April–May 1930, 200–203.

[41]Theodor Gruschka, "Die Sterilisierung Erbkranker," *Jugendfürsorge* 17, December 1933, 502.

national community. Middle-class German and Czech nationalists in the provincial commissions were far less concerned with finding a "final solution" to the problem of working-class deviance or racial inferiority than with *including* as many children as possible into a unified national community in order to prevent children from being "Czechified" or "Germanized." In this case, popular indifference to nationalism in the Bohemian Lands may have had progressive outcomes as nationalists competed to expand their numbers and win nationally ambiguous families to their side through social welfare activism. In the context of an ongoing demographic competition between German and Czech nationalists, no child could be left behind. Yet the assumptions and pedagogical methods of the DLS clearly faced challenges from within the Sudeten German nationalist community as well as from Nazi Germany in the late 1930s. If Germans in Czechoslovakia largely agreed that autonomy, unity, and self-help were necessary to secure the survival of the nation, they remained far from unified about the meaning of these terms or about how best to secure their claims on children.

Autonomy in Heimat

In contrast to the DLS social workers, Heimat education activists in interwar Czechoslovakia vehemently rejected the fundamental legitimacy of the Czechoslovak state. In a 1923 treatise, Emil Lehmann, already a committed National Socialist, elaborated his understanding of the relationship between nationalist education and politics. The problem with politics in general, he insisted, and with German party politics in particular, was that "politicians are content with goals that can be reached within the existing system, and that can be realized through the permissible, official political means." Nationalist educators in the Heimat movement, in contrast, strove to create an entirely new kind of human being, capable of enacting a revolution. Germans in Czechoslovakia found themselves in a situation in which "any kind of satisfactory development is impossible through political means," Lehmann argued. He therefore concluded that radical pedagogy should replace politics, urging, "Leadership must be transferred to the educator."[42]

As explained in chapter 2, the Heimat education movement originated squarely within a broader progressive education movement that had blossomed across Europe at the turn of the century. Children and youth were to learn through active engagement and play in their immediate environments, gradually building from concrete local relationships to abstract reason. In interwar Czechoslovakia, Heimat activists continued to insist that curriculums be grounded in concrete experiences and activities in the child's immediate

---

[42]Emil Lehmann, *Sudetendeutsche Stammeserziehung* (Eger, 1923), 6.

environment. At the same time, however, they increasingly defined the supposedly organic local Heimat in highly idealized and abstract terms, redefining the child's "immediate environment" to suit the needs of a growing pan-German nationalist movement.

Nationalist education reformers typically depicted Heimat as an autonomous, ethnically pure homeland—an ideal that children's actual communities could hardly live up to in the Bohemian Lands. Joseph Blau's own descriptions of the borderland communities in which he lived and worked blatantly undercut idealized visions of the Sudeten German *Heimat* as a nationalist utopia. Shortly after the revolution of 1918, Blau and Emil Lehmann founded *Heimatbildung,* a magazine that became the pedagogical and political organ of the German nationalist Heimat movement in Czechoslovakia. In an article entitled "The Teacher on the *Sprachgrenze,*" he described the many obstacles confronted by a young teacher in an unspecified multilingual town in Bohemia. Teachers there, he lamented, were forced to contend with the negative influence of nearby Czech-speaking towns, poor land, dependence on nobles or Czech landowners, and the constant threats posed by Czech schools and kindergartens. Even more demoralizing, however, were the inner weaknesses of German locals, the "mixed families, weak characters, derelicts, and other national comrades who waver for every reason."[43] Another Heimat educator attempted to square the circle between idealized nationalist visions of Heimat and these grim realities, arguing, "The Heimat is on the one hand what is given in the hearts of men and what is still becoming through human desire. To fuse together what is given and what is still becoming is the task and very reason for the school."[44] Joseph Blau ultimately insisted that the Heimat was really much more than a literal place: it was rather a spiritual homeland. The ostensibly "concrete" local Heimat was thus a fantastic abstraction. "Its breadth [the Heimat] has widened and now encompasses the entire nation, and not simply the narrow territory of the childhood years, the family and Heimat village in district X. We are no longer searching for the Heimat simply in space [*Raum*] but within ourselves, in the districts of our souls."[45]

Heimat activists thereby denied the charges of imagined detractors that they were providing children with an overly "narrow" education, restricting them to learning "how many sheep" grazed in their local village. Such literal, territorial interpretations of Heimat were misleading. August Sauer maintained that Heimat education could open the entire world to German children while simultaneously keeping them firmly attached to their national

---

[43]Joseph Blau, "Der Lehrer an der Sprachgrenze," *Heimatbildung* 11, March 1930, 134.

[44]Ignaz Goth, "Die Entwicklung des Heimatgedankes für Schule und Bewegung," *Heimatbildung* 18, 1937, 1–14.

[45]Joseph Blau, "Zur Heimaterziehung," *Heimatbildung* 7, March 1926, 129.

homeland. German teachers, he argued, "should search out and cultivate every talent, make the child capable for any profession for which he seems determined, educate him in all the languages of the world, so that the entire world is open to him. He should learn to love any nation: but all this on the deep, solid nationalist foundation of the Heimat school. . . . A young German should never experience the faintest doubt about which nation he belongs to, he should never waver about which language he has to pray in, in which language blessings and curses rush from his lips."[46] Yet the wide-open world evoked by these activists increasingly seemed to resemble a vaguely defined German diaspora in Central Europe. Joseph Blau explained in 1924 that the concept of Heimat "is expanding with the travel of humans from their narrow Heimat villages, which only encompass the family and town, to the tribal Heimat [*Stammesheimat*], which is bound by a common language and a common national life, and from there outward to a national Heimat, encompassing all the tribes of the entire nation, in which the written language, common history and national cultural traditions, above all literature and customs, are the unifying factors."[47] August Saurer was also confident that the risk of an overly "narrow" Heimat education could be easily avoided if teachers emphasized that the Germans in Bohemia were merely one branch of a German national tribe that had been "flushed out over the border's ramparts."[48] Heimat education thus provided interwar German nationalists with a pedagogy that did not seem outwardly hostile to the Czechoslovak state but that nonetheless cultivated children's loyalty to an imagined German diaspora in Central Europe rather than to Czechoslovakia.

The meaning of Heimat thus shifted in important ways with the transition from the Habsburg Empire to the Czechoslovak nation-state. In the late Austrian Empire, German nationalists had promoted an elitist self-image as Kulturträger in Central Europe. German nationalists held themselves to be cosmopolitan, distinguished from the supposedly provincial and backward Czechs by their world language, education, and culture. The Heimat movement's civilizing pedagogy served this self-image. In interwar Czechoslovakia, however, Peter Bugge has suggested that a reversal of roles took place. German nationalist Heimat activists now typically represented themselves as simple, provincial Sudeten German peasants, wearing folk costumes and singing folk songs. The civilizing component of Heimat education largely disappeared. As interwar German nationalists promoted an image of themselves as a victimized minority, they linked the German nation

---

[46] August Sauer, "Noch ein Wörtchen über Heimatbildung," *Heimatbildung* 1, January 1920, 4–5.
[47] Blau, "Zur Heimaterziehung," 129.
[48] Sauer, "Noch ein Wörtchen über Heimatbildung," 4–5. See also Sauer, "Deutsche Bildung," *Heimatbildung* 2, February 1922, 93.

less to social mobility and high culture and more to the virtues of hearth, home, handicrafts, and racial purity in an authentic rural Heimat. The image of Germans in Bohemia was provincialized, even as Sudeten German nationalists asserted their cultural affinities with Germans in the Third Reich. Czechs, meanwhile, now enjoyed an international reputation as a cosmopolitan, modern, cultured people, an image Czech nationalists actively cultivated between the world wars. The Czech nation was deprovincialized after 1918 through its claimed role in bridging East and West, its alleged place as the easternmost outpost of Western democracy, and the cultivation of an avant-garde, modernist high culture.[49]

Heimat activists sought to achieve the overriding German nationalist pedagogical goals of autonomy and unity with an entirely different set of strategies than those deployed by the nationalist social welfare activists in the DLS. These nationalist educators typically stood outside the institutional mainstream. They were not typically responsible for the fate of real children. While the DLS targeted middle-class children as well as poor children in Czechoslovakia, many German Socialists and Jews found a welcome place in the nationalist child welfare movement. The Heimat movement, in contrast, was explicitly anti-Socialist and anti-Semitic and claimed to offer internal unity to the German nation without requiring the redistribution of wealth. The strict self-reliance promoted by Heimat educators actually rendered attempts to redress social inequality unnecessary, argued Franz Stowitschek: "Only after we overcome the world of laziness and venality, of selfishness and exploitation, of the striver and profiteer, the money-digger and the work-shy, can we build the new world of Socialism. Even better, we will have rendered Socialism unnecessary, because social justice immediately follows from a character educated in this fashion. That is why Heimat education, as character education, is also the primary social question."[50] While both groups of activists strove for unity and autonomy, Heimat educators built pedagogy around a fantastic, imaginary, and radically autonomous Heimat rather than on the more mundane psychological dynamics and child-rearing practices within German families or hard negotiations for administrative autonomy within the Czechoslovak state. The "autonomy" promoted by Heimat activists required alienation from the Czechoslovak state and from parliamentary politics. And when their demands were rejected by the Czechoslovak state, Heimat activists

---

[49]I am grateful to Peter Bugge, who first made this argument in a panel on Liberalism and Nationalism in the Late Austrian Empire at the American Association for the Advancement of Slavic Studies Annual Meeting in Boston in 2004. For a recent history of the Bohemian Lands that stresses the modernist and cosmopolitan qualities of Czech high culture, see Derek Sayer, *The Coasts of Bohemia: A Czech History* (Princeton, 2000).

[50]Franz Stowitschek, "Grundsteine der Heimatbildung," *Heimatbildung* 1, February 1920, 3.

were more than ready to look toward the Sudeten German Party and Nazi Germany for more radical solutions.

The Sudeten German Party Strikes Back

While the Heimat movement cultivated alienation from the state, the legitimacy of the DLS was dependent on its ability to meet the needs of real German children. In the mid- to late 1920s, economic prosperity enabled the DLS to fuse its social obligations with larger nationalist political goals successfully. The commission's activist politics seemed to bear fruit as Heller and the Socialists worked within the state to protect the organization's social and national claims on German children. The Depression and Hitler's seizure of power severely threatened these achievements. Predominantly German-speaking border regions of Czechoslovakia bore the brunt of the economic crisis, suffering higher rates of unemployment and poverty than Czech-dominated regions. German nationalists blamed their economic misfortune on the Czechoslovak state and increasingly placed their hopes in Konrad Henlein's right-wing, nationalist Heimat Front or set their sights on "liberation" by the Third Reich from national and economic woes.[51] Local offices of the DLS, meanwhile, were flooded by demands for material assistance from impoverished Germans. The DLS was now dependent on a state that was both financially depleted and increasingly illegitimate in the eyes of German citizens. In 1933 the agency lamented that there was "very good lawmaking, which cannot be effective in the desired ways because no money is available to carry out the law."[52]

Following Hitler's seizure of power in Germany, the Czechoslovak state banned the Nazi Party and the German National Party in Czechoslovakia. Konrad Henlein's Sudeten German Heimat Front thrived in the vacuum. The Heimat Front, which espoused both nationalist and corporatist ideologies, developed out of the German nationalist gymnastics movement, where Henlein first made his mark as a nationalist agitator and leader. After the Heimat Front itself was banned, it was reconstituted as the Sudeten German Party (SdP) in 1935 and won two-thirds of the German vote in parliamentary elections that year.[53] There was nonetheless still hope for German activism and for the DLS in 1933–34. In an expression of loyalty to their

[51]Kracik, *Die Politik des deutschen Aktivismus,* 221–24, Václav Kural, "Die Tschechoslowakei als Nationalstaat? Das Sudetendeutsche Problem," in *Tschechen, Deutsche und Slowaken in der ersten Republik,* ed. Jorg Hoensch and Dušan Kováč, 67 (Koblenz, 1994).

[52]"25 Jahre deutsche Jugendfürsorgearbeit in Böhmen," *Jugendfürsorge* 17, August–September 1933, 352–56.

[53]For background on the rise of the Sudeten German Party see Kracik, *Die Politik des deutschen Aktivismus,* 248–61; Volker Zimmermann, *Die Sudetendeutschen im NS-Staat. Politik und Stimmung der Bevolkerung im Reichsgau Sudetenland* (Munich, 1999), 17–54.

state, more Germans celebrated the Czechoslovak national holidays with their Czech neighbors in 1933 than ever before. The liberal *Prager Tagblatt* meanwhile encouraged Germans to support the activist, democratic German parties to avoid the growing danger that Germans would be collectively stigmatized as treasonous Nazis. "For the Germans of Czechoslovakia, whose only hope is democracy, the fatal situation has developed that their undeniable national commonalities with Germandom in the Reich put them in danger of being seen collectively as supporters of the Swastika. It is therefore doubly important that we emphasize the existence of a strong, activist, democratic German camp," editors urged.[54]

The newspaper's warning proved prescient. Local Czech nationalists and state agencies responded to the rise of Hitler largely by reviving and intensifying the denunciatory educational policies and "reclamations" of the Revolution of 1918–22. Between 1933 and 1938, as we have seen, local Czech nationalists aggressively lobbied the state to mobilize against German teachers and schools, to protect Czech children from Germanization in the name of protecting the Republic from Nazism. Movement toward compromise on national issues was largely abandoned, since Czech nationalists feared that any compromise would play into the hands of the Nazis and the SdP.[55] Meanwhile, the rising Sudeten German Party turned Czech nationalists' educational policies against the state between 1935 and 1938, using them in a blistering campaign to mobilize support domestically and win international sympathy. In doing so the SdP, including Heimat activists, earned legitimacy as the most effective representatives of overriding German nationalist educational goals such as autonomy and unity and as the best guardians of the nation's "rights" to German children.

Education activists within the SdP solicited popular support by intervening on behalf of aggrieved German parents and teachers in their local battles with the state or Czech school authorities. One long-standing German nationalist grievance was the physical condition of German school buildings. In 1936 the SdP ordered local party members to photograph the most dilapidated German schools in Czechoslovakia, alongside examples of so-called Czech "School Palaces." The photos were exhibited in Great Britain and Germany and sent on to the League of Nations, in spite of belated attempts by the Czechoslovak Ministry of Education to prevent the stunt.[56] Children themselves also became valuable vehicles of SdP propaganda in Germany. Beginning in 1934 the Heimat Front/SdP covertly supported small-scale Bund der Deutschen and DLS programs to send working-class children from Bohemia to Nazi Germany for the summers.[57] The program was considered a

---

[54] *Prager Tagblatt,* 5 October 1933, cited in Kracik, *Die Politik des deutschen Aktivismus,* 253.

[55] Johann Brügel, *Tschechen und Deutsche, 1918–1938* (Munich, 1967), 307.

[56] Pres. ministerstva školství a národní osvěty. č. 7060 1936, SdP, Fotografování českých škol, 11 November 1936, carton 377, MŠ, NA.

[57] Sudetendeutsches Kinderhilfswerk, Dortmund-Asseln, 25 July 1935, carton 67, SdP, NA.

great success, not because of what the children learned from Reich Germans but because of what Reich Germans learned from the children. The young Germans reportedly entertained their hosts in the Reich with colorful stories of national victimization and cultural repression under Czechoslovak rule. These children, reported SdP officials, "were able to depict the immoral persecution and maneuvering of the Czech powermongers and their organs in a truly childlike but purely German way, such that one was personally angered about the injustice of the treatment of Germans in Czechoslovakia.... In response to the question of one representative of the press about how long his father has been unemployed, a fourteen-year-old answered: 'My father has been unemployed since 1932 and he had to leave his job because he stayed true to Germandom.'"[58]

Alongside these propaganda efforts, the SdP began to serve as an advocacy group for aggrieved German parents and teachers. In 1935 the party distributed leaflets to German parents, featuring a familiar appeal not to let opportunism dictate their choice of schools: "You must now decide to whom you trust your child: to the German school, in which every German child belongs, or the Czech school, which through outward glitter ... campaigns for the souls of our German children!" The leaflet went on to explain how to legally reclaim a German child from a Czech school through the Lex Perek.[59] The SdP also began to represent German parents in their conflicts with the state and local schools. In 1936, the party released a memo to local Gau leaders, requesting that they report any incident in which German parents were pressured to enroll their children in Czech schools.[60] Soon the SdP even established an official "School Division," led by teacher Robert Herzog, which handled parental complaints—and transformed them into a powerful genre of propaganda.[61]

In Fürstenhut in 1937, for example, Lukas Weishäupl was allegedly approached by local civil servants and Czech teachers, who offered him a job, as well as a new suit, a pair of shoes, one hundred crowns, free lunches, and Christmas gifts for his stepson, Walter Böchl, if only he would enroll the boy in the local Czech minority school. Weishäupl was presented with a contract stating these conditions, which he signed. The boy's mother and legal guardian, Emma Weishäupl, had not, however, agreed to the plan because she believed her son was too weak to make the long journey to the Czech school.[62] Böchl was nonetheless forced to attend the Czech school

---

[58] "Bericht über die Ferienkinder, aus Haida und umgegend die im Schulungslager der H.J. in Duisburg-Hamborn untergebracht waren," 10 September 1935, carton 67, SdP, NA.

[59] "Deutsche Eltern! Deutsche Vater, Deutsche Mutter, Deutscher Vormund!" carton 30, SdP, NA.

[60] An alle Kreis u. Bezirksleitungen, sowie Ortsgruppen! 13 July 1936, carton 30, SdP, NA.

[61] Ergeht an alle Bezirks und Kreisleitungen, 13 August 1938, carton 30, SdP, NA; Ministerstva vnitra, SdP zřízení Schulkanzlei v Praze, č. 1554, Pres. Prague, 8 February 1937, carton 377, MŠ, NA.

[62] Protokoll, aufgenommen am 2 September 1937, Aussage der Herrn Lukas Weishäupl, Fürstenhut nr. 22, carton 30, SdP, NA.

that fall by the district school board in Prachatice/Prachatitz. Stories like this one had inflamed nationalist passions since the late nineteenth century. This time, however, Emma Weishäupl filed a complaint with her local SdP party office. The SdP and the German School Association appealed to a Sudeten German deputy in the Czechoslovak parliament, Wilhelm Eichholz, who successfully pressured the provincial school board in Prague to allow the child to return to the German school. The case and its successful resolution were prominently featured in the German Kulturverband's international press releases as well in SdP propaganda.[63] Between 1935 and 1938 such dramas became routine. These incidents reinforced the SdP's image as the champions of aggrieved local parents who had been denied their "rights" to a German education and as frontline soldiers in the battle against denationalization.[64]

The party also intervened on behalf of parents whose children were reclaimed through the Lex Perek. In 1935 in Fulnek, the children of textile worker and German Social Democrat Franz Petrek were reclaimed from the German elementary school. All of Petrek's appeals were rejected, and in the fall of 1937 the local Czech school board sent him a letter ordering him to immediately transfer his children to the local Czech school. The letter explained why the Ministry of Education had classified Petrek and his children as Czechs in spite of his adamant claims to be a German:

> The father of the reclaimed children, František Peteřek, was born in . . . a purely Czech family, and according to several witnesses he could not speak a word of German before his arrival in Fulnek in 1922. . . . The former census commissioner and teacher Augustin Tovačovský testified that at the time of the last census the father of the reclaimed Czech children admittedly attempted to speak German, but still could not speak German well. It has also been ascertained that the father of the reclaimed children is organized in the German Social Democratic Party, from which he receives the magazine *Textilarbeiter.* It was not, however, proven that the father of the reclaimed children could actually read the magazines and that he could understand them.[65]

[63]Walter Böchl, 5 March 1938; Deutscher Kulturbund an Abgeordneten Dr. Wilhelm Eichholz, Prague 26 February 1938, carton 30, SdP, NA; Pressebericht des Deutschen Kulturverbands, "Der Landesschulrat schafft Ordnung," 9 March 1938, carton 65, SdP, NA.

[64]See, for example, Memo from Ortsgruupe Waltersdorf to the Arbeitsamt of the SdP, 12 March 1937; Marie Vavřinčinková ve Valteřovicích, reklamace z německé skoly pro českou školu ve Fulneku, 2 March 1937; Versuchter Seelenkauf in Bittersdorf, Bez Wigstadtl, Fulnek, 20 November 1936; Interpellation des Senator Wilhelm Maixner an den Herrn Minister für Schulwesen und Volkskultur, wegen Auffüllung tschechischer Schulen mit deutschen Kinder, 30 July 1937, all in carton 30, SdP, NA.

[65]Herta Petřková, reklamace z německé skoly v Fulneku. 13 November 1936, carton 30, SdP, NA.

Petrek still refused to send his children to the Czech school and was subsequently arrested and sentenced to fourteen days in jail. The children dutifully attended the Czech school for a few days and then ostensibly became ill and stopped attending school altogether. Meanwhile, Petrek appealed to local SdP party leaders. The SdP not only intervened on Petrek's behalf but used the case in its zealous propaganda campaign against the Czechoslovak state. The party's press releases stressed that these children spoke only German at home and had attended only German schools in the past and that their German mother "even has a higher wage than her husband," implying that as the family breadwinner she was entitled to choose her children's school and nationality.[66]

While defending the rights of men like Petrek to choose German schools, many German nationalists by the 1930s had actually embraced the idea of mandatory national classification. In 1925 German Social Democrats had submitted a plan for the creation of national cadastres in Czechoslovakia whereby citizens could enroll in the cadastre of their choice; these were to become the basis for national autonomy in education.[67] In the spring of 1937 the Sudeten German Party put forward a far more restrictive proposal, stipulating that every citizen would have the right and duty to "declare his allegiance to the nation that he has belonged to since his birth" by registering in the appropriate national cadastre at age eighteen. These cadastres, modeled on those created through the Moravian Compromise, would have created a semicorporatist form of citizenship, requiring every Czechoslovak resident to register on a national list as a precondition for voting, schooling, and receiving government services. Citizens would be permitted to choose a nationality other than their nationality "at birth" only if they did not speak their "mother tongue" at home and if they spoke the language of their claimed nationality flawlessly. A declaration of nationality was to be irreversible. German and Czech nationalists were in agreement on at least one question by the late 1930s: the nationality of citizens in the Bohemian Lands had to be legally determined and recorded in order to secure "national property" (including children) and restrict the disruptive potential of nationally labile hermaphrodites.

The long, bitter, and ultimately violent school conflicts in Hlučín/Hultschin offer the most potent example of how the Sudeten German Party and the Nazis harnessed local nationalist school conflicts for their own political ends in the late 1930s. Hlučín/Hultschin, a region outlying Opava/Troppau in Silesia, was populated mostly by German-identified, Catholic families who spoke a Moravian dialect. The region, with a population of 48,005, according

---

[66]Rechtschutz, an das Arbeitsamt der SdP, 9 March 1937, carton 30, SdP, NA. This case never made it to the Supreme Administrative Court.

[67]Bohemicus (pseudonym for Emil Sobota), *Czechoslovakia and the Sudeten Germans* (Prague, 1938), 65–79, carton 28, SdP, NA.

to the 1921 census, belonged to Prussia between 1740 and 1918, when it was awarded to Czechoslovakia at Versailles. In the early 1920s Czechoslovak officials, who considered the region's population to be authentic Czechs who had been forcibly Germanized by the Prussian government, reduced the number of German schools in the region from forty-one to three. The 1921 Czech census meanwhile counted 39,209 "Czechoslovak" residents and 7,707 Germans in Hlučín/Hultschin, since census officials classified all residents who spoke the Moravian dialect as Czechoslovaks, even if they claimed to be Germans. Jan Kapras, professor of law at Charles University, leader in the Czech School Association and chairman of the Czech National Council, explained in a speech on Hlučín/Hultschin in 1935, "Our task after the liberation of Hlučín is to bring back the Czech roots and Czech cultural unity to Hlučín's national consciousness and to force out the foreigners whose rule came between us."[68]

In spite of these efforts to Czechify the region, German political parties secured 43.6 percent of the votes in the region in the parliamentary elections of 1924 and 61.8 percent of the votes in 1929, with the German Christian Social Party in the leading position. In 1935, Henlein's Sudeten German Party won 65 percent of the votes in Hlučín/Hultschin, a rate of support on par with that among Germans in Czechoslovakia as a whole.[69] Many parents in the predominantly Catholic region, mistrustful of the Czech schools for both nationalist and religious regions (the new Czech teachers were seen as "Hussites"), responded to the state's education policies by enrolling their children in the nearby German schools of Opava/Troppau or sending their children to the private German schools supported by the German Kulturverband.[70] In 1936, thanks largely to SdP agitation, 2,232 pupils from Hlučín/Hultschin registered for German schools in Opava/Troppau. In response, the government closed ten more German elementary school classes and two secondary schools in the city, so that places remained for only 277 of these children. The parents of 1,800 children in Hlučín/Hultschin then requested permission from the state to homeschool their children, but their petitions were rejected.[71] Shortly thereafter, SdP representatives intervened on behalf of the German parents.[72] Throughout the crisis, German nationalists continued to draw attention to Hlučín/Hultschin and its struggle for German schools in propaganda aimed at Germany, which responded with

---

[68] Jan Kapras, *O naše Hlučínsko* (Prague, 1935), 6.

[69] Jaroslava Němečková, "Vývoj školské problematiky na Hlučínsku v letech 1920–1938 a její politický obsah," in *Z dějin českého školství, 1918–1945*, ed. Ervín Koukal, 76–83 (Prague, 1970).

[70] Ibid., 233.

[71] Ibid., 130.

[72] Präsidium des Landesschulrates in Brünn z. 1507 präs. 38, Aufnahme von Kindern aus dem Hultschiner Ländchen in Troppauer Schule, R 1501/127120, BA.

financial contributions to support private German education.[73] The school conflict in Hlučín/Hultschin escalated until the final weeks before the annexation of the Sudetenland by the Nazis. On September 7, 1938, three hundred German mothers demonstrated in front of the offices of the district school board in Opava/Troppau and then marched toward the SdP headquarters in a rally, demanding German schools. Two days later, President Beneš received a delegation of SdP representatives who repeated these demands. Beneš made no promises to the delegation, and that night a Czech nursery school in Hlučín/Hultschin was blown up by Nazi terrorists.[74]

Gleichschaltung from Below

While the DLS largely maintained its positive relationship with the Czechoslovak state into the 1930s, it became increasingly difficult for the activist organization to retain the faith of its German clients or its independence from the growing Henleinist movement. Heimat activists, meanwhile, were now rising to positions of authority within the Sudeten German and Nazi parties and fashioned themselves as the more genuine advocates of values such as autonomy and unity that were promoted by Germans across the political spectrum. "Unity," in the eyes of activist parties like the German Socialist, German Christian Social, and Agrarian parties, implied that all Germans should stand together on national issues and that working-class, Catholic, and rural Germans should at long last join the German national community. In the late 1930s, however, the SdP redefined the ideal of national unity to render the very existence of competing parties and associations illegitimate. Party propaganda asserted, "The union of Sudeten Germandom is not yet complete, as long as there are still party-political enemies of the SdP."[75] In the name of achieving national unity, the SdP soon absorbed all the competing nationalist educational and social welfare organizations in a process of *Gleichschaltung* (coordination) that mirrored the one in Nazi Germany. In Czechoslovakia, however, Gleichschaltung was relatively bloodless. It was achieved largely from below, before the Nazi invasion, without the help of a police state.

The activists in the Heimat education movement were among the earliest and most enthusiastic supporters of Henlein's Sudeten German Heimat Front and the Nazi Party in Czechoslovakia. Emil Lehmann himself was

---

[73]See, for example, Hermann Janosch, *Das Hultschiner Ländchen* (Ratibor, 1930). For an early Sudeten German protest on the Czechification of Hlučín, see Deutsch-mährischer Volksbund, *Die Not des mährischen Anteils* (Ratibor, 1919). In 1935–36, Nazi Germany was reportedly providing 40,000 kč a month for German instruction. Němečková, "Vývoj školské problematiky," 135, 158.

[74]Němečková, "Vývoj školské problematiky," 178.

[75]Erziehungs und Schulungsarbeit als Aufgabe unserer Bewegung, Vortrag 8, Eger, 24 February 1936, carton 28, SdP, NA.

tried and sentenced to a year's imprisonment for treason in 1935. He fled to Germany, but his son Ernst continued to publish *Heimatbildung* until the Nazis annexed the Sudetenland.[76] In 1939 Ernst Lehmann congratulated Heimat activists for their role preparing the ground for the Nazi occupation of Czechoslovakia, boasting that the "Heimat education movement . . . with its wide-reaching influence . . . made us ripe for our liberation by Adolf Hitler."[77] Several members of the Heimat movement were rewarded for their loyalty with posts as education officials in Nazi-occupied Czechoslovakia. Prominent writers for *Heimatbildung* who later joined the Nazi Party or served as education officials in occupied Czechoslovakia included Emil and Ernst Lehmann, Fritz Slawik, Theo Keil, Rudolf Lochner, Eugen Lemberg, Ignaz Göth, and Gottfried Preissler. In 1938, Emil Lehmann and Hans Krebs, the Nazi Party leader in Czechoslovakia, authored a propaganda tract entitled "We Sudeten Germans." This appeared in multiple editions, promoting the notion of a German diaspora and advertising the plight of the "oppressed" Sudeten Germans to Germans in the Altreich.[78] In 1940 Krebs officially paid tribute to Lehmann's early and open devotion to the National Socialist cause, writing, "I personally got to know Emil Lehmann 20 years ago. . . . He came to National Socialism through his activity as an educator and Heimat researcher. A clear path, without fuss, without wavering. . . . He was drawn early on to the Nazi movement and has always joyfully professed to it, even when it was cursedly difficult."[79]

While the SdP endorsed Heimat education as the "natural basis" for "the defensive education of German youth," the party typically stripped Heimat education of its original affiliation with progressive pedagogy and values.[80] Nationalist pedagogues had once urged educators to cultivate children's individualism and agency so that they would resist the threats of Czechification, the Socialist Party, and the Catholic Church. Now the SdP sought hope for the German nation through self-sacrifice and disciplined subordination to a greater German community and to the Third Reich. The individualist and romantic theories of progressive pedagogues were hopelessly outdated in this context, according to the SdP leadership. An SdP newsletter informed German

---

[76]Heinrich Eppinger, "Erinnerung am schwere Tag," in *Aus dem Sudetengau. Emil Lehmann, der Volksforscher und Volksbildner,* ed. Hugo Herrmann (Reichenberg, 1940).

[77]Ernst Lehmann, "Zur Volkskunde in der Sudetendeutsche Volksschule," *Der Sudetendeutsche Erzieher,* 1 June 1939, 253–56. See also Fritz Slawik, "Ist Dr. Ewald Haufe's Werk heute noch zeitgemäß?" *Der Sudetendeutsche Erzieher,* 15 March 1939, 141–43.

[78]See Hans Krebs and Emil Lehmann, *Wir Sudetendeutsche!* (Berlin, 1938), and Hans Krebs and Emil Lehmann, *Sudetendeutsche Landeskunde* (Kiel, 1992) (original publication in 1937). See also Ignaz Göth, "Hauptschule-Heimatschule," *Der Erzieher in Böhmen und Mähren* (July 1944), 118–19. Another striking example of Nazi propaganda written by a former Heimat education activist is Ernst Lehmann, *Volksgemeinschaft aus Nachbarschaften* (Prague, 1944).

[79]Hans Krebs, "Emil Lehmann, ein nationalsozialistischer Grenzland und Heimatkämpfer," in *Aus dem Sudetengau,* ed. Hugo Herrmann, 9.

[80]"Leitsätze für die staatsbürgerliche Erziehung der Schuljugend," Kulturauschuß der sudetendeutschen Lehrerverband, Reichenberg, 15 February 1937, carton 30, SdP, NA.

mothers in early 1938, "Through our upbringing we want our children to achieve . . . consciousness that they are a subordinate part of the superior national community, self-discipline and obedience." SdP activists therefore rejected the permissive spirit of earlier nationalist pedagogy, encouraging German mothers to resist "fulfilling the child's every selfish impulse and desire out of motherly love. Our special task will instead be to bring our children up with a self-evident, voluntary obedience, which is the unshakable foundation of life in the national community. . . . The time in which one sought to achieve joy in work and achievement through the promotion of childish games and excessive attention to the individuality of the child is, thank God, over. We mothers, who wish to ease the lives of our children, will shed no tears for this education for incompetence."[81]

The DLS, meanwhile, managed to retain its independence from the SdP far longer than any other German nationalist child welfare or educational organization in the Bohemian Lands. In January of 1937 the Czechoslovak Ministry of the Interior noted that while most of the other German nationalist associations, youth groups, and educational organizations had long ago been "coordinated" by the SdP, the "DLS and Reichverband are still mostly in the hands of members of the German Socialist Party and the German Progressive Party. The same is true of the district branches of the DLS."[82] The SdP was hardly pleased that an institution with so much authority over German children remained in enemy hands, and it undertook an active campaign to infiltrate from below. Party officials did not expect this to be easy. In a 1936 memo they conceded that "taking the DLS and the Reichsverband fully into our hands would be difficult and also not clearly purposeful" and decided to focus instead on controlling local branches. The memo elaborated that Socialists were particularly dominant in Moravia and in the central leadership of the Reichsverband but were less numerous in Bohemia. "In the Reichsverband they comprise a closed front that can paralyze any great measures from the *völkisch* side," SdP informants warned.[83]

The party strategized to infiltrate and coordinate the DLS by sending an army of loyal SdP women to invade the organization's local branches as activists and clients.[84] A newsletter for SdP women urged readers, "The

[81]Weisung des Frauenamtes OG-18/1938, 18 August 1938, carton 22, SdP, NA.

[82]The Bund der Deutschen was also closely affiliated with the SdP throughout the late 1930s. The Deutscher Kulturverband (successor of the School Association), in contrast, maintained some independence until late in 1937, resisting pressure to merge with the Bund der Deutschen on the grounds that it was neutral with respect to party politics. See Deutscher Kulturverband, press reports from 15 February 1937, 15 March 1937, 15 April 1937. Carton 65, SdP, NA. Presidium Min. vnitra, č. 2750, 8 February 1937, carton 377, MŠ, NA.

[83]"Die deutsche Jugendfürsorge," 1936, carton 67, SdP, NA.

[84]Ibid. See also "Mitgliedschaft bei der Deutschen Jugendfürsorge," 26 August 1936; "Aufruf für den Kinderschutzmonat Oktober (1936)"; "Unpolitische Verbände der Sudetendeutsche, die Deutsche Jugendfürsorge," 5 October 1936; "Herein in die Deutsche Jugendfürsorge!" 1 March 1937; all in *Beilage zur Frauenschaftsweisung*, carton 22, SdP, NA.

DLS is a nonpartisan association. Nonpartisan, however, does not mean that the parties stay away, but to the contrary that they strive such that their members are represented to a degree that corresponds to their importance. We hope that our women will devote themselves more and more to working with the DLS, as is fully suited to their profession as wives and mothers."[85] Several months later the party issued a more strident call to arms: "We do not want to wait and will not wait until the DLS approaches us with a plea to join!"[86]

In the spring of 1938 the DLS finally succumbed. On April 25, 1938, the Reichsverband held a meeting in which its leaders at long last declared their "allegiance to the Sudeten German Volksgemeinschaft (national community)."[87] They simultaneously abandoned their commitment to working with the Czechoslovak government, rejecting the latest reform plan from the Ministry for Social Welfare. Margarete Roller, leader of the DLS in Moravia, sent a memo to the ministry elaborating the organization's new stance: "A legal regulation of specific questions of a national character does not seem possible to us so long as a fundamental regulation of the national question has not been achieved by the state."[88] On May 26, 1938, the SdP appointed Eduard Rohn as the new director of the DLS, a post he held until the Nazi social welfare organization, the Nationalsozialistische Volkswohlfahrt (NSV) took over local branches of the DLS in November of 1938. Ludwig Czech, Socialist and Jew, was deported to Terezín not long after, where he died in 1942. The SdP had achieved its goals of coordination, unity, and autonomy months before the annexation of the Sudetenland. Sudeten German Heimat activists now had the education of real German children in their hands. They set out to transform their imagined utopian Heimat into a reality as leaders of the educational and social welfare system in the new Nazi state.

[85] "Mitgliedschaft bei der Deutschen Jugendfürsorge," 26 August 1936, carton 22, SdP, NA.
[86] "Aufruf dür den Kinderschutzmonat Oktober (1936)," carton 22, SdP, NA.
[87] "Bekenntnis der Deutschen Jugendfürsorge zur Volksgemeinschaft," *Jugendfürsorge* 22, May 1938, 197.
[88] Eduard Rohn and Margarete Roller, "Memo an das Ministerium für Soziale Fürsorge," Reichenberg, 26 April 1938, *Jugendfürsorge* 22, May 1938, 197.

6 Borderland Children and Volkstumsarbeit *under Nazi Rule*

The Nazi annexation of the Sudetenland in early October of 1938 was followed quickly by a homework assignment. Shortly after the invasion, teachers instructed thousands of children in the German schools of the Bohemian Lands to testify to their own personal experiences of "liberation." E.G., aged ten, recalled a life of struggle and hardship in Czechoslovakia. "In the first grade, we already painted swastikas on the houses where the Czechs lived and had to be punished by our teacher for it. On the way to school we had to go past the Czech kindergarten. The Czech children hit us and called us names, so pretty soon we were afraid to go by. Then we learned the Czech national anthem in school, which we didn't like to sing. Later my father went to the Salzkammergut on vacation and brought us back pretty pictures of the Führer. My brother and I hung them up above the bed."[1] The National Socialist Teachers' Association distributed a circular outlining the assignment and its historical significance: "The liberation of the Sudeten German people from twenty years of serfdom has also aroused the unrestrainable enthusiasm of our youth. It would be unforgivable if fresh memories of the liberation weren't preserved in a worthy form." These memories were quickly collected, edited, and published, ostensibly without so much as correcting the grammatical errors.[2]

The much-vaunted authenticity of these stories is certainly questionable, but they do attest to one reality of 1938–39—the Nazis rode into the Bohemian East on waves of propaganda fomented by Austrian and interwar nationalist educational activists. Nazi propaganda invoked stories of victimized German children in the East to portray the regime's *Drang nach*

---

[1] *Endlich Befreit! Sudetendeutsche Jugend erzählt von der Befreiung ihrer Heimat* (Reichenberg, 1939), 13.
[2] Ibid., preface.

Osten as a liberation of an oppressed German diaspora. Under the new regime, moreover, children were no longer simply the subjects of nationalist propaganda or the objects of nationalist pedagogy. In their first writing assignment, they became the authors of the propaganda intended to educate the world.

The Nazi occupation of the Sudetenland is typically remembered, with good reason, as the most radical of all turning points in Czechoslovak history. In the days leading up to the invasion, the Czechoslovak government resigned, while in the name of "peace in our time" Western leaders signed the Munich Agreement, enabling Hitler to dismember the Czechoslovak state without firing a shot. An authoritarian coalition led by the Czech Agrarian Party's Rudolf Beran seized power in what remained of the Bohemian Lands and implemented a program designed to rehabilitate and purify a humiliated nation. The Czech Second Republic—similar in many respects to the Vichy Regime in France, which took power after France's 1940 surrender to Germany—quickly took measures to expropriate Jewish property for Czechs before the Nazis could get to it, to remove women from the workforce, and to curb the emigration of Jewish, Socialist, and Communist refugees from Nazi Germany and from the Sudetenland.[3]

Sudeten Germans, meanwhile, almost universally welcomed the German troops as "liberators" in a spirit of ecstatic jubilation. Twenty years later, Josef Hübler recalled that in his town of Libavá/Liebau, the German troops "were enthusiastically welcomed, in the opinion that paradise on Earth had arrived for the Sudeten Germans."[4] Many Sudeten German Nazis depicted the events of 1938–39 as the fulfillment of Austrian and interwar German nationalists' dearest dreams. Heimat activist Eugen Lemberg proclaimed triumphantly, "The new border has eliminated the fear of denationalization with a single blow. . . . The Sudeten German is happy . . . that he no longer has to learn the hated state language, that he and his children no longer have to learn the dull details of Czech political and cultural history, and that above all the danger of spiritual Czechification . . . has been banished."[5]

The Second Republic lasted only until March of 1939, when the Nazis invaded the Czech rump state and established the Protectorate of Bohemia and Moravia as an "autonomous" administrative unit within the Third

---

[3] On the Second Republic see Theodore Procházka, *The Second Republic: The Disintegration of Post-Munich Czecho-slovakia* (Boulder, CO, 1981), 56; Jan Rataj, *O autoritativní národní stát: ideologické proměny české politiky v druhé republice, 1938–1939* (Prague, 1997), 230–34; Alice Teichová, "The Protectorate of Bohemia and Moravia: the Economic Dimension," in *Bohemia in History*, ed. Mikoláš Teich (Cambridge, 1998); Melissa Feinberg, "The Politics of Difference in the Czech Lands After Munich," *East European Politics and Societies* 17 (May 2003): 202–30.

[4] Ost Doc. 20/37, Josef Hübler, Stadt Liebau, 8 December 1960, 2, BB.

[5] Eugen Lemberg, "Erzieher und Grenzlandaufgabe," *Der sudetendeutsche Erzieher*, 1 March 939, 105.

Reich. While the Sudetenland was directly integrated into the Third Reich and its Gau system, the Protectorate was ruled by a Nazi Reichsprotektor, appointed by Hitler. A weak Czech government, led by Emil Hácha and composed of approximately four hundred thousand Czech officials, was directly subordinated to approximately two thousand German civil servants, many of whom were themselves Sudeten Germans, including Deputy Reichsprotektor Karl H. Frank. One of the first priorities of local Sudeten German Nazis was to reclaim children allegedly lost to interwar Czechification. In doing so, the Nazis built upon interwar practices of national classification. However, both the justification for and the consequences of national ascription transformed dramatically during the Second World War. While children had been assigned national identities in interwar Czechoslovakia in the name of guaranteeing minority rights, the Nazis used national categorization in order to create a new racial order, subordinating Czech subjects to German citizens. On the surface it seemed that hardly a trace remained of the First Republic's democratic political system or culture.

Yet while the Nazi occupation of Czechoslovakia brought radical change and previously unimagined brutality, these transformations were justified and understood in terms borrowed from a long history of German-Czech nationalist struggle. Nazi officials, like Czech and German nationalists before them, saw both a grave threat and seductive potential in borderland children. Children blatantly exposed contradictions between Nazi understandings of the nation as a racial, descent-based community and the social and cultural ambiguities of language frontiers, where individuals often moved easily between national communities. In her work on French and Dutch colonialism, Ann Stoler has discussed the ways in which racism presumes that an individual's inner worth can be assessed on the basis of his or her outer qualities, or racial appearance.[6] In the Bohemian Lands, however, Nazi occupation officials never established clear guidelines for distinguishing between Germans and Czechs. Rather than assessing the political and cultural "value" of individual human beings according to their physical or racial appearance, local administrators often determined the alleged race (Czech or German) of members of a so-called ambiguous *Zwischenschicht* (in-between stratum) on the basis of their political and cultural values. These officials racialized traditional local understandings of national belonging and practices of national ascription in Czechoslovakia in order to implement Nazi Germanization policies. National indifference, long a force propelling nationalist activism in the Bohemian Lands, now directly shaped Nazi Germanization policies.

This and the next two chapters explore the many ways in which both Nazi Germanization policies and popular responses to Nazi rule in the occupied

---

[6] See Ann Stoler, "Sexual Fronts and Racial Frontiers: European Identities and the Cultural Politics of Exclusion in Colonial Southeast Asia," in *Becoming National: A Reader,* ed. Geoff Eley and Ronald Grigor Suny, 286–322 (New York, 1996).

Bohemian Lands were shaped by a longer history of German and Czech nationalist activism around children. Nazi *Ostpolitik* has become a subject of considerable interest among German historians as they have turned their attention toward what Helmut Walser Smith has called the "vanishing point" of 1941, when Hitler's armies invaded the Soviet Union and the genocidal campaign against European Jewry accelerated into its final and most deadly stage.[7] Many excellent studies have productively explored the relationship of Nazi occupiers to the East, examining daily life and policymaking on the "peripheries" of the Nazi empire.[8] Policies of Germanization certainly acquired radical new meanings and consequences in the context of Nazi plans to reengineer the racial demography of Europe. There is, however, much to be gained by situating Germanization policy in particular local contexts over a longer period. "Germanization" represented far more than simply a policy applied by Reich German Nazis to Eastern *Raum*, or to a population self-evidently divided into Czechs and Germans. Rather, Germanization was a contested set of ideologies and practices whose very meanings were powerfully shaped by a longer history of nationalist claims on children.

From Germanization of *Raum* to Germanization of People

In the beginning, Hitler hoped to Germanize *Raum*, or space, rather than individuals in the Bohemian Lands. He justified this strategy with reference to the nationalist conflicts of the late Habsburg Monarchy, which he had witnessed in his youth in Austria. Germans in Imperial Austria, Hitler wrote in *Mein Kampf*, had naively assumed that Czechs could be assimilated into

---

[7] Helmut Walser Smith, "The Vanishing Point of German History: An Essay on Perspective," *History and Memory* 17 (Spring/Summer 2005): 269–95. Geoff Eley argues that growing interest in Nazism during the Second World War corresponds to a general shift away from class and toward race as the central category of analysis in German history. Geoff Eley, "Hitler's Silent Majority? Conformity and Resistance under the Third Reich," *Michigan Quarterly Review* 42 (Spring 2003): 389–425; Geoff Eley, "Hitler's Silent Majority? Conformity and Resistance under the Third Reich (Part II)," *Michigan Quarterly Review* 42 (Summer 2003): 550–83.

[8] Recent examples include Chad Bryant, *Prague in Black: Nazi Rule and Czech Nationalism* (Cambridge, MA, 2007); Götz Aly, *Final Solution: Nazi Population Policy and the Murder of the European Jews* (London, 1999); Isabel Heinemann, *"Rasse, Siedlung, deutsches Blut": Die Rasse und Siedlungshauptamt der SS und die rassenpolitische Neuordnung Europas* (Göttingen, 2003); John Connelly, "Nazis and Slavs: From Racial Theory to Racist Practice," *Central European History* 32 (March 1999), 1–33; Vejas G. Liulevicius, *War Land on the Eastern Front: Culture, National Identity, and German Occupation in World War I* (New York, 2000); Elizabeth Harvey, *Women in the Nazi East: Agents and Witnesses of Germanization* (New Haven, 2003); Wendy Lower, *Nazi Empire Building and the Holocaust in Ukraine* (Chapel Hill, 2005); Karl C. Berghoff, *Harvest of Despair: Life and Death in Ukraine Under Nazi Rule* (Cambridge, MA, 2005); Christoph Dieckmann, Babette Quinckert, Tatjana Tönsmayer, eds. *Kooperation und Verbrechen. Formen der "Kollaboration" im östlichen Europa, 1939–1945* (Göttingen, 2003); Melissa Feinberg, *Elusive Equality: Gender, Citizenship, and the Limits of Democracy in Czechoslovakia, 1918–1950* (Pittsburgh, 2006), 159–89.

the German nation. "I remember how in my youth Germanization led to incredibly false conceptions," he maintained. "Even in Pan-German circles the opinion could then be heard that the Austrian Germans, with the promotion and aid of the government, might well succeed in a Germanization of the Austrian Slavs; these circles never even began to realize that Germanization can be applied to soil and never people."[9] Instead of Germanizing the Czechs of the Bohemian Lands through a "civilizing" mission, Hitler and other Nazi ideologues initially planned to Germanize territory through the ruthless seizure of political and economic institutions, the expulsion of Czechs, and an infusion of fresh German blood.[10]

Not surprisingly, however, Nazi occupiers encountered many obstacles as they set out to Germanize Raum. While Nazi ideology insisted that Germans required *Lebensraum* (living space) in the East, few Germans could actually be found to settle there once they had it. Plans to resettle ethnic Germans in other areas of occupied Eastern Europe, such as the Warthegau in occupied Poland, were stymied by the lack of food, supplies, and space.[11] Deputy Reichsprotektor (and Sudeten German) Karl H. Frank lamented in a key 1940 memo that there was both a shortage of Germans to fill the conquered Bohemian and Moravian Raum and no place to move evacuated Czechs. Moreover, Frank maintained that the war required the integration of the Protectorate, including a pacified Czech labor force, into the Reich economy. "Humans are the empire's capital, and in the new Reich we cannot do without the labor of seven million Czechs," he concluded. By the fall of 1940, Nazi leaders had shifted away from Hitler's initial dreams of Germanizing Raum in the Bohemian Lands. Instead, they settled on the more pragmatic policy of Germanizing people, or at least those 50 percent of Czechs whom Nazi racial scientists estimated to be racially worthy. Frank concluded that the Czech nation as a whole could not be "reduced to a servant nation on

[9] Adolf Hitler, *Mein Kampf*, cited by Brigitte Hamann, *Hitler's Vienna: A Dictator's Apprenticeship*, trans. Thomas Thorton (New York, 1999), 323.

[10] Peter Němec makes a useful distinction between the Germanization of "Raum" and the Germanization of individuals. "Das tschechische Volk und die nationalsozialistische Germanisierung des Raumes," *Bohemia* 32 (1991): 425–55. For more on Nazi plans to expel the Czechs see Václav Král, ed., *Lessons from History: Documents Concerning Nazi Policy for Germanization and Extermination in Czechoslovakia* (Prague, 1960); Miroslav Kárný et al., eds., *Deutsche Politik im Protektorat Böhmen und Mähren unter Reinhard Heydrich, 1941–42* (Berlin, 1997).

[11] On the lack of Germans to fill the new Nazi Lebensraum, see Peter Němec, "Český národ a nacistická teorie germanizace prostoru," *ČČH*, 1990, 538; Bryant, *Prague in Black*, 110–19; Ralf Gebel, *Heim ins Reich! Konrad Henlein und der Reichsgau Sudetenland* (Munich, 1999), 289–93; Detlef Brandes, *Die Tschechen unter deutschem Protektorat*, vol. 1 (Munich, 1969), 34–35. Approximately 1,590 families were resettled into Bohemia and Moravia by late 1944. On resettlement see Aly, *Final Solution*; Harvey, *Women in the Nazi East*; Valdis O. Lumans, *Himmler's Auxiliaries: The Volksdeutsche Mittelstelle and the German National Minorities of Europe, 1933–1945* (Chapel Hill, 1993); Robert Kohl, *RKFDV: German Resettlement and Population Policy, 1939–1945* (Cambridge, MA, 1957).

racial grounds." Rather, through economic incentives, "sugar and the whip," the Nazis would entice or cajole Czechs into joining the Nazi *Volksgemeinschaft*. Those unsuitable for Germanization were to be relocated in the East after final victory.[12]

By the summer of 1941, however, both sugar and the whip seemed to be faltering. The Nazi Secret Service reported that resistance from Czech workers, in the form of strikes and sabotage, was noticeably on the rise. Protectorate Germans who had been successfully registered as Reich citizens grumbled loudly about rationing (they were allocated less fat than Germans in Germany), labor service, the draft, and Czech economic boycotts. Production for the war appeared to be threatened by social unrest on both sides of the national divide. Meanwhile, internal tensions plagued the Protectorate administration. Since the creation of the Protectorate in March of 1939, neighboring administrative districts (Gau Sudetenland, Bayerische Ostmark, Oberdonau, and Niederdonau) had jockeyed for power and influence over cultural and political life in the Protectorate with Minister of State Karl H. Frank and Reichsprotektor Konstantin Freiherr von Neurath. At the same time, Frank and von Neurath themselves vied with each other for authority.[13]

In response to reports of growing social strife, Hitler replaced von Neurath with Reinhard Heydrich, head of the SS, as Reichsprotektor in Bohemia on August 28, 1941. Heydrich's ascension to power in the Protectorate brought a violent wave of terror and arrests to repress Czech resistance, as well as a shift in Germanization policy in the Bohemian Lands. The appointment of Heydrich as Reichsprotektor coincided with the radicalization of Hitler's war for Lebensraum in the East. Only two months earlier, in June of 1941, the Wehrmacht had invaded the Soviet Union. Four months after Heydrich took power in the Protectorate, on January 20, 1942, he chaired a meeting of high-ranking civil servants and SS officers in Wannsee, near Berlin, the purpose of which was to consolidate and coordinate plans to systematically murder all of Europe's Jews. Shortly after he took office, Heydrich began the deportation of Bohemia and Moravia's Jews to Terezín/Theresienstadt, a small garrison town north of Prague that the Nazis had converted into a ghetto and transit point for Jews and political prisoners on their way to the new death camps.[14]

---

[12] Karl H. Frank, "Denkschrift über die Behandlung des Tschechen Problem," esp. 10–13, carton 1, Sb NÚIČ, VÚA. For Germanization plans outlined by von Neurath and Frank in fall of 1940, see Král, *Lessons from History*, doc. 6, 54–63. For analysis of these policies, see Bryant, *Prague in Black*, 114–28. See also Kárný et al., *Deutsche Politik*, doc. 77, 221–34, doc. 22, 107–22.

[13] Gebel, *Heim ins Reich*, 345.

[14] On the radicalization of Nazi racial policy after the invasion of the Soviet Union, see Omer Bartov, *The Eastern Front, 1941–45: German Troops and the Barbarisation of Warfare* (New York, 2001); Hans Mommsen, "Umvolkungspläne des Nationalsozialismus und der

At the same time that the Nazis accelerated their war for Lebensraum and their genocidal campaign against European Jews, Nazi leaders in Berlin decided to postpone any "final solution" to the so-called Czech problem until after the war's end. Germanization, however, took on a new tone under Heydrich's more brutal and centralized authority. Beginning in late 1940, agencies charged with carrying out Germanization policy in both the Sudetenland and the Protectorate had been gradually transferred to the hands of SS officials versed in the language of racial selection. In the process, Sudeten German nationalists associated with Konrad Henlein's Sudeten German Party were often displaced by Reich Germans or Sudeten Germans with SS credentials. This shift was the culmination of a long history of tensions within the Sudeten German Party between former members of the Nazi Party in Czechoslovakia, which had been outlawed and disbanded in 1934, and the ranks of the *Kameradschaftsbund,* Sudeten German Party members recruited primarily from the interwar German gymnastics associations and youth movements. In January of 1940 these tensions came to a head when many members of the old Kameradschaftsbund were purged from the Nazi administration under the pretext of homosexual misconduct.[15] Konrad Henlein's own authority as governor of the Sudetenland also suffered under Heydrich's rule, as power shifted toward Frank and SS-controlled agencies such as the *Rasse und Siedlungs Hauptamt* (RuSHa). Founded to police the racial purity of SS members and their wives, this agency's mission now included settling Germans in the newly occupied East. The RuSHA also took charge of the *Lebensborn* program, which provided support to Aryan single mothers and their children, and later participated in programs to Germanize children from Eastern Europe.[16] Once the war began, the RuSHa was subsumed under Himmler's Reichskommissar für die Festigung der deutschen Volkstums (RKfDV). Heydrich himself assumed leadership of the RKfDV during his tenure as Reichsprotektor, and after his death Frank took charge of the agency in the Protectorate.

Holocaust," in *Die Normalität des Verbrechens. Bilanz und Perspektiven der Forschung zu der Nationalsozialistischen Gewaltverbrechen,* ed. Helge Grabitz et al. (Berlin, 1994); Aly, *Final Solution;* Robert O. Paxton, *The Anatomy of Fascism* (New York, 2004); Ulrich Herbert, *National Socialist Extermination Policies* (New York, 2004); on Wannsee, see Christian Gerlach, "The Wannsee Conference, the Fate of German Jews, and Hitler's Decision in Principle to Exterminate All European Jews," *Journal of Modern History* 70 (December 1998): 759–812; Christopher Browning, *Nazi Policy, Jewish Workers, German Killers* (New York, 2000), 26–57.

[15] Kameradschaftsbund members included Walter Brand, Hans Neuwirth, Heinz Rutha, and Wilhelm Sebkowsky. For a more detailed discussion of the purge see Volker Zimmermann, *Die Sudetendeutschen im NS-Staat: Politik und Stimmung im Reichsgau Sudetenland, 1938–1945* (Munich, 1999), 241–69; Mark Cornwall, "Heinrich Rutha and the Unraveling of a Homosexual Scandal in 1930s Czechoslovakia," *GLQ: A Journal of Lesbian and Gay Studies* 8, no. 3 (2002): 319–47.

[16] On the RuSHa in the Bohemian Lands, see Heinemann, *"Rasse, Siedlung, deutsches Blut,"* 127–86.

Heydrich discreetly introduced new measures to begin the selection and separation of Germanizable from non-Germanizable Czechs. In March of 1942 several thousand Protectorate residents were required to fill out surveys on their racial and political credentials in order to acquire identity cards. One month later, under the pretense of a campaign to prevent tuberculosis, Heydrich sent five mobile X-ray teams to Czech schools, along with teams of racial experts from the RuSHA. These teams were charged with "examining the entire population in order to lay the scientific foundation for future Germanization."[17] In an October 1941 speech before leading Protectorate authorities, Heydrich explained that the Czech population would ultimately be sorted into four categories. Aside from the racially worthy, well-intentioned Czechs, who were to be Germanized, and the undesirable, bad-intentioned Czechs, who would be expelled, racially undesirable but politically loyal Czechs could remain in the Reich so long as they were sterilized. The most dangerous group, the "racially good, ill-disposed" (*gut-rassige, schlecht-gesinnte*) Czechs, were to be forcibly Germanized or shot, since they would otherwise lead the Slavs in the East in an uprising against the Germans.[18]

If these radical actions had to wait for final victory, Heydrich insisted that more subtle policies of Germanization were compatible with military priorities. The line between compensating old Germans for alleged injustices suffered under Czech rule and recruiting new Germans into the Volksgemeinschaft was already deliberately blurry. Germanization efforts in the Bohemian Lands quickly extended well beyond the circle of committed Sudeten German nationalists to what was recognized as a strategically important class of nationally ambiguous Bohemians and Moravians and their children, labeled the *Zwischenschicht* by Nazi observers. If the Zwischenschicht was numerically small by 1939, nationally contested children featured prominently in the reports of Nazi officials and education authorities precisely because such individuals forced the Nazis to define the boundaries of the German nation.[19] Nazi attempts to secure the loyalties of the children of the Zwischenschicht reveal both the centrality of racial thinking to the Nazi administration and the extent to which, in the absence of any real and visible marks of "racial" difference between Germans and Czechs, local administrators were forced to rely on the Sudeten Germans' more traditional,

[17] Zpráva R. Heydricha o stavu v Protektorátu, March 1942, 42, folder 21, carton 1, Sb NÚIČ, VÚA.

[18] Kárný et al., *Deutsche Politik*, doc. 22 107–22.

[19] While it would be nearly impossible to calculate the precise number of parents in the Protectorate or Sudetenland with ambiguous national identities, contemporaries estimated that approximately three hundred thousand individuals who had identified as Czechs in the interwar period became Reich citizens in the Nazi Protectorate during the war. Benjamin Frommer, *National Cleansing: Retribution against Nazi Collaborators in Postwar Czechoslovakia* (New York, 2005), 18, 199–204; Bryant, *Prague in Black*, 50–57.

cultural definitions of Germanness when putting Nazi racial ideology into practice. Even as Germanization policy in the Bohemian Lands was directed toward carrying out novel and radical Nazi practices of racial selection, these policies often relied on traditional modes of national classification, many of which had been established through the nationalist battles over children in the Bohemian Lands since the late Austrian Empire.

Nazi Postcolonialism

Volkstumsarbeit, or Nazi activism aimed at strengthening the German nation in the borderlands, began shortly after the occupation of Czechoslovakia with the "coordination" of the existing autonomous German social welfare apparatus in Bohemia and Moravia. Continuity, rather than radical change, marked this transition. When the 534 district offices of the German Provincial Commission for Child Welfare passed into the hands of the Nationalsozialistische Volkswohlfahrt (NSV) on November 16, 1939, occupation authorities discovered with pleasure that *Gleichschaltung* (coordination) was hardly necessary. The Sudeten German Party in the Bohemian Lands had achieved from below what had been accomplished only by force in Germany after Hitler's seizure of power: "In the many years of the Sudeten Germans' national struggle before the liberation, kindergartens, maternal and child welfare institutions and nurseries were the essential weapons in the fight for self-determination. The successful unification of Sudeten Germandom through the nationality struggle led early on to the unified leadership of this social work," Nazi officials in the Sudetenland reported to Berlin.[20] Czechoslovakia's nationally segregated child welfare system, now four decades old, was ideally structured to serve the Nazis' racial vision. It enabled the regime to accord differential social rights and privileges to Reich (German) "citizens" and Protectorate "subjects."

At the same time, officials in Berlin and Prague created several overlapping agencies with responsibility for "strengthening Germandom" in the East. Volkstumsarbeit was carried out by no fewer than eleven agencies. As will become clear, moreover, local differences of opinion on how to distinguish between a German and a Czech were never really resolved. In the Sudetenland a new *Gaugrenzlandamt* (Borderland Office), headed by Sudeten German Party leader Franz Künzel, initially led efforts to shore up Germandom in the newly annexed territory. Nazi officials quickly established a fund for Borderland Relief (*Grenzlandfürsorge*) to serve the cause by providing money for new German kindergartens, swimming pools, and nurseries

---

[20] NSDP Gauleitung Sudetenland, Amt für Volkswohlfahrt, An das Reichskommisariat für die sudetendeutschen Gebiete, Reichenberg, 1 April 1939, R 1501/127120, 303, BA.

in regions allegedly "neglected" by the interwar Czechoslovak state or threatened by ongoing Czech resistance. In the tradition of both the wartime Austrian and interwar Czechoslovak states, the fund channeled significant amounts of money toward German child welfare programs through local branches of the NSV, the former local offices of the DLS. In 1939 the NSV outlined ambitious plans to build 950 new kindergartens, 500 new mother-counseling centers, and 300 new social work centers in the Sudetenland with money from the Borderland Fund.[21]

Meanwhile in the Protectorate, a fund for Germanization (Volkstums-fond), controlled by the Reichsprotektor himself, served similar goals. The Volkstumsfond brought approximately 5.5 million RM (Reichsmarks) into the Protectorate in 1939.[22] In 1941 and 1942 the office of the Protectorate requested 9 million RM for Volkstumsarbeit, one-third of which was to be directed toward children. Funds were also earmarked for German busi-nesses threatened by Czech boycotts, renovating "German" tourist resorts and spas on the language frontier, and German language courses, as well as the expected kindergartens, swimming pools, day-care centers, movie the-aters, libraries, and nurseries. Families even applied for money from the Volkstumsfond to purchase expropriated Jewish furniture and property.[23] The money thus supported precisely the causes that had long been dear to German nationalist associations in the Bohemian Lands.

The war dampened the boom in school construction, but the number of German middle schools in the Protectorate more than doubled during the occupation, from 36 to 78, and the number of German elementary schools increased from 130 to 333. New German schools, day-care centers, and youth homes were frequently erected in homes expropriated from Jews or in former Czech minority schools.[24] After 1941 no more children were ac-cepted into Czech secondary schools, and the diplomas of children of Czech parents or mixed marriages who attended German schools were marked to indicate their heritage. In November of 1939 all Czech universities were closed for the duration of the war, following student protests.[25] The Nazi

---

[21] NSDP Gauleitung Sudetenland, Amt für Volkswohlfahrt. An das Reichskommisariat für die sudetendeutschen Gebiete, Reichenberg, 1 April 1939, R 1501/127120, 303, BA; Zimmermann, *Sudetendeutschen im NS-Staat,* 289.

[22] Brandes, *Die Tschechen,* 1:162–63.

[23] For an overview of the requested budget and projects supported by the Volkstumsfond, see Volkstumsfond 1942, Einzelübersicht, carton 269, ÚŘP, NA. In 1942 the Protectorate was granted only 5.6 million of the requested 9 million RM. "Beauftragten der Reichskommissars für die Festigung des deutschen Volkstums," 24 October 1942, sig. I-1b 2145, 1939–45, carton 269, ÚŘP, NA.

[24] Brandes, *Die Tschechen,* 1:160, cited from *Zprávy státního úřadu statistického,* 1945, 63 ff; Reichsprotektor an Befehlshaber der Sicherheitspolizei, Inanspruchnahme des Sokolsver-mögens für deutsche Volkstumsarbeit, 11 August 1941, sig. I1b-4218, carton 269, ÚŘP, NA.

[25] Zimmerman, *Sudetendeutschen im NS-Staat,* 302; *Zpráva z domova,* 22 January 1944, and *Situační zpráva o Československu,* 8 August 1944; both in sig. 91/7, fond 37, VÚA.

occupation brought dramatic changes in the content of Czech education as well. "Elementary schools are completely run in a German spirit," a Czech informant reported to London in 1944. In Czech elementary schools in the Protectorate, students received four, then six, then eight hours of German language instruction per week. Czech curricula were overhauled to reflect Nazi ideology, promoting the notion of a German-ruled Central Europe and erasing the history of the Czechoslovak state. One Czech resistance activist remarked bitterly in 1944, "It is as if there was no history in Europe before 1933. . . . In elementary schools the main activity is the collection of trash, paper, bones, etc."[26]

Under the banner of Volkstumsarbeit the Nazis gutted the Czech educational system while erecting new German schools on the language frontier as monuments to the new regime. Sudeten German nationalists demanded new schools, kindergartens, and nurseries as a form of postcolonial reparation and revenge for the degradation they had allegedly suffered under Czech rule. The Nazis, meanwhile, eagerly turned their attention toward rehabilitating and Germanizing borderland children in the East from the alleged damage they had suffered under foreign rule. Six months after arriving in Moravský Beroun/Bärn, for example, the Reich German nurse Helen Kissek reported to a local Nazi administrator that most of the Germans she encountered "know of no baths." Their sanitary needs had been deliberately neglected by the Czechoslovak government, she claimed. Older children were particularly dirty and uncared for, and "in many cases relatively young men and women lack their upper teeth completely."[27] In 1940 a Nazi Security Service informant lamented that even the best German specimens in the Protectorate, small farmers from the so-called national island of Jihlava/Iglau in Moravia, showed signs of racial degeneration. Mixed marriages and incest were taking their toll, claimed Nazi relief workers, and the population was rapidly aging. These Volksdeutsche hardly displayed the desired nationalist fervor expected by Nazi observers. The informant lamented, "The overly conservative mentality of island Germans is expressed through their strong loyalty to the church as well as in their lack of willingness and energy for the reclamation of denationalized carriers of German blood."[28]

While the Nazi colonization project was superficially directed against the apparent sea of "Slavic disorder and lack of culture," these observations suggest that the real mission of the Reich German Nazis who performed Volkstumsarbeit was to Germanize and civilize the *Germans* in the East. The Nazi Empire thereby radicalized and racialized the very mission that

---

[26] Zpráva z domova, 2 September 1944, sig. 91/7, fond 37, VÚA; Zprávy o školských poměrech v českých zemích, 16 October 1944, sig. 91/7, fond 37, VÚA.

[27] "Bericht an den Herrn Landrat in Bärn," Bärn, 13 April 1939, R 1501127120, 239, BA.

[28] Die politische Entwicklung im Protektorat Böhmen und Mähren im Jahre 1940, SD Leitabschnitt Prag, 6, no. 50, carton 8, Sb NÚIČ, VÚA.

had inspired nationalist pedagogical reformers since the turn of the century. While Heimat activists had once labored to bridge a troubling gap between the liberal myth of the German Kulturträger in Central Europe and lamentable working-class and peasant culture and hygiene, the Nazis confronted an equally problematic contradiction between their ideology of racial superiority and the perceived physical and cultural (now understood as racial) degeneration of German speakers in the East.

Nazi propaganda compared female *Ansiedlerbetreuerinnin* (settlement caretakers) in the East to the Freikorps of the early Weimar years. This time around, however, the fight against the "Slavic hordes" began in the German home and school, where German women from the Reich taught Volksdeutsche girls to do laundry, sew, and sing German songs.[29] Not surprisingly, local Sudeten Germans did not always receive this instruction gracefully. In early 1940, for example, Czech resistance activists reported a brawl between local German women and Reich German women in the town of Frývaldov/Freiwaldau. Sudeten German women there resented that while they were mobilized for mandatory factory labor, Reich German women were assigned cozy office jobs. The Reich German women replied to the Sudeten Germans that they were all "degenerate" and didn't have the "smattering of an idea about discipline and order." These embassaries of the Third Reich explained that they had been sent to the Sudetenland to "reeducate" and civilize German locals. The conflict soon came to blows, requiring police intervention. The following day, the aggrieved Sudeten German women were sent to work in factories in Germany.[30]

Ordinary Sudeten Germans may have resented the colonizing efforts of the Third Reich but many Sudeten German administrators eagerly appropriated and reinforced Nazi images of the colonized and victimized Volksdeutsche in order to realize their own local agendas. The leaders of the three administrative regions in the Sudetenland (Troppau, Karlsbad, and Aussig) flooded officials in Berlin with petitions for new schools, nurseries, and social welfare institutions following the Nazi annexation of the Sudetenland. They insisted that these institutions were necessary to avenge the post-1918 settlement and to shore up the loyalties of the labile Zwischenschicht. In a typical appeal, Emil Beier, mayor of Opava/Troppau, petitioned the Ministry of the Interior for new German schools. These schools were necessary, he maintained, in order to reverse two decades of Czechification in the region. He reminded authorities in Berlin that "Troppau has led the Sudeten German Raum for

---

[29] Reichsfrauenführung, Schutzwehr im Osten, NS 44/62, BA. For more on the "civilizing" roles of women in German colonial movements in Weimar and Nazi Germany, see Lora Wildenthal, *German Women for Empire: 1884–1945* (Durham, NC, 2001); Nancy Reagin, "The Imagined Hausfrau: National Identity, Domesticity, and Colonialism in Imperial Germany," *Journal of Modern History* 73 (March 2001): 54–86; Harvey, *Women in the Nazi East*.
[30] Zpráva z domova, 6 February 1940, sig. 91/1, fond 37, VÚA.

centuries and has proved itself nationally and politically, above all through the fight with the Czechs."[31] Sudeten German administrators frequently invoked local histories of nationalist struggle and victimization in their appeals to the Reich, fashioning themselves as expert advisers to the Nazis based on their intimate understanding of the native terrain and history. Heimat activist Eugen Lemberg, for example, reminded Sudeten German teachers of their "special task on the national borderland" in 1939, urging them to serve the Nazi state as anthropological experts on the Czech nation and on borderland societies.[32]

If local Sudeten German officials despaired of the damage wrought by Czech colonialism on the German population, they seemed confident in the power of kindergartens to rehabilitate Germandom in the East. Hans Krebs, *Regierungspräsident* (district president) of Ústí nad Labem/Aussig, thus demanded a state-of-the-art kindergarten in order to repair the damaged pride of the German nation in the city of Podsebice/Podsebitz. "The current kindergarten is housed in a hygienically insufficient building and offers a shameful image of a German kindergarten on the language frontier," he explained. "It is therefore necessary for national and educational reasons that a new kindergarten be built precisely in this highly contested language frontier village. It cannot be forgotten that in the Czech era it is precisely in these endangered regions where the Czechs did nothing for Germandom."[33] When the Nazis complained that the Germans they encountered in the East seemed embarrassingly less civilized than their Czech-speaking neighbors, Sudeten German officials were often happy to agree and to request money to help Germanize and civilize their German constituents.

Czechs, historians have frequently noted, occupied a relatively "privileged" place in the Nazi racial hierarchy. While 50 percent of Czechs were seen as suitable for Germanization, only 3 percent of Poles and Russians were accorded this honor. These hierarchies are typically understood either as a product of Nazi ideologues and racial scientists or as a function of pragmatic economic or military calculations, such as the need to maintain high production in Czech war factories.[34] In fact, the respect accorded to Czechs by Nazi occupation officials was also clearly grounded in the local history of nationalist conflict

[31] Memorandum an das Reichs und Preußische Ministerium des Innern, from Bürgermeister der Stadt Troppau, 10 October 1938, R 1501/127120, 19, BA.

[32] Eugen Lemberg, "Erzieher und Grenzlandaufgabe," *Der sudetendeutsche Erzieher,* 1 March 1939, 105–6.

[33] Grenzlandfürsorge Sudetenland, Reg. Bezirk Aussig, 28, Anträge auf Gewährung von Beihelfen zur Pflege und Förderung des Deutschtums, 1941, R1501/127121, BA.

[34] For analysis of Nazi Ostpolitik centered around ideology, see Michael Burleigh, *Germany Turns Eastward: A Study of Ostforschung in the Third Reich* (Cambridge, 1988); Lumans, *Himmler's Auxiliaries;* Paul Weindling, *Epidemics and Genocide in Eastern Europe, 1880–1945* (Oxford, 2000); Michael Burleigh and Wolfgang Wipperman, *The Racial State: Germany 1933–1945* (Cambridge, 1991); Heinemann, *"Rasse, Siedlung, deutsches Blut."* For interpretations that privilege "pragmatics," see Connelly, "Nazis and Slavs"; Aly, *Final Solution.*

in the Bohemian Lands. As they attempted to secure Nazi investment in the educational and economic infrastructure of the occupied Bohemian Lands, Sudeten German Nazis drew on long-standing nationalist images of Czechs as worthy nationalist foes. Without more Nazi-funded kindergartens, nurseries, and schools, Sudeten German nationalists claimed, nationally indifferent and culturally backward Germans would easily succumb to the superior organization, zeal, and national discipline of the Czech nation.

These fears were now racialized, ironically supporting an image of the Czechs as worthy candidates for Germanization. In August of 1940, Deputy Reichsprotektor Karl H. Frank explained in a critical memo on the "Czech question" that thousands of years of intermarriage between Germans and Czechs had resulted in a "considerable racial equality of the two nations in the Bohemian Raum." The "strong absorbtion of German blood explains the ability of the Czech nation to realize important cultural achievements . . . to a much greater extent than, for example, the Slavic Poles."[35] Likewise, in 1940, SS anthropologist Hans Joachim Beyer concluded on the basis of a study of Czechoslovak draft records that the Czech population actually displayed more "German" traits than did Germans in the Bohemian Lands.[36] These views of Czechs as potentially valuable additions to the German nation helped to justify measures to entice nationally ambivalent Czech speakers into the Nazi Volksgemeinschaft. In doing so, the Nazi occupiers often deployed strategies that had been perfected through decades of nationalist competition for the souls of children.

Negotiating Consent in the Borderlands

Volkstumsarbeit was not only a means of compensating Volksdeutsche for their alleged victimization by the Czechoslovak government. It also served as a pragmatic form of coalition building, a strategy for maintaining the consent and cooperation of German citizens in the Sudetenland and Protectorate. Nazi administrators deliberately harnessed and adapted traditional forms of German nationalist activism to achieve these goals. The regime's claims on children became increasingly important as the Nazis faced the embarrassing reluctance of many German parents in occupied Czechoslovakia to register as German citizens.

As early as August of 1939 officials began to complain about the lethargic support of the Volksdeutsche. Local Nazi administrators, who were charged

---

[35] Karl H. Frank, Denkschrift über die Behandlung des Tschechenproblem und die zukünftige Gestaltung des böhmisch-mährischen Raumes. Prague, 28 August 1940, 2–3, carton 1, Sb NÚIČ, VÚA.

[36] Chad Bryant, "Either German or Czech: Fixing Nationality in Bohemia and Moravia, 1939–1946," *Slavic Review* 61 (Winter 2002): 693.

with explaining this indifference to their superiors in Berlin, quickly pointed their fingers at Czech nationalists. The Office of the Reichsprotektor lamented, "To a great extent the Germans hold back with their registrations, and are apparently openly influenced by the harassment of the Czech population."[37] Even Germans who registered their nationality frustrated officials by refusing to show their German identification cards on demand, not least because they (correctly) suspected they might be drafted into the Wehrmacht. Nazi officials fumed that fully one-sixth of the German population in Brno/Brünn had not been "secured" for Germandom by March of 1940, while the number of delinquent Germans reportedly reached one-third in Zlín/Zlin. After the war, a Sudeten German statistician estimated that one-fourth of all Volksdeutsche in the Protectorate had neglected to register for German citizenship by the fall of 1940.[38]

The refusal of many German speakers to declare themselves German provoked great bitterness among Nazi authorities. Exasperated officials in the Office of the Reichsprotektor echoed the frustration of Austrian and Czechoslovak nationalists with nationally indifferent parents, fuming, "It is indeed the legal situation that every Volksdeutsche will become a citizen of the German Reich, no matter what his personal opinion of the matter." Schools promised to eliminate these conflicts between Nazi officials and nationally indifferent or disloyal parents. "Through the proven work of National Socialist education there is no doubt that the offspring of today's indecisive, madly behaving Volksdeutsche will become the most valuable members of the German citizenry," Protectorate officials reassured themselves.[39] The only realm in which administrators consistently reported progress in terms of bolstering popular support was in the development of Nazi social services for children. The NSV had been a boon to Nazi authorities from the very first days of the occupation, when NSV units and the charity train "Bayern" followed soldiers during the invasion to distribute meals. The Sudetenland was so saturated with provisions that Erich Hilgenfeldt, the local chief of the NSV, requested in early October 1938 that the Reich stop the relief effort in the Sudetenland. Henlein claimed a year later that the NSV had provided 41 million RM worth of assistance in the first twenty-five days of the occupation alone.[40] In Podmokly/Bodenbach, an impoverished Northern Bohemian industrial town, one German expellee who worked in the city government reported that the number of recipients of welfare support in his city increased from 296 in October of 1938 to 517 in December

---

[37] Generalreferat für politische Angelegenheiten, Prague, 12 August 1939, carton 520, ÚŘP, NA.

[38] Bryant, "Either German or Czech," 688.

[39] Generalreferat für politische Angelegenheiten, Prague, 12 August 1939, carton 520, ÚŘP, NA.

[40] Zimmerman, *Sudetendeutschen im NS-Staat,* 76.

of 1939, while the amount distributed also increased from 3,071 RM to 9,885 RM per month.[41]

Memoirs of Sudeten Germans confirm that the NSV provided a positive image for the Nazi regime in the early years after the annexation. One expellee recalled that in Jihlava/Iglau, "day-care centers were welcomed by the population of the language islands. They were all new and clean and provided real relief for women who so often took over the work of their husbands during the war."[42] Contemporary reports from Nazi informants also confirmed the popularity of NSV programs among Germans in the occupied Bohemian Lands. "A positive national-political development can only be numerically confirmed in the realm of German education, and especially through the NSV. Its activity through kindergartens, nurseries for mother and child, social work, and the admirable use of Reich German nurses is universally applauded, and the NSV in Olmütz is the strongest of the Nazi organizations," boasted a 1940 SD report.[43] Nazi informants also praised the work of the NSV in borderland regions, where they claimed that Nazi welfare programs immediately made a "strong impression" among Germans and "doubtlessly contributed a great deal to winning these people for Germandom."[44]

While invoking local Czech domination to explain flagging applications for German citizenship, officials also emphasized the importance of "meeting German expectations" in the Bohemian Lands through appropriate investments in schools and children's welfare. In spite of prevailing discourses about Sudeten German and Volksdeutsche "backwardness," the Nazis were actually hard-pressed to maintain the high educational standards developed through fifty years of nationalist pedagogical activism in the Bohemian Lands. In 1939 the Security Service warned, "In building the school system, the current standards will have to be maintained, or the most serious disappointments will develop, especially among the labile Zwischenschicht."[45] These demands reveal the slippery boundaries between providing restitution for alleged suffering under Czech colonialism and a policy of actively enticing members of the "labile Zwischenschicht" into the German nation. New kindergartens, for example, would serve not only to compensate Germans

[41] Ost Doc. 20/17, Richard Rolf, Bodenbach, October 1958, 36, BB.

[42] Ost Doc. 20/66, Iglau und der Iglauer Sprachinsel, 1918–45, 25, BB.

[43] Heinz Boberach, ed., *Meldungen aus dem Reich, die geheimen Lageberichte des Sicherheitsdienst der SS* (Pawlak, 1984), no. 146, 2 December 1940, Lage des Olmützer und Mährisch Ostrauer Deutschtums, 1828.

[44] Die politische Entwicklung in Protektorate Böhmen und Mähren seit 15. März 1939, SD Leitabschnitt Prag, 15 March 1940, carton 7, VÚA, Sb NÚIČ.

[45] Reichminister des Innern No. VI d 2504/39 Berlin, 14 April 1939, R 1501/127120, 235, BA. See also Theo Keil, ed. *Die deutsche Schule in den Sudetenländern* (Munich, 1967), 113. In particular, the average class size in German schools in the Bohemian Lands (thirty-four children) was smaller than that in most Reich German schools. Sudeten Germans also claimed that their schools had lower dropout rates, were better equipped with kitchens and gardens, and had better-trained teachers.

for past suffering but also to "firmly win children over to Germandom early on," maintained officials in Šternberk/Sternberg.[46]

The Nazis also attempted to secure the loyalties of the liberated Germans by harnessing other traditional forms of mass nationalist politics to the Nazi state. In 1940, in response to a claimed spike in Czech resistance, the RKfDV ordered Künzel's Borderland Office in the Sudetenland to re-invent popular Sudeten German nationalist associations such as the Bund der Deutschen and German Kulturverband under the banner of a new SS-controlled Bund der Osten. The Bund der Osten enabled the Nazis to mobilize Germans in the Bohemian Lands through familiar forms of associational activity. Reports from the RKfDV declared the association a resounding success: "The population of the Gau saw in the Bund der Osten the successor to their old protective associations and happily offered their services." The reactivated Nazi Bund der Osten and Volksbund für das Deutschtum in Ausland (Association for Germans Abroad) collected 550,000 RM in donations from its members in the Gau Sudetenland in 1942 and 705,930 RM in school collections in 1941, more than in any other area of the Reich.[47] A well-established tradition of women's activism in nationalist voluntary associations in the Bohemian Lands also served the Nazis well. Under the direction of former German Kulturverband leader Isabella Pompe, the National Socialist Women's League enrolled a greater percentage of German women in the Sudetenland than in any other district in the Third Reich.[48]

Sudeten Germans seemed to respond most enthusiastically to the Nazi call to arms when the Nazis appropriated local forms of nationalist politics. They welcomed Nazi initiatives that strengthened the nation's claims on children through social welfare programs, new schools, and mobilization against alleged Czechification. There is considerable debate over the role of Sudeten Germans within the Nazi State. The question has been highly politicized, given expellees' later claims that they enjoyed no real authority in the Nazi administration or responsibility for Nazi atrocities—that they, too, were victims of a foreign occupation. Such claims have been overwhelmingly discredited by ample evidence of Sudeten German participation in and enthusiasm for the regime, even if many local Sudeten German interests ultimately took a backseat to Nazi war aims.[49] It is nonetheless helpful to our understanding of Nazi Ostpolitik and the dynamics of occupation to

[46] Der Landrat Sternberg an den Herrn Regierungspräsident in Troppau, 6 June 1939, R 1501/127120, 281–83, BA.

[47] Reichskommissar für die Festigung deutschen Volkstums, Berichte des Ansiedlungsstabes für September 1942–43, 2 October 1943, R 49/3541, BA.

[48] Stanislav Biman, "Podíl sudetských Němců na správě říšské župy Sudety," in *Historie okupovaného pohraničí*, vol. 6 (Ústí nad Labem, 2000).

[49] Ralf Gebel maintains that while Sudeten Germans participated in the regime in considerable numbers, their political and economic interests were ultimately overruled by those of the Reich. Gebel provides a useful statistical account of the percentage of Sudeten Germans in

retain a sense of the diverse interests and identities of Reich Germans and Volksdeutsche Nazis. Making such distinctions does not excuse Germans in the East from their responsibility for Nazi violence but rather helps us to understand the terms on which accommodation to the Nazi regime was negotiated and secured. Many Sudeten Germans eagerly participated in the Nazi administration in the Bohemian Lands, especially in the realms of educational and social activism, and many more were committed Nazis. Equally important and less understood, however, is the degree to which Nazism itself became "Bohemianized" in the occupied East. Nazis and Sudeten German nationalists used each other under the occupation to achieve ideological and social goals that were parallel but not always identical.

From National Ascription to Racial Classification

The mission to "secure" the nationally ambivalent Zwischenschicht in the Bohemian Lands necessarily began well before Heydrich's assent to power, with the Third Reich's earliest attempts to define Germanness itself. Nationality was the basis for citizenship in the Nazi state, determining labor and service obligations, the amount of fat one ate, school attendance, and marital privileges. It was therefore an ideological and administrative priority for the regime that Germans and Czechs be easily identified and distinguished. This task, never simple on the language frontiers of the Bohemian Lands, became even more complicated after 1939. As American diplomat George Kennan noted of one Bohemian town shortly after the invasion, "It became difficult to tell where the Czech left off and the German began."[50] Officials were frequently forced to rely on long-standing civic definitions of Germanness that had been promoted by German nationalists since the late nineteenth century in order to implement new policies of racial classification. In March of 1939, shortly after the occupation of the Protectorate, Karl Frank specified, "A German national is one who himself professes to the German nation, as long as this conviction is confirmed by certain facts, such as language, education, culture, etc. Persons of alien blood, particularly Jews, are never Germans. . . . Because professing to be a member of the German nation is of vital significance, even someone who is partly or completely of another race—Czech, Slovak, Ukrainian, Hungarian, or Polish, for example—can be considered a German. . . . Any more precise elaboration of the term 'German national' is not possible given current relationships."[51]

Henlein's governor's office and in the provincial Landratsämter, estimating that about 50 percent were Sudeten Germans. Gebel, *Heim ins Reich*, 217–18.

[50] Cited in King, *Budweisers into Czechs and Germans*, 176.

[51] Ie 5062 IV-39, Der Reichsminister des Innern, Berlin, 29 March 1939, carton 520, ÚŘP, NA.

Under Nazi rule, this "civic" understanding of the nation ironically kept the door open to Czech-speaking converts to Nazism in the Bohemian Lands. Local Nazi officials were instructed to seek "proof" of Germanness in candidates' political and moral outlook, to decide whether or not each potential German represented a "desirable addition to the population," on the basis of his or her race, "total character," and above all, loyalty to Nazism.[52] This confused understanding of Germanness grew out of the encounter between Nazi racial ideology and native conceptions of nationhood in the Bohemian Lands. Local Sudeten German officials did not reject Nazi racism; they rather relied on their own cultural or political understandings of Germanness to put Nazi racial policy into practice. Reich German Nazis were sometimes even more eager to include Czech speakers in the Nazi Volksgemeinschaft than local Sudeten German nationalists, especially for the sake of securing their children for Germandom. Hans Kaiser recalled that in his town of Suché Vrbné/Dürnfellen near Budějovice/Budweis, many so-called Also-Germans (*Auch-Deutschen*) registered for German organizations after the invasion of the Protectorate. Such individuals, he claimed, "had for many years been active as Czechs and now became '150 percent Nazi.' The old native Germans, who had of course maintained their Germanness under the most difficult hardships and tribulations, could not understand this. . . . But the order came from above not to hold it against anyone, to accept everyone, it is about the children."[53]

These guidelines created awkward situations in the Protectorate's new German schools. The local head administrator (Oberlandrat) in Budějovice/Budweis, for example, reported in 1941, "The children currently attending school have in no way become competent in the German language, given the pressures of the political relationships and the Czech surroundings. In countless cases, the Czech language is at the fore even in their parents' homes, and is even used by some parents in the ostensible interests of their children." These children, assured the Oberlandrat, were nevertheless good Germans, since, "in spite of their lack of German language abilities they make a very good racial and behavioral impression, and to the extent that it is possible among children, they feel German."[54]

On the basis of this circular logic the first decisive regulations on admitting Czech children to German schools were passed by the Reichsprotektor in June of 1940. Von Neurath ruled that Czech-speaking children should be admitted into German schools only to the extent that they would not threaten the German character" of the classroom. Hence Czech-speaking children should make up no more than 25 percent of the students in a classroom (a

[52] Ie 5062 IV-39, Der Reichsminister des Innern, Berlin, 29 March 1939, carton 520, ÚŘP, NA.

[53] Ost Doc. 20/64, Hans Kaiser, Dürnfellen, 17 November 1958, 6, BB.

[54] Der Oberlandrat für die Bezirk Budweis an den Herrn Reichsprotektor in Böhmen und Mähren, 2 August 1940, carton 508, ÚŘP, NA.

rule that was repeatedly violated, judging from Nazi informants' reports). The regulations further specified that "decisive for enrollment is the position of the parents [regarding] current political relationships." The first Czech-speaking children accepted (indeed, required) to attend German schools were the children of mixed marriages, followed by children from families that were "certainly counted as members of the Czech nation, but were however German in previous generations and only Czechified over the course of time." Last in line were "children from pure Czech families." School authorities were given no guidelines with which to distinguish between children in the second and third categories, between "Czechified" Germans and "Germanizable" Czechs.[55]

The ordinance was followed by a list of criteria for the racial assessment and classification of Czech students. Those children placed in the "purely Czech" category were questioned about their previous disciplinary record in school, current and previous views of the parents on the German nation and National Socialism, the type and strength of the parents' national consciousness ("nationally conscious, nationally weak, or nationally unaware") as well as the parents' social and cultural position, professional achievements, and economic and property relationships.[56] Those who answered these questions to the satisfaction of local German school officials were classified as Germanizable and admitted to the German school. Another decree specified more precisely the qualities that differentiated racially worthy from unworthy Czechs. Slavic Czechs (as opposed to Czechified Germans) displayed "a disorderly, careless family life with a complete lack of feeling for order, personal and domestic cleanliness," as well as "lack of any ambition to advance oneself." Moral behavior, political behavior, and the "achievements of the individual" all weighed heavily alongside claims to have German blood or ancestry.[57]

Nazi officials also used welfare payments from the Volkstumsfond and Borderland Relief Funds to secure potential German children, indirectly giving the category of the Zwischenschicht new purchase. In interwar Czechoslovakia parents had already learned to deploy a language of national rights and national victimization in order to obtain welfare assistance. Nazi welfare grants offered citizens new financial incentives to narrate their stories in nationalist and Nazi terms. The most successful requests came from parents who claimed to have raised their children to be good nationalist Germans in spite of (claimed) overwhelming pressures to become Czech. One such appeal was made in Budějovice/Budweis by Irene Jeschuta, who was deemed needy and worthy of 150 RM by the Reichsprotektor. The Oberlandrat approved the grant since "we are concerned here with a woman who is always ready to serve her nation, who raised the children in her care to be upstanding Germans

---

[55] Aufnahme tschechisch sprechender Kinder in deutsche Schulen, Prague, 28 June 1940, carton 295, ÚŘP, NA.
[56] Merkblatt für die Begutachtung von Vorhaben eines Besuchs deutscher Schulen durch tschechische Volkszugehörige, carton 295, ÚŘP, NA.
[57] Kárný et al., *Deutsche Politik*, 105.

in spite of all Czech pressures."[58] Olga Střeka likewise had been forced after the death of her Czech husband in 1928 to move with her four children to Plevnice/Plewnitz, where "she raised her children to be upstanding Germans in purely Czech surroundings, in spite of the most bitter poverty, without ever succumbing to the influences of Czechdom."[59] Keeping one's children German in interwar Czechoslovakia was now recognized as a valuable service to the Volksgemeinschaft, and she was rewarded with 400 RM. It was one thing to reward deserving families who preserved their children for the German nation, but what if those parents were Czechs? Josef Stanek, father of three, requested a grant from the Volkstumsfond to support his family in Olomouc/Olmütz. The security police chief in the city recommended approving the grant, even though Stanek's father was Czech and Stanek himself had attended Czech schools for several years. Authorities saw in Stanek (and his children) good potential members of the Volksgemeinschaft and a chance to secure his loyalty to the regime through the Volkstumsfond: "Politically Stanek has not yet come out, but he sympathizes with Germandom. The Race and Settlement Main Office has determined that he and his family are Germanizable."[60]

In another case, the family of Heinrich Tousek requested permission from the Office of the Protectorate to move from the Protectorate to the Sudetengau, ostensibly on account of his economic victimization at the hands of the local Czech population. Unfortunately for Tousek, a local investigation revealed that while he and his wife were of "German origins," he had also been an active member of a Czech building cooperative and the secretary of the local branch of the Czech Provincial Commission for Child Welfare in Znojmo/Znaim. The report elaborated, "In spite of his German origins [Tousek's] activity was directed to the fullest extent against Germandom, as is proven by the fact that he not only raised his three children to be members of the Czech nation, but was forced to leave the Sudeten German area of Znaim when it was occupied."[61] Tousek had apparently been driven out of the Sudetenland into the Protectorate along with many other Czechs after the annexation and now hoped to return as a German. His appeal was rejected. In these individual cases, administrators' primary concern was securing the loyalties of children, and so applicants with school-age children were at a considerable advantage. Tousek's file indicates that had his children still been in school, his request would have been granted.

It was children of the Zwischenschicht who attracted the attention and sympathies of these Nazi officials. Appeals by Germans to move to the Sude-

---

[58] Irene Jeschuta, Gewährung eine einmalige Beihilfe aus Volkstumsmittel, 25 September 1942, carton 269, ÚŘP, NA.

[59] Olga Střeka, Unterstützung aus Volkstumsmitteln, 22 September 1942, carton 269, ÚŘP, NA.

[60] Letters from Josef Stanek, Olmütz, 26 September 1942, and Befehlshaber der Sicherheitspolizei, 20 November 1942, carton 269, ÚŘP, NA.

[61] Übersiedlung des Offizials Heinrich Tousek von Brünn nach Znaim, 28 May 1941, carton 292, ÚŘP, NA.

tenland from the Protectorate were authorized only for "those families who had not been able to reveal their Germanness under the Czech republic and who once again profess the German nationality," Nazi regulations stipulated. "It is well known that in these families the older children, especially those between 15 and 20 years of age, are frequently completely incapable of speaking German."[62] The cases of Střeka, Stanek, and Tousek merit further consideration. While it is impossible to know for certain, these individuals may well have declared themselves members of the Czech nation in interwar Czechoslovakia. Were they actually Germanized by the Nazis, as the Nazis themselves or Czech nationalists might have argued? Or did they simply choose Nazism?

Germanizing Nazis and Nazifying Germans

Tousek and Stanek were hardly alone in the Bohemian Lands. Everywhere Nazi authorities turned, they found insufficiently "Nazified" Sudeten Germans and insufficiently "German" Nazis. A 1943 report to Himmler from Ernst Müller, leader of the RKfDV in Moravian Fulnek (and himself a Sudeten German), estimated, "The German national body in the Sudetenland has taken a nationally unstable class of questionable worth of about 100,000 people, for whom a great deal of educational work, social welfare and care had to and must still be undertaken, in order that they be made and remain reliable and fully useful."[63] In the Protectorate, meanwhile, the number of registered Germans increased from 189,000 in March of 1940 to 245,000 in October of the same year. While many of these new Germans were Reich German transplants, the number of individuals registering as Germans clearly increased dramatically with the German army's victory over France in the spring of 1940.[64] Nazi officials soon developed anxieties and suspicion toward new Germans who appeared to be *overly* opportunistic. This suspicion reflected ongoing dissent within the administration about the meaning of Germanness and qualifications for Germanization. Local authorities were left considerable discretion to register German citizens, enroll students in schools, and recruit members to the Hitler Youth as they saw fit. For instance, in November of 1940 local Oberlandräte in the Protectorate awarded German citizenship to 81 percent of applicants. The Oberlandrat in Jihlava/Iglau, however, accepted 98 percent of applicants, while the more discriminating Nazi officials in Pardubice/Pardubitz accepted only 47 percent of candidates for the Volksgemeinschaft.[65]

---

[62] Abwanderung von Deutschen Volksangehörigen nach dem übrigen Reichsgebiet, 8 August 1940, carton 292, ÚŘP, NA.
[63] RKfDV, Berichte des Ansiedlungsstabes für September 1942–43, 2 October 1943, R 49/3541, BA.
[64] Die politische Entwicklung im Protektorat Böhmen und Mähren im Jahre 1940, SD Leitabschnitt Prag. no. 50, carton 8, Sb NÚIČ, VÚA.
[65] Bryant, *Prague in Black,* 74.

These local authorities developed varied and competing understandings of what made a good German. Some Sudeten German administrators, for example, racialized old Austrian and Sudeten German discourses that emphasized the fearsome national discipline and superior cultural quality of Czechs. The political "fanaticism" of Czech nationalists, even if directed against Germandom, was now cited as evidence of superior racial quality. In this view, the most dangerous former enemies of the German nation were potentially the most valuable recruits to the Nazi Volksgemeinschaft. Gustav Adolf Schulte-Schomberg, leader of the party Liaison Office (*Verbindungstelle*) in the Office of the Reichsprotektor, wrote a letter to Heydrich in March of 1942 asking him to resolve a long-standing conflict between himself and Franz Künzel, head of the Borderland Office in Liberec/Reichenberg.[66] In defense of what he saw as purely "racial" criteria he argued, "I myself am of the opinion that the child of one of the fanatical Czechs from the past 20 years is more valuable for Germanization than any of the characterless lumps who changed his viewpoint from one day to the next."[67] Officials in Liberec/Reichenberg, meanwhile, made their decisions solely on the basis of Nazi political convictions, a policy fairly generous toward the "characterless lumps" despised by Schulte-Schomberg. Künzel placed the greatest emphasis on "political behavior before annexation to the Reich" and opposed forcible Germanization. In fact, however, both officials used the term "race" to stand in for political values. Schulte-Schomberg merely disagreed with Künzel about the nature of the desirable convictions, insisting that Czech nationalist chauvinism was a better indicator of underlying racial worth than superficial loyalty to Nazi values. Heydrich responded in favor of the criteria favored by the SS, and Künzel was replaced by the Sudeten German SS member Ernst Müller in 1942.[68]

Yet this was far from the final word on the subject. Given the fundamental—and inevitable—lack of clarity about the meaning of race, local differences and disagreements persisted. While Nazi frustration with opportunism among so-called new Germans might seem to reflect the consistency and dogmatism of the regime's racial ideology, suspicion of opportunists actually reflected rivalries within the regime. These discussions about the suspect loyalties of the Zwischenschicht constituted an internal debate about where and how to set the boundaries of the Nazi Volksgemeinschaft. By early 1941, frustration with so-called new Germans was mounting among Nazi officials. Authorities in Tábor/Tabor reported that about sixty to eighty new Germans registered each month, lamenting, "Those registering were led by

---

[66] For more on Künzel's views of Germanization and this conflict, see Gebel, *Heim ins Reich*, 298–305.

[67] Letter from Gustav Adolf Schulte-Schomberg to Heydrich, 11 March 1942, in Kárný et al., *Deutsche Politik*, 242–44.

[68] Gebel, *Heim ins Reich*, 299–301.

various motives. To a large extent we are dealing with an opportunistic element, which is striving to attain German citizenship for the sake of better social welfare benefits."[69] A report from February 1941, meanwhile, noted that there were far too many applications from individuals who "only hope a criminal or civil penalty will be lifted, or hope to make claims on German institutions for social assistance for their children. . . . It can rightly and justifiably be claimed that this part of the population is truly the worst of Czechdom."[70] In Prague, Nazi informants lamented that following the defeat of France, many "undesirable elements" with ambiguous national loyalties had registered as Germans. "We are concerned with members of the national Zwischenschicht or full Czechs, who want to enjoy benefits from the NSV."[71]

Anxieties about opportunistic Czechs were especially pronounced in the school system. German students who didn't speak German were a constant thorn in officials' sides. In 1940 Reichsprotector von Neurath wrote that he was disturbed by reports that students in German schools frequently spoke Czech among themselves. "We are concerned with children from families who were included in the German nation after 15 March 1939, although they previously, for whatever reason, stood on other ground," he elaborated. Children were soon forbidden to speak Czech in German schools, and officials urged "new" German parents to refrain from speaking Czech at home as well. The Protectorate government finally ordered that German language tests be administered to all schoolchildren who had enrolled in German schools after March of 1939. Students who didn't devote sufficient effort to learning German or continued to "carelessly" speak Czech in spite of the rules would now "have to reckon with the consequences of their noncompliance." Nazi political convictions, of course, could still earn a child leniency. The order specified, "In these examinations the school leader should lay the decisive weight on whether the student, through his diligence and his overall behavior, has shown a serious determination to assimilate into the German nation."[72] The Office of the Reichsprotektor claimed that the regime had generously allowed families of ambiguous national origins to join the Nazi Volksgemeinschaft so that their children could become productive Germans. These families, unfortunately, sometimes lacked awareness of their obligations to their new national community. "This offer from the German side must not be misused," warned the memo. "There is no place in the German Volksgemeinschaft

---

[69] *Meldungen aus dem Reich*, no. 194, 16 June 1941.

[70] Verwaltungsbericht für die Zeit vom 24.1 bis 23.2 1941, 25 February 1941, carton 295, ÚŘP, NA.

[71] Die politische Entwicklung in Protektorate Böhmen und Mähren, June 1940, SD Leitabschnitt Prag, 1 July 1940, 16, carton 7, Sb NÚIČ, VÚA. See also *Meldungen aus dem Reich*, no. 205, 24 July 1941, 2566.

[72] Nr. EIU 118/40, Abschrift, Der Reichsprotektor Böhmen und Mähren, Prague, 1 May 1940, carton 508, ÚŘP, NA.

for a youth who only wants to use the German school in order to later find greater economic advancement, who in general remains unstable in his inclinations and doesn't break off this bridge to Czechdom."[73]

These disciplinary measures brought little relief to frustrated Nazi officials. In 1941 the work of the Hitler Youth was still hindered by the fact that the majority of its members in the Protectorate spoke no German, according to the SD. In the Hitler Youth in Prerau, for example, 80 percent of the members reportedly spoke Czech, and the leader there was often forced to give commands in Czech out of necessity. The Hitler Youth in Bat'ha/Bata were also composed mostly of children of mixed marriages who spoke only Czech.[74] Meanwhile, in the German schools in Tábor/Tabor in 1941, authorities proudly boasted that very soon 40 percent of the pupils in German schools would be able to speak German.[75]

The racial populism within the Reich, whereby belonging to the German race was supposed to guarantee some kind of "equality" within the Volksgemeinschaft, simply did not map cleanly onto the occupied East.[76] In occupied Poland, newly registered Volksdeutsche were classified into four categories. At the top of the hierarchy stood Germans who were active in the nationality struggle. "Outside belonging to a German organization, actively engaged denotes any other conscious intervention for the Germans against a foreign race," the decree specified.[77] Next came Germans who had not actively fought for Germandom but had clearly retained their cultural Germanness. The third category consisted of children of mixed marriages, alongside Poles who might once have been German. Finally, there were the traitors, Germans who had become "politically" Polish.[78] If these distinctions were not codified in the Protectorate, it was nonetheless clear to officials in the Bohemian Lands that some Germans were more German than others and that Germanness was most easily read through loyalty to Nazi ideals. Once again, it was national indifference and ambiguity, rather than the clarity of national fault lines, that drove debates over Germanization and citizenship in the occupied East. Nazis, like earlier nationalists in Austria and Czechoslovakia, claimed to be locked in a bitter struggle with

[73] Ibid.

[74] *Meldungen aus dem Reich,* no. 180, 22 April 1941.

[75] Ibid., no. 152, 9 January 1941.

[76] For more on the "populist" dimensions of Nazi racism see David Schoenbaum, *Hitler's Social Revolution: Class and Status in Nazi Germany, 1933–1939* (Garden City, NJ, 1966); Burleigh and Wipperman, *The Racial State;* Robert Gellately, *Backing Hitler: Consent and Coercion in Nazi Germany* (Oxford, 2001).

[77] Doris Bergen has described how this provision acted as an incentive to anti-Semitic violence in the occupied East: questionable candidates for Germandom could "prove" their Germanness through attacks on Jews. Doris Bergen, "The Nazi Concept of Volksdeutsche and the Exacerbation of Anti-Semitism in Eastern Europe," *Journal of Contemporary History* 29 (October 1994): 569–82.

[78] Abschrift der Reichsführer SS, RKfDV, Erlass über die Überprufung der Bevölkerung in den Eingegliederten Ostgebieten. Berlin, 12 September 1940, carton 520, ÚŘP, NA.

the national enemy. In fact, their real struggle was against the perceived scourge of national indifference, opportunism, and side switching, phenomena that showed no signs of abating in Nazi-occupied Czechoslovakia (and that were encouraged by the Nazis' own welfare policies).

Nazi anxieties about Czech "opportunism" also suggest the extent to which attempts to Germanize self-identified Czechs resulted mostly in disappointment for the Nazi occupiers. In 1942, Hans von Watter, Oberlandrat in Prague, lamented the failure of Nazi Volkstumsarbeit to transform the identities of the new Germans. "It is clear to me that to a large degree these German citizens still feel attached to Czech cultural circles, and without resettlement in the German language area they simply cannot be educated to be valuable National Socialists," he concluded.[79] From the exasperated criticism of local officials and government informants over insufficiently Nazified Germans and insufficiently German Nazis, we might conclude that many families in the Bohemian Lands may have maintained a German identity without becoming self-identified Nazis. At the same time, many bilingual or nationally ambivalent families seem to have accepted Nazism without significantly altering their cultural or linguistic practices or identities. They Nazified without becoming Germans. Race and conduct ultimately offered two different paths into the Nazi Volksgemeinschaft.

Lex Perek Avenged

Frustration with reluctant Volksdeutsche and opportunist Czechs gradually led the Nazi occupiers to make more coercive claims on children. Through fifty years of nationalist educational and social activism, Czech and German nationalists had gradually redefined parental rights and duties in the Bohemian Lands. The Nazis built on these native nationalist understandings of family and parental obligations. German parents enjoyed, under Nazism, a right to a nationalist education and the right to certain social services, also provided by the nation to its clients. Parental duties to the nation were meanwhile redefined as duties to the Third Reich. Sudeten German Nazis acted on these understandings of parental rights and duties as they began to set up boarding schools for the children of the so-called *Streudeutsche* families in the Protectorate, families that did not live in a predominantly German community.

These schools built on traditional Sudeten German fears about the malleable identities of children and their accompanying distrust of parental loyalties. A November 1940 report from the Oberlandrat in Olomouc/Olmütz

---

[79] Aus der Niederschrift des Prager Oberlandrates Dr. Hans von Watter über die Stellung und Stärke des Deutschtums in Prag zu Beginn des Jahres 1942, reprinted in Kárný et al., *Deutsche Politik*, doc. 67, 209.

concluded that only boarding schools would "enable a lasting influence in the German educational spirit outside of school hours. Through a greater support network the student can interact in German circles in his free time, and so grow up into the German nation."[80] Like the nationalist orphanages of the Habsburg Monarchy and Czechoslovakia, such institutions were to provide children with an immersion in Germanness, now defined exclusively as adherence to Nazism. Only now the plans were more ambitious in that the children claimed by the Nazis were not only orphans but sometimes forcibly separated from their parents. In the spring of 1941 local officials in Pilsen drew up a list of sixty-six allegedly German children in the Protectorate who still had not been enrolled in German schools.[81] In the tradition of Lex Perek, thirteen such children were reclaimed for German schools in Jičin/Jitschin in 1941–42.[82] Nazi law was clear: German parents and children had a right to German schools, but German schools and the German nation also had a right to German children. Interestingly, not all Nazi officials applauded these reclamations, particularly in Moravia. One administrator from Brno/Brünn criticized the Nazis' forced reclamation policy in 1941, with explicit reference to the Lex Perek:

> Similar regulations, which stem from the time of the so-called Moravian Compromise of 1905 and are based on nationality rather than citizenship, are still formally in effect in Moravia (the so-called Lex Perek), but are however not put to use by German school inspectors. . . . Such a one-sided regulation deliberately undermines current political thought. . . . Through the good, and the legitimacy that they achieve, through the increased status of the German citizenry in the Protectorate, German schools must and will naturally develop an ever stronger power to attract pupils. It must be the task of the Party and cannot be handed over to a legal mechanism to win over and strengthen the loyalty to German schools of all those circles determined to be German.[83]

His opinion was overruled. In December of 1940 the Office of the Reichsprotektor had already declared that German children were required to attend a boarding school if there was no German school in the vicinity of their homes, whether or not their parents were enthusiastic about the idea. "Membership in the German nation brings with it not only rights, but duties, of which the parents must occasionally be reminded," the memo explained. The order clearly specified that the mere sentimental attachment of parents to their children could not override the nation's preeminent claim

---

[80] Schulwesen im Oberlandbezirk Olmütz, I 1b- 2573, carton 508, ÚŘP, NA.

[81] Der Oberlandrat in Pilsen, Abschrift an den Herrn Reichsprotektor und Böhmen und Mähren, 16 June 1941, carton 508, ÚŘP, NA.

[82] No. 7-1-1-0, Besuch tschechischer Schulen durch Kinder von Eltern deutscher Volkszugehörigkeit, 20 June 1942, carton 508, ÚŘP, NA.

[83] I1b- 3881, Prague, June, 1941. Carton 292, ÚŘP, NA.

on youth, insisting, "In no case can a child be sent to a Czech school by his Volksdeutsche parents because the parents don't want to be separated from the child through enrollment in a boarding school, or because they don't find the designated schools . . . to be good enough for their child."[84]

The Oberlandrat in Pardubice/Pardubitz began petitioning early and actively for a Nazi boarding school in his own district. In November of 1939 he appealed to the Office of the Reichsprotektor, "The danger of Czechification of German children is extraordinarily large. Among these children we are especially concerned with the children of large, racially healthy families and the children of small farmers and farm workers."[85] Two years later his requests were granted, and a new school was erected in a former Czech military building. The school was located in the predominantly Czech town of Chrudím/Chrudim, could accommodate up to two hundred children, and was advertised to parents with a glossy catalog, beginning with the proclamation, "While German youth here once had to attend Czech schools, it is now the will of our Führer Adolf Hitler and of the state President Emil Hácha that the old wish finally become a reality, that German children have to attend German schools and Czech children Czech schools."[86]

Once again the occupying regime depicted Nazi educational policy as a triumphant realization of old nationalist visions from the Austrian Empire and interwar period. The pamphlet emphasized the modern technology the school offered, the impeccable hygiene of its facilities, the high quality of the teachers, and the beauty of the grounds and surrounding areas. Pictures of sunny classrooms, athletic fields, fruit trees, and modern kitchen facilities were designed to entice the skeptical parent. Only in closing did authorities discreetly acknowledge that some parents might be reluctant to entrust their offspring to a Nazi boarding school. Parents were reassured, "It goes without saying that children will not be estranged from their parents [at Chrudim]. Although it may be difficult for some parents not to be able to see their boys and girls every day, in exchange they will feel all the happier that their children will grow up to be true Germans, and will fulfill the holy duty of youth to be an eternal source of power for the nation."[87]

These institutions aimed to force the children of insufficiently Nazified Germans and insufficiently Germanized Nazis into ideological conformity. Soon after his appointment, Heydrich hatched even more radical plans to Germanize self-identified Czechs and their children. In October of 1941 he ordered guardian courts and social service agencies throughout the Reich to intervene "in every case, and with every means available to them . . . if the German

---

[84] An die Gruppe I 1 im Hause, Gr. Unterricht und Kultus, Prague, 3 December 1940, carton 508, ÚŘP, NA.

[85] Oberlandrat in Pardubitz an den Herrn Reichsprotektor in Böhmen und Mähren, Gruppe Volkspolitik, 9 August 1939, carton 508, ÚŘP, NA.

[86] "An alle Eltern deutscher Kinder!" Oberlandrat in Pardubitz, carton 508, ÚŘP, NA.

[87] Ibid.

education of German youth is endangered by the influence of Czechdom." In practical terms this meant that if a child was born to a German father and unwed Czech mother, or to a mixed couple in which the family refused German education, local social workers were empowered to accuse the Czech parent of "abusing parental power" and to assume guardianship of the child such that the "Czech influence is fully shut out." Heydrich's office further instructed the courts that in custody disputes, German interests alone were decisive. Decisions should be made "to keep German-blooded or partly German-blooded children for Germandom, and to raise them with a strong national consciousness. The personal interest of the Czech parent is completely irrelevant."[88]

The short-lived campaign to forcibly Germanize Czech children reached a dystopian climax after the assassination of Heydrich in May of 1942. Unlike most of the other Germanization policies pursued during the war, these measures were not designed to entice the Zwischenschicht into the Volksgemeinschaft but rather to humiliate and terrorize the Czech population into submission. On the morning of May 21, 1942, Heydrich was attacked in Prague by Czech partisans and died a few days later. In retaliation, on June 10, 1942, Nazis rounded up all the men in the small village of Lidice and executed them en masse. The village was then burned and razed to the ground. Meanwhile, the town's women and were shaken out of their beds at 3:00 a.m. and driven to a high school in Kladno. Two children were immediately seized for Germanization and the rest sent on to Poland. Seven more children were selected for Germanization in Poland, while the remaining women and children of Lidice were sent to concentration camps. Nazi officials took these nine children to an SS Lebensborn home in Puschkau, near Poznan, for Germanization. Maria Hanfová, who was twelve years old at the time, later testified at Nuremberg that in Puschkau the children were taught to speak German and beaten or denied food if they spoke Czech. Her name was changed twice, first to Maria Hanff and then to Marga Richter.

At Nuremberg Hanfová was asked, had the Germans in Puschkau "ever said anything about Czechs being inferior, or no good?" She responded negatively. "You were never told that?" the prosecutor repeated, surprised. Hanfová answered, "no never."[89] In fact, the kidnappings were justified less by Nazi beliefs about German racial superiority over the Czechs than by their "respect" for (or fear of) the Czechs as racially "valuable" foes and disciplined nationalist adversaries. These were the children, who, according to Himmler, "could of course become the most dangerous avengers for their parents if they are not humanely and correctly raised."[90] The Nazis ultimately planned to expand this program of kidnapping, to seize all the children of executed resistance fighters

[88] Betreuung deutscher Minderjähriger, Prague, 21 October 1941, carton 295, ÚŘP, NA.
[89] *Trials of War Criminals Before the Nürnberg Military Tribunals*, vols. 4–5 (Washington, 1950), 1033–38.
[90] Tgb. Nr. 26/31/43g, Himmler to Sollmann, 21 June 1943, NS 19/345, BA.

or Czech parents interned in concentration camps and place them for adoption into Reich German families. Children under the age of six were to be routed through Lebensborn homes and passed off as Volksdeutsche orphans, whereas children between six and twelve years of age were to be sent to a camp in the Reich for Germanization and then put up for adoption.[91]

Yet placing these children in German families ultimately proved far more complicated than anticipated. In July of 1943 Max Sollmann, chief of the Lebensborn program, reported that the selection, Germanization, and adoption of the Lidice children were proceeding slowly. By June of 1944, it was still unclear that any children had actually been transferred to the care of German families.[92] Frank's closest adviser, Robert Gies, also reported dismal progress on efforts in Brno/Brünn and Prague to kidnap children of executed resistance fighters. They had identified a few dozen candidates for Germanization but were unable to carry out the actual adoptions. He reported, "The planned further measures could not be carried out, since it would have cost us a considerable disturbance in the Czech population. The mere examination of the children would have caused some sensation and would have brought about a state of affairs unbearable with regard to the present situation in the Protectorate, and especially to the maintenance of labor peace necessary for the unlimited production of war material." Frank ultimately conceded failure, ordering that "further measures are not to be undertaken."[93]

By any account, attempts to forcibly Germanize Czech children failed miserably. Things developed very differently in Poland, where the systematic Germanization of children was both far more widespread and typically carried out strictly on the basis of racial examinations. In the city of Łódź in occupied Poland, for example, ambitious plans to Germanize "racially valuable" Polish foster children and orphans developed partly in response to a perceived shortage of German children to adopt. A January 1942 memo to the Public Health Office from a Nazi city councilman in Łódź reported an insatiable demand among Germans for foster children: "In the Altreich there is a strong and widespread demand for foster children, but no supply. I know from my own experience that at some adoption centers there are hundreds of applicants who have been waiting to be assigned a child suitable for adoption for years, and whose wishes typically cannot be fulfilled. . . . We must attempt to reduce this considerable shortage of children for adoption through the re-Germanization of suitable children."[94]

---

[91] N. St. M IV C- 35 j/43 g, An den SS Standartenführer Dr. Brandt von Deutsche Staatsminister für Böhmen und Mähren, 13 June 1944, NS 19/345, B Archiv. Also published in *Trials of War Criminals*, 1030–32.

[92] Tgb. Nr. 26/31/43g, Himmler to Sollmann, 21 June 1943, NS 19/345, BA.

[93] N. St. M IV C- 35 j/43 g. An den SS Standartenführer Dr. Brandt von Deutsche Staatsminister für Böhmen und Mähren, 13 June 1944. NS 19/345, BA.

[94] Memo from Herrn Stadtrat Lindner to Public Hygiene Office, 29 January 1942, reel 7, folder 32, Stadtverwaltung Litzmannstadt, United States Holocaust Memorial and Museum Archive (USHMMA).

Officials cited conflicting reasons for this "brisk demand" for foster children. One Nazi official in the Office of the Reichstatthalter in Poznan/Posen claimed that parents were typically motivated by nationalist enthusiasm. He reported "increasing numbers of married couples from the Altreich who approach the most diverse organizations in the Warthegau, requesting children to adopt. Very often, their request is connected with the desire to do something special for Germandom, in that they ask for a child whose parents were murdered by the Poles."[95] Another Nazi official, however, suspected that many parents had less selfless motivations, complaining in 1943 that too many German women sought out foster children (especially infants) simply to evade mandatory labor service in the war factories.[96] In any event, local officials in Łódź responded to this pressing demand for children. Dr. Herbert Grohmann, an SS doctor and anthropologist who led the Nazi Public Health Office, was charged with screening Polish foster children and orphans for potential re-Germanization. In a single week in January 1941, he examined 448 Polish foster children and orphans, although he declared only 32 of them to be racially valuable and therefore suitable for adoption by German parents. Another 54 were deemed "racially usable," and the rest were ruled unworthy of Germanization and returned to Polish foster parents or orphanages (3 children were judged to be "suspiciously Jewish").[97]

In contrast to the practice in the Bohemian Lands, where children were selected for German citizenship and German schools largely on the basis of cultural traits and their parents' political beliefs, these evaluations focused almost exclusively on physical traits. Grohmann made detailed notes on each child's skin coloring, facial features, bone structure, eye and hair color, and medical history. Nazi racial scientists in the Reich estimated that in theory 50 percent of Czechs were Germanizable, but only 3 percent of the Poles.[98] Yet many more Polish children than Czech children were systematically taken from orphanages, Polish families, and Polish laborers in the Reich and routed through Lebensborn homes for adoption. It is difficult to provide a precise estimate of the number of Polish children who were kidnapped for Germanization because these numbers were heavily politicized after the war.[99] Relying on a survey of postwar documentation, historian Isabel Heinemann

[95] Memo from Gaujugendamt in the Office of the Reichstatthalter in Poznan to the Stadtjugendamt in Litzmannstadt, 7 January 1941, reel 7, folder 32, 7, Stadtverwaltung Litzmannstadt, USHMMA.

[96] Beitrag zum volkspolitischen Lagebericht, 18 March 1943, reel 6, folder 8, 2, Stadtverwaltung Litzmannstadt, USHMMA.

[97] An St.A.40/Jugendamt, 13 January 1941, reel 7, folder 10, 46, Stadtverwaltung Litzmannstadt, USHMMA.

[98] See Vojtěch Mastný, *The Czechs under Nazi Rule: The Failure of National Resistance, 1939–42* (New York, 1971); Connelly, "Nazis and Slavs," 1–33.

[99] For a memo from the director of the International Tracing Service to the deputy director General of the International Refugee Organization disputing Polish claims about the number of kidnapped Polish children, see memo from M. Thudicum to Sir Arthur Rucker, 31 January 1949, 43/AJ/600, AN.

has credibly estimated that around twenty thousand children were kidnapped from Poland and up to fifty thousand from all of Europe. But the numbers also depend on the definition of "kidnapping." German, Czech, Polish, and Yugoslav officials alike in the 1940s would have made little distinction between the removal of a child from his or her parents and the removal of a child from an orphanage to be placed for adoption with a German family. According to the nationalist logic of the time, children could be kidnapped not only from their parents but from a national collective.[100]

In Łódź most of children selected for Germanization appear to have been taken from foster homes and orphanages. These policies of Germanizing Polish orphans and foster children, moreover, were justified in the name of reclaiming lost German blood, children who had allegedly been Polonized in interwar Poland: "Investigations have shown that the Poles formerly systematically took all orphans from Volksdeutsche parents as foundlings into Polish orphanages or placed them with Polish foster parents. The children received Polish names," a 1942 memo from the RKfDV claimed.[101] Some children of mixed unions, however, were forcibly removed from their living parents. For example, in December 1941, the Nazi District Court in Łódź ordered Janina Rutkiewicz, an unmarried Pole, to relinquish custody of her eleven-month-old son, Henryk Rutkiewicz, for the purpose of Germanization. Henryk's father was a German police officer. Shortly after his birth, Dr. Grohmann had determined the child to be racially valuable and recommended that he be immediately transferred to a German children's home. The court order elaborated, "Although this measure is, in reality, fully in accordance with the child's own best interests, his mother has resisted it with all her energy. She thereby denies her child the possibility of a future education and professional training, and deprives the German nation and community of valuable German blood." According to the court ruling, Janina R. was therefore guilty of "neglecting the child's spiritual well-being, to the extent that she places her own motherly feelings ahead of his best interests."[102]

Why were Czech families largely spared this fate? If the Nazi regime enjoyed some success in its attempts to entice nationally ambivalent Bohemians and Moravians into the Nazi Volksgemeinschaft, it failed miserably in

[100] Heinemann, *"Rasse, Siedlung, deutsches Blut,"* 508–9. For more on Nazi policies to kidnap and Germanize children from Eastern Europe (and translated documents concerning kidnapping and Germanization), see Kiryl Sosnowski, *The Tragedy of Children under Nazi Rule* (Poznan, 1962), 46–55; Ulrich Herbert, *A History of Foreign Labor in Germany, 1880–1980: Seasonal Workers/Forced Laborers/Guest Workers,* trans. William Templer (Ann Arbor, MI, 1991), 170–72; *Trials of War Criminals,* 4:990.

[101] Anordnung Nr. 67/I Reichskommissar für die Festigung deutschen Volkstums, 19 February 1942, reprinted in *Trials of War Criminals,* 4:995–98.

[102] Beschluss, Amtsgericht Litzmannstadt, Aktenzeichen 8.VII.R.6, 8 December 1941, reel 7, folder 12, Stadtverwaltung Litzmannstadt, USHMMA.

the attempts to Germanize self-declared Czechs and their children through kidnappings, violence, and terror. The crucial role of Czech workers in the Nazi war economy demanded restraint, as Frank himself made clear. Yet this "restrained" Nazi regime had, by 1943, already suspended Czechs' civil and political rights, begun to deport and murder Jews, expropriated property, and imposed a dictatorial regime of terror on the occupied Bohemian Lands. The Germanization of Czech children promised to provoke an intolerable level of resistance where other injustices had not. This resistance, which is the subject of the next chapter, is perhaps best understood as the culmination of a fifty-year-long Czech nationalist movement to secure its claims on Czech children.

In practice Nazi Volkstumsarbeit in the Bohemian Lands developed out of a longer history of nationalist education and child welfare activism. Policies described by Nazis, by Czech nationalists, and later by historians as the Germanization of Czech children might often be better understood as the (willing) Nazification of nationally ambivalent or intermarried parents. The Nazi administration's use of the term "Germanization" to describe these cases was deliberate and had several important consequences that continue to shape historical analysis. First, the conflation of Germanization with Nazification and German with Nazi papered over significant political and cultural differences among Sudeten Germans, Volksdeutsche, and Reich Germans. The invasion, conquest, and occupation of the East were justified to the Reich German population and to the world by ideological visions of a united German diaspora. Nazis deliberately conflated the terms "Nazi," "Reich German," and "Sudeten German" in order to obscure the weak points of this diaspora, to exclude dissenters from the German national community.

Second, by defining Germanness primarily in terms of loyalty to Nazism and to its cultural and political values, the Nazis deliberately left the door open for binational, bilingual, or nationally ambivalent Bohemians and Moravians to become Nazis. Local officials attempted to draw this so-called Zwischenschicht into the ranks of the Nazi Volksgemeinschaft with a host of social and educational enticements for their children. In doing so they used the time-tested strategies of Bohemian and Moravian nationalists on both sides of the national divide. We can certainly question the extent to which those individuals who responded to these enticements acted out of free will. Many individuals faced extraordinary psychological, family, or economic pressures to join the Nazi Volksgemeinschaft (or not to). Yet there were very few successful cases of forced Germanization of individuals under the Nazi regime in the Bohemian Lands.

Nazi Germanization policy had real meaning and tragic effects if understood as a system of transferring social, political, economic, and educational power and privileges into Nazi hands. Ultimately, however, Nazi officials could not realize their totalitarian ambitions to transform Czech children into Germans. Borrowing an analytic framework that has been used to debate the origins and dynamics of the Holocaust, historians have largely explained these failures, as well as the general dynamics of Germanization policy in Eastern Europe, as a product of carefully calculated choices between a coherent racial ideology and war-driven pragmatism (intention vs. function).[103] While both racial ideology and pragmatic wartime imperatives shaped decision making in the Protectorate, it is helpful to situate both the ideology and the pragmatic decisions that shaped the Nazi occupation in a longer history of local Czech-German relations as well as in the larger context of Nazi-occupied Europe. Germanization was at least partly the product of negotiation among German officials, Sudeten German administrators, and ordinary Bohemians and Moravians.

Nationalist frameworks nonetheless continue to shape writing on accommodation and resistance in Bohemia and Moravia. Czech speakers who sympathized with the Nazis are still typically identified by historians as opportunists, while German-speaking collaborators are depicted as true believers. Czech-speaking collaborators are thereby assumed to have betrayed their apparent "objective" national or collective interests for the sake of fleeting personal gain. This analysis denies Czech speakers the agency and responsibility of conviction, refusing the possibility that a Czech speaker could have believed in Nazi ideology or that a Czech could have actually become a German in the course of five years. This framework also obscures the extent to which opportunism and ideology blended together within the entire Nazi administration, pervading the relationship between Sudeten Germans and the Reich. "Conviction" and "opportunism" were not so easily distinguishable between 1939 and 1945.

This chapter has situated the development of Nazi Germanization policy in a longer local history of Habsburg and interwar German nationalist traditions. The nationalist campaign to wipe out national indifference escalated under Nazi rule, driving new policies of racial classification and Germanization. These policies built on well-established traditions of national classification developed in the Austrian Empire and Czechoslovakia. As the failure of the plot to Germanize Lidice's orphans suggests, however, many citizens did respond to Nazism within the frameworks advanced by nationalists over the course of fifty years. Conflicts between Nazis and local nationalists, which will be the subject of the next chapter, also had important consequences both for Nazi policy and for the dynamics of collaboration and resistance in the occupied Bohemian Lands.

---

[103] See, for example, Zimmerman, *Die Sudetendeutschen im NS-Staat;* Gebel, *Heim ins Reich;* Burleigh, *Germany Turns Eastward;* Connelly, "Nazis and Slavs," 33; Heinemann, "*Rasse, Siedlung, deutsches Blut*"; Bryant, *Prague in Black,* 136–37.

7   Stay-at-Home Nationalism

Not long after the Nazi occupation of the Protectorate, the underground Czech resistance magazine *V boj* issued an urgent message of warning to Czech mothers. "With great fanfare, the Germans are opening new German schools where there used to be none. This is your business, women. It lies in your hands whether our children grow up to be Czechs or Germanized, patriots or traitors," an editorial urged.[1] This call to arms contained both familiar and novel elements. On the one hand, it reflected the extent to which Czech nationalists responded to the new circumstances of Nazi occupation with time-tested strategies. They rallied Czechs for the penultimate battle in the long-standing war against Germanization. From a contemporary perspective, Nazism's greatest crimes were certainly committed in the name of promoting so-called racial purity. But from the perspective of many Czech nationalists during the Second World War, Nazism's greatest crime was Germanization—understood as an assault on the precious ethnic or national purity of Czech children.

There was also something new in this appeal, however, as it reflected a growing nationalist emphasis on education in the home and the family. Parents, once objects of nationalist suspicion and mistrust, were now being called upon to take the lead in nationalizing their children. Czech nationalists on the right and left insisted that only a mother's influence in the home could protect Czech children from the ongoing threat of Germanization under Nazi rule.

On the eve of the Nazi invasion, German and Czech nationalists shared a nationalist political culture centered on nationalist rights to educate children. The Nazi administration initially attempted to harness this culture to

---

[1] "Germanisace," in *V boj: Edice ilegálního časopisů* (Prague, 1992), 1939, 333.

realize its racial program, while Sudeten German bureaucrats in turn sought to use the Nazi state to expand their own claims on German children. This euphoric moment of apparent unity proved all too ephemeral for the Nazi administration. Nazi Volkstumsarbeit built on but also clashed with both native Sudeten German and Czech nationalist political cultures. In turn, six years of Nazi rule fundamentally transformed and ultimately discredited many nationalist assumptions about the relationship between children, the nation, and the state in the Bohemian Lands.

During World War II the family, presided over by a stay-at-home mother, increasingly took precedence over the institutions for collective education built by nationalist activists in the Habsburg Monarchy and interwar Czechoslovakia. Since the late nineteenth century, a conditional form of nationalist feminism had thrived in German and Czech nationalist circles.[2] Women were idealized as guardians of national culture within the family and in educational and social institutions. Simultaneously, however, nationalists harbored deep suspicions of the loyalties of real parents, especially working-class parents, who were often denounced for their indifference to nationalism. This suspicion justified the creation of extensive, nationally segregated institutions for child welfare and education outside the home. While Czech and German nationalists may not have overtly celebrated women's employment outside the home, they generally accepted it as an inevitable fact of economic life. They sought to assist working mothers and guarantee a nationalist education for their children through kindergartens, nurseries, and counseling centers throughout the Bohemian Lands.

The Nazi invasion of the Bohemian Lands disrupted this culture in different ways for both German and Czech women. For both groups, the nationally segregated pedagogical spaces created under the Habsburg Monarchy and interwar Czechoslovakia no longer seemed adequate to protect children against the threat of denationalization. Nationalists increasingly called upon women to fill in for institutions discredited by Nazism. Both Czech and German nationalists radically resituated nationalist education in an imagined private sphere during the Second World War as they mobilized to protect their claims on children against the competing claims of the Nazi state.

German Nationalists Stay at Home

The Nazis occupied the Bohemian Lands in the name of rescuing a supposedly colonized German diaspora and acquiring German Lebensraum in

---

[2] For analysis of the relationship between feminism and nationalism in Bohemia and Moravia see Pieter Judson, "The Gendered Politics of German Nationalism in Austria," in *Austrian Women in the Nineteenth and Twentieth Centuries: Cross-Disciplinary Perspectives*, ed. David F. Good, Margaret Grandner, and Mary Jo Maynes, 1–17 (Oxford, 1996). On Czech feminism see Katherine

the East. This diaspora was, however, a potent ideological construction. The diaspora myth papered over differences in the histories, cultures, and loyalties of German speakers across Central Europe with the myth of a united German community with common origins in the German Reich. Until 1918, however, the patriotic loyalties of German speakers in the Bohemian Lands were firmly bound to the supranational Austrian Empire. Only in the 1930s, following the Depression, Hitler's seizure of power in Germany, and the rise of Henlein's Sudeten German Party, did a majority of Germans in Czechoslovakia truly begin to demand a return "home to the Reich."[3]

Once Nazi troops had rolled into the Sudetenland, however, the new Nazi administration faced the immediate task of transforming their vision of a unified diaspora into a political and social reality. Despite a plethora of new Nazi boarding schools and kindergartens, a yawning gap between ethnic Germanization and ideological Nazification remained. Even those Sudeten Germans who enthusiastically embraced the Nazi regime also continued to assert their own particular understandings of national community to Nazi authorities. Bohemian and Moravian Nazis were above all concerned to see their children and families protected from an alleged ongoing threat of Czechification under Nazi rule. Many Germans in the occupied Bohemian Lands ultimately expressed their disappointment with the Nazi regime's failure to fulfill its social and educational promises to German children in the Sudetenland and Protectorate.

Parents in the Bohemian Lands had long frustrated nationalist activists with their indifference to nationalist demands. National opportunism and side switching continued to impede the efforts of Nazi administrators to classify citizens of the occupied Bohemian Lands as Czechs and Germans. By 1939, however, many parents did identify with a single national community. In interwar Czechoslovakia social and educational rights had largely been accorded to national communities rather than to individuals. The much touted "minority rights" of the new Central European democracies were understood as entitlements of national collectives. It had been necessary to

---

David, "Czech Feminists and Nationalism in the Late Habsburg Monarchy: The First in Austria," *Journal of Women's History* 3, no. 2 (1991): 26–45, and Melissa Feinberg, *Elusive Equality: Gender, Citizenship, and the Limits of Democracy in Czechoslovakia, 1918–1950* (Pittsburgh, 2006).

[3] On the rise of homeland nationalism in interwar Germany see Rogers Brubaker, *Nationalism Reframed: Nationhood and the National Question in the New Europe* (New York, 1996), 107–47; Ronald Smelser, *The Sudeten Problem, 1933–38: Volkstumspolitik and the Formulation of Nazi Foreign Policy* (Middletown, 1975); On shifting German loyalties and the issue of German diaspora, see Pieter Judson, "When Is a Diaspora Not a Diaspora? Rethinking Nation-Centered Narratives about Germans in Habsburg East Central Europe," in *The Heimat Abroad: The Boundaries of Germanness*, ed. Krista M. O'Donnell et al. (Ann Arbor, 2005); Karl Bahm, "The Inconveniences of Nationality: German Bohemians, the Disintegration of the Habsburg Monarchy, and the Attempt to Create a 'Sudeten German' Identity," *Nationalities Papers* 27 (1999): 377–99.

strictly define who belonged to those collectives. The Czechoslovak state and German nationalists both avidly pursued these ends in the interwar period through their educational policies and practices of national ascription. By the time Czechoslovakia was dismembered at Munich, most Bohemians and Moravians had become Czechs or Germans. The majority of Czech and German parents had also learned to articulate their social and educational demands for their children in nationalist terms. If these parents largely accepted the nation's superior claims on their children, as well as a notion of children as national property, they also asserted their rights to a national education for their children and to the social and pedagogical services now traditionally provided by nationalist institutions. Parents themselves demanded that their children be protected from the perceived threat of denationalization. During the Second World War, parents in the Bohemian Lands deployed these nationalist understandings of parental rights, minority rights, and family to assert their agency vis-à-vis the Nazi state.

As early as July of 1939, the *New York Times* observed a mood of growing disappointment among Sudeten Germans, reporting, "While no one regrets the Czech regime, being included in the Reich is not the elysium people expected—and which they had been promised."[4] Two years later, tensions between Reich Germans and Sudeten Germans were boiling over. In 1941 occupation authorities reprimanded the population with a gag rule, insisting, "It is dangerous and it contradicts the principles of a true National Socialist attitude, when here and there disagreements of opinion between national comrades from the Reich and those from the Sudetenland are carelessly and thoughtlessly raised to the level of an alleged enmity between the Reich and the Sudetenland. Enmity between the Sudeten Germans and the Reich may not be discussed, either in the party, or where members of the party are present."[5] These tensions had been seriously exacerbated by the onset of the Second World War. If Sudeten German nationalists had expected the Nazi state to realize all their interwar fantasies of re-Germanization and revenge against the Czechs, they were bitterly disappointed once the war began and it became clear that the Nazis had other priorities, such as maximizing the output of Bohemian and Moravian factories. These conflicts between Nazi administrators and local Germans in the Bohemian Lands amounted to more than petty battles for autonomy or prestige among political leaders—they were often expressed in terms of differing nationalist priorities.

---

[4] *New York Times*, 23 July 1939, cited in Ralf Gebel, *Heim ins Reich! Konrad Henlein und der Reichsgau Sudetenland* (Munich, 1999), 239. Gebel and Volker Zimmermann both chronicle the ways in which Sudeten Germans were often disappointed with the Nazi regime because of their high expectations. See Volker Zimmermann, *Die Sudetendeutschen im NS-Staat. Politik und Stimmung der Bevolkerung im Reichsgau Sudetenland* (Munich, 1999).

[5] Richtlinien des Gauleiters zur Frage Altreichdeutsche-Sudetendeutsche, 8 July 1941, cited in Gebel, *Heim ins Reich*, 231.

As the war dragged on, evocations of Volksgemeinschaft by the Nazi administration increasingly centered around demands for wartime sacrifice. Men were to serve on the front and women in war factories, each struggling for final victory. Many German nationalists in the Bohemian Lands never fully accepted this definition of the German nation or the sacrifices demanded. The real war, as they saw it, was against the menace of Czechification in their communities and families. These Germans were disappointed with the Nazis' waning interest in the borderland struggle once the war began. A German expellee from Jihlava/Iglau recalled years later, "The Reich Germans who came to the Iglau language island only rarely had any sympathy for the national struggle between Germans and Czechs, since they had never experienced it. One often heard remarks such as 'the Czechs are really not so bad' or 'we get along very well with them,' since they did not recognize that the Czechs very cleverly understood how to win the favor of the Reich Germans, thereby creating a division between them and the locals."[6] Another Sudeten German expellee lamented that following the annexation of the Sudetenland, many civil servants unfortunately arrived who didn't understand the borderland struggle of the Sudeten Germans. They underestimated the guile of the Czechs and also did not know how to properly value their cajolery."[7]

This is not to posit a categorical hostility between Sudeten Germans and Nazis or to contrast Sudeten German innocence with Nazi guilt. As the above recollections suggest, Sudeten German Nazis frequently bemoaned the allegedly mild treatment of Czechs by Reich German officials. Many Sudeten Germans nationalists who grumbled about the regime were devoted Nazis who supported the occupation and benefited socially and politically from the regime. Far from being an expression of fundamental hostility to Nazi rule, Sudeten German dissatisfaction typically reflected a gap between their extraordinarily high expectations of the Third Reich and the realities of daily life once the euphoric moment of "liberation" had passed. Many individual policies that stirred Sudeten German resentment, such as the mobilization of female labor, were no more popular within the Altreich. Nonetheless, Germans in the Bohemian Lands often articulated their grievances about daily life under Nazism in the well-worn language of Austrian and interwar nationalist educational activists and social workers.

Money drove the first wedge between the Nazi regime and its Sudeten German citizens. After the war began, there was less of it for Volkstumsarbeit, and the whining complaints of Sudeten German administrators fell on deaf ears. The Reich Finance Ministry initially allocated a generous 35 million RM for borderland development projects in the Sudetenland in 1939,

[6] Ost Doc. 20/66, Iglau und der Iglauer Sprachinsel, 1918–45, 23, BB.
[7] Ost Doc. 20/65, Oskar Koblischke, Mähr. Weißwasser, BB.

but the onset of the war demanded austerity, and so only 5.5 million RM in funds was ultimately distributed for new schools, nurseries, and kindergartens.[8] In 1940 the Ministry of the Interior announced that funds for Borderland Welfare were being redirected toward winning the war. It was difficult to convince officials in the Interior Ministry that new German swimming pools and movie theaters were essential to the war effort, although Sudeten German administrators certainly made an effort to do so.[9] In Karlový Vary/ Karlsbad, *Regierungspräsident* (District President) Fritz Zippelius wasted no time registering his dissatisfaction with wartime austerity, predicting dire consequences for the besieged Germans in his region. "I am unfortunately duty-bound to report that . . . what has been accomplished is not in the least sufficient to create a crisis-proof barrier against Czechdom. . . . The execution of almost all the plans was inhibited by the effects of the war. This lack of progress certainly affects all districts, but the consequences are far more severe for the borders of the Sudetenland than for the other districts of the Reich," he complained. Although 1,000,000 RM had been allocated to Karlový Vary/Karlsbad for Volkstumsarbeit in 1939, only 236,370 RM was actually put to use, because of budget cuts and labor and material shortages.[10]

Above all, Sudeten Germans bitterly experienced the failure of the Nazis to fulfill their social and educational promises to German children. Because of a slow bureaucracy and wartime austerity, many of the promised schools were opened only after embarrassing delays, if they were built at all. In the village of Rejchartice/Reigersdorf in Moravia, Emil Hartel recalled that the Nazis announced ambitious plans to build a modern new schoolhouse with a state-of-the art gymnastics facility. The school was to be a "model for the Sudetengau." The town was allotted 40,000 RM for the construction, but the entire project came to a halt when the war with Poland began.[11] In 1940, Otmark Sedlacek, local Nazi block leader in Kolín/Kolin, ordered all German parents in the district to immediately remove their children from the Czech schools in town. His superiors had assured him that a new German school was on the way. Three months later the school had not materialized, and parents who attempted to reenroll their children in the Czech schools were penalized with large fees. Sedlacek himself, who

[8] NSDP Gauleitung Sudetenland, Amt für Volkswohlfahrt. An das Reichskommissariat für die sudetendeutschen Gebiete, Reichenberg, 1 April 1939, R 1501/127120, 303, BA; Zimmermann, *Die Sudetendeutschen im NS Staat,* 289.

[9] Reichsministerium des Innern, Grenzlandfürsorge Sudetenland, Regierungsbezirk Karlsbad Reichsminister des Innern an Herrn Regierungspräsidenten, 11 May 1940, 93, R 1501/127122, BA.

[10] I/5a no. 2100/40, Reichsministerium des Innern, Grenzlandfürsorge Sudetenland, Regierungsbezirk Karlsbad, Betrifft: Grenzlandfürsorge 1941, 4 December 1940, 123, R 1501/127122, BA.

[11] Ost Doc. 20/37, Emil Hartel, Reigersdorf, BB.

earned a monthly income of only 1,100 crowns, paid 450 crowns a month to send his own son to a private German school in Prague, even though Nazi officials had repeatedly promised the child a scholarship.[12] Other newly erected schools closed after only a few months because teachers were called up for the Wehrmacht and the schools lacked supplies. Until 1940, moreover, German teachers in the Sudetenland and Protectorate earned less money than those in the Altreich, even as wartime mobilization caused a severe shortage of teachers. Sudeten Germans also bitterly resented the appointment of Reich German officials to leading posts in local universities.[13]

New Nazi schools, moreover, did not always measure up to Sudeten German standards. In Southern Moravia, the SD reported in 1940 that new German schools still seemed shabby in comparison with the local Czech schools, provoking considerable grumbling among the German population.[14] After the war many Sudeten German educators claimed to have been disappointed with the Nazi school system, boasting that their native schools and pedagogy had been far superior. Hermann Tannich, for example, reported that Nazi pedagogical methods "failed due to resistance from teacher's organizations, since the methods in the Sudetenland were better."[15] While postwar expellees were inclined to retrospectively emphasize their dissatisfaction, Nazi officials at the time also worried that they had done little to improve the German school system in the Bohemian Lands. In March of 1940, for example, the SD in Prague conceded that there had been "no real improvement" in the German school system over the past year.[16] Sudeten Germans also faced obstacles when they attempted to claim the much-vaunted marriage loans from the Nazi state. These loans were designed to encourage young Aryan couples to marry and have large families. Each German infant produced for the Volksgemeinschaft reduced a newlywed couple's debt, and with the birth of a fourth child the loan was forgiven.[17] The SD reported that in Jihlava/Iglau,

---

[12] Anlage, Zur Lage im Protektorat. SD report from 8 March 1940, R 58/149, BA.

[13] SD Bericht, 1 December 1939, R 58/145, BA; Zpráva z domova, 6 February 1940, sig. 91/1, fond 37, VÚA.

[14] Heinz Boberach, ed., *Meldungen aus dem Reich, die geheimen Lageberichte des Sicherheitsdienst der SS* (Pawlak, 1984), no. 147, 5 December 1940. For other Sudeten German complaints about Nazi schools, see Theo Keil, ed., *Die deutsche Schule in den Sudetenländern* (Munich, 1967), 112–13, 117–24, 462, 509.

[15] Ost Doc. 20/65, Hermann Tannich, Friese. See also Ost Doc. 20/17, Fr. Rollwagen, Bodenbach, October 1958; Ost Doc. 20/30, Matthias Hromada, Mies, 30 June 1960; Ost Doc. 20/37, Hermann Terk, Schönwald, undated; Ost Doc. 20/17, Franz Karsch, Böhm-Kamnitz, 15 March 1959; all in BB.

[16] Die politische Entwicklung in Protektorat Böhmen und Mähren seit 15. März 1939, SD Leitabschnitt Prag, 15 March 1940, carton 7, Sb NÚIČ, VÚA.

[17] On Nazi pronatalism and antinatalism see Gisela Bock, "Antinatalism, Maternity, and Paternity in National Socialist Racism," in *Nazism and German Society 1933–1945*, ed. David Crew (London, 1994); Claudia Koonz, "The Competition for Women's Lebensraum, 1928–1934," in *When Biology Became Destiny*, ed. Renata Bridenthal et al., 199—236 (New York, 1984).

many Germans, even proven nationalist pioneers, were forced to postpone their marriages because the loans never materialized. "This situation has an especially negative effect on the mood of the Volksdeutsche, in that they feel neglected in comparison to the Reich Germans, as 'Second Class Germans,'" informants warned.[18]

The gap between the Nazis' promised nationalist utopia and wartime realities only widened as the war expanded to two fronts. Mobilization actually reversed the progress of Volkstumsarbeit in the eyes of many Sudeten Germans and Volksdeutsche, and not only through budget cuts. As German men were called into the army and German youth sought employment in the Reich's war factories, Czechs at home took over their jobs. Many Czechs who had fled the Sudetenland after the annexation returned in response to the increasing demand for factory labor. In October of 1940 Henlein himself appealed to Berlin to stop the influx of Czech workers into the Sudetenland, to no avail.[19] Between 1942 and 1944, the number of Czechs living and working in the Sudetenland more than doubled, thanks to the mobilization of German soldiers and increasing demand for labor in the war factories. From Karlový Vary/Karlsbad, administrators complained that if strong incentives were not created for the more "culturally demanding Germans—as compared with the Czechs" to remain in threatened borderland regions, they would soon be fully re-Czechified.[20]

Reports from the SD and Sudeten German administrators increasingly pitted native Sudeten German understandings of "national defense" centered around fighting Czechification against Reich German military demands. Local Germans complained that there simply weren't enough Germans to fill in for mobilized men and that Czech businesses even benefited from government contracts. Czech farmers still had their sons and neighbors available for seasonal labor, whereas Germans complained that they had to make do with reluctant prisoners of war and Poles. Meanwhile, German women were forced to shop at Czech-run businesses, where they paid higher prices than Czechs or were refused service altogether, while German businesses suffered under the oppressive weight of Czech boycotts. Worst of all, instead of studying and bettering themselves in new German schools, German boys were dying on the battlefields, while Czech youth behaved provocatively in public and enjoyed undeserved privileges.[21] Echoing these contemporary

---

[18] *Meldungen aus dem Reich*, no. 100, 27 June 1940, 1315.

[19] I/5a no. 2100/40, Reichsministerium des Innern, Grenzlandfürsorge Sudetenland, Regierungsbezirk Karlsbad, Betrifft: Grenzlandfürsorge 1941, 4 December 123, R 1501/127122, BA; Gebel, *Heim ins Reich*, 247–51.

[20] I/5 a. 1225/4, Reichsministerium des Innern, Grenzlandfürsorge Sudetenland, Regierungsbezirk Karlsbad, 12 June 1941, 128, R 1501/127122, BA.

[21] *Meldungen aus dem Reich*, no. 147, 5 December 1940; Auszug aus einem Bericht über die Lage der tschechischen Volksgruppe in Regierungsbezirk Aussig, Prague, 16 April 1940, carton 269, ÚŘP, NA.

gripes, Margarete Kallab, a German dance teacher who had been expelled from Brno/Brünn, insisted in 1959, "The Czech population of Moravia never had it so good as during the Second World War."[22]

Sudeten German leaders in the occupied Protectorate and Sudetenland increasingly conveyed the opinion that Germans in the East served the Nazi Volksgemeinschaft best by staying at home, where they could protect their jobs, families, and children from the continued threat of Czechification. As early as 1939, the SD reported the view of authorities in the Protectorate that "every Volksdeutsche who in the Czech region has a nationally politically important position to hold and to defend" was injured by the policy of drafting *Volksdeutsche* into the Wehrmacht.[23] German understandings of Volksgemeinschaft in the Bohemian Lands centered largely around nationalist claims on children. It was precisely these claims that were threatened by the thoughtless Nazi demand that Sudeten German teachers and fathers serve in the army and that Sudeten German mothers work in war factories. Nazi informants' reports repeatedly articulated this alternative understanding of national service, maintaining, "In total contrast to the Reich or in other closed language areas, most national comrades leave their women and children behind among the Czechs with the greatest anxiety."[24] As the war dragged on, the sexual and national dangers Czech men posed to German women and children on the home front grew increasingly ominous in the German nationalist imagination. In 1940, the SD in Prague reported threatening letters and harassment directed toward German women and children in the Protectorate whose husbands and fathers had been mobilized. Volksdeutsche children were allegedly spit on, called names, or assaulted on their way home from school or while wearing Hitler Youth or BDM uniforms. By 1942 the SD was warning ominously, "The German women in this area cannot hold out in the long run against the strong Czech element without sufficient masculine protection."[25] Such appeals seemed to have little resonance with authorities in Berlin.

The stay-at-home nationalism invoked by Sudeten Germans in response to wartime mobilization required stay-at-home mothers as well. Conflicts between Nazi officials and Sudeten German nationalists soon began actively to transform fundamental principles of nationalist pedagogy. In the past, the nation's claims on children had often superseded those of parents. German nationalist educators and social workers stood between parents and the state, seeking to minimize the negative effects of parental indifference to

---

[22] Ost Doc. 20/63, Brünn, Margarete Kallab, November 1959, BB.

[23] F. 1–1 SD Bericht, 1 December 1939, R 58/145, BA.

[24] *Meldungen aus dem Reich*, no. 37, 8 January 1940.

[25] Ibid., no. 333, 9 November 1942, 5008; Die politische Entwicklung in Protektorate Böhmen und Mähren, 15 March–30 April 1940, SD Leitabschnitt Prag, 1 May 1940, 4–5, carton 7, Sb NÚIČ, VÚA.

nationalism. In practice, this meant that nationalist, collective educational institutions had supported women who worked outside the home. The left-wing nationalists in the German Provincial Commission for Child Welfare, for example, actively encouraged mothers to entrust their children to collective pedagogical institutions for the good of their children and the community. The Sudeten German party had continued this tradition, advising mothers in 1938, "Every child belongs in the community. Community creates discipline and order. Community, however, also creates irreplaceable happiness for youth. Even the most tender mother, the most careful education in the parental home, cannot replace an education to become a communal being through the camaraderie of the *Volksjugend*. Mother should have no exaggerated fears of the dangers that could threaten her child when he is far away from her."[26]

The Nazis initially built on these ideals. As early as 1940, Nazi propaganda in the Protectorate celebrated German kindergartens as liberators of women as well as a tool of nationalist education. Nazi publications boasted that their new kindergartens enabled Sudeten German mothers to serve the Reich by leaving their children in the competent hands of Nazi educators. "The infants' nurseries, kindergartens, and day-care centers of the NSV now give every working and productive mother the possibility to trust her children to the oversight of responsible people," *Die Zeit* advertised.[27] While money for other Volkstumsarbeit projects dried up during the war, funds from Berlin continued to flow generously toward new German kindergartens in order to promote women's labor. A 1941 memo from the Ministry of the Interior in Berlin explained, "The promotion of child care (nurseries, kindergartens, day cares) is an urgent duty of national education and national protection. The war increases this urgency, since the requirements of the war economy also demand the labor of women with children to a high degree. It is therefore a critical task, especially during the war, to ensure that a sufficient number of day care centers are at hand."[28]

Nazi administrators thus attempted to harness long-standing local traditions of collective, nationalist education to meet the wartime demand for female labor force participation. Initially it seemed that the mobilization of female labor in the Bohemian Lands would provoke less controversy than in the Altreich itself, where women were mobilized for the war factories only with great consternation. Given the downward mobility of many middle-class Sudeten German families during the Depression and the traditional

[26] Weisung des Frauenamtes OG-18/1938, 18 August 1938, carton 22, SdP, NA.
[27] "Kindergartenarbeit im Sudetenland," *Die Zeit* (Prague), 26 June 1940, 357 R 1501/127120, BA.
[28] Runderlass der Reichsministerium des Innern, Zusammenarbeit der Gemeinden und Landkreise mit der NSV zur Förderung der Kindertagesstätten, 21 March 1941, 359, carton 269, ÚŘP, NA.

concentration of German women in industry in the Bohemian borderlands, the administration expected few obstacles to the mobilization of female labor for factory work. In 1943 the SD reported, "In view of the fact that the demand for German labor or the social position of German women already caused women in large numbers to exchange their places in the household with work in an office or factory, the introduction of total female employment is not so meaningful for the widest segment of the German population."[29] German women in the Bohemian Lands, however, responded to the Nazi mobilization with their own articulation of "national service." If many women welcomed the new kindergartens and schools for their children, most also bristled against the "duty" to serve the Nazi war effort in factories. "Liberation," especially in the eyes of middle-class German women, promised national and social privileges on the local level, including the privilege not to work, while their Czech neighbors kept the factories running.

In a speech on May 4, 1940, Hitler appealed to German women to seek employment for the sake of the war effort. Official Nazi policy toward women's work within the Altreich continued to waver between a popular ideological commitment to racist pronatalism and stay-at-home motherhood and a growing pragmatic need for wartime labor power. The speech nonetheless marked a shift toward actively encouraging women to serve the Volksgemeinschaft in war factories as well as in the nursery.[30] Two months later the Ministry of Labor in Berlin issued a decree encouraging all women who had been professionally active before the war to return to work. Sudeten German officials in the Protectorate responded by construing the right to stay at home as a national privilege for German women in the Bohemian Lands, justified by their unique duties to defend their families from Czechification. This stay-at-home nationalism challenged the war-centered vision of national service promoted in Berlin by invoking the special national challenges and dangers allegedly confronted by families in borderland regions. Shortly after Hitler's May 1940 speech, Sudeten German and Deputy Reichsprotektor Karl H. Frank called a meeting of officials from industry and

---

[29] *Meldungen aus dem Reich*, Stimmen zum Frauenarbeitzeinsatz in Protektorat Böhmen und Mähren, 22 July1943, 5525.

[30] Within the Third Reich Nazi officials initially legislated women out of the workforce, providing incentives for women to stay at home and raise large families, as part of a larger racist and pronatalist program. Wartime labor shortages nonetheless increasingly required the deployment of female labor in factories. Conquest in the East and the use of forced labor provided one "solution" to the crisis, while another was found in the articulation of a discourse about the suitability of women for low-paid assembly-line labor. Nonetheless, ambivalence and contradiction characterized Nazi policy toward women's work in the Altreich throughout the war. See Tim Mason, "Women in Germany, 1925–1940: Family, Welfare and Work," in *Nazism, Fascism and the Working Class: Essays by Tim Mason*, ed. Jane Caplan, 131–211 (Cambridge, 1995); Annemarie Troeger, "The Creation of a Female Assembly-Line Proletariat," in Bridenthal et al., *When Biology Became Destiny*, 237–70; Claudia Koonz, *Mothers in the Fatherland: Women, the Family, and Nazi Politics* (New York, 1987).

government in the Office of the Protectorate to discuss the latest order to mobilize female labor. Frank insisted, "In the Protectorate women cannot be used in the same way as in the Altreich. The special relationships and the position of the German woman in the Protectorate, in foreign Raum, must be taken into account."[31] Sudeten German officials ultimately agreed upon the following guidelines, which were intended to protect the national and class privileges of German women vis-à-vis their Czech neighbors:

1. The German woman in the Protectorate has tasks to fulfill for Germandom (*Deutschtumsaufgaben*).
2. Child rearing requires greater effort from the German woman in the Protectorate than in the Altreich.
3. The German woman in the Protectorate has more difficulty managing the household because of wartime conditions.
4. The German woman is disadvantaged by her lack of knowledge of the Czech language.
5. The German woman is active in various party organizations.
6. Most wives of civil servants have been separated from their spouses for a long period of time.
7. As a matter of principle, German women should be called up for labor only if there are no Czechs available.
8. The use of German women should be limited to those positions that unconditionally must be filled by German labor power.
9. Czech firms must be infiltrated with well-trained German labor.
10. In Czech firms German women should be placed in subordinate positions as infrequently as possible.[32]

Factory labor was hardly suitable for the German Kulturträger in the Bohemian Lands, Frank argued in August of 1941, insisting, "In general there are plenty of Czech women and girls available for use as workers and for other subordinate activity."[33] Frank himself hoped to use the gradual deployment of German women to strengthen the "German character" of threatened German businesses in the Protectorate. In appeals to the Nazi Women's League, the Office of the Protectorate also reminded local organizations responsible for recruiting women that German women in the Bohemian Lands had "special national-political duties reserved for them, which demand extensive consideration."[34]

---

[31] Protokoll über die Sitzung von 23 August 1941, carton 868, ÚŘP, NA.

[32] Leitgedanken zum Fraueneinsatz, 11 July 1942, carton 868, ÚŘP, NA.

[33] Arbeitseinsatz der deutschen Frauen im Protektorat, Prague, 4 August 1941, carton 868, ÚŘP, NA.

[34] Der Reichsprotektor in Böhmen und Mähren an die Kreisleitung der NS Frauenschaft, 18 July 1941.

While the stay-at-home nationalism of Sudeten German officials may have shaped resistance to labor force mobilization, these tactics failed to keep German women out of the war factories. Sudeten German officials nonetheless continued to create forms of national privilege within the workplace. They segregated German women from Czech workers and brought them into factories with great fanfare in order to endow mandatory factory labor with the desired aura of "honorable" service. On 11 May 1943, when 140 German women began work in the Letov factory in Prague, they were greeted with coffee, cake, flowers, a band, and speeches from local party leaders extolling their special role within the predominantly Czech firm.[35] These attempts to entice German women with a privileged status on the factory floor created new problems for employers and officials. In the Letov factory, for example, supervisors once again confronted the problem of the ambivalent Zwischenschicht as they attempted to distinguish between German and Czech women. Many women who possessed German citizenship and were mobilized for the privileged "German" jobs actually spoke no German. When these non-German-speaking Germans were integrated into the German workforce, Sudeten German women's nationalist sensibilities were offended. Nevertheless, officials feared that if "new Germans" were allowed to work with Czech women, they would soon be "lost to the German nation" for good.[36]

Meanwhile, the Ministry of Labor in Berlin demanded the mobilization of more women and deemed progress in the Protectorate unsatisfactory. Following another order to mobilize female labor in February 1943, employment offices in the Protectorate began a drive to bring fifty thousand more German women into the metalworking industry. In early 1944 representatives from Berlin and Prague issued yet another demand for female labor.[37] Nazi bureaucrats within the Ministry of Labor in Prague virtually ceased to distinguish between Czech and German women under these pressures. The goal of keeping German women out of factories and away from farms was largely forgotten. Single women, women with grown children, and married women without children were required to register for labor service in spite of Frank's earlier promises to refrain from such measures. Even so, the Ministry of Labor in the Protectorate reported that in August 1943, 2,189 German women had been "invited" to the German Labor office in Prague. While 1,591 showed up, only 419 unlucky souls were actually put to work.[38] Much to the chagrin of occupation authorities, the labor force

[35] Errichtung einer deutschen Betriebsabteilung zur Beschäftigung deutscher Frauen bei der Firma Letov Prag, Prague, 15 May 1943, carton 868, ÚŘP, NA.

[36] Der Fraueneinsatz in Kreise Prague, 27 August 1943, carton 868, ÚŘP, NA.

[37] Ministerim für Wirtschaft und Arbeit, Prague, 20 March 1943, carton 868, ÚŘP, NA.

[38] Fraueneinsatz 1943, Ministerium für Wirtschaft und Arbeit, Prague, 19 May 1943; Der Fraueneinsatz in Kreise Prague, 27 August 1943; both in carton 868, ÚŘP, NA.

participation of German women in the Bohemian Lands actually declined between 1937 and 1942, with the sharpest drop right after the outbreak of the war and the onset of Nazi "mobilization," between 1939 and 1942. The situation gradually improved in late 1942, but officials lamented that "the number of working women is still not satisfactory in comparison with other areas of the Reich."[39] By August of 1944, the Employment Office in Prague called up around 607 German women each month but deployed only 131 of those in factories. Meanwhile 1,500 Czech women a month were sent to work by the same office.[40]

Czech women formed the reliable core of the labor force in the Bohemian Lands throughout the war. They were perceived to be less politically dangerous than Czech men and did not require the special nationalist privileges demanded by German women. In 1941 officials in the Office of the Protectorate reported, "Female Czech workers are available to the employment offices in sufficient numbers, or can be won over through local advertising campaigns, so that special legal measures would be excessive. On these grounds we can also refrain from any kind of forcible seizure of Czech women for use as workers."[41] Nazi officials therefore faced difficult choices, between satisfying the demands of Sudeten German women and maintaining the morale of a valuable female Czech labor force. Czech women openly resented the privileges accorded to German women, from their general evasion of labor duties to the flowers and cake in the Letov factory. In July of 1943 the wife of a factory owner in Brno/Brünn complained to Nazi authorities that Sudeten German women were blatantly evading their duty to serve the Nazi Volksgemeinschaft in her factory: "It is a scandal that these Germans call themselves 'German.' Since individuals have refused the assigned work without any justification whatsoever, it has created a certain amount of ill will among the Czech women." Czech women reportedly refused to show up at local employment offices because of "alleged statements in Party circles" that German women would be employed only after every last Czech woman was sent to work, allegations that Nazi officials publicly denied.[42]

By 1943, Nazi officials in Berlin had decisively rejected the stay-at-home nationalism of Sudeten German men and women. This did not stop German women from voicing their dissatisfaction in these terms. In the city of Mladá

[39] Ministerium für Wirtschaft und Arbeit, 12 October 1942, carton 868, ÚŘP, NA. For interwar statistics on women's labor force participation, see *Statistisches Jahrbuch der Tschechoslowakischen Republik* (Prague, 1934), 16–17; Leiter der Sektion A1 an Frau Berghaus im Hause, Betrifft: Verstärkung des Fraueneinsatzes, Prague, 1 March 1943, carton 868, ÚŘP, NA.

[40] Arbeitseinsatz deutscher Frauen, Prague, 1 August 1944, carton 868, ÚŘP, NA.

[41] Arbeitseinsatz der tschechischen Frauen, Prague, 1 October 1941, carton 868, ÚŘP, NA.

[42] *Meldungen aus dem Reich*, Stimmen zum Frauenarbeitseinsatz in Protektorat Böhmen und Mähren, 22 July 1943, 5525.

Boleslav/Jungbunzlau, for example, Aline Komendera sent a bitter letter of denunciation to Karl Frank, complaining that although she was an upstanding local party leader and active in the Nazi Women's League, she was the only German woman deployed in a team of Czech female farm workers. Meanwhile, she denounced three local women, all "former" Czechs who had opportunistically acquired German citizenship and were not yet legitimately employed: "Herain, Elisabeth, 24 years old, single, previously a Czech and Sokol member, is employed by her father, who is a self-employed builder. She can travel to Prague during the week, relax Saturday and Sunday or enjoy her hobbies. . . . The family socializes only with Czechs. In the 1930 census the whole family declared itself Czech."[43] Komendera's denunciation was received with little sympathy. The war-centered vision of Volksgemeinschaft favored by the Reich ultimately put the national, social, and educational privileges demanded by Sudeten Germans on the back burner.

Nazi authorities not only demanded that Sudeten German women enter the workforce but insisted that the Czech population be treated with a certain amount of restraint. SD reports confirmed that rumors were spreading of a "strong enmity between the Germans from the Altreich and the Sudeten Germans," attributed to the fact that the "Czech problem is seen much more humanely in the Altreich."[44] Czech resistance activists themselves observed that Sudeten Germans were more brutal toward Czechs and more universally despised by Czechs than Germans from the Reich.[45] While social and educational promises to Germans in the Bohemian Lands remained unfulfilled by the Nazis, Reich German "liberators" provoked resentment among Sudeten Germans with their ostentatious behavior and a tendency to provocatively befriend "good Czechs."[46] Local Germans, "who cannot allow themselves such an extravagant lifestyle, are naturally thoroughly angered by the behavior of these Altreich Germans . . . above all their instinctless behavior with respect to Czech hypocrites," the SD reported in 1941.[47] Sudeten Germans' understanding of national community and national service still centered around protecting German families from the perceived threat of Czechification, a battle that justified social privileges for German women and children in the name of national "defense." The friendly behavior of Reich German invaders toward the national enemy therefore seemed nothing less than treasonous.

---

[43] An Herrn Staatsminister SS Obergruppenführer Frank from Aline Komendera, Tschelakowitz, 30 October 1944, carton 330, ÚŘP, NA.

[44] *Meldungen aus dem Reich*, no. 333, 9 November 1942, 4446.

[45] Zprávy z domova, 7 December 1943; Protektorát, 2 April 1943, sig. 91/6, fond 37, VÚA.

[46] Unwürdiges Benehmen von deutschen Reisenden im Protektoratsgebiet, 8 December 1939, R 58/146, BA.

[47] Misstimmung der Volksdeutschen gegenüber den Reichsdeutschen, IIa 1941, carton 341, ÚŘP, NA.

In the eyes of many local nationalists and parents, Nazi officials from the Altreich failed to meet their educational and social promises to German children during the Second World War, leaving them vulnerable to the ever-present threat of Czechification. The relationship among child, family, and state soon shifted dramatically, since the nationalist, communal educational institutions long favored by nationalists had fallen into the hands of Reich German authorities. These authorities substituted ideological Nazification for traditional policies designed to ward off ethnic Czechification. The private sphere therefore gradually became the privileged site of nationalist education for embittered Sudeten Germans. Protecting the "Germanness" of the nation's property, including its children, seemed to require that both mothers and fathers stay at home.

Rumors and Modernity

Toward the end of the war a rumor circulated among Czechs that powerfully expressed a growing popular association of Nazi terror with forced Germanization. German soldiers traveled door-to-door in Czech neighborhoods, the story held, asking each Czech family if they wanted to register as Germans. Anyone who declined was automatically sent to a concentration camp.[48] The occupied Bohemian Lands were awash with such rumors, which bolstered both Sudeten German and Czech assertions of stay-at-home nationalism. These rumors evoked the barbaric threat of modern pedagogical and social institutions to denationalize and destroy the family. Such rumors not only informed Nazi policy during the war but ultimately framed memories of the Nazi occupation, shaping postwar educational and social institutions.

Recently many scholars of the Third Reich, following Detlev Peukert and Zygmunt Bauman, have located the potential for genocide within the disciplinary logic of modernity and modern social welfare institutions.[49] The potential "dark side" of modernity and a growing interventionist welfare state was, however, far from invisible to those who experienced these

---

[48] Leitsabschnitt Prag, SD Tagesbericht, 22 August 1944, 5, no. 72, carton 8, Sb NÚIČ, VÚA.

[49] See Detlev Peukert, *The Weimar Republic: The Crisis of Classical Modernity* (New York, 1992); Zygmut Bauman, *Modernity and the Holocaust* (Ithaca, 2001). For more specific accounts of the relationship between Nazism and modern social welfare (many of which attempt to provide less teleological analysis) see Atina Grossmann, *Reforming Sex: The German Movement for Birth Control and Abortion Reform, 1920–1950* (Oxford, 1995); Edward Ross Dickinson, *The Politics of German Child Welfare from the Empire to the Federal Republic* (Cambridge, MA, 1996); David Crew, *Germans on Welfare: From Weimar to Hitler* (New York, 1998); Young-Sun Hong, *Welfare, Modernity, and the Weimar State, 1919–1933* (Princeton, 1998).

developments firsthand. The barbaric potential of Nazi social institutions was the subject of intense discussion, of rumors, fears, and fantasies in daily life in the Protectorate. These rumors contributed to the development of stay-at-home nationalism in different ways for both Sudeten German and Czech nationalists. Through such rumors, Czech nationalists depicted the evil of Nazism as an attack on their distinctive nationalist culture and national autonomy and on the nation's claims on its children. Rumors in the Protectorate often centered precisely around the dangerous potential of a Nazi-controlled social welfare apparatus to invade and destroy a presumably nationalized family.

In its appeals to women, the underground Czech publication *V boj* repeatedly portrayed Nazi charity and social welfare organizations as hidden traps to infiltrate the Czech family. It was true, *V boj* conceded, that the "Germans festively come into Prague and all the cities of the former Czechoslovakia with Bavarian help trains, distributing goulash, soups, making a lot of pork and blood sausage . . . with sufficient assistance from photographers and photography equipment." In reality, however, the paper asserted, all the food distributed had come from outside the Third Reich, and the city of Prague was later forced to pay 8 million crowns for partaking of this so-called Nazi charity. Soon enough, the magazine warned Czech mothers, they would watch helplessly as their children grew hungry and sick on fake foods: "Prepare for the future, when you will read articles signed by medical experts, as is already the case in Germany, on how butter is actually very damaging to your health! You will observe how your children's faces will grow pale, because substitute products never contribute to our health, but always detract from it."[50] Other Czech rumors warned that money collected by Czech charities for poor families actually went to support the German war machine and that all Czech schools would be closed so that they could serve as hospitals or shelters for German refugees fleeing the Russians from the East.[51]

Czech rumors also referred to the threatening potential of Nazi eugenics to cripple the Czech nation's reproductive power. One such story asserted that beginning in 1940, Czechs would be prohibited from marrying for five years and that every Czech woman was to be sterilized.[52] Likewise, Nazi public health measures were widely construed as subversive attacks on the Czech family and the health of Czech children. For example, Czechs spread the word that immunizations against diphtheria administered by the NSV to Czech children would actually sterilize their children or even kill them.

[50] "Českým ženám!," *V boj*, 1939, 329.

[51] SD Leitsabschnitt Prag, SD Tagesbericht, 2 June 1944, Anlage zum SD-Tagesbericht no. 43/44, no. 43, carton 8, Sb NÚIČ, VÚA; Leitsabschnitt Prag, SD Tagesbericht, 1 August 1944, no. 66, carton 8, Sb NÚIČ, VÚA.

[52] F. 1–1, SD Bericht, 6 December 1939, R 58/ 145, BA.

This rumor provoked such a panic in the towns of Kladno and Kročenhlav/ Krotschenlav that countless mothers showed up at school on the day of the scheduled immunizations and frantically dragged their children home, according to Nazi informants. By 8:30 a.m. all of the towns' schools were empty after the Czech police tried in vain to convince mothers that the vaccinations were harmless. A similar rumor asserted that all Czech children born in German hospitals in Prague were sterilized by Nazi doctors. In both Prague and Brno/Brünn, Czech resistance activists meanwhile spread the word that Nazi immunizations would cause insanity or sterilization among children, again resulting in empty Czech classrooms on the days when German doctors were scheduled to visit schools.[53]

Not surprisingly, rampant rumors surrounded the introduction of youth service in the Protectorate. As the Nazis began to enroll Czech children for new summer camps in the fall of 1942, the illegal Communist newspaper *Rudé právo* published an article entitled "Serfdom for Czech children older than 11!" arguing that the lists were being used to gather Czech children to serve as slave labor in German factories. Parents whispered in the streets that their children would be sent to the Reich as forced labor or drafted for military service. Some suspected that young Czech girls were being forced to serve as prostitutes on the Western front.[54] The Nazi regime was forced to address these concerns through its propaganda, reassuring parents, "There is no cause for any worries because the care and education of the children will be assigned only to experienced and expertly trained individuals, whose sense of responsibility is the best guarantee that the children will get a true education for their future calling and duties in life."[55] Young unemployed people meanwhile suspected that if they failed to find employment in their hometowns, they would be forced to work in the Reich, where they would be Germanized or sterilized. Not taking any chances, many young people, especially women, soon found themselves some kind of fake or real work as protection.[56] Wartime rumors thus reinforced stay-at-home nationalism by focusing precisely on the barbaric potential of large-scale modern social welfare and educational institutions in the hands of the national enemy. These perceived threats shaped everyday responses to Nazi authorities and institutions and encouraged the romanticization of the home as both the authentic site of national pedagogy and a domain requiring protection from social intervention.

[53] *Meldungen aus dem Reich*, no. 20, 24 November 1939; Anlage, Zur Lage im Protektorat für die Zeit vom 15.2 bis 28.2 1940, 3 March 1940, R 58/149, B. Archiv; Zpráva z Prahy, 5 December 1939, sig. 91/1, fond 37, VÚA.

[54] "Pracovní knížky pro české dětí od jedenácti let!" *Rudé právo, 1939–45 (1942)* (Prague, 1971), 284. See also "Braňte své děti!" *Rudé právo*, 1941, 215; SD Bericht, 15 December 1939, R 58/145, BA.

[55] "Povinná služba mládeže," *Národní práce*, 6 February 1943, carton 83, MSP-London, NA.

[56] *Meldungen aus dem Reich*, no. 34, 29 December 1939; ibid., no. 115, 15 August 1940.

To a lesser extent, Sudeten Germans also circulated such rumors, though their rumors named Czechs and Nazis alike as a threat to German children. By late in the war, for example, teachers in Nazi evacuation camps for German children as well as Hitler Youth camps came under fire for allegedly abusing children.[57] More often, however, Sudeten German rumors focused on the mistreatment of Germans by Czech social and medical institutions. Since few of these institutions were still in Czech hands after 1939, a popular genre emerged around the evil of Czech-run hospitals, a product of the shortage of German doctors in the Protectorate. Pregnant German women, in these stories, were left at the mercy of Czech midwives and doctors. German women complained that Czech nurses were far more likely to read to them out of a prayer book than help them through their delivery. In Brno/ Brünn, meanwhile, Germans were agitated by rumors of homosexual molestation in a Czech hospital, the SD reported. In Mladá Boleslav/Jungbunzlau a Czech doctor reportedly told German parents that their child's illness was harmless even though the child had days to live. Another Czech doctor was rumored to have refused to X-ray a German child on the grounds that public Czech health insurance should not be expected to pay for the treatment of the wealthy Germans.[58]

For Germans and Czechs alike, these rumors confirmed an argument that had been implicit in nationalist mobilization against Czechification and Germanization since the turn of the century: modern social welfare and educational institutions were dangerous weapons in the hands of the national enemy and therefore needed to be nationally segregated. A cyclone of such stories flourished at the very moment that the barbarity of the Nazi racial state was most fully realized in Eastern Europe. These rumors themselves had ambiguous consequences for the dynamics of collaboration and resistance. Clearly, rumors obscured the lines between truth and fiction under the Nazi occupation. Anything seemed possible, but which rumors were true, which worth believing and acting on?[59] Such rumors also helped to precipitate the demise of the nationalist political culture built around the collective education of children in the Bohemian Lands. In the Austrian Empire and interwar Czechoslovakia the German and Czech nationalist movements had competed to provide for the educational and social welfare

---

[57] SD Leitabschnitt Prag, 19 August 1943, 6/410, BA.

[58] *Meldungen aus dem Reich*, no. 137, 31 October 1940, 1725; Zur gesundheitlichen Betreuung der Deutschen im Protektorat, 27 May 1940, R 58/151, BA; *Meldungen aus dem Reich*, no. 120, 2 September 1940, 1531.

[59] Maureen Healy has described a similar "crisis of truth" in wartime Vienna during the First World War. See Maureen Healy, *Vienna and the Fall of the Habsburg Empire: Total War and Everyday Life in World War I* (Cambridge, 2004), 141–48. On rumors in wartime see also Ute Daniel, "Informelle Kommunikationen und Propaganda in der deutschen Kriegsgesellschaft," in *Medien, Kommunikation, Geschichte*, ed. Siegfried Quandt, 76–89 (Giessen, 1993).

of children. The seizure of large-scale modern social and pedagogical institutions by the Nazi state helped to discredit that culture in the eyes of both Sudeten Germans and Czechs. The Nazi experience seemed to confirm that Czechs and Germans themselves, rather than simply schools, hospitals, and welfare agencies, needed to be physically separated.

Homeschooling for the Czech Nation

The rumors of denationalization that permeated Czech society under the Nazi occupation encouraged an even more dramatic shift toward stay-at-home nationalism in Czech nationalist circles. In December of 1938, a self-declared "authoritarian democracy" led by Rudolf Beran of the Czech Agrarian Party took power in what was left of Czechoslovakia. In the name of national defense, the Czech Second Republic, much like Petain's France, began preemptively to fulfill Nazi demands, rousing antiforeigner sentiment, limiting the access of Jews to higher education and retiring them from the civil service in January of 1939. The new government discussed at length plans to expel all Jews who had emigrated to Czechoslovakia after 1917.[60] Nazi informants also reported widespread efforts among Czechs, especially in business circles, to expropriate Jewish property before the Germans could get to it: "Aryanization has become a method through which both sides, the Germans as well as the Czechs, attempt to win back their lost position [in the national struggle]."[61] Right-wing Czech conservatives and collaborators, like many other nationalist regimes in occupied Eastern Europe, accented linguistic and racial purity in their appeals for national unity. All Czech political parties meanwhile merged into two blocks, the National Union Party and the National Labor Party, while the Communist Party was banned altogether.[62] After March 15 both the conservative bureaucrats surrounding Czech President Emil Hácha and less influential Czech fascists collaborated in the name of national defense.

---

[60] Jan Rataj, *O autoritativní národní stát: Ideologické proměny české politiky v druhé republice, 1938–1939* (Prague, 1997), 108–19. On parallel measures in Vichy France, see Miranda Pollard, *Reign of Virtue: Mobilizing Gender in Vichy France* (Chicago, 1998); Robert Paxton, *Vichy France: Old Guard, New Order* (New York, 2001).

[61] Die politische Entwicklung in Protektorate Böhmen und Mähren seit 15. März 1939, SD Leitabschnitt Prag, 15 March 1940, carton 7, Sb NÚIČ, VÚA.

[62] Rataj, *O autoritativní národní stát,* 35; Vojtěch Mastný, *The Czechs under Nazi Rule: The Failure of National Resistance, 1939–42* (New York, 1971), 22. For more on the ways in which Eastern European nationalists used the Nazi occupation to realize their own domestic nationalist ambitions, see Christoph Dieckmann, Babette Quinckert, Tatjana Tönsmayer, eds. *Kooperation und Verbrechen. Formen der "Kollaboration" im östlichen Europa, 1939–1945* (Göttingen, 2003). On collaboration in Eastern Europe, see also "Resistance and Collaboration in Europe, 1939–1945: Experience, Memory, Myth, and Appropriation," *East European Politics and Societies* 9 (Spring 1995), 207–94.

They officially sought to protect Czech cultural autonomy by working with Nazi authorities.[63]

Under the Second Republic, Czech nationalist leaders urged Czech women to serve the national cause by embracing their role in the home, protecting children from foreign influences. On the day it was founded, the National Unity Party proclaimed in Czech newspapers, "The family is the true base of national life. We will return women to their calling, happy motherhood. Peaceful homes and working men. For children we guarantee a happy youth and moral education. We will be a national state, and therefore foreign influences cannot be allowed to shape our new lives. We will quickly solve the problem of emigrants, especially Jews."[64] National discipline, unity, and ethnic purity were to rehabilitate the Czech nation from its humiliation in Munich. Nationalist and conservative women in the Second Republic encouraged Czech women to embrace domesticity in the name of protecting Czech national purity. Married women were dismissed from the civil service in December of 1938. Conservative women formed a women's auxiliary to the Second Republic, the Women's Center, which was organized under the auspices of the Czech National Council (Ústředí žen při české národní radě). The Women's Center planned educational reforms to encourage a "nationally efficient" gendered division of labor, shuttling women toward female fields such as nutritional science, tourism, and massage, where they would be less likely to compete with Czech men. During the war these women planned exhibitions promoting motherhood and distributed recipe books to help women prepare traditional Czech foods with ersatz ingredients.[65]

It is hardly surprising that women on the Czech right promoted maternalism in the late 1930s, urging women to embrace motherhood and femininity for the sake of the nation's future. Yet in the face of Beran's "authoritarian democracy," Czech Socialists, feminists, and Communists also retained a stubborn nationalist faith that democracy and freedom were inherent in Czech national character. While a great deal still separated the Czech right and left, this tautology enabled left-wing antifascists to join right-wing nationalists and collaborators in a defense of ethnic Czechness during the Second World War and to allow this battle to stand in for all others. Rather than offering Czech society two mutually exclusive paths, organized collaborators and the organized resistance together cleaved to

---

[63] See Chad Bryant, *Prague in Black: Nazi Rule and Czech Nationalism* (Cambridge, MA, 2007), 20–45, 180–207; Jan Rataj, "Obraz Němce a Německa v protektorátní společnosti a československém odboji," in *Obraz Němců, Rakouska a Německa v české společnosti 19. a 20. století*, ed. Jan Křen and Eva Broklová, 209–10 (Prague, 1998); Mastný, *The Czechs under Nazi Rule*, 23.

[64] "Národe český!" *Večer*, 18 November 1938, reproduced in Rataj, *O autoritativní národní stát*, 33.

[65] Národohospodářské komise, 8 March 1938, carton 288, NRČ, NA. On the program of the Women's Center see Feinberg, *Elusive Equality*, 170–74.

the common priority of defending ethnic Czechness against Nazi Germanization. Historians tend to agree that the ethnic strand of Czech resistance under Nazism was the product of an erosion of options, given the brutality of Nazi rule.[66] Yet when Czech resistance activists, feminists, and Communists rallied around the defense of Czech ethnicity, it was not solely because they had no other option but to abandon their originally individualist values. This argument overestimates both the power of the occupying regime and the traditional Czech commitment to a democracy understood in individualist rather than communal terms.

The Communist Party began to conflate the struggle against Nazism with a struggle to defend Czech ethnicity the day the Nazis marched into Prague. In a manifesto released that day the party declared, "After a series of violent acts against other nations, the German Nazis have grabbed the freedom-loving, democratic, progressive, Czech nation by the throat with bloody hands, so as to force them under the iron heel of brutal, German fascist tyranny."[67] Nine months later, however, references to democracy, social justice, and individual freedom had largely disappeared from most Communist propaganda since such values were now supposedly subsumed by the larger effort to preserve the Czech nation from the threat of Germanization. Drawing on decades-old nationalist discourses that linked Germanization with class oppression, as well as the Communist view of fascism as the highest stage of capitalism, the illegal Communist newspaper *Rudé právo* declared in September 1940: "The colonial regime of German enslavers and their Czech footmen will inflict great damage and suffering on the Czech people. The occupiers will, however, certainly never achieve two things. First they will never succeed in Germanizing Czech teachers, Czech pupils, and Czech schools. Czech teachers, parents, and pupils . . . will defend themselves, they will fight tooth and nail to uphold their cultural and national values, their language and their spirit."[68]

---

[66] Detlef Brandes, *Die Tschechen unter deutschem Protektorat,* vol. 1 (Munich, 1969), 78; Bryant, *Prague in Black,* 179–208; Melissa Feinberg, "Dumplings and Domesticity: Women, Collaboration and Resistance in the Protectorate of Bohemia and Moravia," in *Women and War in Central and Eastern Europe,* ed. Nancy Wingfield and Maria Bucur, 95–110 (Bloomington, IN, 2006); Ralf Gebel, "Die tschechische Gesellschaft unter deutscher Besatzungsherrschaft in Protektorat Böhmen und Mähren," in *Tschechen, Deutsche, und der Zweite Weltkrieg,* ed. Robert Maier, 23–27 (Hannover, 1997); Jiří Doležal, *Česká kultura za Protektorátu: Školství, písemnictví, kinematographie* (Prague, 1996).

[67] Manifest der kommunistischen Partei der Tschechoslowakei vom 15. März 1939, document 4 in *Die kämpfende Tschechoslowakei: Dokumente über die Widerstandsbewegung des Tschechoslowakischen Volkes 1938–1945,* ed. Jiří Doležal and Jan Křen, 25–27 (Prague, 1964).

[68] "Zahájení školního roku na českých školách," *Rudé právo,* September 1940, 123. The Communist Party's turn toward nationalism began even before the invasion of the Protectorate. See Doležal and Křen, *Die kämpfende Tschechoslowakei,* document 4, Manifest der kommunistischen Partei der Tschechoslowakei, 25, and document 7, Aufruf der illegalen kommunistischen Partei der Tschechoslowakei an das gesamte tschechische Volk, 33. For an overview

These appeals marked a shift in Communist Party rhetoric that would have significant postwar implications, since the Czechoslovak Communist Party had traditionally remained aloof from nationalist politics.[69] They also represented an ironic reversal in nationalist pedagogy: Czech and German nationalists had spent most of the twentieth century wresting children from the control of nationally indifferent parents to serve the needs of the nation. In the face of the Nazi threat, Czech nationalists on the right and left now construed nationalist education in the home as the last and best hope for national survival. They called upon Czech women, in turn, to devote themselves fully to the task of national defense within the family.

In March of 1939 the National Partnership (*Národní souručenství*, NP) was created as the sole official body to represent Czech national interests and autonomy in the Protectorate. Women, who had enjoyed the right to vote in Czechoslovakia since 1918, were denied the right to join. Leaders of the NP argued that Czech women had to be protected from the dirty work of governing under the Nazis.[70] While women on both the right and left protested their exclusion from the NP, they articulated their objections in the name of defending Czech ethnicity. Left-wing Czech women defended the rights of women to political participation by claiming that feminism was essential to Czech nationalism and innate to Czech "character" itself. They defended women's rights in the name of preserving Czech ethnicity in its truest form. The goal of all women's education in Germany, according to one editorial in the Czech feminist magazine *Ženský obzor,* was to transform German women into obedient mothers. Political education in Germany was limited to education for motherhood, a system that perfectly corresponded to the essential "nature" and "mentality" of German women. With all due respect to German women, who "happily devote themselves to their assigned tasks," this system was hardly suited to the feminist, democratic, freedom-loving nature of the Czech people, who had always prized the participation of women in public life, feminists insisted.[71] Another article in the same issue maintained, "If we want to follow the example of the Third Reich, we must resolutely move forward as they did. Every movement, political, literary, social, was characteristically colored in a national spirit. It must be the same in our case." Therefore, fidelity to Czech national character required

---

of the program of the Communist resistance throughout the war see Detlef Brandes, *Die Tschechen unter deutschem Protektorat* (Munich, 1975), 2:82–87. See also "Připravují velké germanizační tažení," in *Rudé právo,* August 1939, 18.

[69] On Communism and nationalism in the immediate postwar years, see Benjamin Frommer, *National Cleansing: Retribution against Nazi Collaborators in Postwar Czechoslovakia* (New York, 2005); Bradley Abrams, *"The Struggle for the Soul of the Nation": Czech Culture and the Rise of Socialism* (Lanham, MD, 2004); Christiane Brenner, "Politické diskurs české společnosti v letech 1945–1948," *Dějiny a současnost* 21, no. 3 (1999): 41–42.

[70] Č. 590, May 1940, carton 1, Ženská národní rada (ŽNR), NA.

[71] "K obzorům ziřtků," *Ženský obzor,* č. 4, 1939. See also Feinberg, *Elusive Equality,* 159–89.

that "rather than senselessly imitat[ing]" the Nazis, the Czechs "count on the high cultural level of Czech women" and include them in the NP.[72] Such arguments did not represent an abandonment of principle. They reflected an effort by feminists to emphasize the common ground they shared with the Czech right in 1938–45 in order to maintain a space for Czech women in formal political life. This common ground demanded that women protect Czech cultural "autonomy" at all costs and that they subsume feminist goals to the more primary struggle to preserve Czech ethnicity.

While Sudeten German Nazis invoked the threat of Czechification and Czech resistance to justify the creation of new German schools, Czech underground publications relied on fears of Germanization to mobilize Czech resistance. In 1939 the underground magazine *V boj* described the violent Germanization of Czech children, directly comparing Nazi methods to those of German nationalists in the Habsburg Monarchy. "The methods of the Gestapo in Germanizing the Czech nation are even more brutal and inhumane than the oppression in the former Habsburg Monarchy," resistance activists claimed. "In mixed regions Czech schools were closed and Czech children harassed. In areas like Jihlava, where the Germans were a minority, Czech families were exposed to the worst terror of the Nazis. Czech families fled into the forest in fear."[73] If that wasn't bad enough, *V boj* also reported a frightening number of new German schools in "purely Czech regions."[74] The newspaper repeatedly published ominous reports about the "purchase" of Czech children by Nazi schools, a favorite trope of Czech and German nationalists alike since the days of the Austrian Empire. Parents were rumored to receive 600 crowns for each Czech child enrolled in a German school. Czech highway workers also reportedly earned a raise from 3.50 crowns to 4.70 crowns an hour—the German rate—for sending their children to German schools. The report continued, "Today's Germanization naturally strives for the destruction of Czech self-consciousness and will to freedom." Fortunately, however, only the worst Czech traitors succumbed to such tactics, which, *V boj* affirmed, "were succeeding poorly."[75]

Although the Czech resistance itself openly questioned the success of Nazi Germanization tactics, the threat remained a powerful tool with which to mobilize the population, particularly Czech women. Articles urged women not to "delude themselves" into sending their children to German schools merely for the sake of attentive teachers or superior facilities. Above all,

[72] "Kratinké nebe," *Ženský obzor,* 1 č. 4, 1939, 51.

[73] "Útisk čs. národa," *V boj,* 1939, 148. *V boj* was the organ of the largest Czech resistance organization, Národní odboj, which SD officials estimated to have 10,000 members in 1940. All Czech political parties were represented in the organization.

[74] "Metody násilníků zůstávají po věky stejné," *V boj,* 1939, 216; "Německé školy v českých městech," *V boj,* 1939, 701.

[75] "Germanisace," *V boj,* 1939, 238.

however, resistance activists urged women to intensify nationalist pedagogy in the home. Although most Czech teachers remained patriots, according to *V boj,* Czech schools had been hopelessly corrupted by the Nazis by 1939. Education in the home necessarily took on greater importance. "The family must exert greater efforts," *V boj* chided readers. The newspaper repeatedly urged parents to read national histories and historical fables out loud each night to their children.[76] The Communist resistance echoed these sentiments. In 1943 *Rudé právo* thus promoted education in the home as the only effective antidote to the ongoing threat of Germanization:

> Just like in Germany they will turn our children into fanatics, such that they would willingly denounce even their own parents, and create an apparatus of spies among the adults. It is true that our six-year-old children have already been educated within the Czech family to such an extent that even this diabolical plan must fail. Yet it is still necessary that we heighten our attention to this matter. A partial danger remains here, especially among parents who are apathetic and indifferent. . . . In every case it is going to depend on the parents themselves to find the Nazi poison in their children, to isolate it and eliminate it.[77]

Czech nationalists on the left depicted this pedagogical activity in the home and on the streets as the most supreme form of national service for Czech women, writing in 1939, "Every day you will find dozens of opportunities to educate your children and create in them beautiful and free human beings. This is your holy struggle with a system that purposefully sets all its power toward creating an unthinking herd." It was the "beautiful duty" of women to strive, through their children, for the "reestablishment of our independent state and in it a free nation," where Czechs would lead their lives "in the only way that accords with their mentality, and that naturally corresponds to their centuries-long growth and development."[78] The Czech resistance thus continued to assert that democratic political values were rooted deep within the essential character of the Czech people. The task of mothers was to keep children ethnically Czech in order to ensure the future of Czech democracy. While no one objected if a woman wanted to take on "some kind of activity in public life," no woman should be fooled into abandoning her most important task. The article reminded Czech women, "No one in the world can take away from us the possibility to form the souls of the next generation of our nation, the souls of our children."[79] *V boj* simultaneously urged fathers

---

[76] "Pravda vítězí-ale dá to fušku," *V boj,* 1939, 643. On Czech teachers see "Český učitel se nazapře," *V boj,* 1939, 750.

[77] "Všem našim instruktorům," *Rudé právo,* January 1943, 380–81.

[78] "Pravda vítěžství- ale dá to fušku," *V boj,* 1939, 647.

[79] "Českým ženám," *V boj,* 1939, 646.

to reassert their role as protectors at home. Goering himself had promised to reach deeply into the private sphere, resistance activists warned readers, and no Czech man should forget it. It was the duty of Czech fathers in occupied society to fight "for your property, for your women and children."[80] Preserving Czech ethnicity also required women to remain sexually loyal to the nation.[81] Nationalists called upon Czech women to resist treasonous sexual impulses for the sake of their future children. "Certainly you want to marry, you want to create a family and your own household—but do you think that the haughty German, loyal to his 'pure race' would marry you, or even once in his life recall the 'bastard Czech' that you are to him? For him you are merely the woman who was good for him in the moment when he 'conquered Bolshevik Czechoslovakia.'"[82]

Czech welfare organizations quickly rallied around the priorities articulated through this stay-at-home nationalism. On the local level this entailed an active pronatalist campaign. M. Machačová, leader of an association for the protection of mothers and children (Ochrana matek a dítě) in Brno/Brünn, reinforced a message now being promoted by the Czech right and left alike, chiding women in 1941, "The number of pregnancies and live births in Bohemia and Moravia offers no quantitative assurance for the development of our nation. We have the solution in our own hands. It is above all a question of education about the responsibility and joy of parenting, the defense of motherhood, love of children and the defense of their physical and spiritual health."[83]

From all sides women were thus urged to embrace their role as mothers and nationalist pedagogues in the home. Czech women responded to this call to arms. "We have to thank the Nazis for a remarkable increase in the birthrate. There have never been so many pregnant women to be seen in Prague or in the countryside—the sole protection against mandatory labor," observed one Czech informant in late 1943.[84] Hans Kaiser, a Sudeten German from Suché Vrbné/Dürnfellen, also recalled that the Czechs triumphed in the nationalist demographic battle during the Second World War. Many Czechs got married young and had children to avoid labor service, he claimed, "and so it happened that the Czech nation grew remarkably while

---

[80] "O smyslu dnešního vlastenectví," *V boj*, 1939 569.

[81] These discourses resonated powerfully in Czech society, as the widespread rape and brutalization of "horizontal collaborators" in 1945 revealed. Benjamin Frommer, "Denouncers and Fraternizers: Gender, Collaboration, and Retribution in Bohemia and Moravia," in Wingfield and Bucur, *Women and War*, 111–32.

[82] "Germanisace," *V boj*, 1939, 337–38.

[83] Karel Kotek, *Naše dobrovolná sociální a zdravotní péče* (Prague, 1941), 19. See also Antonin Roček, "Budujeme stát od rodiny," *Ženský obzor*, č. 2, 1939, 20, and "Česká rodina," *Ženský obzor*, č. 3–4, 1939, 47.

[84] Zpráva o poměrech ve vlasti, 6 October 1943, 91/6, fond 37, VÚA.

the German nation bled on the Russian fields."[85] In a reversal of long-term trends, the number of Czech women between the ages of twenty and twenty-four per 1,000 women who married increased from 130.2 in 1935 to 165.4 in 1941 and to 200.1 in 1942. Teenage Czech girls between the ages of fifteen and nineteen were twice as likely to marry in 1942 as in 1935. Likewise, the number of Czech births increased from 103,642 in 1938 to 153,953 in 1944, the highest rate since 1932.[86] In 1962 German demographer Albert Eissner estimated that the Czech population had enjoyed a net increase of 236,000 people by the end of the war. During the war, Walter Gross, head of the Office for Racial Politics (Rassenpolitische Amt) in Berlin, attempted to depict this surprising increase in the Czech birthrate, which surpassed the German birthrate in the Protectorate, as evidence of the Third Reich's "humane" treatment of the Czechs.[87] In reality these demographic trends probably reflected the shift from mass unemployment in the 1930s to the full employment of the war years. In addition, childbearing may have represented an attempt by Czech women to avoid forced labor in war factories. Pregnancy, however, provided little protection from labor mobilization, according to one Czech correspondent—soon after the birth of a child Czech women were required to return to the factory and entrust their children to the care of family members or a nursery.[88]

During six years of occupation, Czech women were bombarded from all sides by a unified message. Resistance fighters, feminists, Communists, and the Second Republic's self-described "Authoritarian Democrats" agreed: there was no higher service or duty for Czech women than preserving the Czech "essence" in the home, keeping their children ethnically Czech. In the summer of 1939 *Ženský obzor* insisted that "especially in current times" the burden fell on Czech women to protect and promote the "healthy nationalism" of their children: "The tepidity of the nation can mostly be blamed on an insufficient understanding of national education in the family. Women too can strive so that our culture is and remains distinctive, pure, and wholly our own," editors urged their readers. Achieving this end required that women take pride in their essential and primary tasks as mothers. "If Czech women are wholly women, if they inspire their children with the internal essence of

[85] Ost Doc. 20/64, Hans Kaiser, Dürnfellen, 17 November 1958, 2, BB.
[86] Brandes, *Die Tschechen*, 2:48; *V dětech je národ věčný. Zpráva o činnosti zemského ústředí péče o mládež v Praze* (Prague, 1946), 23; "Fünf Jahre Protektorat Böhmen und Mähren," *Wirtschaft und Statistik* 24 (1944): 17; Albin Eissner, "Die tschechoslowakische Bevölkerung im Zweiten Weltkrieg," *Aussenpolitik* 13 (1962): 334. For statistics on birthrates in interwar Czechoslovakia see *Statistisches Jahrbuch der tschechoslowakischen Republik* (Prague, 1936), 17.
[87] Walter Gross, "Rassenpolitische Leitsätze zur Fremdvolkpolitik des Deutschen Reiches," April 1940, carton 63, ÚŘP, dodatky 1, NA.
[88] Jak smýšlí lid doma? August–September 1944(?), 91/7, fond 37, VÚA.

the nation, the spirit of human sensitivity and national consciousness, the value of collective work and endurance . . . the nation will succeed to the greatest extent."[89] The Czech left was not unique in identifying democratic values with patriotism or essential national character under the Nazi occupation. This strategy was also embraced by antifascist movements across occupied Europe, especially in France, Italy, and Poland.[90] But these tactics had unique historical dimensions in the Bohemian Lands. Between 1900 and 1945 Czech nationalists had already vigorously promoted the battle against the Germanization of children in the name of a larger struggle against class injustice, violence, and political repression. When representatives of the Czech right and left encouraged Czech mothers to resist the Germanization of their children under Nazism, this call to arms was particularly potent. Czech nationalists resisted Nazi rule in the Bohemian Lands but not with the goal of combating Nazi racism. To the contrary, they understood Nazism as a menace to their own ethnic or national purity and mobilized zealously to protect that purity.

If the struggles over children during the Second World War reflected many continuities with Austrian and Czechoslovak political culture, the stay-at-home nationalism promoted by Czech and Sudeten German nationalists marked a radical departure in both the location and the form of nationalist pedagogy. Before 1939, nationalists made claims on children that often superseded those of parents, creating a network of nationally segregated pedagogical and social institutions to educate children collectively outside the home. The activism of nationalist educators and social workers reflected an underlying suspicion of the loyalties of nationally indifferent parents in bilingual regions. With the Nazi seizure of power, however, both Sudeten Germans and Czech nationalists radically resituated authentic national pedagogy in an imagined private sphere in order to protect children from the national enemy and from the competing claims of the Nazi state. While Sudeten Germans demanded that mothers and fathers be excused from service in the war factories and on the battlefields to protect their children from Czechification, Czech nationalists construed the family as the only refuge from Nazi attempts to Germanize Czech youth. These activists did not depoliticize the private sphere, nor did they denounce the involvement of mass political movements in children's education. Rather, they depicted the home and family, presided over by a stay-at-home mother, as the last and best hope for protecting the nation's overriding claims on children.

[89] "Žena má zůstati ženou," *Ženský obzor,* č. 7–8, 1939, 1–2.
[90] Geoff Eley, *Forging Democracy: The History of the Left in Europe, 1850–2000* (Oxford, 2002), 299–329.

8 *Reich-Loyal Czech Nationalism*

In late 1943 a member of the Polish resistance reported his observations of occupied Prague to the Czech exile government in London. He observed many differences between the harsh occupation of Poland and the relatively mild conditions in the Protectorate. Above all, this contemporary observer was startled by the persistence of Czech national life in the Bohemian Lands under Nazi rule:

> The Czechs live under relationships that are so different from ours that they seem almost improbable to us, even though they are real. The living conditions are without a doubt difficult and full of restrictions but remain at a far distance from the horrors in which we live. . . . For the Czechs there remains a certain appearance of national life, a quantitative production of newspapers that has not been limited up to this point. The Czech reads his favorite magazine just like he did before the war, which is, however, just as coordinated as the entire German press. Every Czech has a radio and hears the program of the Czech radio station, which cultivates Czech music, broadcasts Czech programs and . . . spreads propaganda. But in spite of this propaganda, one hears Czech news from London. Czech sports teams organize competitions just like before the war, and the sports fan goes to the arena every Sunday, to be inspired by the accomplishments of his favorite athlete.[1]

These observations provoke an obvious question: why and how did Nazi rule operate in the Bohemian Lands with less violence, repression, and resistance than in other areas of the occupied East such as Poland, Russia, and Greece? What was the meaning of Czech nationalism under Nazi

[1] Život v dnešních Čechách, 18 May 1944 (written in second half of December 1944), 91/7, 280–81, fond 37, VÚA.

rule?[2] These questions cannot be answered through reference to Nazi racial ideology alone or by studying the pragmatic military calculations of Nazi leaders in Berlin. If it was indeed pragmatic to introduce many forms of expropriation, repression, censorship, violence, and terror into daily life in the Bohemian Lands, forcibly Germanizing Czech children ultimately promised to provoke more resistance than it was worth. The Nazi occupiers adapted their strategies of rule accordingly. Nazi Germanization policy thus developed partly in dialogue with Czech society. In particular, thanks in large part to Czech mobilization against Germanization, the Nazis failed to realize their ambitions to Germanize self-identified Czech children. The assassination of Heydrich and the retaliatory massacre at Lidice proved to be a critical turning point in Nazi Germanization policy in the Bohemian Lands. Maria Hanfová, kidnapped at Lidice, may have briefly become Marga Richter, but the vast majority of Czech children were spared her fate. This failure represented a victory for a Czech nationalist political culture mobilized around its claims on children. It also marked the beginning of a subsequent policy of accommodation between Nazis and Czechs.

Czech nationalists resisted Nazism in the name of protecting Czech ethnic purity. Such resistance entailed the daily assertion of Czechness in the face of the Nazis' presumed determination to Germanize everything Czech. Rejecting German culture, speaking Czech, cooking Czech dumplings, telling Czech jokes, singing Czech songs, and above all, protecting the ethnicity of Czech children thus supposedly constituted important forms of agency for the Czech people in occupied society. But what were the consequences of this nationalist resistance for daily life in the Bohemian Lands and for Czech political culture more broadly? It has been tempting for historians to celebrate assertions of Czech nationalism during the Second World War as heroic forms of resistance, small triumphs of national will in everyday life.[3] In fact, following Heydrich's assassination and the failed attempts to Germanize Lidice's orphaned children, the Nazis increasingly authorized Czechs to continue singing their songs and eating their dumplings by developing a

---

[2] For a sense of the differences between occupation policies in Czechoslovakia and other parts of Eastern Europe see especially Detlef Brandes, *Die Tschechen unter deutschem Protektorat*, vol. 2 (Munich, 1975); John Connelly, "Nazis and Slavs: From Racial Theory to Racist Practice," *Central European History* 32, no. 1, March 1999, 1–33; Mark Mazower, *Inside Hitler's Greece: the Experience of Occupation, 1941–45* (New Haven, 1993); Bernhard Chiari, *Alltag hinter der Front. Besatzung, Kollaboration und Widerstand in Weißrußland, 1941–44* (Düsseldorf, 1998); Jan Gross, *Polish Society under German Occupation: The Generalgouvernment, 1939–1944* (Princeton, 1979); Wendy Lower, *Nazi Empire-Building and the Holocaust in Ukraine* (Chapel Hill, 2005); Karel Berkhoff, *Harvest of Despair: Life and Death in Ukraine under Nazi Rule* (Cambridge, MA, 2004).

[3] See, for example Jiří Doležal, *Česká kultura za Protektorátu: školství, písemnictví, kinematographie* (Prague, 1996); Vojtěch Mastný, *The Czechs under Nazi Rule: The Failure of National Resistance, 1939–42* (New York, 1971); Detlef Brandes, *Die Tschechen unter deutschem Protektorat*, vol. 1 (Munich, 1969), 78–80.

policy of harnessing Czech cultural nationalism to the Third Reich. It may therefore have been the norm in occupied Czechoslovakia to collaborate and resist at the same time. This is not simply because the terms "collaboration" and "resistance" are relics of an outdated positivist or politicized history.[4] As we have seen, broad sectors of Czech society united around defending Czech children from denationalization during World War II. This response to Nazi rule emerged from the logic of fifty years of Czech nationalist activism in the Bohemian Lands. It was the common ground shared by self-identified right-wing nationalist collaborators and the left-wing Czech nationalist resistance.

Nor did Czech nationalists on the left or right abandon their ideals as they coalesced around the defense of Czech ethnicity. When Czech Communists, Socialists, and feminists appealed to the public to keep Czech children ethnically Czech, they followed a path carved out by Czech nationalist educational and social activists since the turn of the century. Since the mid-nineteenth century, Czech nationalists had claimed to represent the masses in a struggle against the allegedly oppressive and undemocratic forces of German hegemony. While always competing with a historical (Bohemian state rights) strand of Czech nationalism, ethnic or descent-based understandings of Czechness increasingly dominated Czech nationalist movements by 1918. Nationalists valorized the Czech nation as *essentially* freedom-loving and democratic and proclaimed that membership merely required a Czech-speaking parent. In this circular logic language, identity, and political values folded into a tautological unity. The democratic credentials and character of the Czech nation were rendered almost unquestionable.

Following Heydrich's assassination and the Lidice massacre in June of 1942, the Nazi regime increasingly adapted to this expression of Czech resistance. Nazi officials attempted to secure Czech accommodation by promoting forms of Czech cultural nationalism harnessed to the Third Reich. The blurring boundaries between collaboration and resistance reached their most absurd extremes in the Nazi Kuratorium for Youth Education. The Kuratorium was established shortly after the death of Heydrich in 1942 as a sort of parody of the Hitler Youth, intended to secure the loyalty of Czech children to the Third Reich through physical and ideological education. By the summer of 1943, the Kuratorium had registered 944,770 Czech youths, employed 674 employees, and organized over 1,300 cultural and sporting events in towns across the Protectorate.[5]

---

[4] Historiography on Nazism in Germany, France, and Greece in the last twenty years has increasingly deconstructed categories of collaboration and resistance, focusing on the shades of gray that dominated everyday life. See Detlev Peukert, *Inside Nazi Germany: Conformity, Opposition, and Racism in Everyday Life* (New Haven, 1989); Robert Gellately, *Backing Hitler: Consent and Coercion in Nazi Germany* (Oxford, 2001); Mazower, *Inside Hitler's Greece.*

[5] "Kuratorium für Jugenderziehung in Böhmen und Mähren, 1943," *Statistisches Jahrbuch für das Protektorat Böhmen und Mähren* (Prague, 1944), 318. On the Kuratorium see also Jan

Nazi officials realized early on that Czech adults might never give up their hopes of reestablishing an autonomous Czech nation-state. Informants' reports were rife with denunciations of Czech parents and teachers who subverted Nazi pedagogical aims. In Zábřeh/ Hohenstadt, where the Czech school was closed in 1942, parents reportedly registered their children in the next village over, where many were taken in by relatives so that they could attend the local Czech schools. Czech children in the region not only rejected food distributed by the Nazis in schools but allegedly threw the food at their German teachers in the streets, according to indignant informants. Czech parents also refused to send their children to Nazi kindergartens, and the NSV finally simply gave up and closed many kindergartens in predominantly Czech areas of the Protectorate.[6] Czech teachers, as during the First World War, were considered the worst enemies of the state. Nazi informants blamed resistance to German schools and institutions directly on the intractable "anti-German attitudes of the Czech teaching profession." The alleged subversion of Czech teachers kept the Gestapo and the SD alike busy throughout the occupation.[7] The Nazi state used money, force, and terror to prevent such subversion. By 1943 the Ministry of Education had spent 5 million crowns to send 12,500 Czech teachers to "reeducation" courses in the Reich and at home. According to postwar Czech estimates, during the Nazi occupation 5,000 teachers were sent to concentration camps, where 1,000 perished.[8]

The Czech teaching profession, Nazi police informants warned, "openly and actively seeks to influence Czech youth through their lessons as well as in their private lives, such that national resistance among young people is becoming especially powerful." In the eyes of German informants, Czech stay-at-home nationalism appeared to be a resounding success. As more and more German teachers were called away to the Wehrmacht, the SD reported, "The education of Czech youth lies solely in the hands of Czech teachers and parents, who may refrain from openly taking a position against the Germans but nevertheless secretly incite their children against us."[9] Czech informants,

---

Špringl, "Protektorátní vzor mladého člověka: Kuratorium pro výchovu mládeže v Čechách a na Moravě, 1942–1945," *Soudobé dějiny* 11, nos. 1–2 (2004): 154–77.

[6] Heinz Boberach, ed., *Meldungen aus dem Reich, die geheimen Lageberichte des Sicherheitsdienst der SS* (Pawlak, 1984), no. 256, 2 February 1942, 3242; ibid., no. 192, 9 June 1941, 2387; Dozvuky německé sociální a dobročinné péče v protektorátu, 21–28 May 1939, 91/1, fond 37, VÚA.

[7] *Meldungen aus dem Reich*, no. 192, 9 June 1941, 2387; see also SD Bericht, Zur Lage der tschechischen Minderheit im Sudetengau, 15 April 1940, R58/150, BA.

[8] Franz Langhaus, "Die Erziehung zum Reichsgedanken," in *Ansprachen und Vorträge, gehalten bei der Dienstbesprechung der tschechischen Bezirksschulinspektoren des Protektorates Böhmen und Mähren am 27, 28, und 29 Mai 1943 in Prag* (Prague, 1943), 442. On reeducation courses for Czech history teachers see also Václav Buben, "Dějepis na školách v době okupace," *Šest let okupace Prahy* (Prague, 1946), 54; Doležal, *Česká kultura*, 51.

[9] *Meldungen aus dem Reich*, no. 41, 17 January 1940, 656.

meanwhile, proudly emphasized that Nazi education failed to sway Czech children, thanks to the patriotic efforts of Czech teachers and parents. In June of 1944, one Czech resistance activist reported to London, "There is no fear over the corruption of Czech children," and recounted an incident in which an eleven-year-old boy made an impertinent comment about a German soldier who had just boarded a tram. All the passengers smiled in sympathy, and fortunately no Germans overheard the remark. Nazi reeducation efforts were futile, the informant concluded, as "the healthy spirit of Czech boys is spread and preserved on the streets."[10]

Nazi occupation officials also agreed that purely repressive measures could not sufficiently counteract the perceived disloyalty of Czech educators and parents. As Heydrich lamented in 1942, "We can't lock up all the Czech teachers."[11] The Gestapo, moreover, repeatedly investigated suspicious Czech schools and teachers but failed to unearth incriminating evidence. The Nazi administration did demand that posters of Beneš and Czech legions be removed in several schools, but many other investigations turned up ambiguous evidence of subversion at best. Was it a form of "resistance," for example, if Czech students from a trade school in Budějovice/Budweis marched in military formation? Officials in the Office of the Protectorate were not entirely sure.[12] Investigations of a Czech school for endangered girls, denounced as "a cell of hidden passive resistance," also produced no evidence of suspicious activity. Nor did reports of a student demonstration in Fridrichov/Friedrichsdorf after extensive police investigation.[13] The Gestapo soon announced that there was hardly sufficient personnel to police every Czech school and complained of being burdened with too many trivial denunciations.[14]

Initial attempts to Germanize children had failed, and the Gestapo was overextended. The Nazi administration in the Protectorate was therefore pressed to develop more creative measures to counteract the subversive influence of parents and teachers on Czech youth. Heydrich was especially

[10] Spojenecký nálet na Most a zprávy z domova, 5 June 1944, 91/7, fond 37, VÚA.

[11] "Aus Heydrich's Ansprache an die leitenden Funktionäre der Okkupationsbehörden," 4 February 1942, document 77 in *Deutsche Politik im Protektorat Böhmen und Mähren unter Reinhard Heydrich, 1941–42,* ed. Miroslav Kárný et al., 230 (Berlin, 1997).

[12] Entwurf an de Herrn Ministerpräsidenten in Prag, March 1940, 11a–9038, carton 271, ÚŘP, NA. For other failed investigations see folder I-1a 1333, 1939–43, carton 271, ÚŘP, NA.

[13] Folder I-1a 1333, 1939–43 B, no. II B/M 1–1222/ 40 u. 880/40 Mähr.-Ostrau, 24 June 1940, carton 271, ÚŘP, NA; Folder I-1b 2320, 1940–1943, no. I 1b-2703, 11 January 1941, and no. I 2 4400/5, Prague, 7 March 1941, carton 269, ÚŘP, NA.

[14] Folder I-1a 1333, 1939–43, no. II BM 1499/39, 12 October 1939, carton 271, ÚČP, NA. Shortages of labor and resources and excessive denunciations were problems faced by the Gestapo throughout the Third Reich. Gellately, *Backing Hitler;* Klaus-Michael Mallman and Gerhard Paul, "Omniscient, Omnipotent, Omnipresent? Gestapo, Society and Resistance," in *Nazism and German Society 1933–1945,* ed. David Crew, 168–71 (London, 1994).

intent on resolving this thorny problem. In his first speech to leading Protectorate officials in 1942, he devoted significant attention to his plans to "reeducate" Czech youth outside the family and schools. Czech children had to be educated in a way that would enable the Nazis "to extract them from the atmosphere" at home, he explained.[15] These ambitions were finally realized a week after his assassination, with the formation of the Kuratorium for Youth Education (Kuratorium für Jugenderziehung) on May 28, 1942. The Kuratorium, led by Czech Minister of Education Emmanuel Moravec, was charged with coordinating youth service for Czech children, now mandatory, and with overseeing all Czech youth organizations and associations. Czech children between the ages of ten and eighteen fulfilled their service requirement by enrolling in any one of the associations affiliated with the Kuratorium, where they were required to spend four hours each week. In each two-hour session, one hour was devoted to physical education and one hour to political education, which was comprised of instruction in four subjects: history, culture, "The Reich and its Founding," and "The New Way of Life."[16] The explicit goal of the organization was to "give to youth that which they cannot get from parents or from the school."[17]

The Kuratorium was initially perceived by Czechs as a pernicious Nazi scheme to Germanize Czech children and was received accordingly by Czech parents. The Communist *Rudé právo* declared, "Czech youth are estranged from the nation, and with the help of the Kuratorium have turned against their fathers, mothers, brothers and sisters."[18] A Czech resistance activist pessimistically reported to London that Czech Kuratorium members marched together with German children and SS units and sang German songs, "proof that the traitors around Moravec [the Czech Minister of Education in the Protectorate] have sold our youth to Nazi Germanization."[19] Meanwhile, only a week after announcing the Kuratorium and the new mandatory service requirements, the Nazis were forced to counter widespread rumors and fears that "Czech youth are going to be sent abroad so that they learn foreign languages and succumb to foreign ways."[20] If Czech youth did go abroad, an article published in *Večerní slovo* countered, it was because

---

[15] "Aus Heydrich's Ansprache an die leitenden Funktionäre der Okkupationsbehörden," 4 February 1942, document 77 in Kárný, *Deutsche Politik*, 230.

[16] Sammlung der Gesetze und Verordnungen des Protektorates Böhmen und Mähren, no. 189–1942, 20 May 1942; Sammlung der Gesetze und Verordnungen des Protektorates Böhmen und Mähren, no. 187–1942, 28 May 1942; I-K8-A, Kuratorium pro výchovu mládeže v Čechach a na Moravě, carton 43, Kuratorium, NA.

[17] Kuratorium pro výchovu mládeže v Čechách a na Moravě, carton 43, Kuratorium, NA.

[18] "Národem prochází stav nejistoty," *Rudé právo*, č. 5, April 1944, 507. See also "Kuratorium a česká mládež," *Rudé právo*, č. 16, December 1943, 492, and "Český den matek," *Rudé právo*, č. 6, May 1944, 516.

[19] Zprávy z ČSR, 23 September 1943, sig. 91/6, fond 37, VÚA.

[20] "Odnárodňování české mládeže," *Večerní slovo*, 25 May 1942, carton 83, MSP-London, NA.

they were among the world's best workers. They would remain Czechs, pioneers who represented Czech national achievements to the world, and enjoy social mobility upon return. Propaganda for the Kuratorium was intense and included magazine articles, window displays, brochures, film and radio programs, and parties in the Lucerna in Prague for "alumni" of the Kuratorium's summer camps.[21]

Mandatory youth service was nevertheless a hard sell. At least initially, Nazi officials reported embarrassing organizational follies and widespread parental resistance. At the first annual Day of Czech Youth in Prague in 1943, which included a series of festive sport and intellectual competitions, one observer reported that the assembled Czech youth "live in the conviction that as sports stars they have to obey no one at all" and that their teachers did little to discipline them. Students made "stupid jokes" and disrespectfully wore their hats and uniforms wrong. One child ran around the marching grounds wearing a costume and a fake beard, causing "the greatest disturbance among the youth."[22] Teachers, as well as leftist activists from the former Czech Provincial Commission for Child Welfare, were to blame for deliberately ridiculing and undermining the activities of the Kuratorium, Nazi reports insisted. "The situation among the youth was impossible and depressing," Eduard Chalupa conceded in his report to authorities in Berlin. "Unfortunately I have to conclude that we are dealing here with an almost organized and deeply rooted resistance, which has infected a good 60–70 percent of the assembled middle school youth."[23]

Outside Prague, however, observers were somewhat more optimistic in 1943. In Pilsen, the SD reported in 1943 that the Days of Czech Youth had clearly given expression to an "inspired unity" among Czech children. Unfortunately, their enthusiasm contrasted starkly with the "complete lack of interest and negative position of the rest of the Czech population, above all the parents."[24] A Czech informant likewise warned that Czech youth in the countryside were increasingly eager to participate in Kuratorium activities, while the youth of Prague turned a cold shoulder to the organization.[25] Similar news came from Brno/ Brünn, Zlín/Zlin, Hodonín/Göding, and Kyjov/ Gaja. Czech youth participated eagerly in the festivities, but disappointing numbers of adults turned out to support them and to take in Nazi propaganda. Informants in Valašské Meziříčí/Wall-Mesertisch emphasized that

[21] Reinhard Heydrich Erholungsaktion 1944 Propaganda, 29 July 1944, carton 107, Kuratorium, NA.

[22] Beobachtungen während des Jugendtages, Prague, 20 September 1943, carton 43, Kuratorium, NA.

[23] Vermerk an Herrn Generalreferat Dr. Teuner, Burgfeier, Rezessionerscheinung, 30 December 1943, carton 43, Kuratorium, NA. See also Tschechische Jugendfürsorge, SD Leitabschnitt Prag, 20 July 1943, NS 6/410, BA.

[24] SD Leitabschnitt Prag, 15 August 1943, NS 6/410, BA.

[25] Zprávy z domova, 28 November 1944, 91/7, fond 37, VÚA.

the Czech intelligentsia was particularly prejudiced against the Kuratorium "as a Germanization organization" and therefore attempted "to hinder the success of the organization in every possible way."[26]

In Moravia Nazi officials were more confident about the Kuratorium's progress, even among adults. In Moravská Ostrava/Mährische Ostrau and in Brno/Brünn the Kuratorium's magazine for youth was well received in 1943, according to Nazi security police. More than before, the magazine's pictures "depict youth the way a Czech would imagine it," reports explained.[27] In Havlíčkův Brod/Deutsch Brod most parents were reported to have made peace with the Kuratorium by the summer of 1943. Participation in Kuratorium activities was regular and youth were enthusiastic. Only the older generation remained skeptical, distrustful of Minister of Education Emanuel Moravec, who enjoyed the worst reputation of all the government collaborators. Among themselves they reportedly claimed, "Moravec was an officer and wants to command at any price. Since he is not allowed to command adults, he is trying it with the youth."[28] Younger children were also typically more receptive to Kuratorium activities than were older teenagers, who could still remember life before the war. In Budějovice/Budweis, for example, local Kuratorium officials reported that a cultural program called "Show What You Can Do," in which Czech children displayed their artwork and musical talents, had been a roaring success. Youth over the age of sixteen, however, "remained completely passive and showed absolutely no interest in participating."[29]

Heydrich's Summer Relaxation Action for Czech Children

If most adults and older youth mistrusted the Kuratorium as a tool of Germanization in 1943, a year later Nazi reports took on a remarkably different and more optimistic tone. It is difficult to draw definitive conclusions about the attitudes of youth themselves toward the Kuratorium, since we have access to their voices almost exclusively through the reports of Nazi and antifascist informants or functionaries. Officials in the Protectorate may have been searching for good news by the summer of 1944. The Czech population might also, however, have been emboldened by events on the Eastern front to resist the Kuratorium's activities. Instead, the Czech public seems to have responded with growing enthusiasm to the programs of the Kuratorium in

---

[26] SD Leitabschnitt Prag, 15 August 1943, NS 6/410, BA.

[27] SD Leitabschnitt Prag, 15 July 1943, NS 6/410, BA.

[28] SD Leitabschnitt Prag, 15 July 1943, SD Leitabschnitt Prag, 22 July 1943, NS 6/410, BA. As a result of Moravec's unpopularity, the Nazis increasingly used the more trusted Karl Theuner to represent the Kuratorium to the Czech public.

[29] SD Leitsabschnitt Prag, SD Tagesbericht, 5 May 1944, carton 8, no. 35, 7, Sb NÚIČ, VÚA.

the final year of the war. The Kuratorium, far from proving itself an instrument of Germanization, had accommodated to the dominant demand of the Czech right and left: that Czech children remain ethnically Czech.

Through trial and error, the Kuratorium came to promote an ambiguous doctrine labeled "Reich-loyal Czech nationalism" (*Reichsgebundene tschechische Nationalismus*) by observers. Through programs such as Heydrich's Summer Relaxation Camps for Czech Children and the Week of Czech Youth, Protectorate authorities attempted to harness Czech nationalist traditions to the Nazi state. It became more and more common for Czech boys and girls to parade the outward signs of Czech ethnicity, singing nationalist songs, speaking Czech, and wearing Czech costumes, all under the Nazi banner. The idea that one could be both a Czech nationalist and a loyal Reich subject was not new in the Protectorate. Conservative Czech elites such as Hácha had promoted precisely such ideas since the beginning of the occupation, as they aligned well with Goebbels's propaganda about a harmonious "New Order" in German-led Central Europe.[30] But policies of deliberately harnessing Czechs to the Third Reich as Czechs and of encouraging the expression of local, patriotic Czech culture under Nazi supervision became more explicit after Heydrich's appointment in 1941. Heydrich notoriously deployed a "carrot and stick" policy in the Protectorate. In addition to intensifying the level of terror and brutality in the Bohemian Lands, he increased rations and wages for heavy workers, planned to encourage Czech sports, and appropriated Czech national heroes such as St. Wenceslas as a leader "who realized the Czech nation can live only in harmony with the German Lebensraum."[31] In the Sudetenland as well, SS officials recommended that Czechs be permitted more space for national expression and cultural development toward the end of the war. They discussed plans to create Czech sports associations and reestablish a Czech newspaper in the Gau Sudetenland.[32] Reich-loyal Czech nationalism was therefore not limited to the realm of youth welfare and education, but it did ultimately find its fullest expression within the ranks of the Kuratorium, where this doctrine was systematically developed in a mass organization for the education of Czech youth in the final years of the war.

The Third Reich's authorization of Czech nationalism within the Kuratorium makes it even more difficult to assess whether the children mobilized within its ranks were loyal or resistant to the Third Reich. Contemporary observers were themselves conflicted about the meaning of nationalism

[30] One organization in Nazi-occupied Europe that may have promoted a similar brand of Reich-loyal nationalism was the Weißruthenische Jugendwerk in occupied Belarus. See Chiari, *Alltag hinter der Front*, 195–230.

[31] Kárný, *Deutsche Politik*, 117; Brandes, *Die Tschechen*, 1:211–14.

[32] Volker Zimmermann, *Die Sudetendeutschen im NS-Staat. Politik und Stimmung der Bevölkerung im Reichsgau Sudetenland* (Munich, 1999), 325.

within the Kuratorium. Some saw evidence of Czech youth's successful incorporation into the Third Reich in these nationalist activities, while others viewed the Kuratorium as a potential source of rebellion and revolution, or at least passive resistance. This contemporary ambivalence and confusion were themselves evidence of the extent to which the Kuratorium responded to a priority shared by Czechs across the political spectrum, that Czech children remain ethnically Czech. The Kuratorium thus rendered already blurry lines between collaboration and resistance in the Protectorate even blurrier. Czech children remained ethnically Czech, the Nazi administration believed that it was gradually winning the loyalty of the next generation, output in Bohemian war factories increased, and everyday life continued, ultimately with less repression and resistance than elsewhere in the occupied East.[33]

The popular rehabilitation of the Kuratorium from rumors of Germanization was facilitated in part by Heydrich's Summer Relaxation Program for Czech Children (officially known as the Heydrich *Erholungsaktion*). In 1944, twenty-seven camps offered approximately twenty thousand Czech boys and girls, mostly teenage workers from the war-essential metalworking industries, two weeks of companionship, abundant food, Nazi indoctrination, and Czech nationalism. In 1944 the administration planned to expand the program to include greater numbers of younger children and rural youth during the winter.[34] Teenagers were recommended by their firms, while children were nominated for the program by local youth welfare centers. Participants were required to have fulfilled their youth service, be "intelligent," and "in need of relaxation." Workers from heavy industries and those who worked under adverse conditions were given preference among the teenagers.[35] The Nazi administration took these camps and their propaganda value seriously. Factory owners and managers in 1944 frequently expressed disbelief that essential workers in war industries were to be released for eight weeks to serve as swimming instructors and camp counselors and refused to surrender their employees to the Kuratorium's camps. With the Ministry of Labor's support and threats of fines and police action, the Kuratorium typically prevailed in these disputes.[36] Nazi inspectors meanwhile prepared detailed reports of their visits to the camps, recording every organizational

---

[33] Postwar Czech economist Vacláv Průcha estimated that industrial production in the Bohemian Lands increased by 12 percent between 1939 and 1945. On industrial output in the Protectorate see Alice Teichova, "The Protectorate of Bohemia and Moravia (1939–1945): The Economic Dimension," in *Bohemia in History,* ed. Mikuláš Teich, 267–305 (Cambridge, 1998).

[34] Carton 106, Kuratorium, NA; Grundlagen der Arbeiten für das Sonderlager der Sozialreferenten, 5 January 1944, carton 92, Kuratorium, NA.

[35] Carton 92, Kuratorium, NA; memo an den Herrn Betriebsführer der Firma, Prague, 3 May 1943, carton 108, Kuratorium, NA; lists of children suggested for camps, 11 May 1943, carton 107, Kuratorium, NA.

[36] Letter from Witkowtizer Bergbau und Eisenhütten Gewerkschaft, 5 October 1943, and reply, carton 105, Kuratorium, NA.

or ideological lapse that threatened to weaken the desired propaganda effect of the Heydrich summer camps.

Kuratorium camp leaders faced serious setbacks in the summer of 1943, many of which stemmed from Nazi policy in the Protectorate itself. In Holasice/Holasitz in Moravia, Kuratorium camp leaders could barely even secure provisions for their camp, explaining to a camp inspector that all the food in the region had been "devoured [by the Nazis], and the people here are only punished now." They could purchase meat only on the black market at exorbitant prices. At first, local farmers in the town refused to sell them anything at all because they thought the food was for the Hitler Youth, but once they found out it was for the Kuratorium (and therefore for Czech children), they were slightly more cooperative.[37] Meanwhile, in Okluky/Okluk the Czech leader of a Kuratorium camp was deemed "weak" by a Nazi inspector because the Czech campers greeted him with the Nazi salute and he did not return it.[38] In Eš/Esch there were spoons but no forks or knives in the dining hall. In Mlač/Lautsch, a dismayed inspector reported, "There is an intensive odor of spoiled food in the entire camp. It pervades the dining hall." Many of the girls in the camp had lice. Other camps reportedly lacked a sufficient supply of Swastika flags and photos of Heydrich.[39] These reports reflected both the challenges of running summer camps in the midst of Total War, and a genuine Nazi concern that the camps function flawlessly as instruments of propaganda. It was critical to the Nazi administration that camps were hygienically sound and that campers returned home happy, since, Kuratorium leaders insisted, "The youth who will return from the camps will always be the best propaganda for the Kuratorium."[40]

In spite of organizational setbacks, the prevailing mood in the camps was positive, at least according to the internal reports of Nazi camp inspectors.[41] The reports may not have been exaggerated, however, given that the camps did offer teenagers a respite from the long hours, discipline, and physically exhausting labor in war factories. In fact, most tensions arose because of the gap between campers' expectations of total freedom and leisure and the minimal level of discipline expected in the camps. At first, leaders remarked, some young Czechs arrived with infuriating attitude problems. Camp leader Kubik reported, "As I've heard, the youth came to the camp with poor information, which the firms had given them. They thought they could do whatever they pleased in the camps (like swim, play, lie in the

---

[37] Josef Jirasek, Die Meldung des Wirtschaftsführers aus Holasitz in Mähren, Prague, 28 June 1943, carton 107, Kuratorium, NA.

[38] Bericht über das Erziehungspersonal im Lager Okluk bei Prossnitz, Prague, 9 June 1943, carton 108, Kuratorium, NA.

[39] Bericht über Erholungslager, 20 May 1943, carton 106; Revision in den Erholungslagern, 28 July 1944, carton 107; all in Kuratorium, NA.

[40] Sommerlager Podhrad, Kolin, 20 May 1943, carton 108, Kuratorium, NA.

[41] Bericht über Erholungslager, 20 May 1943, carton 106, Kuratorium, NA.

sun, all according to their mood) and that the most that would be expected is that they come eat at a certain time." With a bit of firm guidance from the instructors, however, the campers reportedly adapted, and even began to enjoy the "relaxing" pedagogical routines in the camp.[42] Czech youth were also far more receptive to the camps in 1944 than in 1943, in part because many had not expected any vacation at all during that summer of frantic military production. The SD in Prague reported that if some teenage workers had attempted to avoid the camps the previous year, in 1944 many young workers actually requested to participate in the program, such that the quality of the youth attending improved considerably. Some Czech youth nonetheless still resented the disciplined routines and exhausting schedule of lectures and activities in the "relaxation" camps, above all being "yanked out of bed" at the crack of dawn. These campers reportedly complained that "a vacation at home would offer far more opportunity for relaxation than the Relaxation Program."[43]

Days in the camps began early, with a flag-raising ceremony. The camp leader read inspirational proverbs from Goebbels, Friedrich the Great, and Nietzsche in Czech before closing the ceremony with the Nazi salute.[44] Campers and instructors spoke to one another only in the informal form of address, a tradition adopted from the Hitler Youth and Sokol.[45] The days continued with sports, singing, political education, swimming, hiking, and plenty of eating. The dining halls served three meals and two snacks each day. At the end of each two-week session the population in neighboring towns were invited to a public festival with music, food, skits, inspirational speeches, sports competitions, and the singing of Czech national songs. Political education emphasized both Czech national achievements and a long history of German-Czech cooperation in their shared Heimat.[46]

Campers submitted hundreds of evaluations of their experience, carefully handwritten in Czech, at the end of each session. The evaluations are certainly not an objective source: the campers were assigned to write them for use in Nazi propaganda campaigns, and they betray a formulaic quality. It is possible, however, to learn something from *what* the Czech campers found to praise in the camps. If these teenagers, many away from home for the first time, complained that their mothers prepared better dumplings at home and that strenuous exercise took getting used to, they enthusiastically praised the camaraderie among youth and instructors, nights spent singing Czech national songs around the campfire, and opportunities to learn

[42] Erholungslager in Okluk, Bericht, 16 June 1943, carton 105, Kuratorium, NA.

[43] SD Leitabschnitt Prag, SD Tagesbericht, 12 May 1944, 7, no. 37, 7–8, carton 8, Sb NÚIČ, VÚA.

[44] Dienstliche Weisung, no. 11, Prague, 4 August 1943, carton 106, Kuratorium, NA.

[45] Dienstliche Weisung no. 10, Prague, 24 July 1943, carton 108, Kuratorium, NA.

[46] Memo an alle Lagerleiter/innen, carton 106, Kuratorium, NA; Dienstliche Weisung no. 14, Prague, 14 September 1943, carton 106, Kuratorium, NA.

about Czech national culture through field trips to Prague. More than a few mentioned the "superb instruction" they received from camp youth leaders. Oldrich Rozehnálek, for example, wrote of his experience in a camp in Tábor, "I liked it in the camp very much. I was happy to be called up for 14 days of vacation, for walks in the woods and to the lake for swimming. Best of all I liked the camaraderie and unity in the camp, the peaceful order, and the national songs we sang."[47] Václav Řehák likewise affirmed, "The national songs that we sang in the evenings had a very impressive effect on me. Before the burning fire I encountered lovely Czech music. It surprised me a great deal."[48]

The Day of Czech Youth

In the final year of the war, the ambiguous successes of the Kuratorium seemed to offer hope to Nazi officials for the future of Czech-German co-operation. The Kuratorium's Day of Czech Youth in May of 1944 proved to be a turning point. A German informant cited the success of the Day of Czech Youth in Prague as evidence that "Czech youth now find themselves in the hands of the Kuratorium and willingly follow its lead. . . . They took things seriously and did not attempt to avoid various exercises as in previous years."[49] Reich-loyal Czech nationalism was at the root of the program's success. Following the festivities, SD informants in Prague elaborated that the improvement in Czech attitudes toward the Kuratorium was almost entirely the fruit of the Kuratorium's new policy of "emphasizing Czech nationalism in youth education."[50]

In a surprising development, the 1944 Day of Czech Youth made a favorable impression among Czech parents as well as youth, according to Nazi informants. Parents and other observers at the festivities were frequently overheard praising the unexpected Czech nationalist tone of the event. "If we had known that our children would be trained like this, we would not have made it so difficult for them to participate in the Kuratorium," remarked one parent. A second surprised observer commented, "The children were educated as Czechs, although we were always of the opinion that it [the Kuratorium] was a purely German affair." Yet another Czech mother

[47] Folder Tábor Es, 1943, Oldrich Rozehnálek; see also letter from Josef Mrásecký, both in carton 107, Kuratorium, NA.

[48] Folder Tábor Es, 1943, letter from Václav Řehák, carton 107, Kuratorium, NA. See also Kuratorium, carton 109 for more letters from boys' camps, as well as carton 108 for news from the camp leader of Medlov, 12 June 1944.

[49] SD Leitsabschnitt Prag, SD Tagesbericht, 9 May 1944, no. 36, 9—10, carton 8, Sb NÚIČ, VÚA.

[50] Anlage zum SD-Tagesbericht no. 40/44, Frühlingstag der tschechischen Jugend am 7.5.1944, 6, no. 40, carton 8, Sb NÚIČ, VÚA.

Fig. 4. The Kuratorium's Day of Czech Youth, Moravská Ostrava/Mährisch Ostrau, June 13, 1944. Národní archiv, Prague, fond Kuratorium, carton 100.

Fig. 5. The Kuratorium for Youth Education in Wenceslas Square, Prague, 1944. Národní archiv, Prague, fond Kuratorium, carton 100.

explained that she had mistakenly believed that the Kuratorium was trying to Germanize Czech youth until the Day of Czech Youth disabused her of this notion: "The Kuratorium is leading youth education in a Czech spirit, as we demanded. Now for the first time we understand the work of the Kuratorium correctly."[51] Local officials within the Kuratorium were also pleased with its new direction. Following the festival in Tábor/Tabor, many young people reportedly appeared in local Kuratorium offices to register for activities, demanding, "We want to sing and march along with the others." From Budějovice/Budweis, the local Kuratorium leader reported, "This political tactic is the right strategy to bring Czechs closer to Reich ideals. The Spring Day of Czech Youth achieved far more in this respect than lectures and newspaper articles have thus far accomplished." Another German-friendly Czech agreed, insisting that "the Czech nation, when allowed . . . his old customs and traditions, will feel more inclined toward the Germans than has previously been the case."[52]

The Kuratorium, explained SD informants, was increasingly taking on the character of an organic Czech nationalist youth movement. Many of the youth leaders involved had previous experience in fascist youth organizations such as the otherwise marginal Czech nationalist Vlajka or in patriotic organizations such as the Sokol.[53] At a conference of functionaries and educators in 1944, Kuratorium chief Karl Theuner was greeted with thunderous applause when he announced that he intended to transform the organization from "an office and a bureaucratic authority to a dynamic movement." This Nazi informant explained that "Reich-loyal Czech nationalism" was not a top-down policy but the spontaneous invention of the Czech pedagogical activists who worked within the Kuratorium: "The activist, Reich-oriented Kuratorium employees, above all, the considerable number of Czech youth leaders, sought within themselves an idea, a program that they believed they had found with the formation and promotion of a Reich-loyal Czech nationalism. They push open themes that have been avoided up until now, like worldview, race, and nation, etc." He concluded, "countless individual observations show that it is only a matter of time until this Reich-loyal Czech nationalism is openly promoted as the ideological basis of education in the Kuratorium."[54]

This program marked a clear change of direction for the Nazi administration in the Protectorate. While Reich-loyal Czech nationalism had not yet shown any "chauvinistic tendencies," SD informants also cautioned that the development clearly rendered any attempt to "denationalize" or "Germanize" Czech youth "difficult, if not impossible." Locally, the work of the

[51] Ibid.
[52] Ibid., 2–6.
[53] Zprávy z domova, 24 January 1944, 91/7, 3, fond 37, VÚA.
[54] Kuratorium für Jugenderziehung im Böhmen und Mähren, 23 August 1944, R 58/1003, BA.

Kuratorium had already contributed to stronger assertions of Czech nationalist consciousness among children and adults alike. "Local events of the cultural division have already become little national climaxes reaching well beyond the youth themselves."[55] These celebrations of Czech culture promoted a depoliticized kind of national folklore that observers hoped would be consonant with loyalty to Reich. At the May festival in Prague, for example, German informants observed, "The mentality of the Czech population was particularly addressed through propaganda marches displaying costumes, games, the singing of Czech folk songs and performances of old Czech folk dances, whereby the 'Spring Day of Czech Youth' partly took on the character of a Czech national festival. The increased support for the Kuratorium that has been achieved is thus in no way attributable to the desired Reich ideals but to the Czech nationalist moments."[56]

The Kuratorium also successfully built on native Czech nationalist traditions of collective education. SD informants reported that many Czech parents appreciated the national discipline cultivated in the Kuratorium. "It is certainly important that our youth are also raised for the community," remarked one Czech observer in praise of the Kuratorium's springtime festival. The SD reported widespread rumors among Czechs "that even Beneš supporters and other enemy elements no longer reject the Kuratorium because they see a conscious Czech-national program in its activities. They are of the opinion that through the preservation of this program, the Czech nation and above all Czech youth will be more unified than otherwise."[57] In September of that year, confusion between collaboration and resistance within the Kuratorium reached a truly absurd (and embarrassing) climax for the Nazis when the Kuratorium actually printed a notice in its propaganda magazine stating that the Czechoslovak National Committee in London (the exiled Czech government led by Beneš) had recognized and endorsed the Kuratorium's activities.[58]

Reich-loyal Czech nationalism was most prominently on display during the Week of Czech Youth in Prague in the summer of 1944. Official propaganda explicitly promoted the festival as a Czech nationalist event. The Czech newspaper *Národní politika* encouraged the entire Czech population to participate as spectators, advertising, "At the Strahovský stadium girls will dance in national costumes from all regions of our homeland and Czech national songs will blare from morning until night. The week of Czech youth is not only an event for youth but a people's event, to which all are summoned. And all of you, who will be the spectators, should remember that

---

[55] Ibid.

[56] Anlage zum SD-Tagesbericht no. 40/44, Frühlingstag der tschechischen Jugend am 7.5.1944, 6, no. 40, carton 8, Sb NÚIČ, VÚA.

[57] Ibid.

[58] Leitsabschnitt Prag, SD Tagesbericht, 12 September 1944, no. 79, carton 8, Sb NÚIČ, VÚA.

it is Czech youth before you, the sons and daughters of your nation."[59] Reports from Hitler Youth officials to Berlin immediately noted the new tone of the festivities and the corresponding enthusiasm of the Czech population. These reports emphasized that many Czech participants and supporters of the Kuratorium now viewed it as "no more than a continuation of the Sokol tradition." Czech children dressed in traditional Moravian costumes were demonstratively greeted with cries of "Nazdar," and noisily applauded as they marched through the streets of Prague, "at which point the mood clearly slid over into chauvinistic extremes." Meanwhile, youth marching in military formation were greeted with icy silence as they appeared suspiciously "German." Only when musical groups began to play well-known Czech songs did the crowd resume its rowdy cheering.[60]

Hitler Youth officials from Germany who attended the festivities in Prague were duly impressed by the discipline and even by the "impressive racial appearance" of the ten thousand Czech youth who marched through the streets of Prague that August, as well as by the eager participation of the adult population. One official reported to Berlin that an exhibition of children's artwork entitled "Show What You Can Do" was "extraordinarily well received" by adults and children alike, in spite of the fact that the work on display was "kitschy and from a German standpoint hardly bearable." The population's enthusiasm reached an awe-inspiring climax at a final performance in which Czech youth led a cheering crowd, including Moravec himself, in the singing of well-known Czech national songs. "In these moments the mood in the room almost corresponded to that of a German Nazi Party assembly during the fight era. Occasionally I could not ward off a certain feeling of uneasiness," the informant confessed.[61]

His uneasiness was shared by a Czech who denounced the Kuratorium in an anonymous letter that summer: "I beg of you to bring order to the Kuratorium camps. The instructors are unreliable rascals. They play forbidden games, drink, listen to foreign radio broadcasts and prepare themselves for the arrival of the Bolsheviks."[62] A Nazi SD informant substantiated these fears, speculating that the young nationalists being trained in the Kuratorium might one day become revolutionaries whom the Reich would be "forced to reckon with in the future."[63] Other observers also concluded that the Czech nationalism on display could only be interpreted as a sign of resistance to the Nazi regime, assuming that any expression of Czech nationalism represented hostility to Nazi ideals. One Czech woman was overheard remarking,

[59] Ohlas nové mládeže, "Praha-hostitelka," *Národní politika*, 30 June 1944. See also "Poznáváme českou mládež," *Přítomnost*, 1 August 1944, carton 103, Kuratorium, NA.

[60] SD Leitabschnitt Prag, 8 April 1944, NS 6/410, BA.

[61] Hitler Jugend, Oberbannführer Riebensahm an Oberbannführer Schmidt, Bericht über die Woche der tschechischen Jugend, Berlin, 17 July 1944. NS 28, BA.

[62] SD Tagesbericht, 19 September 1944, no. 81, carton 8, Sb NÚIČ, VÚA.

[63] SD Tagesbericht, 23 May 1944, no. 68, 5, carton 8, Sb NÚIČ, VÚA.

"If the Germans believe that they can educate Czech youth in Reich ways of thinking they're barking up the wrong tree. . . . These costumes can only strengthen national feeling."[64]

A July 1944 report by a Hitler Youth official to Berlin confirmed these ambivalent impressions. The Kuratorium had succeeded, wrote Oberstammführer Krome, in promoting "the immediate impression not of a Czech youth that is dying out and brooding with dark plans against the Reich, but of a Czech youth that is marching, dancing, and singing for a better European age, under the leadership of their great German neighbors." Krome corroborated SD reports that the entire event was "truly a Czech nationalist demonstration." The Hitler Youth, he explained, had deliberately held back as Kuratorium officials organized the Week of Czech Youth, precisely in order to "allow the impression that this is actually an internal affair of the Czech youth."[65] The Nazi coordination of Czech youth had successfully neutralized private political resistance against the Reich, he claimed. Yet "lasting and deliberate" supervision and guidance was necessary to ensure that this impressive "will to demonstrate" in the Kuratorium youth took on the desired political accents.[66]

Nazi observers were themselves well aware that Reich-loyal Czech nationalism was a double-edged sword. Informants both within and outside the Nazi administration were confused and conflicted when confronted with Czech nationalism in the ranks of the Kuratorium. Was participation in the Kuratorium a form of collaboration? Of resistance? There could be no clear answer. While Communists and Socialists were certainly not welcome in the ranks of the Kuratorium, Reich-loyal Czech nationalism did represent a Nazi attempt to accommodate the dominant concerns of the Czech right and left, that Czech children should remain ethnically Czech. Nazi informants emphasized that they had successfully harnessed Czech nationalism to their own cause with popular Kuratorium programs, but they were unsure about the extent to which they could control this nationalism. Czech resistance activists were equally conflicted about the meaning of Reich-loyal Czech nationalism. An informant writing to London assured the Czech government in exile that the Kuratorium posed little threat to Czech children in October of 1944, optimistically emphasizing the national resistance within the Kuratorium: "Our children look better than the Germans, healthier and more spirited. The Kuratorium is causing no harm, young people see it as a temporary replacement of the Sokol and the propaganda is not taking one bit. Resistance to Nazism is deeply rooted."[67] Only five months earlier,

---

[64] SD Tagesbericht, 23 May 1944, no. 40, 6, carton 8, Sb NÚIČ, VÚA.
[65] Teilnahme an den Abschlußfeierlichkeiten der Woche der tschechischen Jugend in Prag am 8. und 9.7.1944, Berlin, 14 July 1944, NS 28, BA.
[66] Ibid.
[67] Vzkaz Fuetera a zprávy z domova, 2 October 1944, 91/7, 4, fond 37, VÚA.

however, in Budějovice/Budweis, a local Czech bureaucrat had observed a successful Kuratorium rally and concluded with dismay, "One can only come to the conclusion that Czech youth and German youth will soon be indistinguishable."[68]

Krome himself was ultimately optimistic, seeing the Kuratorium as a broader model for Nazi rule and future Czech-German cooperation. Czech youth, he reported, had "doubtlessly" rejected Bolshevism, and it was also widely acknowledged that "the young Czechs fulfill their duties in the workforce conscientiously and with discipline."[69] Young skilled workers and craftsmen were reported to be particularly receptive to the Kuratorium and its camps, even if they still faced pressures to resist the Nazis from teachers and family members at home.[70] It was impossible to imagine, Krome speculated, "that in the case of a direct threat to their Heimat through a danger from the East, the 500,000 young people organized through the Kuratorium would take on any other position than that which furthers the interests of the Reich."[71]

The Nazi administration had learned something from reports about Czech attitudes toward the Russians. Those Czechs who favored Russian rule did not necessarily believe that Stalin would offer the possibility of autonomous or democratic self-government. Rather, Russophile Czechs often asserted that Stalin was less likely than the Nazis to impose a regime of cultural and educational denationalization.[72] The Kuratorium's doctrine of Reich-loyal Czech nationalism took these attitudes to heart. If Sudeten German Nazis initially imagined the Nazi regime as the ultimate German nationalist state, in this context the Nazi state appeared as a new kind of empire. Like educational activists in the Habsburg Monarchy, Czech educators active in the Kuratorium promoted nationalist cultural "autonomy" alongside (outward) loyalty to the state. Indeed, Reich-loyal Czech nationalism may have been similar in certain respects to the nationalities policies pursued by the former Soviet Union, which sought to promote symbolic forms of cultural nationalism in order to domesticate political nationalism.[73] It was the imagined imperial quality promoted by the Kuratorium that enabled some Czechs to envision a nationalist potential for themselves under Nazi rule, even while other participants and

[68] SD Tagesbericht, 23 May 1944, no. 40, 6, carton 8, Sb NÚIČ, VÚA.

[69] Teilnahme an den Abschlußfeierlichkeiten der Woche der tschechischen Jugend in Prag am 8. und 9.7.1944, Berlin, 14 July 1944, NS 28, BA.

[70] Unser Einfluss auf die ältere Schuljugend, Prague, 21 April 1944, Kuratorium, carton 43, NA.

[71] Teilnahme an den Abschlußfeierlichkeiten der Woche der tschechischen Jugend in Prag am 8. und 9.7.1944, Berlin, 14 July 1944, NS 28, BA.

[72] *Meldungen aus dem Reich,* SD Bericht zu Inlandsfragen, 10 February 1944.

[73] Terry Martin, *The Affirmative Action Empire: Nations and Nationalism in the Soviet Union, 1923–1939* (Ithaca, 2001); Yuri Slezkine, "The USSR as a Communal Apartment, or How a Socialist State Promoted Ethnic Particularism," in *Becoming National: A Reader,* ed. Geoff Eley and Ronald Grigor Suny, 203–39 (Oxford, 1996).

observers saw the Kuratorium as a bubbling cauldron of resistance and subversion.

Aftermath

The Kuratorium's successes were short-lived. By late 1944 the Czech population of the Protectorate was biding its time until the German defeat and the arrival of the Russians. Discipline and order were impossible to maintain among youth and especially among Kuratorium functionaries. In Kuratorium camps, lamented the SD in August 1944, "fistfights and brawls are a daily occurrence. . . . Sabotage of work due to laziness and conscious political obstruction is steadily increasing."[74] In Hradec Králové/Königgrätz, a group of sixteen- to eighteen-year-olds, convinced that the Russian invasion was imminent, refused to attend mandatory Kuratorium events. They informed their instructor that he should "go look for a tree on which he wanted to hang."[75]

If the Kuratorium's popularity was fleeting, the doctrine of Reich-loyal Czech nationalism had much deeper roots in the history of the nationalist battle for children in the Bohemian Lands. Reich-loyal Czech nationalism emerged from a society in which both right-wing collaborators and left-wing antifascists, for all their significant differences, shared a common nationalist priority. It was a product not only of self-declared Czech collaborators, who organized and staffed Heydrich's relaxation camps, but of a left-wing Czech nationalist milieu that insisted that democratic political values were innate to Czech ethnicity. If democracy was essential to Czech character, protecting ethnic Czechness could stand in for a larger battle in defense of progressive values. Reich-loyal Czech nationalism represented a largely improvised Nazi response to the specificities of Czech nationalist political culture, the vehicle through which the occupying regime traded in its failed dreams of ethnically Germanizing Czech children for the far less contentious program of ideologically Nazifying them as Czechs.

Czech parents succeeded in keeping Czech children Czech during World War II. But they fought their battle against Nazism in a shared language of protecting ethnic purity. These nationalist priorities authorized indifference to the fate of those seen to be outside the boundaries of the national community, including Jews and antifascist Germans, and helped to justify the violent expulsions of the postwar period. In a startling example of this indifference, Czech resistance activists commented, toward the end of the war,

---

[74] SD Tagesbericht, 19 September 1944, no. 81, carton 8, Sb NÚIČ, VÚA.
[75] SD Tagesbericht, 8 June 1944. See also SD Tagesbericht, 8 August 1944, no. 68. Both in carton 8, Sb NÚIČ, VÚA.

on the growth of anti-Semitism among ordinary Czechs. These informants often blamed anti-Semitism on the Nazi example, even as they located its primary roots in a (now tragically ironic) long-term association of Jews with Germandom and Germanization in the Bohemian Lands. A typical report explained, "Anti-Semitism will probably be the only thing that we will partly take from Nazi ideology. Our people certainly don't approve of the bestial German methods of breaking the Jews, but they do believe that the majority of Jews deserve what is coming to them. As far as national reliability is concerned, our people are of the belief that in reality there were very few Jews who spoke Czech correctly and were Czech-oriented. Only such people will be granted residence in the new state."[76] Another Czech informant reported, "Memories of Germanization here, of Jewish indifference to our national cause, disloyalty to the state, are still alive. The general opinion is that they will not be missed."[77] A few months later, a Czech resistance activist reported widespread bitterness that Jews had not at least left Czechs with more of their property when they were deported by the Gestapo to concentration camps or fled the country: "The anti-Semitism of our people at home is growing. They [Jews] reciprocated our favors badly. They fled to us from the Sudetenland. We protected them. But they left nothing behind for us. It would have been better to put them all in the hands of the Gestapo."[78]

Through their campaign to protect the ethnic purity of Czech children against the overriding threat of Germanization, Czech nationalists across the political spectrum answered the Nazi occupiers in the Nazis' own terms. By depicting the violence of denationalization as the Nazis' greatest offense, Czech nationalists also placed themselves first in an imagined hierarchy of victims. If denationalization had been the crime, national purification was the imagined solution. Many Czech nationalists ultimately understood the Nazi experience not as a failure of tolerance or pluralism in the Bohemian Lands but as the consequence of diversity itself, of the presence of non-Czechs in the Czechoslovak nation-state. In this view, nothing but ethnic cleansing could prevent social and educational institutions from again becoming instruments of Germanization.

[76] Zpráva z Turecka, 20 December 1943, sig. 91/6, fond 37, VÚA.
[77] Zpráva o domově, 14 August 1944, sig. 91/7, fond 37, VÚA.
[78] Zprávy z domova, 5 May 1944, 3, sig. 91/7, fond 37, VÚA.

Epilogue

After the Nazi defeat, the doctrine of Reich-loyal Czech nationalism was quickly forgotten. Postwar journalists, Czech officials, and humanitarian activists typically remembered the barbarity of Nazi rule in Eastern Europe in terms of the violence of forced denationalization.[1] The prevailing opinion in Czech society, according to an informant's report from May 1944, was that Czech children would not be safe until every German was purged from the Bohemian Lands. In July of 1944 a Czech informant reported to London, "After the last speech of Dr. Beneš there was disappointment in Bohemia because he wants to keep the loyal Germans here. There are no loyal Germans, they are all alike, and in the best case the children of loyal Germans will grow up to be pan-Germans again. They cannot stay even if they attend Czech schools, because the German spirit will be preserved privately. We are doing the same thing ourselves under the Nazi regime, and we are not as sneaky as the Germans would be."[2] A growing consensus emerged among Czech nationalists and political leaders that every last German would have to be sent "home to the Reich" after the war. The very ideals of national homogeneity and practices of demographic engineering promoted by the

---

[1] For some contemporary examples see Dorothy Macardle, *Children of Europe: A Study of the Children of Liberated Countries, Their Wartime Experiences, Their Reactions, and Their Needs* (Boston, 1951), esp. 37–65, 65–83, 231–41; Czechoslovak Ministry of the Interior, *Pohřešované československé děti* (Prague, 1946); Václav Buben, ed. *Šest let okupace Prahy* (Prague, 1946); Ira Hirschmann, "The Lost Children," in *The Embers Still Burn* (New York, 1949), 244–61. For accounts emphasizing the Germanization of children, see Václav Král, ed., *Lessons from History: Documents Concerning Nazi Policy for Germanization and Extermination in Czechoslovakia* (Prague, 1960); Kiryl Sosnowski, *The Tragedy of Children under Nazi Rule* (Poznan, 1962); Jiří Doležal, *Česká kultura za Protektorátu: školství, písemnictví, kinematographie* (Prague, 1996).
[2] Zprávy z domova, 10 July 1944, sig. 91/7, fond 37, VÚA.

Nazis (and by Sudeten German and Czech nationalists before them) therefore emerged triumphant from the Second World War.

Soon after the allied victory, Czech soldiers, local security forces, and militias began their campaign to rid the Bohemian Lands of their German citizens, expelling over seven hundred thousand Germans by the end of 1945. Two million more Germans were stripped of their citizenship and shipped westward in cattle cars during the "organized" transfers that began in January of 1946, with the blessing of the international community. Rhetorically, expulsion may have seemed like the cleanest solution to the nationality conflict in the Bohemian Lands. Not surprisingly, however, the persistence of bilingualism, mixed marriages, and national hermaphroditism made for a more complicated reality on the ground. The expulsions forced officials to deal with the thorny problem of national classification one last time.

In July of 1945, the Czech Provincial Commission for Child Welfare in Bohemia sent an urgent memo to the Ministry of the Interior, demanding new solutions to an old problem: how were they to distinguish between German children and Czech children? This time the results would determine which children could stay in liberated Czechoslovakia and which would join the cattle cars of expellees. Children of mixed marriages, in particular, forced officials to choose between two conflicting nationalist goals—an ambition to cleanse the Bohemian Lands of every last trace of Germandom and the impulse to save every last drop of Czech blood for the "small" Czech nation. Widespread rumors that internment camps and trains bound for Germany were crowded with Czech-speaking children and mothers provoked noisy public debate and concern. In the face of continuing confusion, the ČZK demanded "that a principled, responsible, and singular decision be taken as to how to determine the nationality and legal standing of these minor children. . . . Children from mixed marriages are very numerous, and because the evacuation of Germans is progressing steadily, it is necessary to decide quickly." Child welfare officials in Ústí nad Labem, the site of some of the most violent "wild" expulsions, recommended in July 1945 that "parents [in mixed marriages] are offered the opportunity to divorce, so that their children can be saved." Otherwise these children received coupons for German rations, which were equivalent to the starvation rations allocated to Jews during the war. The provincial commission, for its part, proposed that "in the greater interests of the nation . . . every child in whose veins Czech blood flows, even if only from one parent, should be considered a Czech child and educated as a Czech so as to undo the damage wrought on the moral development of these children during the period of unfreedom, whether that damage was caused by German persecution or the negligence of their parents."[3] A year later, the ČZK even requested permission

---

[3] Národnost dětí ze smíšených rodičů, 9 July 1945, carton 1421, Ministerstvo vnitra-nová registratura (MV-NR), NA.

from the Ministry of the Interior to forcibly remove children of mixed marriages from their German parent in order to keep them in Czechoslovakia and
raise them as Czechs (while their German mothers or fathers were expelled).
When the Nazis had deployed such tactics, they were denounced as a barbaric
form of kidnapping and denationalization, but postwar Czech nationalists
considered the same policies a just and humane measure, a necessary defense
against Germanization.[4]

One concerned citizen even suggested that expelling Germanized Czech
children (by which he meant any child whose ancestors had allegedly been
Germanized over the past hundred years), amounted to nothing less than a
concession of defeat in the nationalist battle for children. Josef Břecka, the
director of a Czech middle school, delivered an impassioned manifesto on
the subject to government officials in 1946, cautioning, "The latest news
from Germany shows that there is a very large population among the young-
est generation. We, however, are increasing that population even more,
through the expulsion of children from mixed marriages and Germanized
regions. Isn't that an extreme form of recklessness?" These children could be
salvaged for the Czech nation, he argued, if they were quickly resettled in the
Czech interior to be reeducated as Czechs. Meanwhile, "The Germanizing
parts of the family . . . must be prevented from exercising any influence on
the family. . . . Even if they are not guilty, they must be sentenced to forced
labor and only permitted to visit [the family] for short periods of time."[5]

Not everyone agreed, but Břecka's proposal was taken seriously and circulated to several government ministries. While the Ministry of Foreign Affairs
found nothing objectionable in the plan, officials in the State Statistical Office
accused Břecka of upholding the "Nazi theory of nationality, which considers
nationality a corporeal and material fact." The Statistical Office countered:

> Nationality is not decided by the dead, but by living individuals. That means
> that so-called Germanized Czechs, or individuals whose ancestors were
> Czechs, are Germans. A Czech man or woman who joined the German na-
> tionality through marriage or German influence and thereby deserted us does
> not deserve any sentimental allowances. It is not in the interest of the Czech
> nation to expand its ranks with the German nation's trash. The few thousand
> German children we expel will not add much to the German nation's many
> millions, but for our Czech nation of a few million, those children would be a
> large germinating embryo of future collaborators and fifth columnists.[6]

---

[4] Dětí ze smíšených manželství, memo from Czech Provincial Commission to Ministry of the
Interior, 12 April 1946, sig. 1364/2, carton 1032, Úřad předsednictva vlády (ÚPV- bez), NA.

[5] Josef Břecka, Opis k č.j. 11560-II-2947/46, 12 March 1946, sig. 1364/2, carton 1032,
ÚPV-bez, NA.

[6] President Státního úřadu statistického, Prague 15. dubna 1946, Napravení germanisace,
Návrh Josefa Břecky, sig. 1364/2, carton 1032, ÚPV-bez, NA.

The Czechoslovak authorities ultimately issued several sets of conflicting guidelines for assessing nationality, guaranteeing ongoing confusion at the local level. In March of 1946 the Ministry of Foreign Affairs specified that in carrying out the expulsions, local officials should "make it a clear priority to preserve as many people as possible for the Czechoslovak nation in whom Czech or Slovak blood flows."[7] Simultaneously, however, a 1946 directive from the Ministry of Interior cautioned that children of mixed marriages should not be repatriated to Czechoslovakia if the "non-Czech elements [in the family] are dominant and there is no hope of changing this situation."[8] Yet another set of rules applied to displaced orphans and unaccompanied children in Germany. Ministry of Interior officials instructed the United Nations Relief and Rehabilitation Administration (UNRRA) that unaccompanied children over the age of fourteen could be repatriated to Czechoslovakia only if they had sufficiently mastered the Czech or Slovak language. Orphans over the age of eight from mixed marriages or of undetermined nationality were subject to an investigation to determine their nationality based on the time-tested "objective characteristics," and only certified Czechs or Slovaks were permitted to return to Czechoslovakia. Orphans under the age of eight, however, could be repatriated even if they were Germans or Hungarians, since they could presumably be reeducated as Czechs in Czech orphanages.[9]

In another (ultimately failed) effort to eliminate national hermaphroditism in postwar Czechoslovakia, Czechoslovak president Edward Beneš proposed that all Czechs and Slovaks with Germanic names be required to Czechify their names by the end of 1945. The Nazis had made similar attempts to force Germans in Eastern Europe and Alsace to Germanize Slavic or French names during the war. According to the postwar plan, citizens would be required to obtain approval for their new Czech names from local committees composed of four Czech-language teachers and a linguistic expert.[10] A government pamphlet entitled "Let's Czechify our names" speculated that eliminating this final trace of national ambiguity would not be easy—some linguists estimated that 28 percent of Czechs in the Bohemian Lands had Germanic names. The law never went into effect, and in spite of widespread propaganda encouraging the "national cleansing of names,"

[7] Ministerstvo zahraničních věci, 16 March 1946, Pátrání po dětech-otázka národnosti, carton 846, Ministerstvo práce a sociální péče-repatriace (MPSP-R), NA; for the Ministry of Foreign Affairs' response to Břecka's memo, see Smíšená manželství a napravení germanisace-návrh Josefa Břecky, memo from the Ministry of Foreign Affairs to the Ministry of the Interior, 13 May 1946, sig. 1364/2, carton 1032, ÚPV- bez, NA.
[8] Repatriace přislínků smíšených manželství, carton 8245, MV-NR, NA.
[9] Ministerstvo vnitra, 28 April 1947, Směrnice pro repatriaci sirotků, carton 847, MPSP-R, NA.
[10] Návrh Dekret presidenta Československé republiky ze dne . . . 1945 o odgermanisování osobních jmen příslušníků českého národa. carton 1439, MV-NR, NA.

fewer than one percent of Czechoslovak citizens changed their names voluntarily. In Hlučín, moreover, a September 1947 article complained that the most popular names for new babies were Inge, Edeltraude, and Horst.[11]

Jewish displaced persons, meanwhile, were subject to regulations that reflected persistent anti-Semitism and an association of Jews with Germandom and Germanization. A decree from the Ministry of Interior in September of 1946 declared that all Czechoslovak Jews were eligible for Czechoslovak citizenship after the war, even if they had declared themselves Germans in the 1930 census, so long as they now "profess to belong to the Czech, Slovak or another Slavic nationality, and never acted against the Czech or Slovak nation."[12] In practice, however, some Jewish requests for repatriation were denied on the grounds that the applicants were Germans. In one such case, officials in the Ministry of National Defense refused Emmanuel Goldberger's application to return to Czechoslovakia on the grounds that he was German, although Goldberger himself claimed to be a Czech and had been an active Zionist. He had escaped a concentration camp in 1942 and then joined the Czechoslovak foreign legion. Ministry of Defense officials nonetheless concluded that he had only opportunistically joined the foreign legion and professed to be a Czech "in order to avoid racial persecution as a Jew" and "in order to remain hidden and avoid attention" and not out of "authentic" Czech national loyalties. Goldberger had attended German schools as a child, "only spoke German at home and read German newspapers," officials explained, and therefore he remained a German and "could not be considered loyal from the perspective of state citizenship."[13]

In the same year, Czech sociologist Josef Hůrský published an extensive study on the problem of ascertaining nationality for the purpose of determining citizenship rights, an emerging field of study he called "natiologie." He recommended detailed investigations into each questionable individual's private life, public deeds, and personal history in order to ascertain his or her capacity for "re-Czechification." His analysis reveals how old nationalist tropes linking national flexibility to a defective character were integrated into new, allegedly more "scientifically objective" investigations of political and national loyalties, criminality, and social psychology. Case RV8, for example, was a married, bilingual father of two children who worked in a sugar factory. His education had been both Czech and German. As an adult he exemplified the nationally labile opportunist. When questioned directly about his own national loyalties, RV8 responded frankly, "It is a matter of who is giving

[11] František Jílek, *Počeštujeme svá příjmení* (Prague, 1945); Jména na Hlučinsku, 10 November 1947, both in carton 1439, MV-NR, NA.

[12] Úřad předsednitcva vlády, Otázka židovské národnosti, 13 dubna 1948, carton 8245, MV-NR, NA.

[13] Ministerstvo národní obrany, Goldberger Emmanuel-Setření národnosti, 5 November 1946, carton 1421, MV-NR, NA.

more." This national flexibility reflected a degenerate character, according to Hůrský: "The lability of his nationality corresponds to the lability of his entire character, which is enormous and borders on immorality. Even in the choice of a wife he was (according to one acquaintance) dictated by greed (hopes for inheritance), which was stronger than his true love for a former classmate whom he had known for some years." Hůrský ultimately warned against granting RV8 Czech citizenship, concluding, "His trembling character would certainly offer no contribution to the national community. His nationality is permanently wobbly, and even under the condition that he was removed from the influence of his family, not capable of true stabilization."[14]

These postwar efforts to establish scientific criteria to distinguish between Czechs and Germans for the purpose of ethnic cleansing drew on and consolidated long-standing traditions of national classification in the Bohemian Lands. In the heat of the postwar moment, the demographic battle to secure the souls of nationally ambiguous children raged on. With time, demands to preserve Czech blood triumphed, and the government adopted policies designed to save the children of mixed marriage for the Czech nation and to protect them from the worst physical and material hardships inflicted on the children of Germans. In the words of *Hlas lidu,* the newspaper of the Czech People's Party in Budějovice/Budweis, "We must not allow ourselves to make Czechs out of Germans, but then again, we must not allow ourselves to make Germans out of Czechs either. Many mixed marriages, and especially the children from those marriages, must be examined very carefully so we do not commit any injustice."[15] The expulsion of the Sudeten Germans can therefore be seen as the final and most decisive battle in a war that had dragged out over fifty years. But who were the actors in this war, and who were its victors? This war was not simply fought between Czechs and Germans for control over territory and state power, as historians have typically claimed. As local officials separated Czechs from Germans one final time after World War II, it was not Czechs who triumphed over Germans, but nationalists who finally triumphed in their long-standing war against national indifference.

Lost Children

Czechoslovak officials did not simply seek to salvage Czech blood among families scheduled for expulsion. An urgent priority of the new government

---

[14] Josef Hůrský, *Zjišťování národnosti* (Prague, 1947), 92–94.

[15] *Hlas lidu,* 27 June 1945, 3–4, cited in Jeremy King, *Budweisers into Czechs and Germans: A Local History of Bohemian Politics, 1848–1948* (Princeton, 2002), 195. On the dynamics of national ascription during the expulsions see Chad Bryant, *Prague in Black: Nazi Rule and Czech Nationalism* (Cambridge, MA, 2007), 208–53; Benjamin Frommer, "Expulsion or Integration? Unmixing Mixed Marriages in Postwar Czechoslovakia," *East European Politics and Societies* 14 (March 2000): 381–410; King, *Budweisers into Czechs and Germans,* 190–202.

was to reclaim the nation's so-called lost children, those allegedly kidnapped for Germanization by the Nazis. The search for the children of Lidice, for example, immediately captivated the public imagination in liberated Czechoslovakia. A radio address on January 8, 1946, rallied all Czech citizens for the hunt, asking that they immediately report any clues or sightings of the 105 missing children to their local national council. In liberated Berlin, meanwhile, German antifascists circulated flyers and posters with the names and pictures of the missing Lidice children. The posters exhorted Germans, "There can be no town hall in Germany, no police officer, no office, no church, no newspaper, no radio station, no political party, no union, no rally, no home, no family, that does not cry out, 'What happened to the children from Lidice?'"[16] Several citizens in Germany and Czechoslovakia responded to the call to arms, reporting sightings of boys and girls who had been adopted after 1942 and spoke suspiciously good Czech. All these sightings merely raised false hopes. Only 17 out of 105 children from Lidice ultimately survived the tragedy—82 had been gassed in Chelmno shortly after the 1942 massacre.[17]

Stories of children from Eastern Europe who had been stolen or kidnapped for Germanization became a powerful symbol of Nazi evil in the immediate postwar years and circulated in the Western press and among humanitarian and relief organizations as well as in Eastern Europe.[18] In 1951 the American journalist Dorothy Macardle recounted an anecdote overheard in the town of Falkenov/Falkenau in Bohemia. A Czech woman there reportedly found six abandoned babies and four puppies in the bottom of an American jeep that was driven to her door by Russian soldiers. Macardle speculated about the children's nebulous origins: "Were some of them kidnapped Czechoslovak children, whose German foster-mothers had abandoned them? They might be children of slave-workers who had been imported by the Germans from Poland and the Ukraine, or perhaps some of them were babies of Nazi women, of the type who regarded their offspring as State property and felt no concern for them." She simultaneously elevated often sensational rumors of widespread kidnappings in the Protectorate to fact: "Children were taken

---

[16] An alle Frauen, an alle Familien in Deutschland, Wo Sind die Kinder von Lidice? carton 849, MPSP-R, NA.

[17] Letter from Marie Jirásková, 9 November 1945, carton 845, MPSP-R, NA; Czechoslovak Ministry of the Interior, *Pohřešované československé děti*; Czechoslovak Ministry of the Interior, *Lidické děti* (Prague, 1945); Relace čsl. rozhlasu, 8 January 1946, Ohledně pátrání po lidických dětech; Letter from Johannes Bergenda to the government of Czechoslovakia, 5 September 1946; Obec Lidice, dotaz po dětech, 5 November 1945; all in carton 849, MPSP-R, NA. On the fate of individual Lidice children see Jolana Macková and Ivan Ulrych, *Osudy lidických dětí* (Lidice, 2003).

[18] For examples in the popular press see Oscar Schisgall, "T stands for Dead," *Coronet*, October 1946; A. J. Fischer, "Background of the German Kidnapping," *Central European Observer*, 13 September 1946; "Returning Europe's Kidnapped Children," *Ladies' Home Journal*, October 1946.

from orphanages, from streets and parks, and even from their homes. It was the sturdy, fair-haired boys and girls who were lost, as a rule. Pairs of twins were found to be in special danger: numbers of these were seized. The German motives were obscure, and appalling rumors and conjectures added to the torment of parents whose children had disappeared."[19]

It is difficult to distinguish between rumor and reality in postwar journalists' reports about kidnapped children, many of which were based on anecdotal evidence. For example, journalists often conflated "missing" children, those separated from their parents through population transfers, deportations, bombings, and abandonment, with children who were deliberately kidnapped for Germanization. They also conflated children who were stolen from their own living parents with orphans who were removed from institutions and placed with German adoptive parents. A child removed from his or her native culture and language was a victim of kidnapping just as much as a child removed from his or her parents, according to the prevailing nationalist logic. Estimates of the number of stolen children therefore varied wildly.[20]

Tracing lost children proved to be challenging detective work. Shortly after the war UNRRA created a Child Tracing Bureau, staffed by one hundred workers who spoke twenty-seven languages. Search teams scoured children's orphanages, hospitals, and institutions throughout Germany in pursuit of Allied children who had been Germanized. In 1947, Jean Henshaw described Polish and Yugoslav children in the UNRRA Children's Center in Prien who had "renounced their country, language, and culture and vehemently claimed they were Germans."[21] Once these children were identified, UN Child Search Officers typically removed them from German foster parents as quickly as possible. The separations could be emotionally wrenching for both foster parents and children. "Very often the separation is extremely cruel; the child is very attached to his adoptive family and no longer remembers having had any other family," reported child welfare consultant Yvonne de Jong in a 1948 memo.[22] While Allied children often resisted removal from their German foster families, UN child welfare officers were confident that returning the children to their homelands represented both

[19] Macardle, *Children of Europe*, 54–56.

[20] While Polish authorities insisted that two hundred thousand Polish children had been stolen by the Nazis, Isabel Heinemann has recently estimated that around twenty thousand children were kidnapped from Poland and up to fifty thousand from all of Europe. Hirschmann, "The Lost Children," 252; Macardle, *Children of Europe*, 234, 295–96; Isabel Heinemann, *"Rasse, Siedlung, deutsches Blut": Die Rasse und Siedlungshauptamt der SS und die rassenpolitische Neuordnung Europas* (Göttingen, 2003), 508–9.

[21] Report on International Children's Center, Prien, Mrs. Jean Henshaw to Cornelia Heise, 28 April 1947, S-0437–0012, UN Archive.

[22] June 1948, Yvonne de Jong, Quels sont les principaux problèmes concernant les enfants réfugiés? 43AJ/599, AN.

political justice and the children's individual best interests. Eileen Davidson, Deputy Chief of the International Refugee Organization's Child Search section, warned that Allied children left in German foster families would surely suffer permanent psychological damage even if they were loved and well cared for. "Far from securing the best interests of the child, one has run the danger with the passage of years of contributing to the development of a warped and twisted personality, a misfit with roots neither here nor in his home country."[23] International humanitarian organizations and child welfare activists thus followed the lead of nationalist pedagogues, insisting that children without a clear sense of national identity were doomed to become psychologically and morally defective adults.

The decision to remove East European children from German foster homes, repatriate, or resettle them became even more contentious as Cold War tensions mounted. In 1951 Ira Hirschmann published a scathing indictment of what he called the American "get-soft-with-Germany" policy, arguing that thousands of kidnapped children from Eastern Europe languished in German orphanages and homes because of Cold War politics. Search efforts had virtually ceased, he claimed, because American government and military officials were reluctant to send the children back to their families in Communist Eastern Europe.[24] Communist officials in Poland and Yugoslavia agreed and directed a wave of bitter propaganda toward British and American military authorities and the United Nations, accusing them of perpetuating the Nazi crime of Germanization. In Yugoslavia, for example, a 1948 article in the Belgrade newspaper *Tanjug* asserted, "In Austria at the present time there are large numbers of Yugoslav children who were taken by force from Yugoslavia during the war. Scattered throughout Austria, exposed to Germanization and education designed to make them hate their own country, these children are unscrupulously exploited as free manual labor. Efforts by the Yugoslav government and Red Cross to find these children and bring them back to their native country are blocked by the occupation authorities in the Western Zones."[25]

In Czechoslovakia, however, the postwar government's own efforts to rescue Germanized children revealed a startling gap between international discourses about the crime of Germanization and the more complicated realities of occupied society in the Bohemian Lands. In December of 1945 Czechoslovak officials ordered local branches of the Czech Provincial Commission in Moravia to search all German children's homes and foster

[23] Eileen Davidson, Removal from German families of Allied children. Reasons why this is to the best interest of the child, 21 February 1948, 43/AJ/599, AN.

[24] Hirschmann, "The Lost Children," 260.

[25] Article from the bulletin of *Tanjug*, 26 October 1949, Repatriation of Yugoslav children in Austria blocked by the IRO. See also (in the same carton), "Les enfants Yougoslaves retenus par force en Autriche," *Tanjug* (Belgrade), 7 January 1948, 43/AJ/601, AN.

families to rescue Czech children who had ostensibly been kidnapped and forcibly Germanized by the Nazis. After a thorough search, however, local Czech social workers reported that they had recovered only twenty to thirty Czech children in German institutions, most of whom turned out to be children of mixed marriages who were abandoned or orphaned and then placed with German families by Nazi welfare authorities.[26] Unconvinced, the state once again ordered a thorough sweep of all German internment camps by Czech social workers in 1946. Before German families were expelled, the Czechoslovak Ministry of the Interior ordered social workers to search the internment camps for any "suspicious" children of Czech or Slovak origins. The memo explained, "It is a well-known reality that there is a large number of missing children who became victims of Nazi terror and were given to German families to be raised after the execution or the torture of their parents—Lidice and other cases. It is therefore not only a matter of service and duty for the relevant institutions but a moral, patriotic duty, that in this respect nothing is neglected that could in certain cases lead to the rectification of these tragic realities."[27] Once again the search turned up a handful of children from mixed marriages. In accordance with the policy of preserving this valuable "Czech blood," one such child was removed from her German grandmother and placed instead with a Czech uncle who remained in Czechoslovakia.[28] The postwar Czechoslovak courts meanwhile punished Czech women who had volunteered with the NSV for their alleged role in Germanizing Czech children. In condemning these accused traitors, retribution courts deployed traditional nationalist rhetoric dating back to the turn of the century. The NSV, courts ruled, had "promoted the purchase of souls in our land, that is to say the attraction of less moral members of our nation to the German side through monetary advantages."[29]

Because the barbarity of Nazi social welfare organizations was located largely in such crimes of denationalization, the solution, in the eyes of the postwar Czech state, was to eliminate national cohabitation. Many argued that even the children of German antifascists would become agents of

[26] Opis, Ministerstvo vnitra, Prague, 18 April 1946, k č. B-300/2878, Zjišt'ování a přešetřování dětí neznámého původu při provádění odsunu Němců. See also memo from Czech Provincial Commission for Child Welfare in Brno, č. 9,000, 16 December 1945, memos from Okresní péče o mládež v Novém Jičíně, 18 January 1945, and Medlov, 24 December 1945 to Czech Provincial Commission in Brno; all in carton 153, Česká zemská komise (ČZK), MZA.

[27] Opis, Ministerstvo vnitra, Prague, 18 April 1946, k č. B-300/2878, Zjišt'ování a přešetřování dětí neznámého původu při provádění odsunu Němců, carton 153, ČZK, MZA.

[28] 3017-46 II B kr, 7 March 1946, carton 153, ČZK, MZA.

[29] Cited in Mečislav Borák, *Spravedlnost podle dekretu: Retribuční soudnictví v ČSR a mimořádný lidový soud v Ostravě, 1945–48* (Ostrava, 1998), 181–82. The Czechoslovak government actually created a new crime after the war, a crime against the nation (as opposed to the state), which allowed local retribution courts to prosecute this kind of national renegade. See Benjamin Frommer, *National Cleansing: Retribution Against Nazi Collaborators in Postwar Czechoslovakia* (New York, 2005).

Germanization if allowed to stay. In May of 1944 a Czech informant reported the widespread opinion that "not a single one of our Germans can stay here, no, not even the Socialists, Sudeten Germans are all alike. . . . We need to be certain that at least our children will have some rest from the Germans."[30] The postwar expulsions ensured that the rights of the Czech nation to Czech children would never again be threatened by "foreign" social welfare and educational institutions. No less important (if unremarked upon), the expulsions guaranteed that nationally indifferent parents would never again have the right to bring up their children in an alien language or culture.

At the same time, stories concerning the alleged theft or Czechification of German children during the interwar period lived on in postwar Sudeten German memory. Expellees used these stories to explain and justify German collaboration with the Nazis in the Bohemian Lands. As late as 1962, Theo Keil, a Sudeten German nationalist and leader of the Protectorate's educational administration, made excuses for the Nazi regime's harsh reduction of the number of Czech schools in these terms. He argued that Czech school closings under Nazism merely compensated for German losses in interwar Czechoslovakia, when "so-called minority schools were erected at the state's expense in the purely German regions of the Sudetenland. . . . These schools seduced the children of poor German parents through gifts. State force also pushed the children of dependent Germans into these schools. . . . These 'minority schools' understandably caused great anger among the Sudeten German population and contributed considerably to national tensions in the state."[31]

Well after the end of the Second World War, German and Czech nationalists alike thus clung to a worldview in which children's souls were Czechified, Germanized, robbed, kidnapped, seduced, bought, won or lost through the mobilization of nationalist collectives. In these narratives, the decision of a parent or child to become a German or Czech, to switch sides, or to identify fully with neither community could never be trusted as a genuine expression of personal agency. These choices were portrayed as symptoms of opportunism, force, economic dependence, or moral decrepitude. "While the German school often faced difficult limitations, Czech schools were often erected in the city or countryside for only a handful of Czech children. In order to fill these schools, the familiar practice of soul robbery was purposefully deployed, especially among German workers' children," recalled K. Schnall in his 1959 report on the village of Česká Kamenice/Böhmisch Kamnitz.[32]

---

[30] Zprávy z domova, 5 May 1944, 3, sig. 91/7, fond 37, VÚA.

[31] Ost Doc. 21/14, fol. 1, Tschechische Schulen im ehemaligen Reichsgau Sudetenland, Theo Keil, 25 September 1962, BB.

[32] Ost Doc. 20/17, K. Schmall, Česká Kamenice/Böhmisch Kamnitz, 19 January 1959, BB.

The Nazi experience thus did little to discredit nationalist worldviews in the immediate postwar years. Among both German expellees and Czechs, nationalism emerged triumphant from the Second World War. Czech nationalists interpreted the Nazi occupation as a confirmation of a stereotyped image of Germans as undemocratic barbarians, intent on violently Germanizing Czech children. Sudeten Germans, meanwhile, justified their participation in the Nazi regime in the name of defending their own children from forced Czechification. Both sides remained convinced that national hermaphroditism was symptomatic of a defective moral character and damaged psyche. Both sides upheld national purity as their highest value. During and after the war, Nazis, Sudeten Germans, and Czechs shared common fears of "denationalization," fears that presumed that every individual had a single, authentic national identity of origins. These concerns disappeared only when the ambition to create homogenous nation-states was finally realized after World War II with the approval of the allies. Ethnic cleansing was not just a radical solution to national conflict in Europe: it was a final solution to the persistent problem of national hermaphroditism and ambivalence.

The Demise of Collective Education

If nationalism itself was not discredited by the Nazi experience, the Nazi occupation did profoundly disrupt a long-standing tradition of collective education and ownership of children in Central Europe. In the Cold War West, memories of Nazi rule reinforced popular arguments against collective education. After the war Sudeten German expellees and West Germans frequently contrasted the ostensibly apolitical pedagogical space of the nuclear family with the "invasive" tactics of collective brainwashing allegedly promoted by the Nazis and Communists alike. The problem with totalitarianism, in this view, was that it interfered with parental rights. In 1962 the expellee Max Mayer recalled, "It is true that some measures of the party were not always endorsed, but no one dared open resistance. Interference in youth education, in particular, was strongly resented, since children were thereby estranged from their parental homes."[33] A former teacher from Mariánské Lázně/Marienbad also retrospectively criticized the Nazi state's alleged attempts to undermine parental authority, insisting that after 1938, the "once fruitful influence of the parental home was lost."[34] Such memories downplayed or ignored the extent to which Nazi claims on children had built on a native Sudeten German nationalist political culture in which children were already seen as collective property. In their recollections of the Nazi

[33] Ost Doc. 20/50, Max Mayer, Nitschenau, 3 May 1962, 3, BB.
[34] Ost Doc. 20/29, Franz Nitsch, Auschowitz, 5 May 1958, 3, BB.

period, Sudeten Germans also attempted to portray themselves as victims, contrasting their own allegedly democratic, nationalist youth movements with the militaristic, undemocratic nationalism promoted by the Nazis. In an essay on Sudeten German youth associations, Eduard Berkert idealized the final days of freedom before Sudeten German youth movements were coordinated with the Hitler Youth: "For a short time, the joyous, youthful, independent life in the youth groups was still to a large extent preserved, before voluntarism became service, hiking became marching, diverse ways of thinking became a prescribed worldview."[35]

The evil of totalitarianism in the Cold War West was soon located in its excessive claims on children and interventions into an imagined private sphere. Alfred Brauner, a French psychologist who worked with children immediately after the war, reported a German Socialist teacher's observations of children in Nazi Germany. Whereas before the war, this teacher recalled, his students "lived only for the life of the school, their friends and their parents," those raised under Nazism "live too much for the political ideal. They knew nothing else. The school is a necessary evil. The family counts for nothing. They no longer have a child's life." According to Brauner such children "denounced, if required, their father, who remained loyal to his old political party, and their mother, who preferred to believe the priest rather than the Führer. They are the youth who blindly executed all orders, and were prepared for this voluntary submission since their earliest childhood."[36] Resistance activists had been circulating tales of Nazi brainwashing since the late 1930s. In 1938, Erika Mann, Thomas Mann's daughter, published *School for Barbarians,* in which she defined the evils of the Third Reich in terms of a relentless assault on parental rights. The destruction of the family, Mann warned, was essential to the Nazi worldview and its drive toward world conquest. "If the world is to go to the Nazis (for no one else, in Hitler's eyes, is German), the German people must first belong to them. And, for that to be true, they can't belong to anyone else—neither God, nor their families, nor themselves."[37] *School for Barbarians* was reprinted in several editions during the war and appeared in English, German, and French.

The demonization of collective education and idealization of the "apolitical" family was an integral part of the reconstruction of postwar West Germany.[38] The process of postwar reconstruction often raised serious

---

[35] Eduard Burkert, "Die Auflösung der sudetendeutschen Jugendbünde und die Einführung der Hitler-Jugend," in *Deutsche Jugend in Böhmen,* ed. Peter Becher, 173 (Munich, 1993).

[36] Alfred Brauner, *Ces enfants ont vécu la guerre* (Paris, 1946), 182, 179.

[37] Erika Mann, *School for Barbarians: Education under the Nazis* (New York, 1938), 15, 28–29. For other examples of this narrative about Nazi education, see Macardle, *Children of Europe,* 19–37; Sosnowski, *The Tragedy of Children,* 12–42.

[38] On the importance of the nuclear family to postwar reconstruction politics in Western Europe, see Robert Moeller, *Protecting Motherhood: Women and the Family in the Politics of*

conflicts between goals of "normalizing" West Germany, on the one hand, through integration in a Cold War alliance against the Eastern bloc, and de-Nazification on the other.[39] Blaming Nazi education for the evils of totalitarianism helped to resolve some of these tensions. Commentators attributed the apparent failure of moral reasoning in German society under Nazism to the brainwashing of German youth and children, which allegedly took place against the better judgment and will of their parents. This argument discursively de-Nazified the adult German population by depicting German parents as hapless victims of Nazi pedagogical institiutions. Dorothy Macardle thus insisted in 1951, "It was almost impossible for parents to save their children from being impregnated by the Nazi creed. . . . There were fanatical little devotees of the Führer who blackmailed their parents by threatening to denounce them in the party for lack of zeal."[40]

At the same time, a focus on totalitarian brainwashing and intrusions into domestic life helped to solidify Cold War divisions and integrate West Germany into the ranks of Western capitalist democracies. After the war West German anti-Communists attempted to mobilize citizens to save East German children from the same terrible fate that had allegedly befallen children under Nazism: being "ripped from the hands of their parents" by the educational and social welfare apparatus of the Communist state.[41] Anti-Communists reserved their harshest criticism for Communist policies that encouraged women to work outside the home and provided state support for child care and collective education. They argued that East German Communists deliberately mobilized mothers to work outside the home in order to brainwash their children at the most tender age. Women were required to send their children to state-run nursery schools in order to ensure "the undisturbed indoctrination of the child with the Communist worldview," claimed activist Käte Fiedler in 1955. In a 1955 government publication, Hans Köhler likewise asserted, "wherever possible mothers have no more

---

Postwar West Germany (Berkeley, 1993), 69–70; Elizabeth D. Heineman, *What Difference Does a Husband Make? Women and Marital Status in Nazi and Postwar Germany* (Berkeley, 1999); Dagmar Herzog, *Sex after Fascism: Memory and Morality in Twentieth Century Germany* (Princeton, 2005); Pat Thane, "Family Life and 'Normality' in Postwar British Culture," in *Life after Death: Approaches to a Cultural and Social History of Europe During the 1940s and 1950s*, ed. Richard Bessel and Dirk Schumann, 193–210 (New York, 2003); Mark Roseman, "The 'Organic Society' and the 'Massenmenschen': Integrating Young Labor in the Ruhr Mines, 1945–1958," in *West Germany under Reconstruction: Society, Politics, and Culture in the Adenauer Era*, ed. Robert Moeller, 287–321 (Ann Arbor, 1997); Atina Grossmann, *Jews, Germans, and Allies: Close Encounters in Occupied Germany* (Princeton, 2007).

[39] See *Jeffrey Herf, Divided Memory: the Nazi Past in Two Germanies* (Cambridge, MA, 1997).

[40] Macardle, *Children of Europe*, 35.

[41] Bundesministerium für Gesamtdeutschen Fragen, *Deutsche Kinder in Stalins Hand* (Bonn, 1951), 78. For similar discussions of Communist education in Cold War propaganda, see Ernst Tillich, "Die psychologische Entwicklung und die psychologische Führung der Menschen hinter dem Eisernen Vorhang," in *Die Jugend der Sowjetzone in Deutschland* (Berlin, 1955).

opportunities to devote themselves to their children."[42] By depicting both Nazi and Communist evil in terms of state intrusions into the private sphere, West German anti-Communists helped to secure their own position in the Western bloc through an embrace of antistate liberalism.[43]

The trope of the child informant became one of the most powerful symbols of the alleged dangers of collective education after 1945 and was even dramatized in a scene in Bertolt Brecht's *Furcht und Elend des dritten Reiches.* Set in Cologne in 1936, the scene depicts a middle-class couple who worry that their little boy has gone to denounce them to the Gestapo because they confiscated his pet frog.[44] I have found no documented examples of children who actually denounced their own parents, but these stories powerfully represented the alleged Nazi destruction of the private sphere, the totalitarian quality of Nazi pedagogy, and the ironic reversals in power in occupied society—a society turned upside down. Tropes about child informants had already gained currency among Czechs during the Nazi occupation. In October of 1943 a Czech resistance activist reported to London that it was now dangerous for families with children to listen to foreign radio broadcasts because German school inspectors and the Gestapo allegedly interrogated children about their parents' listening habits.[45] In August of 1944 another Czech correspondent warned, "at home many cannot speak in front of their children because children prattle and betray their father and mother."[46] Shortly after the liberation, Czech school inspector Josef Blažek recalled, in an essay on Czech schools under the occupation, that "the Gestapo had agents and informants even among children."[47] These stories about children who denounced their parents affirmed both the innocence of ordinary parents and the impossibility of resistance under Nazi rule.[48]

Suspicion of collective education and state intrusion into family life was reinforced in part by Central European émigrés, pioneers in the field of

---

[42] Käte Fiedler, "Der Ideologische Drill der Jugend in der Sowjetzone," in *Die Jugend der Sowjetzone,* 36; Hans Köhler, "Erziehung zur Unfreiheit," in *Die Jugend der Sowjetzone;* Arbeits und Sozialminister des Landes Nordheim-Westfallen, *Jugend Zwischen Ost und West* (Nordheim-Westfallen, 1955), 60.

[43] On de-Nazification and education in postwar West Germany see Karl-Heinz Füssl, *Die Umerziehung der Deutschen: Jugend und Schule unter den Siegermächten des Zweiten Weltkriegs 1945–1955* (Paderborn, 1994).

[44] Bertolt Brecht, "Der Spitzel," in *Furcht und Elend des III Reiches* (New York, 1945), 61–70, trans. Eric Bentley as *The Master Race* (New York, 1944), 71–84.

[45] Zpráva o poměrech ve vlasti, 6 October 1943, sig. 91/6, fond 37, VÚA; Zpráva z domova, 24 January 1944, sig. 91/7, fond 37, VÚA.

[46] Zpráva o domově, 14 August 1944, sig. 91/7, fond 37, VÚA.

[47] Jaroslav P. Blažek, "Národní školy za okupace," in *Šest let okupace Prahy,* ed. Václav Buben, 47.

[48] Klaus-Michael Mallman and Gerhard Paul, "Omniscient, Omnipotent, Omnipresent? Gestapo, Society and Resistance," in *Nazism and German Society 1933–1945,* ed. David Crew, 168–71 (London, 1994); Robert Gellately, *Backing Hitler: Consent and Coercion in Nazi Germany* (Oxford, 2001).

psychoanalytic pedagogy. Many leading psychoanalysts from Vienna, such as August Aichhorn and Siegfried Bernfeld, had once promoted the virtues of collective education to repair the alleged damage wrought on families by the First World War. By contrast, in the wake of the Second World War, analysts such as Anna Freud, Melanie Klein, and Bruno Bettelheim focused instead on the importance of psychological relations between mothers and children and rarely advocated collective education as a substitute for a flawed parental upbringing.[49] The writings of Anna Freud and Dorothy T. Burlingham on young children evacuated from London during the war played a key role in this shift. Freud and Burlingham concluded that while evacuated children may have been far safer from the threats of bombs, infections, malnourishment, and neglect than those who remained in London, "all of the improvements in the child's life may dwindle down to nothing when weighed against the fact that it has to leave the family to get them."[50] These principles found practical application almost immediately in UNRRA's displaced persons camps after the Second World War, where psychoanalytically informed social workers from Great Britain and the United States sought to rehabilitate thousands of so-called unaccompanied children by strengthening the family. "Educational psychologists are very generally in accord with Dr. Anna Freud in the conclusion she has expressed repeatedly; that for little children even a mediocre family home is better than the best of communal nurseries," wrote Dorothy Macardle in 1951 in her survey of efforts to rehabilitate postwar children.[51]

Memories of Nazism and Nazi pedagogy, soon widespread in the postwar West, bolstered the claim that children were best cared for by stay-at-home mothers rather than left to the mercy of the state and political activists. Nationalist claims on children in the Habsburg Monarchy and interwar Czechoslovakia had initially been motivated by suspicion of parents' wavering national and political loyalties. During the Nazi occupation, however, many German and Czech nationalists had relocated authentic nationalist pedagogy into a heavily politicized private sphere, urging mothers to protect their children from denationalization through nationalist education in the family. The family, in their view, was the last and best hope for preserving the nation's overriding political claims on children. In the wake of the Nazi defeat, however, pedagogues and psychoanalysts in the Cold War West promoted a suspicion of politics itself, demanding that children be brought up in a domestic realm that was ostensibly free from politics. Yet parents

---

[49] On links between psychoanalysis and familialism in postwar Britain, see Laura Lee Downs, "A 'Very British' Revolution? L'évacuation des enfants urbains vers les campagnes anglaises, 1939–1945," *Vingtième siècle* 89 (January–March 2006): 47–60; Denise Riley, *War in the Nursery: Theories of the Child and the Mother* (London, 1983), 85–110.

[50] Anna Freud and Dorothy T. Burlingham, *War and Children* (London, 1943), 45.

[51] Macardle, *Children of Europe*, 270.

themselves were under no less scrutiny after the Second World War. They were now seen to be both exclusively responsible for their children's development and fundamentally irreplaceable by social workers, pedagogues, activists, and analysts, the utopian and disciplinary agents of mass political movements.

Conclusion

In his memoir, *Der siebente Lebenslauf,* writer Ota Filip reflected on the ironic legacies of his experiences as a nationally contested child: "On the first of September 1939, I was violently dragged by my father, howling and miserable through the streets of Schlesische Ostrau out of the Czech and into the German linguistic community. This day sealed my fate with a powerful shot of irony and absurdity. While I had many reasons to hate the German language and everything that stank of Germandom because of my father Bohumil, 40 years later I would be designated a German writer in every lexicon. Should I be grateful to my father, or should I seek revenge on him?"[52]

In the first half of the twentieth century, nationalists in the Bohemian Lands depicted children as the nation's most valuable collective assets, symbols of hope for the nation's future. In 1936, for example, the Czech Provincial Commission for Child Welfare had promoted its annual fund-raising campaign under the banner, "In Children, the Nation is Eternal." Filip's story, however, underscores the extent to which the provincial commission's slogan more accurately reflected the wishful thinking of nationalists than the reality of many children's lives. In spite of the hard work of nationalists, the nation was often far from fixed or eternal in the hearts of children in the Bohemian Lands. Sometimes, "eternity" lasted only as long as a political regime; sometimes it lasted until the "other" nation made a better offer of welfare benefits; and sometimes nationality simply never became the most compelling source of self-understanding for these children and their families.

This book builds on several decades of scholarship that has historicized and denaturalized nations and nationalisms, as well as more recent work that has emphasized the surprising flexibility of national loyalties in the Bohemian Lands. The story of nationalist mobilization around children contributes to this larger project through several related strategies. First, this study has deliberately followed nationalist efforts to eradicate national indifference across four regimes. Nationalist histories tend to emphasize the radical changes that marked the transitions from the multinational Austrian Empire to the Czechoslovak nation-state to the Nazi occupation. And yet striking institutional, legal, and discursive continuities flowed beneath

---

[52] Ota Filip, *Der siebente Lebenslauf: Autobiographischer Roman* (Munich, 2001), 31.

a surface marked by revolutionary political upheaval. Simultaneously, it is clear that the state itself played a critical role in the nationalization of East Central Europe. The meaning and extent of "national indifference" transformed dramatically when the Austrian Empire dissolved into self-declared nation-states and changed again when Czechoslovakia was overrun by the Nazi regime. Individuals (and their children) were obliged to choose sides after 1918 as the government forcibly disciplined and classified nationally ambiguous citizens through the census and the Lex Perek. With the triumph of the nation-state, fewer individuals could claim to be neither Czech nor German.

Many parents gradually identified themselves in the binary terms demanded by nationalists over the course of the twentieth century. And yet, even as the nationally ambivalent Zwischenschicht shrank to a small minority, so-called hermaphrodites retained prominence beyond their numbers in the imagination and rhetoric of nationalists. They forced nationalist activists to define and police the boundaries of the national community. This book has argued that popular indifference to nationalism, as much as nationalist fervor, was a driving force behind the radicalization of nationalist politics in Habsburg Central Europe. The nationalist confrontation with indifferent and nationally ambiguous parents and children shaped understandings of democracy and minority rights. It prompted nationalists to devise increasingly disciplinary practices of national ascription as well as new forms of social welfare activism and pedagogical reform. Finally, concerns over national indifference dramatically shaped Nazi Germanization policies and popular responses to the Nazi occupation and transformed ideas about the proper relationship between parents, children, and the state in the Bohemian Lands.

The persistence of national ambiguity forces us to rethink many of the categories, terms, and assumptions that tend to structure histories of East Central Europe, including the assumption that we can write confidently about German-Czech relations, Czech history, or German history without minimally exploring the question of who was a German and who was a Czech. In particular, the meaning and consequences of Nazi Germanization policies must be understood in local historical contexts, as well as in the larger context of Nazi-dominated Europe. The conflation of Germanization with Nazification in the Bohemian Lands, as we have seen, traded heavily on the politics of Czech nationalist educational activists in the Habsburg Monarchy and interwar Czechoslovakia, as well as the Nazis' own rhetoric. At the turn of the century Czech nationalists had mobilized to keep Czech children in Czech schools in the name of class justice and democratization. Throughout the interwar period, the Czechoslovak state intensified its campaign against alleged Germanization, as census takers and school officials reclaimed children and adults for the Czech nation against their will in the name of minority rights and national self-determination. Following the dismemberment of the first Czechoslovak Republic between October of 1938 and March of 1939, charges of Germanization took on unprecedented political and emotional force in Czech society, shaping responses to the occupation on the right and left. It is not clear who ultimately "won" the contest to reclaim children for the nation in the Bohemian Lands, since Czech nationalists finally protected the ethnicity of their children within a system of Reich-loyal Czech nationalism authorized by the Nazis themselves.

In recent years Germanization in the East has attracted the attention of historians of Germany, who seek new contexts in which to explore the complexities of Nazi racial policy and the origins of the Holocaust. Historians have situated the Holocaust not only in the dynamics of a "cumulative radicalization" on the Eastern front but within a larger population policy designed to transform the racial demography of Eastern Europe.[53] Yet the Nazi ambition to forcibly Germanize children in Eastern Europe signaled a radical departure from Nazi policy toward Jews. The term "Germanization" itself implied that there were some Czechs who could (and should) become part of the German Volksgemeinschaft, requiring a flexible approach to racial categorization. Nazi officials promoted Germanization policies by explicitly evoking and capitalizing on a longer history of national ambiguity and flexibility in Eastern Europe, using discourses of "re-Germanization" to recruit candidates with questionable ethnic credentials. Debates over the identification and classification of Jews also continued throughout the Nazi regime, but Jews could almost never be Germanized or re-Germanized in the eyes of Nazi ideologues, nor could they be Nazified.[54]

Moreover, policies designed to forcibly remake Czech children and families into self-identified Germans were a disappointing failure to the Nazis. Given the actual development of Nazi Germanization policy during World War II, we should be skeptical of narratives about the Germanization of children under Nazism, many of which perpetuate nationalist myths and discourses born in the nineteenth century. These myths ascribe authentic Czech or German nationalities to parents and children who may not have

---

[53] For example, see Doris Bergen, "The Nazi Concept of Volksdeutsche and the Exacerbation of Anti-Semitism in Eastern Europe," *Journal of Contemporary History* 29 (October 1994): 569–82; Bryant, *Prague in Black*, 104–79; Connelly, "Nazis and Slavs"; Elizabeth Harvey, *Women and the Nazi East: Agents and Witnesses of Germanization* (New Haven, 2003); Vejas G. Liulevicius, *War Land on the Eastern Front: Culture, National Identity, and German Occupation in World War I* (New York, 2000); Götz Aly, *Final Solution: Nazi Population Policy and the Murder of the European Jews* (London, 1999); Heinemann, *"Rasse, Siedlung, deutsches Blut,"* 165; Omer Bartov, *The Eastern Front, 1941–45: German Troops and the Barbarisation of Warfare* (New York, 2001); Hans Mommsen, "Umvolkungspläne des Nationalsozialismus und der Holocaust," in *Die Normalität des Verbrechens. Bilanz und Perspektiven der Forchung zu der Nationalsozialistischen Gewaltverbrechen*, ed. Helge Grabitz et al. (Berlin, 1994).

[54] On ambiguity in the Nazi classification of Jews, see Thomas Pegelow, "Determining 'People of German Blood,' 'Jews' and 'Mischlinge': The Reich Kinship Office and the Competing Discourses and Powers of Nazism, 1941–1943," *Contemporary European History* 15 (2006): 43–65.

identified themselves in national terms and efface a long history of national indeterminacy in East Central Europe. Germanization narratives also validate a logic of ethnic purity that was at the heart of Nazi racism, the long Czech nationalist struggle to prevent the Germanization of Czech children, and the forced population transfers of the postwar years.

A critical reader might justifiably question why we should worry so much about the actions of Czech nationalists. Czech speakers were unjustly persecuted by a militarized Habsburg state and by German nationalists during the First World War. Czechoslovakia clearly did a better job than most interwar states of protecting the rights of minorities. The interwar Czechoslovak Republic also impressively outlasted almost every European democracy before being dismembered by the Nazi regime. Why focus so much on the agency of individuals who were often subjected to forces beyond their control?

Czech nationalists merit this scrutiny precisely because they acted in the name of democracy, more proudly and over a longer period of time than most other mass nationalist movements in modern Europe. The lesson, however, is not that interwar Czechoslovakia should now be recategorized among the bad and undemocratic nationalist states of Central and Eastern Europe. Like all interwar democracies, Czech national democracy was rife with contradictions. Democratic societies today still face powerful tensions between collective rights seen to be critical to the functioning of a pluralist, democratic, egalitarian society and the liberal rights of the individual. Interwar Czech and German nationalists alike promoted a particular ideal of *national* democracy, in which principles such as minority rights and national self-determination centered around collective rights (such as national claims on children) rather than on the principles of liberal individualism. In this framework individual parents often lost the right to determine the nationality of their children, a question that only the state was competent to rule on.

In spite of nationalist rhetoric that insisted on the essential differences between Czechs and Germans and between Czech and German political culture in the Bohemian Lands, this book has revealed that the two movements shared far more than nationalists themselves were willing to admit. The potential within Czech society for collaboration with the Nazis, national ascription, denunciation, ethnic cleansing, and participation in a Communist dictatorship did not result from the corruption of a liberal democratic tradition by the Nazi experience or from imitation of the Nazi example. These events in Czech history were made possible by a shared political culture developed over more than fifty years, in which children stood at the center of political mobilization and nationalist self-understanding.

Across four regimes in the Bohemian Lands, nationalists insisted that their rights to educate and provide for children trumped parental rights. Their claims on children were based on an explicit critique of the family, especially the working-class family, which activists deemed incapable of providing for the well-being and education of children on its own. During and after the Second World War, however, the evil of Nazism and Communism was increasingly defined in terms of intervention into a so-called private sphere. Popular and scholarly assertions about how Nazism and Communism colonized, invaded, or destroyed the private sphere should be greeted with skepticism. These arguments rest on an idealized conception of the family as an apolitical space that must be protected from intervention, an ideology that has historically protected the rights of fathers to rule over women and children with impunity. The idea that nationalists, Nazis, or Communists destroyed the private sphere does not do justice to the historical experiences of women and children in the family or to the complexity of the relationship between society and state in the twentieth century. It may in fact be a sloppy shorthand for more convincing claims: about the depth of penetration of political ideologies into daily life, for example, or about the limits or barriers to resistance under dictatorial regimes.[55]

Ernst Renan, in his 1884 speech at the Sorbonne, famously defined a nation as a voluntary community, "a daily plebiscite." A nation, he insisted, "has no more right than a king does to say to a province 'You belong to me, I am seizing you.'"[56] But as they sought to combat widespread apathy and indifference to the very concept of national belonging, nationalists in the Bohemian Lands created a political culture in which people, as well as provinces, were seen as the property of national communities. The decision about who was Czech and who was German was transferred from the hands of individuals to panels of judges, school officials, teachers, welfare activists, and census-takers, who seized children for the nation in the name of democracy and minority rights. This lost political culture had both progressive and disciplinary potential. The nationalist battle for children not only helped to first constitute and consolidate national communities in the Bohemian Lands, forcing the nationally indifferent to call themselves Czechs or Germans, it also defined real and imagined boundaries between state and society, public and private, democracy and totalitarianism. When mass political movements campaigned for children's souls, they simultaneously transformed the very meaning of nation, family, and democracy in modern Europe.

---

[55] See Geoff Eley, "Hitler's Silent Majority? Conformity and Resistance under the Third Reich," *Michigan Quarterly Review* 42 (Spring 2003): 389–425.

[56] Ernst Renan, "What is a Nation?" in Geoff Eley and Ronald Grigor Suny, ed. *Becoming National: A Reader* (New York, 1996), 41–55.

Index